A HISTORY OF AIR POWER

by the same author

THE DEFENCE OF THE UNITED KINGDOM

THE BATTLE OF BRITAIN

A SHORT HISTORY OF THE SECOND WORLD WAR

THE WAR IN THE FAR EAST, 1941–1945

THE LION AND THE EAGLE : BRITISH AND ANGLO-AMERICAN STRATEGY, 1900–1950

A HISTORY OF AIR POWER

BASIL COLLIER

MACMILLAN PUBLISHING CO., INC.
NEW YORK

Macmillan Publishing Co., Inc.
866 Third Avenue, New York, N.Y. 10022

Library of Congress Catalog Card Number: 73-20991
First American Edition 1974

Printed in the United States of America

CONTENTS

When my brother and I built and flew the first man-carrying flying machine, we thought that we were introducing into the world an invention which would make further wars practically impossible.

Orville Wright

If men were all virtuous . . . I should with great alacrity teach them all to fly. But what would be the security of the good, if the bad could at pleasure invade them from the sky?

Samuel Johnson

I would make it death for a man to be convicted of flying.

William Cowper

ILLUSTRATIONS

between pages 160 *and* 161

MAPS

I

THE GENESIS OF AIR POWER

Long before men held the keys to powered flight, poets and philosophers warned mankind of the perils to which the innocent would be exposed if the wicked could attack them at pleasure from the sky. Francesco Lana, an Italian Jesuit priest who was also something of a physicist, pointed out in 1670 that the occupants of an airship would be able to escape unscathed after dropping missiles which could capsize ships or damage buildings. In the following century Samuel Johnson drew attention to the danger that 'a flight of northern savages' might descend on the capital of a fruitful region. The poet Cowper wrote in a letter to a friend that he would make flying a capital offence. He added that doubtless historians would censure him for imposing such a ban, but that meanwhile it would make the world a safer if not a better place.

The use of aircraft for warlike purposes did not begin, however, with the aeroplane, the airship or even the balloon. The kite, invented in China at least 2,300 years ago, is essentially a tethered glider and hence undoubtedly an aircraft. The Chinese are believed to have used man-lifting kites for military reconnaissance before or soon after the beginning of the Christian era. Much later, having invented gunpowder about the time of Charlemagne, they made the first recorded use of self-propelled ballistic missiles as weapons of war by bombarding their enemies with rockets. The term 'rocket arrows', applied to missiles used against the Mongols in 1232, suggests rockets stabilized by fins.

Both the kite and the rocket reappeared in Europe in the Middle Ages or shortly afterwards. No serious attempt to use man-lifting kites for military purposes seems, however, to have been made by Europeans before the last decade of the nineteenth century. Captain B. F. S. Baden-Powell of the Scots Guards then carried out experiments in Britain with the box-kite, invented in 1893 by the Australian Lawrence Hargrave. Rockets were employed as siege weapons from the middle of the fifteenth century, or perhaps earlier; but most of those used before William Congreve introduced a finned rocket early in the nineteenth century were very unstable and inaccurate.

Early introductions which pointed the way to mechanical flight included a miniature helicopter, rotated before release by the pulling of a string, or in some instances by movement along a helical spindle. This pleasing device was in use as a child's toy by the first quarter of the fifteenth century and can still be bought today. From very early times aspiring aviators showed much interest, too, in the possibility of free flight by means of artificial wings, moved either directly by the wearer or mechanically. Leonardo da Vinci (1452–1519) committed to his notebooks some interesting designs for such aids to aviation. A keen interest in the flight of birds did not save him, however, from drawing a false analogy between flying and swimming. In addition to a number of devices too cumbrous to be effective, his proposals included an ornithopter powered by a bow-string mechanism and a helicopter supposedly meant to be worked by clockwork.

In the seventeenth century the Englishman Robert Hooke and the Italian Giovanni Borelli came independently to the conclusion that a man's muscles were not strong enough to sustain him in the air without help from some form of engine. Hooke is believed to have made a successful working model of a powered ornithopter and to have gone on to design a man-carrying machine, but no drawings or detailed descriptions of either appear to have survived. Francesco Lana accompanied his warning of the disagreeable uses to which air power might be put with an elegant but impractical design for an airship driven by a sail and sustained by hollow metal spheres devoid of air. Since the spheres would have collapsed under atmospheric pressure when the air was withdrawn from them, his design was useful only in so far as it prompted other men to consider how an airship might be made to fly.

In 1749 Alexander Wilson, of the University of Glasgow, used a thermometer attached to a train of kites to measure the temperature of clouds about 3,000 feet above the earth. Three years later Benjamin Franklin, the American statesman, diplomat and natural philosopher, narrowly escaped electrocution by employing a kite to investigate the nature of thunder. Substantial progress in the design of heavier-than-air flying-machines was made in the course of the next half-century or so, but the lack of a power-unit suitable for man-carrying aircraft limited trials of powered craft to models small enough to be driven by clockwork or kindred mechanisms.

In 1766 the Englishman Henry Cavendish isolated hydrogen and devised a method of producing it in useful quantities. His work and that of his disciples attracted so much attention that an acquaintance with the nature and properties of gases soon became widely diffused on both sides of the Channel. In Paris especially, keen interest was aroused by the publication in 1776 of a French translation of a work on experiments with gases by the English chemist and physicist Joseph Priestley.

Among Priestley's foreign readers was a French paper manufacturer named Joseph Montgolfier who lived and worked at Annonay, about 35 miles south-south-west of Lyons. In 1782 Montgolfier began a series of experiments with hot-air balloons. Apparently unaware that hot air rises because it is lighter than cold air, he seems to have supposed that the combustion of organic materials produced an unidentified buoyant gas. He is said to have claimed when he began his investigations that hot-air balloons would enable the French Army to mount an airborne invasion of Gibraltar.

Montgolfier's first experiment was made indoors at Avignon with a small balloon made of fine silk, which rose to the ceiling when burning paper was held beneath it. Enlisting the help of his brother Etienne when he returned to Annonay, he went on to test much larger balloons in the open air. At a public demonstration at Annonay on 5 June 1783 a balloon with a circumference of 110 feet, made of cloth lined with paper, rose to 6,000 feet or so and came to earth about a mile and a half away after a 10 minute flight.

This achievement by men with no known scientific background prompted the French Academy to accept an offer from a 37-year-old physicist, J.-A.-C. Charles, to experiment with a hydrogen balloon. Hydrogen balloons had been proposed in 1782 by Joseph Black of Glasgow, but experiments with a bladder and a paper envelope by Tiberius Cavallo, an English-domiciled

Neapolitan, had failed because the bladder was too heavy and the paper too porous. Charles commissioned two craftsmen, the Robert brothers, to construct an envelope of fine silk coated with what was said to be a solution of rubber. About 12 feet in diameter and perfectly spherical when inflated, it weighed 25 lbs and had a capacity of 943 cubic feet.

Charles and his helpers began on 23 August to inflate the envelope with hydrogen produced by the action of sulphuric acid on iron filings. Satisfied by 26 August that inflation was as complete as they could make it, they allowed the balloon to rise to a height of 100 feet at the end of a rope. Such huge crowds gathered that the authorities insisted on transferring the trial ascent from the workshop of the Robert brothers in the Place des Victoires to the relatively open spaces of the Champ de Mars. The balloon, still inflated, had therefore to be trundled at night through the streets of Paris on a cart escorted by an armed guard. Released late on 27 August, it rose quickly to 3,000 feet and remained airborne for three-quarters of an hour before coming to earth about 15 miles away.

On 19 September the Montgolfiers demonstrated a large hot-air balloon, some 40 feet in diameter, before the royal family at Versailles. Carrying a sheep, a cock and a duck in a wicker cage, it reached a height of 1,700 feet and stayed aloft about 8 minutes. Joseph Montgolfier, who had expected it to reach 12,000 feet and remain airborne for 20 minutes, attributed its relatively poor but still impressive performance to rents in the fabric.

The Montgolfiers then prepared a man-carrying balloon of tougher material, with a capacity of 79,000 cubic feet. The King at first proposed that two condemned criminals should make the first flight on the understanding that they would be pardoned if they survived its rigours. The Marquis d'Arlandes, a nobleman of Languedoc, persuaded him to change his mind by bringing feminine influence to bear on him through friends at court. In October Jean-François Pilâtre de Rozier, a 26-year-old physicist who had watched the demonstration at Versailles with keen interest, made a number of trial ascents with the balloon tethered. Taking aloft a store of fuel, he found that the rise and fall of the balloon could be regulated to some extent by controlled firing. On 21 November he and Arlandes became the world's first aeronauts by making a 25-minute flight from the Château de la

Muette in the Bois de Boulogne to the Butte-aux-Cailles, about 5 miles away.

A few days later, Charles exhibited in Paris a small man-carrying hydrogen balloon of advanced design. He believed, probably correctly, that expansion of the hydrogen as his previous balloon ascended had shortened its flight by bursting the envelope. His new design provided a twofold means of escape for surplus gas, in the shape of an open neck at the bottom of the envelope and a valve at the top, remotely controlled by a long cord. A wicker car, large enough to carry two or more aeronauts with their clothing, equipment and provisions and a quantity of ballast, was slung from a hoop suspended from the upper half of the envelope by a network of cords.

In this handsome vehicle, which set the pattern for future hydrogen balloons, Charles and the elder of the Robert brothers ascended from the Tuileries in perfect weather on 1 December. They made a 2-hour flight over the northern outskirts of Paris, followed by a controlled descent in the Ile-de-France. Charles followed with a lone ascent to a height estimated from barometric readings at 10,000 feet.

In the following February Paolo Andreani of Milan made the first ascent from Italian soil. He used a hot-air balloon built to his design by two local craftsmen who accompanied him on his 20-minute flight.

Seven months later Vincenzo Lunardi, a native of Lucca at one time employed at the Neapolitan Embassy in London, ascended from the Honourable Artillery Company's parade ground at Moorfields in a hydrogen balloon, with a dog, a cat and a pigeon in a cage as his sole companions, After making an intermediate descent at North Mimms to disembark the cat, he completed the first sustained flight from British soil by descending in a cornfield near Ware, about 20 miles in a direct line from his starting-point. A bizarre feature of Lunardi's flight was that he carried oars and so-called wings, with which he believed he could influence his direction of movement both laterally and vertically.

The title of first British aeronaut is generally awarded, for his courage rather than his achievement, to James Tytler of Edinburgh, who used a crude hot-air balloon to make brief leaps into the air in the late summer of 1784. The first of these was made on 25 August, about 3 weeks before Lunardi's historic flight. The second and last was made on 1 September.

The first English aeronaut, and also the first British subject to remain airborne for any length of time, was James Sadler, son of an Oxford pastry cook and afterwards a successful inventor and engineer. Sadler made a brief flight on 4 October 1784 from Oxford to the neighbourhood of Islip in a hot-air balloon of his own devising. On 12 November he flew in a hydrogen balloon from Oxford to Hartwell, near Aylesbury, covering 14 miles in 17 minutes. He made 5 flights in 1785 , including one of 50 miles, but then gave up ballooning for nearly a quarter of a century.

Other feats which helped to make ballooning a fashionable pastime included some remarkable flights by Jean-Pierre Blanchard, with the possible exception of Lunardi the first professional aeronaut. Accompanied as far as Sunbury by the celebrated anatomist John Sheldon, Blanchard flew in a hydrogen balloon on 16 October 1784 from Chelsea to Romsey in Hampshire, a distance of more than 70 miles. On 7 January 1785 he crossed the Channel from Dover to Guisnes in 2 hours. His companion on the cross-Channel flight was the American Dr John Jeffries, a generous and long-suffering patron who paid all the expenses of the voyage and went out of his way to ensure that Blanchard received all the credit.

Between 1785 and 1789 Blanchard made a number of exhibition flights in various European countries, usually with hydrogen balloons but sometimes with hot-air balloons. He also set up a long-distance record by making a flight of 300 miles in a hydrogen balloon from Lille. After the outbreak of the French Revolution he was arrested in Austria on a charge of spreading anti-monarchist propaganda in the Hapsburg dominions, but escaped to the United States. On 9 January 1793 he made the first flight over American territory by ascending in a hydrogen balloon from Philadelphia. Returning to France in 1798, he continued to receive the pension awarded to him by Louis XVI in recognition of his cross-Channel flight until, in 1809, he died of a heart-attack after making his sixtieth ascent.

Until the introduction of coal gas—first used to fill a balloon by the Englishman Charles Green in 1821 – a serious disadvantage of gas-filled balloons was the prodigious expenditure of time and effort needed to inflate them with hydrogen which had to be manufactured on the spot. Moreover, a hydrogen balloon could be inflated or topped up only where the cumbrous equipment and relatively scarce materials required were available. By contrast, a hot-air balloon needed nothing to bring it to life but a match or a tinder-box and a supply of combustible matter procurable almost anywhere. On the other hand, its range was limited by the quantity of straw or other fuel that could be carried.

A shortcoming shared by the hot-air balloon with the gas-filled balloon was, of course, its utter dependence on the wind. Lunardi with his oars, Blanchard with a manually-rotated airscrew which he called a *moulinet*, could no more direct the course of a free balloon than Canute could arrest the rising tide.

Had a suitable engine been available, a dirigible airship could none the less have been constructed by the end of the eighteenth century. J.-B.-M. Meusnier, a French army officer who was also a gifted engineer and physicist, submitted to the Academy in 1783 a paper in which he described a method of improving the stability and endurance of a gas-filled balloon by the incorporation of an internal reservoir of air, or *ballonnet*. It soon became apparent that this device, besides enabling the pilot of a free spherical balloon to conserve gas and ballast and thus make longer flights than would otherwise be possible, could be applied to an aspherical balloon as a means of maintaining the elongated shape desirable for powered flight. In 1784 Meusnier designed a 260-foot-long non-rigid dirigible balloon of ellipsoid form, with a rudder, a rudimentary elevator and 3 large airscrews. This remarkable design anticipated most of the salient features of the non-rigid dirigible airship of the future. Its only serious shortcoming was that lack of an engine forced Meusnier to rely on the manpower of the crew to rotate the airscrews by rope and pulley.

No further advance of major importance was made up to the time when the French found themselves simultaneously in the throes of a revolution and at war with Austria and Prussia. Meusnier was killed at Mainz in 1793, and his airship was never built. Balloons based on his design were constructed by Charles and the Roberts brothers, but they were unpowered.

In the same year a scientific advisory commission appointed by the revolutionary government in France recommended that captive hydrogen balloons should be used for military reconnaissance. The government accepted this recommendation with the proviso that sulphuric acid should not be used for the manufacture of hydrogen, since all the available sulphur was needed to make gunpowder. On the advice of the distinguished chemist Antoine Lavoisier, experts adapted to large-scale production a laboratory method of making hydrogen from superheated steam. An experimental station was established at Meudon, and the first of a series of specially strong two-man observation balloons was constructed and given the name of *L'Entreprenant*. After a successful trial at Meudon in the early spring of 1794, a balloon corps with an initial establishment of one company was formed as a branch of the artillery and despatched to Maubeuge, at that time besieged by Austrian and Dutch troops.

Before *L'Entreprenant* could be used in the field, the large generator provided for its inflation had to be installed in a massive furnace constructed on the spot. Nevertheless the balloon gave good service when it did go into action. After a satisfactory performance at Maubeuge it was hauled, still inflated, some twenty-four miles across country to Charleroi. In the light of favourable reports from the front, a second company was added to the balloon corps on 23 June. At Fleurus 3 days later, the French gave a striking demonstration of the value of air power by basing their tactics throughout a highly successful ten-hour battle on the aerial observations of a senior officer sent aloft for the purpose. By the summer of 1796 4 balloons, each with its complement of aeronauts, ground crew and equipment, were in service on various fronts.

A balloon unit accompanied Napoleon to Egypt, but little use was made of it and its equipment was destroyed by the British at Aboukir. On his return to France in 1799, Napoleon disbanded the balloon corps and abolished the experimental establishment, depot and balloon school at Meudon. This decision has been generally attributed to the vanity of a tyrant unwilling to admit that he could not divine the enemy's dispositions by the light of his genius alone. That may well be the true explanation. On the other hand, Napoleon was keenly interested in the artillery and had a good grasp of technical problems. He may have been genuinely convinced that, in view of the notorious instability of captive spherical balloons and the difficulty of transporting the equipment needed to inflate them, the balloon units were more trouble than they were worth.

Free ballooning continued after the Napoleonic Wars to provide sport for the rich and a livelihood for the intrepid. On 22 July 1817 Windham Sadler, younger son of James Sadler, crossed the Irish Sea from Dublin to Anglesey in 5 hours in a hydrogen balloon. In 1836 Charles Green, the pioneer of balloons filled with coal gas, made with 2 companions a record-breaking flight of nearly 500 miles from London to Weilburg, near Frankfurt. A rope trailed from the car to check the tendency of a gas-filled balloon to rise to uneconomic heights was used for the first time on this flight, although its use had been suggested half a century earlier. Finally, in 1839, an American aeronaut, John Wise, introduced the ripping panel as a means of ensuring prompt deflation on landing. This device substantially reduced the perils of ballooning, and was afterwards generally adopted.

Twenty years later Wise and another professional aeronaut, John La Mountain, with a patron named Gager and a journalist, made a remarkable flight of roughly 800 miles from St Louis to Henderson, NY, in a large gas balloon with which they hoped to cross the Atlantic. A still larger balloon designed by Wise's rival, Thaddeus Lowe, for the same purpose was wrecked by a sudden squall half an hour before it was due to begin its transatlantic flight.

Hot-air balloons were used for the first time in war in 1849, when the Austrians attempted an aerial bombardment of Venice with small time-fused bombs, each carried by a small balloon. About 200 such missiles are said to have been prepared. Many went astray or were blown back over the Austrian lines, and those which reached the target did negligible damage. The French experimented with a hot-air balloon during Napoleon III's Italian campaign in 1859, but it did not remain airborne long enough to be put to practical use.

Progress towards powered flight entered a new phase in 1850, when Pierre Jullien, a French clockmaker, demonstrated in Paris an elegant streamlined model airship with 2 airscrews driven by clockwork. The success of Jullien's model inspired Henri Giffard, a brilliant engineer and inventor, to design and build a non-rigid dirigible airship 144 feet long. This was propelled by a single large airscrew driven by a 3 hp steam engine weighing, with its boiler, about as much as 2 fair-sized men. The envelope was completely symmetrical in longitudinal section, sharply pointed at both ends and of elegant shape. In the interests of safety the car was slung more than 40 feet below it, the fire-door of the boiler was screened by wire gauze except when stoking was in progress, and the chimney pointed downwards and backwards so that no sparks which it might discharge were likely to reach any inflammable part of the structure.

In this handsome airship Giffard made, on 24 September 1852, the first powered flight ever made by man. Wearing a frock coat and a top hat, he flew some 17 miles from Paris Hippodrome to Trappes, where he landed safely. On a subsequent occasion he showed that the airship was under control by describing a circle in the air.

Giffard's aerial steamer was, without question, the first successful dirigible airship ever built. The fact remains that 'dirigible' is a relative term. Giffard's airship attained a speed of 6 miles an hour in still air. Thus it was dirigible only in a calm or in light airs. In even a gentle breeze it would have attained a spanking pace down-wind, but could not have returned to its starting-point.

Giffard recognized that he needed a better power-weight ratio to make his airship controllable in everyday conditions, but was unable to attain it with the means at his disposal in 1852. He tried attaching his existing engine to a longer, slimmer envelope in order to reduce wind resistance and gain added lift, but the new version came to grief for lack of an effective means of restoring its fore-and-aft trim when the nose tilted sharply during a trial flight. He then planned a vast airship nearly 2,000 feet long, and designed for it an engine calculated to give it a speed of 45 miles an hour in still air, but the immense cost of the project prevented him from carrying it out.

The invention of the gas engine by Etienne Lenoir in 1860 opened new possibilities to designers of airships, not because early gas engines were particularly efficient but because no heavy boiler was needed. In 1865 Paul Haenlein, an Austrian, took out a patent in London for an airship powered by a gas engine, but it was not built until 7 years later.

On the outbreak of the American Civil War most of the leading American aeronauts offered their services to the Union. John

Wise designed a field generator for the production of hydrogen by the steam process, but the authorities refused to meet the cost of making it. Later, 12 generators designed by Thaddeus Lowe were built. These used sulphuric acid and iron filings and could inflate a balloon in less than 3 hours, but were heavy and cumbersome. Other innovations sponsored by Lowe included the use of a converted coal barge on the Potomac as a mobile base for a captive balloon, of gas-burning searchlights to aid night ascents, and of the electric telegraph to pass messages from air to ground. A transmitter carried in a balloon was first used to direct artillery fire against the enemy at Falls Church on 24 September 1861.

By the end of 1862 at least 7 captive balloons built specially for military use were in service with the Union forces. In addition, John La Mountain made a number of free flights over the Confederate lines, relying on the varying direction of the wind at different heights to bring him back. The balloon corps was credited with averting a panic in Washington after Bull Run by reporting that no Confederate troops were in sight, and with saving the Union forces from defeat at Four Oaks and Gaines's Mill. But the professional aeronauts who provided the backbone of the corps were not particularly easy men to handle. The authorities made the mistake of not bringing them under military discipline by giving them commissions. They quarrelled amongst themselves, they fell out with their superiors and especially with Cyrus B. Comstock, Chief Engineer of the Army of the Potomac. After Comstock was made responsible for the corps it soon fell into disarray, and from the early part of 1863 it ceased to play any significant part in the war.

The Confederates had to manage with more limited resources. In the early stages of the war they made some use of a hot-air balloon manned by John Randolph Bryan. Bryan's balloon could remain aloft only for brief periods, since it had no brazier, and it is said have rotated freely about its cable. It was replaced by a coal-gas balloon whose manufacture from bolts of silk of different colours and patterns gave rise to the legend that the ladies of Richmond, Va, had sacrificed their dresses to make it. The original 'silk dress' balloon was captured by Union forces at Turkey Bend on the James River in the summer of 1862. It was replaced by a similar balloon which gave good service until, some twelve months later, it was blown over the Union lines and captured without its pilot.

The achievements of Lowe and other aeronauts in the early stages of the American Civil War made a powerful impression on Captain F. Beaumont, a British officer attached as military observer to the Union forces. On his return to England Beaumont and a brother officer, Captain C. E. Grover, tried to enlist the interest of the War Office in ballooning by making demonstration ascents at Woolwich and Aldershot with balloons hired from Henry Coxwell, the best-known British aeronaut and balloon-maker of the day. Grover, a man of means, spent considerable sums on attempts to make the army balloon-minded, but it was not until some 15 years had elapsed that he managed to persuade the War Office to take much interest in the subject.

At the beginning of the Franco-Prussian War of 1870–1 the Prussians possessed 2 balloons bought from Coxwell, but had no means of inflating them in the field. The French made a limited use of captive balloons for military reconnaissance after the fall of Sedan, but these were privately-owned balloons intended for free flight and were not very suitable for the purpose. Ballooning came into its own so far as the French were concerned when Paris was invested and the beleaguered garrison felt the need to communicate with the Provisional Government at Tours. On the initiative of a group of professional aeronauts, the postal authorities then organized a balloon-mail service and set up improvized factories at temporarily disused railway stations where seamstresses and sailors stitched envelopes and prepared lines, nets and baskets. Between September and January 66 balloons left Paris carrying 10 tons of mail, about 100 privileged passengers, some hundreds of pigeons and 5 dogs. The balloon post was also used to scatter propagandist leaflets and broadsheets over the Prussian lines. About 60 pigeons returned safely to Paris carrying microfilmed letters, some of them making 2 or more flights. The dogs were intended to make their way back to the city with messages concealed in their collars, but none arrived.

In the light of these experiences the French Government appointed in 1874 an advisory commission on air communications. On the recommendation of the commission a revived military aeronautical establishment was installed at the old site at Meudon. Between 1878 and 1893 the British, the Italians, the

Germans, the Austrians and the Russians all followed the example of the French by setting up balloon schools or aeronautical research establishments. During the same period the Americans resumed the use of balloons for military purposes after a lapse of nearly 30 years. In 1884 the British introduced portable cylinders of compressed hydrogen. In the same year a balloon detachment of the Royal Engineers accompanied a British military expedition to Bechuanaland. Balloons were also used on active service by the British in the Sudan in 1885, and by the Italians in Eritrea in 1887 and 1888.

After the Franco-Prussian War designers of airships made little or no attempt to develop steam propulsion on the lines sketched by Giffard, but experimented with a variety of other methods. A large non-rigid airship ordered by the French Government during the war was tested on 2 February 1872. The designer was Stanislas Dupuy de Lôme, a marine engineer and naval architect. No engine was installed, but 8 men rotated a large 4-bladed airscrew by means of cranks and gears. A speed in still air approximately equal to Giffard's was attained, but the effort was prodigious and the experiment was not reckoned a success.

Paul Haenlein's airship, with an engine which drew gas from the envelope, was ready for trial by the following December. The envelope was 164 feet long and of a shape which suggested two ships' hulls of different draught placed deck to deck. Tests were made at Brunn (Brno) on 13 and 14 December, but on both occasions the airship was restrained, as if it had been a dangerous wild beast, by ropes held by soldiers. A speed of 9 miles an hour in still air was claimed. How the airship would have behaved in free flight remains unknown, since further experiments were ruled out by lack of money.

A one-man airship designed by Charles F. Ritchel of Corry, Pa, was tested at Hartford, Connecticut, in 1878. Twenty-five feet long, with a propellor driven by pedals, it made a circular flight in still air at a speed of 3½ miles an hour.

In 1881 an Electrical Exhibition was held in Paris. Two brothers, Gaston and Albert Tissandier, showed a model electric airship which aroused so much interest that they went on to build a man-carrying version. This was not unlike Giffard's aerial steamer, but with a shorter and more bulbous envelope. It was driven by a Siemens electric motor rated at 1½ hp. Since the batteries alone weighed more than Giffard's engine and boiler, it is not surprising that barely half his speed in still air was attained.

A more powerful electrically-propelled airship designed by Charles Renard and Arthur Krebs was completed in 1884 and named *La France*. The envelope was about a foot longer than that of Haenlein's airship, and of the same rather ungainly shape. With a $7\frac{1}{2}$ and later an $8\frac{1}{2}$ hp motor, *La France* made 7 flights in 1884 and 1885, and on all but two occasions was able to return to her point of departure under her own power. Her speed in still air was $14\frac{1}{2}$ miles an hour. Thus she was truly dirigible only in a calm or in light airs or a light or gentle breeze.

At that stage fate decreed that the German inventor Gottlieb Daimler, following a path pointed out by his compatriot N. A. Otto, should develop a derivative of the gas engine which used as fuel the volatile liquid known in English-speaking countries as petrol or gasoline. From the point of view of safety, a more unsuitable power unit for an airship kept aloft by highly inflammable hydrogen might seem hard to imagine; but the high power-weight ratio of the boilerless internal combustion engine was attractive. Daimler read in 1887 of some experiments with a small, manually propelled airship by a certain Dr Karl Wölfert. He wrote to Wölfert, offering his collaboration.

Wölfert's one-man airship gave a satisfactory performance when tested in 1888 with a single-cylinder Daimler engine rated at 2 hp. Since the car was very close to the envelope and ignition was by a tube which projected from the cylinder and was kept hot by a naked flame the airship could, however, scarcely be called safe.

In the course of the next few years Wölfert built a much larger airship with a 6 hp twin-cylinder engine. This engine, too, had hot-tube ignition, as indeed had all Daimler engines completed before 1900. The new airship was exhibited at the Berlin Trade Fair in the late summer of 1896. It attracted favourable notice from the Emperor Wilhelm II, but was said to lack lift. Furthermore, no *ballonnet* was fitted and again the car was much closer to the envelope than was customary. Wölfert's critics feared that the envelope might touch the heads of the crew if it sagged in consequence of the loss of hydrogen by valving as the airship ascended. There was also an obvious risk that hydrogen so released might come into contact with the burner of the ignition system. Wölfert's disregard of these hazards is hard to understand unless he counted on always flying so low that no valving would occur.

As a result of the Kaiser's interest in the airship, a distinguished audience assembled at the aeronautical establishment at Tempelhof on Saturday, 12 June 1897 to see her put through her paces. It included representatives of Germany's armed forces and members of the diplomatic corps. An officer of the Prussian balloon corps was to have accompanied Wölfert and his mechanic on the trial flight, but he stood down when the net which distributed the weight of the car over the envelope was found to have broken in two places. The change was intended to give a better distribution of weight, but possibly the amount of ballast needed to adjust matters was miscalculated. Perhaps for that reason, or perhaps because the original calculations were faulty, the ship rose rapidly to a height of 3,000 feet when Wölfert gave the order to let go. A few minutes later the envelope was seen to be on fire. An explosion was heard, and the ship plunged to the ground in flames. Both occupants were killed, and the blazing wreckage started a fire in a timber yard.

Five months later an airship of entirely different construction, designed by an Austrian engineer named David Schwartz and completed under the supervision of his widow, was tried at Tempelhof. In 1886 a Frenchman, P.-L.-T. Héroult, and an American, C. M. Hall, had independently invented an electrolytic process suitable for the production of aluminium in commercial quantities. The envelope of the Schwartz airship, 156 feet long and elliptical in cross section, consisted of sheet aluminium on a tubular framework, also of aluminium, and the car or gondola was attached to it by aluminium struts. Propulsion was by belt drive from a 12 hp Daimler engine.

The Schwartz airship was the world's first rigid airship. Unfortunately she was entrusted on her maiden flight to a mechanic or engineer with no aeronautical experience. To make matters worse, the authorities allowed her to depart in a moderate breeze. As no previous airship had proved dirigible in such conditions, this was certainly unwise. The pilot, alone in the gondola, found himself blown along by the wind and unable to gain control. In the course of his attempts to do so, the driving belt came off its pulley. He then brought the ship heavily to the ground by opening the valve. He escaped injury by jumping clear at the last moment, but the ship was wrecked.

This mishap did not deter Count Ferdinand von Zeppelin, a retired German cavalry officer who was determined to perfect a large rigid airship in order, as he said, to give his country a new weapon. In 1900 he completed an airship 420 feet long, driven by 2 Daimler marine engines. These were rated at 16 hp each, but their combined output is said in practice to have been about 24 hp. Unlike Schwartz, Zeppelin did not rely on sheet aluminium to make his envelope gas-tight. He covered his tubular frame with fabric and divided the interior into 17 compartments. With two exceptions, each of these contained a lined gasbag. This remarkable ship, designated LZ.1, flew for 18 minutes on 2 July from a floating hangar on Lake Constance, and on 17 October made a flight of 80 minutes. But the method of controlling fore-and-aft trim was unsatisfactory, and the frame buckled on the first flight. Although this trouble does not seem to have recurred on the second flight, a third trial on 24 October convinced the indomitable designer that he would do well to suspend his experiments until a new and stronger ship could be built. Pending the appearance of a sympathetic backer, he sold his hangar, workshops, engines and stock of aluminium to pay his creditors.

Not surprisingly the fate of Wölfert's airship gave non-rigid dirigibles with petrol engines a bad name in official circles. Balloonists continued, none the less, to aspire to powered flight. In 1898 the Aéro Club de France was founded in Paris and acquired a flying ground at Saint Cloud. Among its most enthusiastic members was Alberto Santos-Dumont, a Brazilian who was well placed to indulge his hobby since he was not only a competent engineer but also a man of means. After an abortive attempt on 18 September, Santos-Dumont made on 20 September the first of a long series of successful flights in small non-rigid airships with De Dion petrol engines. In 1901 he won a large cash prize by flying from Saint Cloud to the Eiffel Tower and back – a distance of roughly 15 miles – in less than half an hour.

As a designer, Santos-Dumont was not among the great innovators. He was, however, an exceptionally skilful pilot and constructor, and he had the advantage over most of his predecessors of not having to curtail his experiments for lack of money or skimp his designs because no engine both light enough and powerful enough for his purpose was available. Above all, he had an almost instinctive understanding of what a lighter-than-air craft could and could not be made to do. If Meusnier, Giffard and Renard showed the world how non-rigid airships should be designed, Santos-Dumont showed how they should be flown.

In England an Aeronautical Society was founded in 1866 and an Aero Club (later the Royal Aero Club) in 1901. Throughout the nineteenth century, and indeed earlier, a keen interest was taken in Britain in the theory of flight, especially with heavier-than-air machines, and in various aspects of ballooning, but little attempt was made to compete with the French in the development of powered airships. It was not until 1902 that Stanley Spencer, an English balloonist, made the first flight in a British airship. This had a small one-man car suspended from an envelope 75 feet long and 20 feet in diameter, with a capacity of 20,000 cubic feet. The power-unit was a Simms water-cooled petrol engine which developed 3½hp at the remarkably high speed of 2,500 rpm and drove a single airscrew through a reduction gear. Spencer flew on 22 September by a roundabout route from the Crystal Palace, in south-east London, to Eastcote in Middlesex, covering an estimated distance of 30 miles in 100 minutes. He made a number of subsequent flights in the same airship, and afterwards built a larger one which gave some trouble.

In the same year Henri Julliot, a French engineer, completed for Paul and Pierre Lebaudy, the proprietors of a sugar refinery, a semi-rigid airship driven by a 40 hp Daimler engine. The envelope was 187 feet long, and of the same rather unattractive shape as that adopted by Haenlein and more recently by Renard. A speed of approximately 25 miles an hour in still air made Julliot's the first airship which could be described as truly dirigible in a fresh breeze. Between the early winter of 1902 and the summer of 1903 she completed about 30 flights from her base near Mantes, on one occasion covering 61 miles at an average speed over the ground of 22 miles an hour. In the following November she flew from Mantes to the Champ de Mars in Paris, where she landed close to the spot from which Charles had released the first successful hydrogen balloon in 1783.

Thereafter the armed forces of most of the leading powers experimented with, and eventually adopted, small non-rigid or semi-rigid airships for naval and military reconnaissance. For some years Count von Zeppelin remained almost the sole champion of the large rigid airship. In 1905 he completed, partly with the proceeds of a state lottery, his LZ.2. Her dimensions were similar to those of the LZ.1, but her engines were much more powerful, and elevators replaced the unsatisfactory sliding weight by which the pitch of the earlier airship had been regulated. Unhappily for her designer, inexperience led him to moor her at both ends when engine failure compelled him to make an emergency landing away from base as the sequel to a trial flight on 17 January 1906. Unable to swing into the wind, she was so severely damaged by a sudden storm that she had to be dismantled on the spot.

Zeppelin followed with the LZ.3, which made a number of successful flights in 1906 and 1907 and was afterwards taken over by the army and renamed Z–1. He then constructed the 450-foot-long LZ.4 and offered her to the German Government. One of the conditions of acceptance was that she should complete a 24-hour non-stop flight. Zeppelin decided to make a round trip of some 450–500 miles by flying from Friedrichshafen to Basle, thence down the Rhine to Mainz, and back to Friedrichshafen by a cross-country route. In good summer weather, such a voyage would be well within the capacity of the ship if her two 110 hp Daimler-Mercedes engines behaved well.

The LZ.4 began her acceptance flight on 4 August 1908, carrying eleven persons in addition to her designer. The day was warm, and conditions must have seemed ideal to watchers at Basle, Strasbourg and Mannheim who saw the great ship pass majestically overhead. In fact, the heat of the sun caused the hydrogen to expand so much that a good deal was lost by valving. Between Mannheim and Mainz, when roughly half the journey was completed, one engine failed. Zeppelin had to make an unscheduled landing at Oppenheim and spend 3½ hours there while it was repaired. The ship then resumed her flight with a reduced load. One the following morning, when she had logged 378 miles and was only about 90 miles from home, engine trouble again forced Zeppelin to make an unscheduled stop. He brought the ship safely to the ground near the Daimler factory at Stuttgart. For lack of a better anchorage, volunteers from a neighbouring barracks moored her to a cart buried in the ground. In the early afternoon a storm blew up. The ship broke from her improvised mooring, caught fire and was wrecked.

For Zeppelin this bloodless disaster proved a blessing in disguise. A sympathetic public subscribed so generously to a fund in aid of his work that he was able to set up an elaborate organization for the manufacture of airships, engines and ancillary equipment. The world's press announced that 8 new airships would be built in the coming year and that their designer was to be decorated in recognition of his services to the Imperial Government.

Zeppelin was not interested in making money. Nor was he interested in producing a mere rival to the non-rigid or semi-rigid airship as a means of reconnaissance. His aim was to contribute to Germany's greatness by providing her with an unrivalled instrument of air power. Nevertheless he agreed towards the end of 1909 that a company should be formed to operate some of his airships on a commercial basis. By this means he hoped not only to make his organization to some extent independent of government orders, but also to foster an interest in flying among the general public. During the next few years the commercial airships *Deutschland*, *Ersatz Deutschland*, *Schwaben*, *Viktoria-Luise*, *Hansa* and *Sachsen* carried about 35,000 passengers on some 1,600 flights without injury to a single one of them. The commercial fleet was also used to train soldiers and sailors to handle airships in the air and on the ground.

The German Army's interest in the LZ.4 caused some alarm in Britain. British anxieties were not allayed when her destruction was followed by the news that more airships were to be built with money contributed by patriotic Germans. At a time when Anglo-German naval rivalry was intense, this announcement seemed to make it all too clear that Germany, not content with the strongest army in Europe, hoped to make herself supreme at sea and in the air.

How the challenge was to be met so far as the air was concerned was a difficult question. In 1907 a small, sausage-shaped airship built in the Army Balloon Factory and rather hopefully called the *Nulli Secundus* had flown from Farnborough to the Crystal Palace by way of St Paul's Cathedral, covering about 50 miles in just under 3½ hours. But the *Nulli Secundus*, even when redesigned and rebuilt in 1908 as the *Nulli Secundus II*, was too slow to be anything but a fair-weather ship. British hopes of competing with the Germans were staked not on such small fry but on a large rigid airship to be built for the Admiralty by Vickers, Sons and Maxim Limited. This firm, which became Vickers Limited when Sir Hiram Maxim left the board, had built the first British submarine. The airship was to be constructed largely of duralumin, a new light alloy of German origin introduced to Britain by Vickers.

When the project was first mooted, the intention was that Captain R. H. S. Bacon, RN, the Director of Naval Ordnance, should not merely satisfy himself by inspection of the finished product that the airship built by Vickers conformed with specifications drafted by the Director of Naval Construction, but should exercise a considerable degree of supervision while the work was in hand. This was an appropriate choice, since Bacon was keenly interested in airships and was largely responsible for the Admiralty's decision to adopt them. However, at an early stage Bacon was forced to relinquish his appointment in consequence of a quarrel about naval strategy between Admiral Lord Charles Beresford and the First Sea Lord, Admiral Sir John Fisher. His successor, Captain Murray Sueter, was an ardent advocate of a strong naval air arm, but he did not profess to know anything about airships. He accepted the post of Captain Inspector of Airships on the express understanding that he should be absolved of responsibility for the design of the Vickers airship. The result was that an unexpectedly heavy burden was thrown on the manager of the marine division of Vickers, who had no experience of aeronautics and no special knowledge of such problems as were likely to arise in the construction of a rigid airship with largely unfamiliar materials.

Vickers began by building at Barrow-in-Furness a vast shed in which the airship was to be constructed. This involved so heavy an outlay as to make it virtually certain that they would incur a substantial loss unless they obtained further orders for aircraft of one kind or another. After sounding Murray Sueter about the prospect of their being asked to tender for more airships, the directors took steps which led eventually to their becoming large suppliers of heavier-than-air machines to the War Office. In the meantime, even without counting the cost of the shed they faced the problem of producing the airship already ordered without spending more on labour, materials and overheads than the contract was worth.

When the ship was not far from completion, a mathematician employed by Vickers predicted that, in consequence of numerous departures from the original design, her structure would prove unsound unless further and more radical changes were made. However, it was decided that she should be completed and thoroughly tested on the ground before she flew.

By the late spring of 1911 the 512-foot-long airship, popularly called the *Mayfly*, was ready for buoyancy and ground-handling tests. She successfully rode out strong winds while moored to a mast built specially for the purpose, but was found seriously deficient in lift. She was therefore returned to her shed for modification. On 24 September she was hauled from the shed for further tests, but broke her back before they could be made. She is said to have bumped against the shed, but a photograph taken immediately before she broke up shows her apparently well clear of it.

Since Count von Zeppelin produced a satisfactory rigid airship only at his third attempt, this experience scarcely suggested that the British were incapable of producing one. A distinguished naval officer declared, however, that a glance at the wreckage of the *Mayfly* was enough to show that that the entire project was 'the work of a lunatic'. A Court of Inquiry attributed the accident to structural weakness and recommended that work on rigid airships be suspended. The £100,000 spent on the *Mayfly* was written off, the Admiralty decided to concentrate for the time being on heavier-than-air machines, and the Germans were left in possession of the field so far as large rigid airships were concerned.

Germany was also well to the fore in the development of a stable aerial platform for artillery reconnaissance. In the South African War, as in earlier campaigns, the British Army used captive spherical balloons for observation in the field. These proved helpful at times, but they could not be flown in much more than a moderate breeze and were seldom stable enough to allow an observer to use field glasses. After the war the British tried, and for a time adopted as a substitute for captive balloons in windy weather, man-lifting kites developed at the request of the War Officer by S. F. Cody, an English-domiciled Texan of pleasing address and picturesque appearance. Cody's kites, like those used tentatively by Baden-Powell before the war, were based on the box-kite of Hargraves. They could be flown – indeed, they could only be flown – in strong winds, but they were even unsteadier than balloons. The attachment of a kite to a captive balloon to improve its stability had been suggested as early as 1885, and this proposal was followed up in Germany about 10 years later. Major August von Parseval and Captain Bartsch von Sigsfeld, of the German Army, then devised an inelegant but highly practical kite-balloon described as stable in winds up to gale force. The Parseval-Sigsfeld 'dragon' or 'sausage balloon' was the ancestor of all the kite-balloons used by the belligerents on both sides in the First World War, and through them of the barrage balloons used much later by the British.

Major von Parseval was also a successful designer and constructor of non-rigid airships. After his retirement from the Army in 1907 he set up as a producer on a commercial scale. Between 1909 and 1913 his firm completed 18 airships, some of which carried passengers while others were applied to military purposes. Orders for *Parseval* airships were placed by the Governments of Austro-Hungary, Britain, Germany, Italy, Japan, Russia and Turkey. Yet another German producer of airships was the firm of Schütte-Lanz, which presented a minor challenge to the Zeppelin organization by offering rigid airships in which wood was used instead of aluminium for the framework.

Before and after the introduction of the hot-air balloon, the gas balloon and the dirigible airship, would-be aviators who aspired to fly in heavier-than-air machines carried out their experiments more or less independently of those made by aeronauts who relied on hot air, hydrogen or coal-gas to buoy them up. For a long time the lack of a light and powerful engine continued, however, to restrict practical trials to tantalizing ventures with models or gliders.

In 1784 two Frenchmen named Launay and Bienvenu demonstrated in Paris a model helicopter with a built-in power-unit consisting of a bow-string mechanism. A model helicopter not unlike theirs, but driven by clockwork, is said to have been flown some 30 years earlier by the Russian writer and natural philosopher M. V. Lomonosov, but contemporary evidence is lacking.

In 1796 Sir George Cayley, a Yorkshire baronet and philanthropist who combined great practical ability with an exceptional capacity for constructive thought, made a model helicopter on the lines of that demonstrated by Launay and Bienvenu. By afterwards improving it and publishing his improved design in a form which secured the attention of serious investigators on both sides of the Channel, he laid the foundations of all subsequent progress towards the man-carrying helicopter of the twentieth century.

The claims made for Cayley as the true inventor of the aeroplane and the father of aerial navigation rest, however, chiefly on his contributions to the theory and practice of flight with fixed-wing aircraft. Envisaging the powered aeroplane as essentially a kite in which the tug of the string is replaced by the thrust of an engine, he defined the central problem of mechanical flight as that of making a surface support a given weight by the application of power to the resistance of air. For lack of an engine, he was able to apply this principle only to gliders, in which (except when they were towed) the power applied to the resistance of air was derived solely from the pull of gravity on the structure and its human or inanimate load. Between 1804 and 1853 he built a series of gliders, starting with a kite-winged model 5 feet long and ending with a large triplane which carried his coachman across a small valley on his estate near Scarborough. His publications included a masterly exposition of the principles of aerodynamics and flight control, and a design for an inherently stable fixed-wing glider, intended to be launched from a balloon.

Among Cayley's warmest admirers was William Samuel Henson, a manufacturer of machinery for the making of lace. In 1843 Henson took out a patent for an 'Aerial Steam Carriage'. This was a monoplane with double-surfaced cambered wings braced by wires, a tail unit comprising elevator and rudder, a tricycle undercarriage and two pusher airscrews. Power was to be provided by a 25–30 hp engine carried in the boat-shaped fuselage. The machine was never built, but engravings based on the drawings which accompanied the specification were reproduced in many countries and eagerly discussed. The essential soundness of Henson's design, and its influence on his successors, are attested by the reappearance of many of its salient features in the first successful monoplanes of the twentieth century.

With the help of a friend, John Stringfellow, Henson went on to build a large model with a wing-span of 20 feet, powered by an elegant small steam engine. This was launched down a ramp in the open air, but failed to sustain itself. After numerous attempts to make it fly, Henson abandoned his hopes of founding an aerial transit company and emigrated to the United States.

Stringfellow then built a smaller model with an improved engine and other modifications. This was launched from an overhead wire in a shed in 1848, and was afterwards demonstrated at Cremorne Gardens in London. It was long regarded as the first model aeroplane to fly under its own power, but whether it ever flew in the sense of maintaining a level or ascending course after the impetus derived from its launching was exhausted is open to doubt.

Doubtless influenced by some adverse comments by Cayley on Henson's monoplane design, Stringfellow switched to a multi-wing configuration when, 20 years later, he contributed to an aeronautical exhibition at the Crystal Palace. The model triplane he then showed looked archaic in comparison with his monoplane of 1848, and it was not very successful when tested. Nevertheless his change of heart is believed to have been largely responsible for the decision of the Wright brothers to experiment with biplanes rather than monoplanes when they built their first gliders a generation later.

About 10 years after Stringfellow's first model was tested, a French naval officer named Félix du Temple de la Croix produced, with the help of his brother Louis, a clockwork model aeroplane which scored a resounding success by taking off, flying and landing safely. Later the clockwork mechanism was replaced by a steam engine. Félix du Temple also designed and built a man-carrying monoplane with swept-forward wings, a tailplane and rudder, a retractable undercarriage and a tractor airscrew driven alternatively by hot air or steam. Unsuccessful when first put through its paces at the end of the 1850s, this ingenious but rather cumbrous machine made a brief flight with a seaman aboard after descending a ramp in 1874.

Another designer with nautical associations who first made his mark with a model of outstanding quality was Alphonse Pénaud, the physically-handicapped son of a French admiral. After making a successful model helicopter in 1870, Pénaud produced in 1871 a tiny monoplane of masterly simplicity, with a wing-span of 18 inches, a diamond-shaped tailplane and a pusher airscrew rotated by twisted rubber. The tips of wing and tailplane were bent sharply upwards in the interests of lateral stability. When demonstrated in Paris on 18 August, this enchanting mini-aircraft flew 131 feet in 11 seconds. Pénaud was not the first model-maker to use twisted or stretched rubber as a source of power, but he was the first to draw attention to its commercial possibilities by adopting it for a model which combined simplicity with an outstanding performance. The result was that model aeroplanes capable of sustained flight were afterwards manufactured and sold in quantities and at prices which enabled enormous numbers of children and adults throughout the world to derive pleasure from them.

Besides making a successful model ornithopter, Pénaud went on to take out a patent, in association with his mechanic Paul Gauchot, for a full-size two-seater monoplane with elliptical wings, a rudder attached to a fixed vertical fin, a domed cockpit and other advanced features. The machine was never built, but the specification provided students of aeronautics with a fruitful field of enquiry for many years to come.

A feature common to Félix du Temple's and Pénaud's designs was that both men set the wings of their monoplanes at a slight upward angle, or in aeronautical terms with slight positive dihedral, in the hope of counteracting a tendency to roll. This arrangement reflected a preoccupation with stability natural in designers who drew their experience from models, since these had to be stable if they were to fly at all. Cayley, who also began with models, and whose gliders flew in ballast or on rare occasions carried a boy or man who was more passenger than pilot, likewise attached much importance to stability, although that did not prevent him from recognizing that a powered aeroplane would be useless if it were so stable that it did not respond to its pilot's will. The broad effect of the precept and example of these pioneers was that their successors and disciples, especially in France and Britain, tended during the latter part of the nineteenth century and the early part of the twentieth to aim at the production of a fixed-wing aircraft with inherent stability, both lateral and longitudinal, at the cost of giving less attention than they might have done to the problem of providing the pilot with adequate means of control in flight.

Important contributions to the theory of flight during the second half of the nineteenth century included the publication of books by Count Ferdinand d'Esterno, L.-P. Mouillard and Otto Lilienthal on the flight of birds, with special reference to gliding and soaring. In 1863 the photographer Félix Tournachon, better known as Nadar, founded in Paris a society for the encouragement of flight with heavier-than-air machines. At the first meeting of the Aeronautical Society of the United Kingdom on 27 June 1866, Francis Herbert Wenham, a marine engineer, initiated the close scientific study of wing-shape and camber by pointing out that the wings of all birds were cambered and were thicker at the leading than at the trailing edge, and that a cambered wing which was long and narrow gave more lift in proportion to its area than one which was short and broad. Thereafter another pioneer of aerodynamics, H. F. Phillips, used a wind tunnel constructed by himself to conduct a series of experiments with cambered wings of diverse curvature and thickness. In 1884 he took out a patent for a number of double-surfaced aerofoils which he described as 'blades for deflecting air'. Phillips also produced evidence to show that the greater part of the lift generated by a thick cambered wing more curved on the upper than on the lower surface was due not to pressure from below the wing but to suction created by a region of low pressure above it.

In the same year, or earlier according to some accounts, a monoplane designed by A. F. Mozhaiski on the lines of Henson's Aerial Steam Carriage, and powered by a British engine, travelled some 30 yards through the air with a man aboard after descending an elevated ramp near St Petersburg. This has been claimed as the first powered flight by a man-carrying heavier-than-air machine; but there is nothing to show that Mozhaiski's aircraft was capable of sustaining itself in the air after the impetus derived from its descent of the ramp was spent.

Despite the wealth of information available to serious investigators by the middle of the 1880s, some oddly archaic machines were produced in the course of the next 20 years or so. In 1890 Clément Ader, a French electrical engineer, completed a grotesque bat-winged monoplane whose best feature was a light but powerful steam engine with an output of some 18–20 hp. This drove a 4-bladed tractor airscrew. No elevator was fitted, and the pilot's view ahead was obstructed by the boiler. On 9 October 1890 this machine covered its designer with glory by rising from level ground and flying some 54 yards, with Ader himself at the controls. Ader afterwards built a twin-screw monoplane for the Ministry of War, but it failed to fly when he demonstrated it to the military authorities at Satory, near Versailles, on 12 and 14 October 1897. He alleged in 1906 that it had flown some 325 yards on the second of these occasions, but his claim was refuted by an official report published in 1910.

Unaware that Ader had forestalled him in 1890, the British-domiciled American inventor Hiram Maxim embarked in 1893 on an elaborate attempt to prove that a man-carrying machine propelled by steam could 'lift itself from the ground'. He built an immense biplane with a lifting area of 4,000 square feet, equipped it with 2 well-designed steam engines of 180 hp each, and installed it on rails at Baldwyns Park in Kent. The all-up weight of the machine, with pilot and a crew of 3, was roughly 3½ tons. Guard rails were provided to prevent this huge contraption from rising more than about 2 feet should it become airborne. When the boiler pressure was raised to 320 lbs to the square inch on 31 July 1894, the machine rose with such force that the axletree of one of the wheels which engaged the guard rails gave way. One of the guard rails then broke and fouled the mechanism. This appears to have been the last, if not the only, occasion on which Maxim tried to raise the machine into the air. At any rate until the summer of 1895 he continued, however, to show it to distinguished visitors, and on one or two occasions it was used to trundle members of the public across the park in aid of a local charity.

In the United States Samuel Pierpont Langley, at one time Secretary of the Smithsonian Institution, constructed in 1887 a large steam-driven whirling arm for the purpose of ascertaining how much power was needed to sustain a given weight in the air and drive it forward at a given speed. After making a large number of experiments with small rubber-driven models he built 6 larger models driven by steam and launched by catapult. None of these was successful in its original form, but 2 of them made flights of up to three-quarters of a mile after he had rebuilt them as tandem-wing monoplanes.

In 1898, after the outbreak of the Spanish-American War,

Langley accepted an invitation from the United States Government to build a man-carrying aircraft in return for a subsidy of $50,000. This was completed in 1903 as a tandem-wing monoplane with a wing-span of 48 feet. It was driven by a petrol engine designed and built by Langley's assistant Charles Manly but based at least partly on a rejected engine supplied by Stephen M. Balzer of New York. Langley made 2 attempts to launch the machine by catapult over the Potomac with the faithful Manly aboard, but on both occasions it fell straight into the water.

Paradoxically, the man who did most in the 1890s to point the way to powered flight with fixed-wing aircraft believed that the future lay with the ornithopter. Otto Lilienthal, a German engineer from Pomerania, made more than 2,000 flights with fixed-wing gliders before he stalled, crashed and was killed in 1896, but he never ceased to hanker after wings more like a bird's. In addition to a large number of tailed fixed-wing gliders, a few of which were biplanes and the rest monoplanes, he built at least 2 monoplanes with movable slats along the trailing edges of their wings. These he intended to use as glider-ornithopters powered by a small gas engine.

Accounts of Lilienthal's exploits, many of them accompanied by photographs or drawings, appeared in newspapers and periodicals throughout the world. Percy Sinclair Pilcher, a marine engineer and naval architect of Scottish antecedents employed for a time by Maxim, was moved to build gliders of his own and to visit Lilienthal in Germany. In the light of his experience of gliding and soaring he designed, patented in 1896 and decided to build a light aeroplane which was essentially a monoplane glider with a hinged tail and a small auxiliary petrol engine driving a pusher airscrew. He completed and tested the engine by 1899, but had not yet built the aeroplane when he was killed in that year while demonstrating a rain-sodden glider. Since Pilcher's combination of technical knowledge with practical experience was unique in Britain at the time, his death was a serious blow to British aviation.

Lilienthal's experiments also came to the attention of Oscar Chanute, a French-born citizen of the United States who practised as a civil engineer in Chicago. The author of a book called *Progress in Flying Machines*, published in New York in 1894, Chanute was familiar with the literature of the subject and aware of the work done by Cayley, Henson, Stringfellow and other pioneers. Lilienthal's example inspired him to exhort would-be designers of heavier-than-air machines to build man-carrying gliders and try them in the air. In 1896, at the age of 64, he built 2 gliders which he persuaded a young engineer named A. M. Herring to test for him. A third followed in 1902. The best of these was a tailed biplane (originally a triplane) derived from Stringfellow's model triplane of 1868 and Lilienthal's biplanes. The wings were braced by struts and diagonal wires and the tail was of a type introduced by Cayley. Herring made a number of successful glides with this aircraft, including at least one of well over 100 yards. He afterwards built, on his own account, a powered biplane driven by compressed air, but it failed to fly when he showed it to Chanute in 1898.

Wilbur and Orville Wright, two brothers who had built up a modest business as manufacturers of bicycles at Dayton, Ohio, were also encouraged by accounts of Lilienthal's flights to take an active interest in aviation. In the first half of 1899 Wilbur wrote to the Smithsonian Institution for information about books and articles on the subject, and was sent a list which included Chanute's book. The brothers then built a biplane kite designed to test a theory of Wilbur's about the flight of birds. Wilbur believed that a buzzard, when partly overturned by a gust of wind, regained its lateral balance by twisting the tips of its wings. He and Orville arranged matters so that they could twist or 'warp', the wings of their kite by pulling on strings.

In the following year, after Wilbur had written to Chanute for advice and information, the brothers built a tailless biplane glider with a wing-span of 17 feet. It resembled Chanute's successful glider in being a biplane with wings braced in accordance with the system he used, but in other respects the design was all their own. The Wrights believed that it was by learning to control a glider that they were most likely to hit upon a successful design for a powered aircraft. They aimed, therefore, at producing an inherently unstable machine which would make demands on its pilot's powers of co-ordination similar to those made by a bicycle on its rider. Lilienthal had sought to control his gliders by adopting a more or less upright posture which enabled him to swing his legs and trunk both backwards and forwards and from side to side. The Wrights, rejecting this method and adopting a prone position, depended for control of their first glider on their wing-warping system and on a forward elevator. A forward elevator would, they hoped, save them from sudden nose-dives such as that which had cost Lilienthal his life.

In the late summer of 1900 the Wrights tested the glider at Kitty Hawk on the coast of North Carolina, a place chosen in the light of weather reports which suggested that strong and constant winds could be expected there. They flew it mostly as an unmanned kite, more rarely as a manned kite, and only on a few occasions as a free manned glider.

In July and August of the following year they tested a larger biplane glider in free manned flight at the Kill Devil Hills, a group of sand dunes about four miles south of Kitty Hawk. The new glider was very similar to the first, but had a wing-span of 22 feet and a more sophisticated method of controlling the warping movement. One of the brothers acted as pilot while the other, assisted by a helper recruited locally, grasped the glider and ran with it until it became airborne. Some successful glides were made, including at least one of nearly 130 yards, but the glider showed a tendency to sideslip when the wings were warped.

After their return to Dayton at the end of the season, the brothers worked out their theories afresh in the light of experiments which included the testing of wing sections in a wind tunnel and on a bicycle. When they came to build their third biplane glider in the late summer of 1902, they increased the wing-span to more than 30 feet and added, as a precaution againts sideslip, a double vertical fin at the rear. In the second half of September they took the new glider to the Kill Devil Hills, but found it tended to slew round when the wings were warped and to go into a spin if corrections were applied. These troubles disappeared when the double fixed fin was replaced by a single movable rudder whose movement was linked with the wing-warping mechanism. In its modified form the glider could be made to perform smooth banked turns and was controllable in winds up to Force 7 on the Beaufort Scale.

The Wright brothers applied in the same year for a patent for their method of control by a combination of wing-warping and rudder movement, but it was not granted until 1906. In the meantime they built three powered aircraft which they called *Flyer*, *Flyer II* and *Flyer III*. Since they were unable to buy a suitable power unit they designed and built an excellent petrol engine with an output of 12 hp, increased in 1904 to 15–16 hp.

The original *Flyer* was transported to the Kill Devil Hills at the end of the summer of 1903, but was not tested until December. It was a biplane with a wing-span of more than 40 feet and a general resemblance to the successful glider of 1902, but both the forward elevator and the rudder at the rear were double. It stalled and nose-dived almost immediately after take-off when launched from a downhill ramp on 14 December, but flew about 40 yards from level ground on 17 December. Three more flights, one of which lasted nearly a minute, were made later on the same day, but the machine was then overturned by a gust of wind and wrecked.

Flyer II, outwardly similar to the original *Flyer* but equipped with the more powerful engine which the Wrights had built since December, made some 80 brief flights in the summer, autumn and early winter of 1904. For these a field near Dayton was used. From 7 September all take-offs were assisted by a weight-and-pulley device which remained in use until 1910.

Flyer III, more robust than *Flyer II* and with larger elevator and rudder surfaces, made some 40 flights from the same field in the summer and early autumn of 1905. Towards the end of the season the Wrights divorced control of the rudder from that of the wing-warping system. Thereafter they were able to correct roll without changing course.

The success of the original *Flyer* on 17 December 1903 was reported in the world's press, but often inaccurately. The New York correspondent of one London newspaper reported, for example, that the aircraft had flown 3 miles and had 'landed at a point selected in advance'. Since this was not only untrue but highly improbable, it is not surprising that accounts of the exploits of the Wright brothers were received in Europe with a good deal of scepticism. One European who nonetheless believed that the Wrights had made a significant advance was Lieutenant-Colonel J. E. Capper, commandant of the Royal Engineers' balloon school and depot at Aldershot and later Superintendent of the Army Balloon Factory at Farnborough. Capper travelled to the United States in 1904 to attend an exhibition at St Louis on behalf of the War Office. He took the opportunity of calling on the Wrights at Dayton. On his return he gave an accurate account of the best flight they had made in 1903, and added that he was convinced of their integrity.

In the light of this visit and of the keen interest taken by the United States Government in Langley's experiments, the Wright brothers concluded that they had in their possession an asset which might be sold for a high price. When their attempt to sell their invention to the United States Army came to nothing, they decided to offer it to the British Government.

However, the aircraft built by the Wrights up to this time were not, in point of fact, very suitable for military purposes. The pilot of *Flyer III*, lying prone in a situation which made him vulnerable to fire from the ground, had to give all his attention to flying her. There was nothing to show that she was capable of carrying an observer or of reaching altitudes suitable for military reconnaissance, and she carried only enough fuel for flights of half an hour to an hour. Colonel Capper, recognizing that the Wrights had proved their ability to make an aircraft that would fly, was none the less extremely interested. He had, indeed, recommended immediately after his return from the United States that a machine should be bought from the Wrights. But negotiations would have been bound to break down, even if the British had been willing to pay the price asked of them, since the Wrights refused to allow inspection of the aircraft before purchase. Between 1906 and 1908 their overtures were rejected twice by the War Office and once by the Admiralty. They also made unsuccessful approaches to the French Government.

Their failure to sell their invention for a large sum was undoubtedly a great disappointment to the Wrights. They seem, too, to have feared that, if they continued to allow *Flyer III* to be seen while negotiations were in progress and patents pending, their secrets might be stolen and exploited by competitors. On 16 October 1905 they made what proved to be not merely their last flight of the season but their last for 2½ years. They then put the machine away, and they did not fly again until the spring of 1908.

In France reports of the experiments carried out by the Wrights with gliders between 1900 and 1902 made a powerful impact on students of aeronautics whose hopes of making the aeroplane a serious rival to the airship had begun to wane. At a time when Lilienthal had been dead for some years and progress with heavier-than-air machines was almost at a standstill in Europe, they did much to revive interest not only in gliding but also in the prospect of powered flight with fixed-wing aircraft.

Early in 1902 Captain Ferdinand Ferber, a French artillery officer and disciple of Lilienthal, received from Octave Chanute a transcript of a lecture on gliding delivered by Wilbur Wright in Chicago in the previous September. He decided soon afterwards to adopt the methods recommended by the Wrights, but the glider he then built bore only a superficial resemblance to theirs.

In the spring of 1903, about 9 months before the Wrights made their first powered flight, Chanute brought to Europe and communicated to the Aéro Club de France a detailed description of their improved No. 3 glider. A glider meant to conform with Chanute's description was commissioned after some delay by Ernest Archdeacon, a prominent member of the club, but the wing-warping mechanism was omitted. It was tested with only moderate success in the spring of 1904 by Ferber, and also by Gabriel Voisin, a young Frenchman who had turned from architecture to engineering. Voisin broke new ground in the following year by opening an aircraft factory at Billancourt in association with his brother Charles.

In 1904 Ferber rebuilt his own Wright-type glider, giving it a fixed tailplane and wing-tip rudders as well as a forward elevator. With this construction he took a significant step towards the inherently stable aeroplane at which the vast majority of European designers of fixed-wing aircraft were to aim during the next decade or so.

Ferber afterwards built a powered aeroplane which was essentially a slightly enlarged version of his rebuilt glider, with the addition of a 12 hp petrol engine driving 2 coaxial tractor airscrews. It could not sustain itself in level flight, but made a successful power-glide when launched from an overhead cable in the early summer of 1905.

Another copy of the No. 3 glider came in 1904 from Robert Esnault-Pelterie, a French engineer who afterwards achieved considerable success as a designer and manufacturer of powered aircraft and aero-engines. Finding after a few months that the wing-warping mechanism and forward elevator did not suit him, he adopted the principle of the aileron by replacing them by elevons. This, too, was a step in the direction which a large number of successful designers were afterwards to take. Esnault-Pelterie's reputation as an innovator was, however, somewhat marred in the eyes of posterity by his subsequently reverting for a limited period to the wing-warping system, although in the meantime he had pronounced it dangerous.

In 1905 Gabriel Voisin built for Ernest Archdeacon a biplane glider on floats. The mainplane assembly was essentially a large box-kite, with side curtains between the wings. Voisin added a box-kite tail and a forward elevator. This aircraft, also a trend-setter, made two successful glides when it was tested by being towed along the Seine by a motor-boat. A somewhat similar float-plane built for Louis Blériot, a prosperous manufacturer of lamps for motor-cars, was unsuccessful.

In England S. F. Cody built and tested, also in 1905, a biplane glider of box-kite form. It was fitted with primitive elevons, possibly suggested by Capper in the light of a published account of Esnault-Pelterie's innovation.

With the Wright brothers temporarily out of the running, 1906 saw only modest progress. Trajan Vuia, a French-domiciled Transylvanian, built a tractor monoplane which made short hops; Santos-Dumont flew some 240 yards in a small inelegant machine of box-kite form; and a Danish engineer, J. C. H. Ellehammer, made a brief flight in a powered biplane tethered to a pole. Louis Blériot, doubtless inspired by Vuia's near-success, abandoned his floatplane glider and took to monoplanes.

In the same year Léon Levavasseur, a French engineer whose *Antoinette* engines were beginning to be widely used in motor-boats, made an important contribution to powered flight by perfecting 24 hp and 50 hp engines eminently suitable for aircraft. Besides finding ready buyers among British and French aircraft constructors, these engines and others developed by Levavasseur were afterwards used in his own highly successful *Antoinette* monoplanes.

In 1907 Blériot and Esnault-Pelterie both made flights of well over a quarter of a mile, and a twin-rotor helicopter designed by a French engineer, Paul Cornu, became the first machine of its kind to make a free ascent with a man aboard. A rival helicopter, also of French design and powered like Cornu's by an *Antoinette* engine, was the first to leave the ground, but it cannot be said to have made a free ascent since it was held by 4 men. More than 20 years were to elapse before the helicopter became a practical man-carrying aircraft.

In the same year the Voisin brothers began a short-lived but fruitful association with Henry Farman, one of the three sons of an English journalist domiciled in France. The Voisins developed from the Archdeacon floatplane a family of biplanes with pusher airscrews, powered as a rule by 50 hp *Antoinette* engines. Henry Farman – a British subject until 1937 although he was more fluent in French than in English – acquired one of these machines and greatly improved it. With it he made, towards the end of 1907 and early in 1908, by far the longest and most impressive flights yet seen in Europe. Since the Voisin-Farman had no ailerons or wing-warping system it could not, however, be banked, and was capable only of wide flat turns.

After their American patent was granted in 1906, the Wright brothers entered into agreements with European firms for the manufacture of their aircraft and aero-engines under licence in Britain, France and Germany. They also accepted an invitation to tender for an aeroplane which the United States Government expressed its intention of buying if it passed stringent tests. They arranged that in the summer of 1908 Orville should submit a machine to acceptance trials at home while Wilbur made demonstration flights in Europe. They then taught themselves to fly without lying on their stomachs and developed an improved version of their *Flyer III*. Known as Model A, this had a 30 hp engine driving 2 geared-down pusher airscrews, a seat for the pilot and another for a passenger, pupil or observer, but again no wheels. Like its predecessor, it was launched by weight and pulley and landed on skids.

In September Orville made 10 flights at Fort Myer, Virginia. Four of them lasted more than a hour. On the tenth flight a faulty airscrew caused the machine to crash. Orville's passenger, a young army engineer and budding aircraft designer named Thomas E. Selfridge, was killed and Orville himself was badly hurt.

Wilbur made more than 100 flights from French soil between 8 August and 31 December. The effect was electrifying. His banked turns, circles and figures of eight astonished all beholders. 'Compared with the Wrights', said one member of the Aéro Club de France, 'we are as children.' 'Wilbur Wright', the kite-flying Baden-Powell declared, 'is in possession of a power which controls the fate of nations.' With his last flight of the year, Wilbur won a prize of 20,000 francs by remaining airborne for 180 minutes and covering nearly 80 miles.

His competitors were not slow to apply the lesson. Early in 1909 Henry Farman broke with the Voisins, alleging that they had sold an aircraft built for him to another customer. He then designed and built for himself a biplane with ailerons, a forward elevator, a tail with twin rudders, and a 4-wheeled undercarriage supplemented by skids as a precaution against fast nose-down landings. It proved more manoeuvrable than the Voisin-Farman and was far more stable than the Wright A. The American Glenn Curtiss produced, in the same year, a very similar machine with the same merits. Meanwhile Blériot continued to improve his monoplanes and Hubert Latham, a newcomer with British and French antecedents, scored some striking successes with elegant *Antoinette* monoplanes designed and built by Levavasseur. By the end of the year Blériot had become a popular hero by making the first cross-Channel flight in a heavier-than-air machine, and the world's speed, altitude and endurance records had passed to him, Latham and Henry Farman.

Developments outside France and the United States in 1909 included the first flights in Germany by a German-born pilot, Hans Grade, who flew a triplane of his own design in January and a light monoplane, also designed by himself, in September. The Austrian-designed *Taube* monoplane of Igo Etrich and F. Wels, afterwards manufactured under licence in Germany, was first flown under power at Wiener-Neustadt in November. In Italy two Italian naval officers took lessons in flying from Wilbur Wright; one of them, A. Calderara, was co-designer with a Frenchman, Ambroise Goupy, of an interesting tractor biplane afterwards developed by Goupy with considerable success.

In Britain an Irishman, J. T. C. Moore-Brabazon, became the first British subject by birth to qualify as a pilot by making a number of brief flights in a Voisin with modifications attributed to Henry Farman. Later in the year he flew a Wright-derived biplane built in England by the brothers Horace, Eustace and Oswald Short. S. F. Cody, who had made one or two short hops in the previous year in a biplane built at the Army Balloon

Factory and known in its original form as 'British Army Aeroplane No. 1', outdid Moore-Brabazon by flying about a mile in May, nearly 6 miles in July and some 40 miles in September; but he was not a British subject at the time. After he had become one in October, the Aeronautical Society honoured him as 'the first Englishman to have flown satisfactorily in England'. The Englishman A. V. Roe, afterwards a successful aircraft manufacturer, also flew in 1909 and was credited with some brief flights in 1908.

A sign of the times was the intense interest aroused by a rally held at Rheims in late summer of 1909 under the auspices of the leading champagne firms. Thirty-eight aircraft were entered. Of the 23 which flew, 18 were built by the Voisins, Blériot, Henry Farman, Levavasseur or Esnault-Pelterie, only 3 by the Wright brothers or their licensees. The other 2 machines were the successful Curtiss biplane and a tractor biplane designed by a Frenchman, Louis Breguet. The most successful pilots were Henry Farman, Glenn Curtiss, Blériot and Latham. Maximum speeds were of the order of 45–50 miles an hour.

In the same year the British Government decided, in the light of a report on aerial navigation from a sub-committee of the Committee of Imperial Defence, to reapportion responsibility for the design and construction of aeroplanes and airships as between the War Office, the Admiralty and other agencies. Cody and W. J. Dunne, a half-pay officer who aimed at producing a tailless but stable aircraft with swept-back wings, were relieved of their part-time appointments, ostensibly on the ground that too much money had been spent on experiments, in reality to make way for radical reforms. Both men were allowed to keep their machines and were encouraged, and to some extent helped, to continue their work. A special department for the study of aeronautical problems was created at the National Physical Laboratory at Teddington, and an advisory committee of scientists and serving officers was appointed to keep the authorities informed of technical progress on the one hand and the needs of the armed forces on the other.

Soon afterwards the Government separated the Army Balloon Factory at Farnborough from the school and depot administered by the Royal Engineers. Reorganized under a civilian chief, the factory became the Army Aircraft Factory in 1911, and was renamed the Royal Aircraft Factory on the formation of the Royal Flying Corps in the following year. The Government's intention was that the factory should continue to build non-rigid or semi-rigid airships, in which commercial manufacturers were not interested, but should not compete with private enterprise by producing aeroplanes or aero-engines in commercial quantities. So far as heavier-than-air machines were concerned, its duties were to undertake modifications and repairs, test aircraft and power-units acquired by or offered to the State, and give private firms a lead by setting standards of workmanship, performance, efficiency and safety to which it would be in the interests of all to adhere. A disadvantage of this system was that manufacturers disliked submitting their products for trial to an organization which existed partly to help their competitors.

The appointment of Superintendent of the reorganized factory was accepted, initially on a part-time basis, by Mervyn O'Gorman, a distinguished engineering consultant with a classical and scientific background. To ensure that the factory did not take the bread out of the mouths of the Government's suppliers, O'Gorman was given terms of reference which forbade him to build new heavier-than-air machines, though these were afterwards relaxed to an extent which allowed him to produce experimental aircraft. Nothing in his instructions precluded him, however, from modifying existing machines. He began by acquiring, by various means, an assortment of largely obsolete or damaged aeroplanes and making discreet additions to his staff. Towards the end of 1910 he bought for £400 a biplane designed and built by a young enthusiast named Geoffrey de Havilland and offered its creator a job in his drawing-office. Thereafter the factory produced a succession of prototype aircraft, designed largely by de Havilland, which set new standards of fitness for military use. Some good designs came, too, from private firms.

In the summer of 1912 about 30 British and foreign aircraft were entered for military trials on Salisbury Plain. Marks were awarded for speed, climb, low landing-speed, ease of handling and other qualities. The highest marks were scored by a Farnborough-built two-seater tractor biplane, the B.E.2, although it was not eligible for a prize since O'Gorman was among the judges. Piloted by de Havilland, the B.E.2 flew at 70 miles an hour, landed at 40 miles an hour, achieved an initial rate of climb of 365 feet a minute, and reached an altitude of 10,000 feet or so with a passenger and fuel for 3 hours' flying.

Other outstanding aircraft which helped to vindicate the Government's decision in 1909 to await developments before placing large orders for military aircraft included the Farnborough-designed B.S.1 and the Sopwith Aviation Company's Sopwith Tabloid, designed by Harry Hawker and F. Sigrist. The B.S.1, a single-seater biplane planned as a smaller and faster follow-on to the B.E.2, attained when tested early in 1913 a speed of 91·7 miles an hour and climbed at 900 feet a minute. The Tabloid, a small two-seater biplane said to have been inspired by the B.S.1, proved equally fast in level flight and could reach 15,000 feet in 10 minutes.

From the B.E.2 Geoffrey de Havilland and E. T. Busk developed the B.E.2c, a moderately fast two-seater biplane whose manoeuvrability and rate of climb left something to be desired, but which had the merit of possessing true inherent longitudinal and lateral stability. Nearly 2,000 aircraft were afterwards built to this design by various British firms.

In 1911 a Dutchman, Anthony Fokker, built at the age of 18 the first of a series of aircraft which soon put him in the front rank of European designers. In Russia Igo Sikorsky pointed the way to the large bombers and passenger aircraft of the future by demonstrating in 1913 a cabin biplane with a wing-span of more than 90 feet and 4 Argus engines of 100 hp.

In the summer of 1912 two pilots crashed in swift succession in England while flying monoplanes. Almost simultaneously the French authorities received from Blériot an adverse report on certain aircraft alleged to be structurally weak. Thereupon the British military authorities imposed a temporary ban on monoplanes, and the French laid down standards to which all monoplanes used by their armed forces must conform. The effect was to strengthen an existing preference on the part of British designers for multiplane configurations. That there was nothing wrong with the monoplane where speed was the aim was shown when, at Rheims in 1913, a monoplane of striking monocoque construction, designed by L. Béchereau for A.-J.-A. Deperdussin, attained the record-breaking speed of 126.67 miles an hour in level flight.

The development of fast, stable and reasonably reliable military aircraft accompanied, and to some extent was prompted by, a decline in international relations which gave European statesmen a strong incentive to take aviation seriously. After the Agadir crisis in the summer of 1911, all the leading European powers made substantial provision in their budgets for aeroplanes as well as airships. In most countries armies and navies organized their own air forces. In Britain the authorities aimed in the first instance at a unified air service. In the spring of 1912 the Government formed the Royal Flying Corps, comprising a Military Wing, a Naval Wing, a Central Flying School, the Royal Aircraft Factory and a reserve. The Navy, always inclined to take an independent line, retained a flying school of its own to which would-be pilots were sent for their initial training, and in the summer of 1914 the Admiralty succeeded in detaching the Naval Wing from the rest of the Royal Flying Corps and forming its own air service. Airships, at first divided between the Army and the Navy, had already been placed exclusively under naval control on the ground that they were particularly suitable for maritime reconnaissance.

In all countries maritime, tactical, and strategic reconnaissance were the tasks for which aircraft other than large airships were felt by the naval and military authorities to be most needed. Nevertheless bombing trials, official or unofficial, were carried out in many parts of the world before the outbreak of the First World War. As early as the summer of 1910 Glenn Curtiss made tests in the United States with dummy bombs, using as target the shape of a battleship marked out with flagged bouys on the surface of a lake. Live bombs were used in tests by the United States Army with a Wright biplane at San Francisco in the following January. Soon afterwards an American army officer, Lieutenant Riley Scott, devised a rudimentary bomb-sight, but failed to persuade the authorities to adopt it. In the summer of 1912 he won the prize for bomb-dropping at a contest at Rheims. Tests with small bombs were made, too, at the military trials held in Britain in the same year. Other early experiments with aeroplanes employed as missile-carriers included tests made by an Italian officer named Guidoni in 1911 with a torpedo launched from a Henry Farman biplane, and by British naval officers in the summer of 1914 with a torpedo, bombs and an improvised bomb-sight.

Powered aircraft were first used in war in 1911. In that year the Italians, seeing in the despatch of a German gunboat to Agadir a possible threat to their hopes of establishing a dominant position in North Africa, declared war on the Turks and occupied Tripoli. Their expeditionary force included a small air component commanded by a Captain Piazza. On 22 October Piazza made a flight of about an hour in a Blériot to observe the Turkish positions near Azizia, about twenty miles from the coast. Further reconnaissance flights were made on a number of days thereafter, and on some occasions after the beginning of November small bombs made from hand-grenades were dropped. The Italians aimed at harassing military encampments, but before long the Turks accused them of bombing a hospital. Enquiries failed to establish the existence of a hospital at the place in question, but the possibility that a tent used to shelter the wounded had received a chance hit could not be ruled out. The Italians pointed out that in any case their warships had aimed a large number of heavy shells at precisely the same locality at an earlier stage of the campaign, and that no one had then suggested that it was not a legitimate military target.

This dispute raised the whole question of the extent to which bombing from the air was permissible under international law. The signatories to the Hague Convention of 1899 had agreed to prohibit bombing from balloons, but no agreement to perpetuate the ban and extend it to aircraft of all classes had been reached at subsequent international conferences. Whether bombing from the air was permissible in a given case could therefore be determined only by reference to the standards governing bombardment in general.

Such standards existed in the form of rules or 'usages' sanctioned by custom and embodied in Article 25 of the Hague Convention of 1907, which forbade the bombardment of undefended places 'by any means whatsoever' in the course of operations by land forces. These rules had sometimes been broken in the past, but in general they had come to be accepted throughout the civilized world as morally binding on all belligerents since, apart from the humanitarian aspect of the matter, soldiers and statesmen in most countries acknowledged the practical utility of a recognized code of behaviour to which reference could be made in case of doubt. If they were to be applied to attacks from the air, then it seemed to follow that military encampments, naval dockyards, arsenals and warlike stores must be regarded as legitimate objectives for bomb-carrying aircraft, even though attacks on them might involve some incidental risk to non-combatants and their property. The bombing of open towns, on the other hand, was clearly inadmissible. According to the rules, towns could legitimately be bombarded only if they were held as defended places by military or naval garrisons, and even then only after the defenders had been given due warning and had been invited to surrender on terms. Eminent authorities held, therefore, that the bombing by aircraft even of defended towns would be legitimate only in conjunction with operations by naval or land forces under a commander who was in a position to give such a warning and to enter into negotiations with the garrison.

2

THE FIRST WORLD WAR

Powered aircraft were first used in substantial numbers to support armies in the field when Germany found herself committed in 1914 to the two-front war long pondered by her strategists. True, the Italians had used such aircraft earlier in Tripolitania, but only on a small scale and against an adversary who himself possessed no aircraft or anti-aircraft weapons.

The plan by which the Germans hoped to destroy the French Army in 6 weeks in 1914 is sometimes loosely called the Schlieffen Plan. In fact, it differed materially from that plan.

Alfred von Schlieffen's plan for war with France and Russia was drawn up at the time of the first Moroccan crisis in 1905, when flying was in its infancy and British intervention in a European war was not expected. Schlieffen aimed, as his successor was to aim in 1914, at enveloping the main body of the French Army from the north. He proposed to do this by thrusting his right across the Meuse, or Maas, in Dutch territory between Maastricht and Wesel and sending a smaller force across the Meuse in Belgian territory at Huy. Having thus circumvented the powerful Belgian forts commanding the crossings of the Meuse at Liège and Namur, his armies of the right were to advance from central Belgium into northern France before attempting a series of encircling movements towards and west of Paris. The essence of his plan was first that the main crossing of the Meuse should be made in Dutch territory, secondly that his troops should pass so close to the French coast near Abbeville that 'the last man on the right' would 'brush the Channel with his sleeve'.

Schlieffen's successor, Helmuth von Moltke, drew up *his* plan in response to the Agadir crisis of 1911. By that time all the leading powers were providing themselves with military aircraft, and 5 years of staff talks and off-the-record exchanges between

British and French officers had almost transformed the *Entente cordiale* into a military alliance. Factors which tended to favour Germany included the development of heavy howitzers capable of tackling the Belgian forts and of large rigid airships which might be used to bomb them.

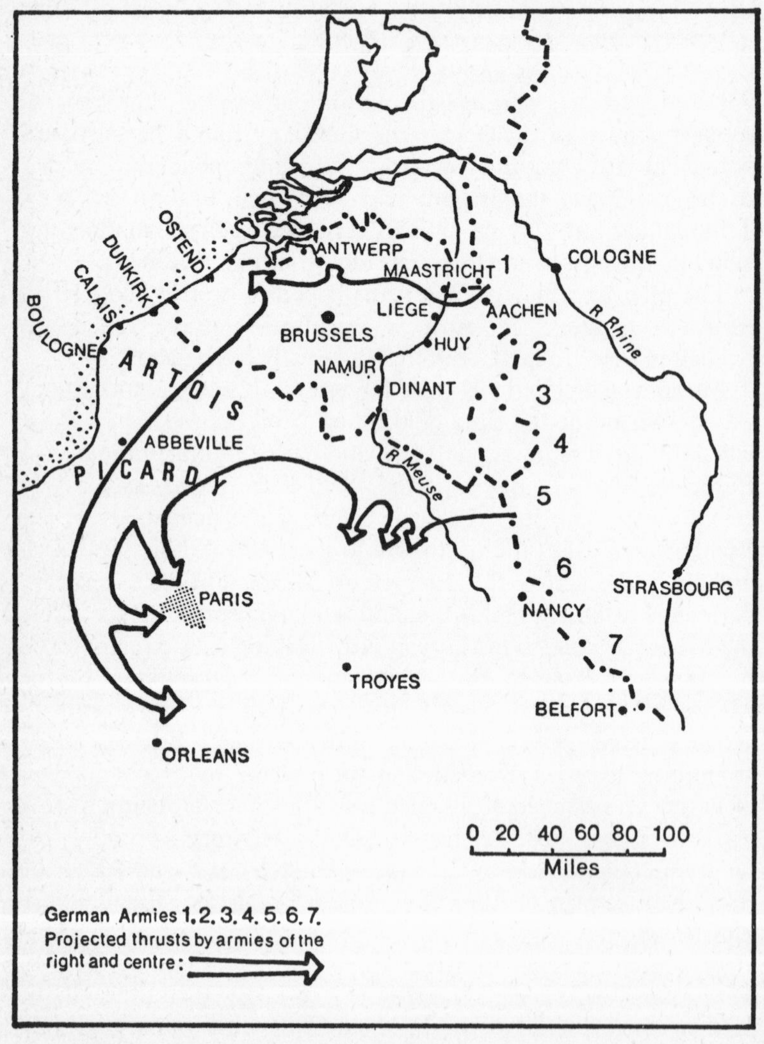

1 The Schlieffen Plan as modified by Moltke

Moltke took his predecessor's plan as the point of departure for his strategic thinking, but his proposals differed from Schlieffen's in much more than detail. Rejecting an advance north of Maastricht, he proposed to push his right across the Meuse entirely in Belgian territory. Fifty-three divisions of his armies of the right and centre would have to make their approach march along 17 roads in the sector between Aachen and Metz, and success would be possible only if the First Army, on the extreme right, gained access to road and rail bridges dominated by the Liège forts. Aircraft as well as cavalry would reconnoitre ahead of the infantry. In the light of the information they provided, Moltke or his successor would control the movements of 7 armies with the aid of a battery of telephones, a powerful wireless transmitter and a staff liberally provided with mechanically propelled vehicles.

The French had 9 years in which to prepare for the war they expected the Germans to force upon them. Until 1911 they intended to meet a thrust from the German right by standing on the Franco-Belgian frontier, but in that year they appointed a new Commander-in-Chief, General Joseph-Jacques-Césaire Joffre, who shared the fashionable belief that French troops were more at home in an offensive than a defensive role. Joffre proposed to defeat the Germans by thrusting at their centre as soon as they attacked him, even at the cost of allowing them to outflank him on the left. He made no provision to stiffen Belgian resistance on the Meuse, and British approaches to the Belgian General Staff in 1912 were rebuffed on the ground that Belgium could not afford to hazard her neutrality. The British then made a tentative plan to block a German advance to the Meuse in the neighbourhood of Namur by sending their small Expeditionary Force to the Ardennes, but it did not square with Joffre's ideas and was never put into effect.

When war came, the Germans made an unsuccessful attempt to capture Liège by a *coup de main* before mobilization was completed. They then sent an emissary under a flag of truce to warn the garrison commander that the city would be bombed if he did not allow them to cross the river. This ultimatum having been rejected, the Zeppelin Z.6 aimed 13 bombs on 6 August at one of the 12 forts which ringed the city. No hits were scored on the fort, but 9 civilians were killed and the Z.6 was hit by gunfire and crashed on returning to her base at Cologne.

In the course of the next few weeks 2 more Zeppelins were brought down by gunfire on the Western Front, a fourth landed behind the Russian lines after fire from the ground had damaged her and killed her commander, and a fifth was destroyed by bombs dropped on her shed at Düsseldorf from a British naval aircraft. These events did not justify any far-reaching conclusions about the relative merits of airships and heavier-than-air machines. But they showed fairly conclusively that large rigid airships were too vulnerable to fire from the ground to be used successfully in close support of troops.

The Germans followed their Zeppelin raid on Liège by opening fire on the city with their field artillery. They succeeded in capturing the citadel, but the forts commanding the principal crossings of the Meuse continued to hold out. They then brought up giant howitzers whose fire they directed from observation balloons and high buildings. Designed to withstand any ordinary bombardment by field or medium guns, the forts were soon knocked out by armour-piercing projectiles which descended almost vertically and were fused to explode after impact. The last of them fell on 16 August, less than a fortnight after the first violation of the frontier by German troops.

On the following day the German First Army, commanded by General Alexander von Kluck, began its roundabout advance on Paris. Leading troops of General Karl von Bülow's Second Army, on Kluck's left, had already crossed the Meuse at Huy.

Moltke soon found that conducting a gigantic war of movement by remote control was anything but a straightforward business. Landline communications with armies not on German soil were at the mercy of hostile populations. Reports sent by wireless sometimes took many hours to reach their destinations, since only one channel was available for all the armies and transmissions were persistently jammed by the French. Despatch riders and staff officers made slow progress along roads thronged with marching troops and horse-drawn transport. Cavalry patrols were misdirected or primed with false information by artful peasants; air reconnaissance was made difficult or impossible by a dearth of trained observers, the short range of most heavier-than-air machines, a lack of airfields in the forward area and the hazards of the weather. The British Expeditionary Force was reported by Kluck's cavalry on 13 August to be disembarking at Ostend, Dunkirk and Calais, by Moltke's staff on 17 August not yet to have landed, by a Belgian newspaper on 20 August to have arrived safely 'on French soil'. Unaware that it had landed at Le Havre, Rouen and Boulogne and was moving by the middle of August to is concentration area near Maubeuge, the Germans continued to guess at its whereabouts until, on 22 August, Kluck discovered that his forward troops were marching straight towards it.

The French failed even more conspicuously to form a clear picture of the enemy's dispositions immediately after the outbreak of war. When invited on 4 August to send troops into Belgian territory for the purpose of 'ascertaining the direction of advance of the Germans and delaying their columns', Joffre ordered his cavalry to reconnoitre both banks of the Meuse as far downstream as a point almost within sight of Liège. They reported on their return from a 3-day gallop through the Ardennes that they had seen German cavalry and light infantry, including cyclist battalions and small bodies of motorized troops, but that there was no evidence as yet that the enemy had reached the left bank of the Meuse in strength. Later reports indicated that the German Second Army was pouring across the Meuse at Huy and that large numbers of German troops – in fact, the spearheads of the Third, Fourth and Fifth Armies – were heading for the right bank on a 90-mile front from Dinant to Verdun. These warnings failed to shake Joffre's determination to attack what he still believed to be the enemy's weak centre. Going forward on 21 August in misty weather which made air reconnaissance impossible and cavalry reconnaissance ineffective, the French Third and Fourth Armies met powerful German forces in wooded country west and south-west of Luxembourg. A series of battles extending over the greater part of three days cost them appalling losses.

The task assigned to the British in Joffre's scheme was to cover the left of the French armies by moving in a northerly direction along the axis of the Maubeuge – Mons – Soignies – Brussels road. This put their 4 infantry divisions opposite the 8 forward divisions of the German First Army. With 4 squadrons of aircraft and a cavalry division to scout ahead of them, the British would

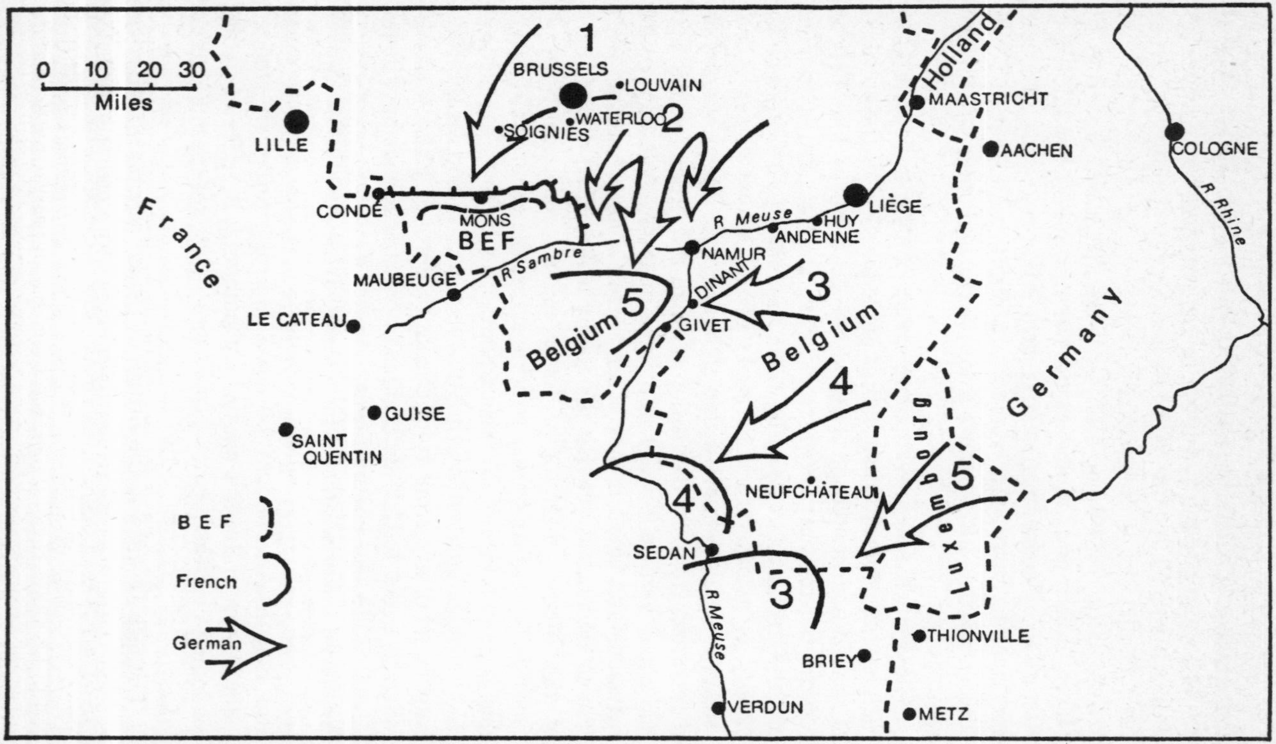

Mons and the Frontier Battles

have felt reasonably secure against a surprise attack if there had not been a gap some 80 miles wide between their left and the Channel coast. This was guarded only by old-fashioned frontier fortifications and two French Territorial divisions of doubtful quality. The British Commander-in-Chief, General Sir John French, asked on 16 August for a French cavalry corps to cover the gap, but his request was refused.

British and German cavalry patrols clashed on 22 August near Soignies. Kluck then learned for the first time that the elusive British Expeditionary Force was ahead of him, Sir John French that German infantry was marching towards him along the road from Brussels. On the same day an air reconnaissance told French that there were also German troops to the north-west and that his left was in danger of envelopment. He decided to halt his infantry on the line of the Condé Canal at Mons and await developments. That evening he told General Charles Lanrezac, commanding the French Fifth Army on his right, that he would hold the line of the canal for 24 hours and then decide what to do in the light of further reports from his aircraft.

This was a fortunate decision. Had the British continued their advance on 23 August, they would almost certainly have been defeated by an enemy superior in numbers and firepower. As it was, by standing in positions of their own choosing they were able to fight a highly successful defensive battle on a day when all the French armies on their right were in dire trouble. They had every reason to be thankful for the timely information provided by their reconnaissance aircraft and also by their cavalry.

About 11 o'clock that evening French learned to his dismay that Lanrezac, attacked by the German Second Army, was in full retreat. Namur was in German hands and a huge gap was opening on the British right.

The British Expeditionary Force then retreated by stages behind the Marne, pausing to fight rearguard actions at Le Cateau on 26 August and Villers-Cotterets on 1 September. To the east of the British, the French Fifth and Fourth Armies also retreated behind the Marne. A gap opened between them, but was filled by a new Ninth Army drawn partly from the Fourth and partly from the Third Army.

During the Allied retreat to the Marne, units and formations made such frequent moves that neither side was able to form a clear picture of the enemy's movements, either by air reconnaissance or by other means. Moreover, such information as could be obtained was often misleading. The French Fifth Army paused on 29 August to deliver a counter-attack at Guise, but resumed its retreat next morning. When its troops were seen streaming from the battlefield on 30 August, the commanders of the German First and Second Armies agreed to set off in pursuit of an apparently defeated enemy. Their consequent change of course initiated a premature turning movement which exposed the First Army's flank to a counter-attack from the direction of Paris.

The Allies did not depend entirely on their aircraft for the information that led them to turn and fight on the Marne, but air reconnaissance provided vital confirmation. As early as 31 August a French cavalry officer reconnoitring between the Somme and the Oise saw a German infantry column heading not for Paris but for Compiègne. On the following day the French took from the body of a German officer killed by one of their patrols a map which showed that the First Army was to wheel to the south-east after crossing the Oise. But it was not until 3 September, when British and French airmen reported independently that German columns were in fact marching in that direction, that General Joseph Galliéni, the Military Governor of Paris, became convinced that the enemy was offering his flank and must be attacked with the least possible delay. Further reports from reconnaissance aircraft on the following day showed that the First Army was moving to positions which would make it vulnerable to attacks not only by the Sixth Army in the outskirts of Paris but also by the British Expeditionary Force and the Fifth Army south of the Marne.

Brushing aside a warning from Moltke that the French seemed to be reinforcing their left, Kluck went on to take the main body of his army across the Marne, leaving only a weak rearguard on the north bank. The main body of the Second Army and part of the Third Army also crossed the river in the hope of contributing to the final defeat of a supposedly disorganized enemy.

After a preliminary skirmish on 5 September, the Sixth Army engaged Kluck's rearguard on 6 September on a front of some 10–15 miles running roughly north and south between the north bank of the Marne and the Paris–Chantilly road. Counter attacks were repulsed with the help of newly-arrived troops, some of whom were rushed through Paris in the famous 'taxis of the Marne'. South and east of the Marne, the British Expeditionary Force and the French Fifth, Ninth, Fourth and Third Armies attacked the German First, Second, Third, Fourth and Fifth Armies on a front of 140 miles from the outskirts of Paris to the Argonne. On 9 September an emissary from Moltke's headquarters found the roads in rear of the First and Second Armies jammed with baggage trains 'retiring in wild haste'. About an hour after his arrival at Kluck's headquarters the emissary used his authority as Moltke's personal representative to order the First Army to fall back on Soissons.

During the afternoon the British learned from their reconnaissance aircraft that the First Army was in full retreat. They succeeded in getting most of their troops across the river before nightfall, but the 'vigorous pursuit' they ordered that evening did not begin until the following day. Between 10 and 12 September the British Expeditionary Force advanced about 30 miles, the French Fifth Army about 20 miles, the Ninth Army scarcely at all.

Moltke, seeing his plan in ruins, reached the logical conclusion that Germany should make peace. His superiors thought otherwise. The retreating armies succeeded in establishing themselves on the Aisne, and the war went on for another 4 years.

Before long the Germans began shifting troops to their right in the hope of turning the Sixth Army's flank and renewing their advance on Paris. These moves were easily detected by air reconnaissance. To counter them, Joffre extended his flank until there was a continuous line of Allied troops in entrenched positions from the North Sea to the Swiss frontier. The Germans tried in October and November to force a decision by breaking through the British front at Ypres, but a series of hard-fought battles left the Allies still in possession of a small part of Belgium and the British holding a salient whose retention was to cost them many lives.

Both sides then set to work to deepen their positions by digging more and more trenches. Since cavalry patrols were no longer feasible, air reconnaissance and the capture of prisoners by raiding parties became the chief sources of military intelligence. Both sides longed to end the deadlock by delivering a surprise attack in overwhelming strength, but neither could hope to complete its preparations without detection as long as the enemy's aircraft were free to reconnoitre.

Many attempts were made by one side or the other to solve this problem by gaining command of the air, at least over its own lines. The Germans took the lead in introducing specially-designed high-trajectory guns intended to keep the enemy's reconnaissance aircraft at bay. Both sides were soon well provided with such weapons, but neither managed to gain the mastery by this means. The best they could do was to force hostile aircraft to fly at heights which made visual observation difficult. This did not rule out photographic reconnaissance, at first with hand-held cameras, later with built-in equipment designed for the purpose. For many purposes, photographic reconnaissance was more effective than direct observation. Air photographs provided objective data, often more reliable than the notes and impressions of a fallible observer. They furnished a permanent record which intelligence officers could study at leisure and interpret in the light of accumulated knowledge and experience. They could be reproduced in large numbers with simple equipment, and could therefore be given a wide distribution.

Photographic reconnaissance created a new skill, that of the photographic interpreter. Large numbers of British, French, German and later Italian officers devoted their working hours to the study of air photographs, noting and interpreting changes in the layout of the enemy's trenches, lines of communication and supply dumps. These efforts were not confined to the European theatre. The offensives by which the Allies drove the Turks from Palestine and Syria in 1917 and 1918 were planned and executed in the light of expert scrutiny of air photographs of the Turkish lines.

In 1914 there was still a tendency among senior officers in Britain and elsewhere to believe that accurate observation was possible only from slow aircraft. This impression was derived from peacetime manoeuvres at which old-fashioned, cumbrous heavier-than-air machines flew only just above the heads of the troops. The test of war soon showed that speed was no bar to effective reconnaissance when aircraft flew at the heights they must maintain if they were not to be shot down by fire from the ground. Recognition of this fact brought demands for fast, high-performance aircraft for reconnaissance or all-round use, though designers were still hampered by the need to produce machines capable of landing on the rough surfaces of small wartime airfields.

On 10 March 1915 the British launched an attack at Neuve-Chapelle, south-east of Merville, after a brief but effective artillery bombardment which demolished the enemy's wire and breastworks. The initial assault was brilliantly successful, but orders to follow-up formations to come forward and exploit the gap made by the assault troops were never given because a German counter-bombardment destroyed landlines between the British front and rear. In the light of this experience, aircraft with wireless transmitters were used by the British in subsequent battles to fly 'contact patrols' in the battle area for the purpose of reporting the progress of the forward troops and thus ensuring, at any rate in theory, that opportunities of exploiting a success would not be missed. Attempts were made to devise a system by which the troops would display signs showing the positions they had reached, or pointing towards objectives they wished their supporting artillery to tackle, but these were not very successful.

Later, when the arming of aircraft with machine-guns became general, machines despatched on contact patrols were also used to attack targets of opportunity. Here again, the difficulty was that the forward troops had no reliable means of making their needs known to pilots of supporting aircraft. Twenty-five years were to elapse before the Germans solved this and other close-support problems by perfecting a radio-based system of communication between ground and air which stood the test of battle.

In all major battles from the spring of 1915, the belligerents on both sides made strenuous attempts to support their land forces by sending bombers to attack objectives beyond the reach of their artillery. Objectives worth bombing proved much harder to hit than might have been expected. The Allied armies were not much troubled by German bombers in the early stages of the war, and an analysis of all bombing done by Allied aircraft between 1 March and 20 June 1915 showed that only 3 out of 141 attempts to bomb railway stations for the purpose of disrupting the enemy's communications were known to have succeeded. On the other hand, some successful attacks by British naval aircraft on airship sheds in Germany and Belgium in 1914 and 1915 proved that large, conspicuous targets could be destroyed or seriously damaged by bombing where attacks were carefully planned and the attacker secured the advantage of surprise.

A question discussed at considerable length both before and after the outbreak of war was whether reconnaissance aircraft should be armed with more effective weapons than the pistols or carbines carried by many observers. Some airmen maintained that all reconnaissance crews should be given adequate means of defending themselves against hostile aircraft, even if this meant that all machines must be provided with machine-guns at the cost of impairing their performance. Others argued that reconnaissance aircraft should not be so encumbered, but should be escorted or supported by 'fighting scouts', or fighters, specially chosen and equipped for the purpose.

As a result of more frequent encounters between German and Allied aircraft, this problem reached an acute stage about six months after the outbreak of war. By that time the British, the French and the Germans had all provided themselves not only with a variety of two-seater aircraft but also with fast single-seater biplanes or monoplanes whose performance would make them eminently suitable for use as fighters if they could be adequately armed. Attempts had been made in France and Germany since 1913 to perfect some form of synchronizer which would make it possible to fire a machine-gun through the area swept by the airscrew of a tractor aircraft, but no such device had been adopted by the military authorities in either country. A French team associated with the firm of Morane-Saulnier had carried their investigations to the stage of practical trials, but the shortcomings of the gun they used compelled them to protect the blades of the airscrew with metal plates as an insurance against their destruction by rounds which hung fire.

In the spring of 1915 a well-known French aviator, Roland Garros, persuaded the authorities to allow him to try a Morane-Saulnier Type L monoplane fitted with gun and deflector plates but not the synchronizer, which he seems to have thought too unreliable for his purpose. After 3 weeks of phenomenal success, Garros was shot down and his machine was captured. The German authorities then commissioned Fokker to design a synchronizer on which pilots could rely. Fokker and his staff succeeded by the late summer in producing a synchronizer which, fitted to a single-seater monoplane, gave the Germans a commanding lead.

To catch up, the Allies were forced to hasten the arming of their own aircraft. By the early spring of 1916 a fast Nieuport single-seater biplane with a remotely-fired machine-gun fitted above the upper wing was in service in British and French squadrons. By May the first of a series of British-made positive synchronizers was also in use. In the meantime machine-guns could be fitted to two-seater tractor aircraft, but this arrangement tended to give a poor field of fire since the observer, who worked the gun, usually sat almost directly beneath the top wing of a biplane. One effect of the demand for a stop-gap fighter was, therefore, to give a new lease of life to the old-fashioned pusher biplane, in which the observer had an unobstructed view forward and over a wide arc on either side. Machine-guns were installed in the noses of well-tried but obsolescent Voisin and Farman biplanes. In addition, the British introduced to squadron service early in 1915 a new pusher biplane, the Vickers F.B.5 Gunbus. Like the F.E.2b which superseded it in 1916, this early British fighter was derived ultimately from the Maurice Farman and more recently from the F.E.2a, an experimental aircraft designed and tested at Farnborough before the war.

The general adoption of fighter aircraft gave rise to a prolonged debate as to whether the fighter should be regarded as an offensive or a defensive weapon. The British, with their traditional pragmatism, might have been expected to hold aloof from this controversy. In fact they took a leading part in it, and may even be said to have launched it. Major-General Sir David Henderson, who had left his post as Director-General of Military Aeronautics at the War Office on the outbreak of war to command the Royal Flying Corps on the Western Front, expressed as early as the summer of 1915 his conviction that fighters ought, in principle, to be used in an offensive role. When he planned his dispositions for the Battle of Loos in September of that year he would have liked to group his fighters together and use them to drive the enemy's aircraft from the sky. Nevertheless he agreed that he must, in practice, distribute them among reconnaissance squadrons so that no squadron should feel that it had been left without protection.

A few weeks before the battle Henderson was recalled to London. His place in France was taken by Brigadier-General H. M. Trenchard, a former infantry officer who had qualified as a pilot and joined the Royal Flying Corps on being told by the War Office in 1912 that he could expect no further employment unless he did so.

Trenchard had made his mark before the war as a forceful, energetic, and none too scrupulous Assistant Commandant of the Central Flying School at Upavon. In recent months he had become a controversial figure as a result of heavy losses suffered by the wing he commanded at the Battle of Neuve-Chapelle. Backward in youth, he had scraped into the Army by way of the militia. His critics described him as dull, unimaginative, overbearing and almost illiterate. But he was capable of hard work, and had shown great courage and determination in overcoming ill-health and other obstacles. He believed that the prime requisite of success in war was an almost unlimited capacity to withstand hard knocks, and on that ground he defended his expenditure of men and machines at Neuve-Chapelle.

Soon after taking up his new appointment, Trenchard made it clear to his staff that he held firmly to the axiom that the commander of an air force should aim at gaining control of the air over the battlefield. Believing that freedom to bomb and reconnoitre could be won only by relentless pressure on the enemy, he intended to use all his resources to force the Germans on to the defensive.

His first major task was to decide how his squadrons should be disposed to support an offensive on the Somme in the summer of 1916. The main assault, so far as the British Expeditionary Force was concerned, was to be delivered by the Fourth Army, but this was only one of 4 British armies on the Western Front.

Trenchard had 27 first-line squadrons with an average of 15 serviceable aircraft apiece. He allotted 6 squadrons to direct support of the Fourth Army and the 5 corps under its command. Four squadrons were to form a Headquarters Wing whose tasks were defined in Trenchard's orders as 'strategical reconnaissance for General Headquarters, the organized offensive against the enemy air service, and distant bombing of communications'.[1] The remaining 17 squadrons were allotted to the First, Second and Third Armies and their corps, but each day 2 of these squadrons, or their equivalent, were to give indirect support to the main assault by bombing communications immediately behind the front attacked by the Fourth Army.

At first sight the chief weakness of these dispositions might seem to be the provision of only 6 squadrons to meet all the demands of the Fourth Army and its 5 corps for tactical reconnaissance, artillery reconnaissance, contact patrols, the bombing of trenches and strongpoints and special missions undertaken for such purposes as destruction of the enemy's kite-balloons. The apparent meagreness of the close-support force was, however, intentional. Trenchard's aim, and indeed the essence of his plan, was to atone for it by providing a Headquarters Wing whose 'organized offensive against the enemy air service' would greatly ease the task of the 6 close-support squadrons by removing hostile aircraft from their path. Had he in fact provided a fighter force strong enough to stand a reasonable chance of dominating the battlefield, his plan would have been a good one. Its true weakness was that, instead of doing so, he provided only a small Headquarters Wing which he burdened with a variety of tasks. To suppose that a heterogeneous wing of 4 squadrons, with some 60 aircraft between them, would be able to drive the enemy from the skies and at the same time undertake strategic reconnaissance for General Headquarters and the distant bombing of communications was, to say the least, unrealistic.

This error was so crucial that a striking success was scarcely to be expected. The close-support force gave such help to the Fourth Army and its constituent formations as 6 squadrons could provide. The Headquarters Wing grappled with tasks which would have taxed the resources of a force twice its size. The aircraft sent day by day from the First, Second and Third Armies' sectors carried out their missions to the best of their ability. But the combined effort of these forces was too small, too widely dispersed over a variety of aims, to make more than a minor contribution to the welfare of the Fourth Army. Some attacks on communications were successful, but they did not prevent the Germans from moving large numbers of troops to the threatened sector.

Nor did Trenchard gain any substantial degree of air superiority over the battlefield. Command of the air remained in dispute throughout the battle. As was only to be expected, the Germans began to build up their air strength in the sector attacked by the Fourth Army as soon as the assault was launched. Trenchard tried to arrest the process by ordering squadrons assigned to the other armies to attack objectives opposite their own fronts. But the Germans, recognizing that the sector opposite the Fourth Army had become for the time being the decisive front, refused the bait. By continuing to reinforce the crucial sector, they succeeding in inflicting heavier losses than they incurred, and they found time about a fortnight after the battle began to improve their organization by grouping their fighter aircraft in separate squadrons. This was a reform to which the British were still groping their way when the battle began, although they had been considering the case for using such squadrons to support their bombers and reconnaissance aircraft for 12 months or more.

Almost simultaneously, Trenchard still further reduced his chances of success by insisting that henceforward the Headquarters Wing's attempt to force the enemy on to the defensive should take the form of continuous patrols over the German lines from dawn to dusk. The commander of the wing, Lieutenant-Colonel H. C. T. Dowding, would have preferred intermittent patrols, since these could be made stronger; but he had to do as he was told. To meet the demand for continuity, he was obliged to despatch so few aircraft at a time that the Germans could nearly always intervene with superior numbers at a moment of their own choosing. The patrols were not altogether ineffective; but they did not give Trenchard undisputed command of the air, and he paid a high price for them in wear-and-tear on his aircraft and in casualties.

In the course of the battle Dowding asked that one of his squadrons, which had suffered fairly heavy losses, should be rested and that a relief should be found for it. The request was granted, but Dowding had the impression that he was under a cloud. Promoted and sent home soon afterwards, he held no further appointment in the field during the remainder of the war. But the lessons learned on the Somme made a powerful impression on him, and he did not forget them when, 20 years later, he found himself responsible for the air defence of the United Kingdom.

The British offensive on the Somme began on 1 July and was prolonged until the middle of November, although the failure of the initial assault was apparent within a fortnight of the start. In order to rebut the storm of criticism evoked by the sacrifice of the flower of the British Army in a hopeless undertaking, attempts were made at the time and afterwards to show that the battle was not the disaster for British arms which it appeared to be, but a success.

So far as the Royal Flying Corps was concerned, the facts speak for themselves. According to Trenchard's staff, between 1 July and 17 November 369 German aircraft were destroyed or damaged and forced down. During the same period the Royal Flying Corps lost 499 pilots and observers killed, wounded or missing, and 782 aircraft were struck off its strength for one reason or another. Starting the battle with 410 serviceable aircraft on all parts of the Western Front, Trenchard ended it with 550, but received in the meantime no less than 1,006 aircraft sent to him from England or flown from Paris.[2] To man them, some training units at home were stripped not only of all their newly-fledged pupils but also of some of their instructors.

While the battle was in progress and before these figures were available, a memorandum on future policy was drawn up at Trenchard's headquarters. This document, afterwards widely read, was not so much an orthodox staff study as an essay on the uses of air power. Its author was Maurice Baring, scion of a distinguished family and an amateur of letters whom the fortunes of war had transformed into an officer on Trenchard's staff.*

The undisguised aim of the memorandum was to bolster the doctrine of the relentless offensive which Trenchard had in-

* Maurice Baring (1874-1945) was the fifth son of Edward Charles Baring, who became the 1st Baron Revelstoke. He was a nephew of the 1st Earl of Cromer and a great-grandson on his mother's side of the 2nd Earl Grey. Educated at Eton and Trinity College, Cambridge, he went down without taking a degree. He entered the diplomatic service in 1898 but resigned his post in 1904 to become a war correspondent in Manchuria, and later a special correspondent in Russia and the Balkans. Baring wrote a number of novels, of which probably the best known was *Daphne Adeane* (1926). He was noted for his gift of satire and mischievous sense of humour.

herited from Henderson. Pointing out that the mere appearance of a hostile aircraft in the sky was often enough to inspire 'exaggerated forebodings', Baring claimed that aircraft used offensively could exert a moral effect out of all proportion to any material damage they might inflict on the enemy. From this he argued that an air commander should always aim at using his aircraft in an offensive role and that this was a rule which should 'guide all warfare in the air'. The temptation to use aircraft for defensive purposes should be resisted because 'the aeroplane is not a defence against the aeroplane'.[3]

Clearly, a good deal of this was not meant to be taken at its face value. Baring cannot really have believed that the aeroplane was not a defence against the aeroplane because, if it had been true that aeroplanes were incapable of shooting down other aeroplanes when used defensively, then they would have been equally incapable of doing so when used offensively. This would have made nonsense of Baring's case. While he was writing his essay, aeroplanes of the Headquarters Wing were being sent over the German lines for the very purpose of shooting down other aeroplanes.

Nor can Baring really have believed that an offensive was always better than a defensive strategy. Although it suited him to make out the best case he could for fighting on the offensive on all possible occasions, he must have known that there would always be times when this was not possible, as well as times when it was not even desirable.

Besides a good deal of special pleading of this kind, the memorandum contained some dubious statements about recent events. Baring claimed, for example, that experience on the Somme supported his hypothesis that the advantage in air warfare always lay with the side that concentrated its forces and assumed an aggressive attitude. This implied that Trenchard, whose attitude was nothing if not aggressive, had concentrated his forces for the Battle of the Somme and was doing well. In fact, he had failed to concentrate his forces and was doing badly. By the time the memorandum was written, his losses were such that he was calling for replacements at a rate which threatened to bring the training organization at home to a standstill. At one time he was so short of aircraft and pilots that he had to call on the Royal Naval Air Service for help.

However, in so far as the memorandum was intended to draw attention to the part played by the moral factor in air warfare, it served its purpose. It also went some way to establish Trenchard's reputation as a strategist, despite the unsatisfactory outcome of his attempt to support the Fourth Army on the Somme. But it did not convince the authorities at home that aeroplanes should never be used in a defensive role and that therefore they could afford to part with all their home defence squadrons for Trenchard's benefit.

At various times during the First World War the British, the French, the Italians and the Russians all had to endure attacks by German or Austrian aircraft on objectives far to the rear of their battlefronts. The facts of geography decreed that by far the hardest to counter, as well as the most persistent and most damaging of these attacks should be those made on objectives in Britain. Since hostile aircraft could reach Britain's nerve centres without making long flights over unfriendly territory, London and the industrial Midlands were always harder to defend against air raids than Paris, Le Creusot, Rome, Milan or even St Petersburg and Moscow.

Some spasmodic bombing of objectives in Britain by heavier-than-air machines was attempted early in the war, but it was not until 1915 that the Kaiser authorized a systematic offensive, to be undertaken under cover of darkness by the Army's and the Navy's Zeppelin and Schütte-Lanz airships. He stipulated that only legitimate military objectives should be selected for attack and that every care should be taken to avoid damage to private property or buildings of historic interest. Such restrictions had, however, little or no practical effect. The airship crews had great difficulty in finding the targets they were told to attack, and in consequence their bombing was in effect, if not in intention, largely indiscriminate.

In 1915 German airships made some 55 sorties for the purpose of attacking objectives in Britain. Bombs dropped from airships which succeeded in crossing the coast killed or injured 740 people, nearly all of them civilians and more than half of them inhabitants of Greater London. No major damage was done to any objective essential to Britain's war economy, but one or two factories had narrow escapes and troops had to be called in to quell disturbances which followed one raid on Kingston-upon-Hull.

When the raids began, the British were very ill-equipped to deal with them. Soon after the outbreak of war the Admiralty had assumed responsibility for air defence at home, not because this was considered an appropriate task for the Navy but because most of the Royal Flying Corps had gone to France. None of the Navy's aircraft or those put at the Admiralty's disposal by units of the Royal Flying Corps left at home carried weapons which could be relied upon to destroy large rigid airships, few had the necessary performance in terms of speed, rate of climb and ceiling, and only small numbers of guns and searchlights were available. One airship whose commander inadvertantly took her over the Allied lines in daylight was shot down by Belgian troops. Another was destroyed by the pilot of a British naval aircraft who was on his way to bomb airship sheds in Belgium when he saw her returning from a raid on Britain and bombed her.

The raids taught the British that they needed not merely more and better aircraft, guns and searchlights but much else besides. Home defence fighters had to be able to close with retreating airships while they were still within reach and to outclimb them even when they tried to escape by dropping ballast and putting up their elevators. They had to be provided with weapons and ammunition which could do more than perforate envelopes and puncture gasbags. Searchlights sited to meet the needs of anti-aircraft gunners were essential, but so were searchlights whose primary purpose was to reveal the enemy's whereabouts to fighter pilots who could not hear the noise made by an airship's engines because they were deafened by the noise made by the engines of their own machines. An organization was needed to co-ordinate the actions of guns, fighters and searchlights, to keep track of the enemy's comings and goings, to issue warnings which would ensure that streetlamps and factory lights were put out at the right moment but not prematurely or needlessly extinguished to the detriment of war production.

The first raid on Britain in 1916 rubbed home these lessons. Nine naval airships were despatched on 31 January with orders to attack objectives in the Midlands or the south of England, and if possible to bomb Liverpool. Nearly all of them lost their bearings and one, the L.19, foundered in the North Sea after wandering over the island of Ameland on the return flight and being driven out to sea again by small arms fire from Dutch troops. But many bombs were dropped, 183 people were killed or injured, and local authorities complained to the Central Government about the inadequacy of the warning system.

About a fortnight later, responsibility for the air defence of the United Kingdom was passed to the Commander-in-Chief, Home Forces, an officer answerable not to the Admiralty but to the War Office. This reform was the outcome of prolonged discussions between naval and military authorities. The War Office was ready with a scheme intended to provide 475 guns and 500 searchlights for the local defence of factories, magazines and arsenals in those parts of England and Scotland which were most likely to be attacked and of specially important or particularly vulnerable objectives elsewhere. An early-warning system based on the national telephone network was worked out by the staff of Home Forces and a central control room was set up in Whitehall.

By the time the change was made, about 300 guns were available for the air defence of all parts of the United Kingdom. Fewer than a third of these were true anti-aircraft guns, but orders already placed would bring the total of modern guns up to the number needed for the War Office scheme. Twelve squadrons of fighters for home defence were formed between November 1915 and the early winter of the following year, and 33 home defence airfields equipped with rudimentary flare-paths for night flying were brought into service by the end of 1916. Home defence aircraft were gradually fitted with machine-guns to replace the small incendiary bombs or fire-darts previously used against airships, and in the summer of 1916 incendiary and explosive bullets were introduced.

These measures made airship raids on Britain increasingly unrewarding and expensive. The Germans devoted three times as many sorties to such raids in 1916 as in 1915, but so many bombs fell in open country, or were dumped in the sea, that the number of people killed or injured by bombing rose by only a third. Between the end of March and the last week in August, airships were hit by anti-aircraft fire on at least four occasions. One of these ships, the L.15, came down off the mouth of the Thames in the early hours of 1 April, and her entire crew, with the exception of one man drowned, were captured. Another ship, the L.20, made a forced descent near Stavanger in Norway at the beginning of May. Finally, between the beginning of September and the last week in November 6 airships were shot down by British fighters, with or without the help of anti-aircraft guns. Among these were the Schütte-Lanz army airship SL.11 and 4 of the newest naval airships, the L.31, L.32, L.33 and L.34. Heinrich Mathy, the German Navy's ablest airship commander, was among those who lost their lives.

After losing the SL.11, the German Army decided to attempt no more airship raids on Britain and to concentrate on the development of heavier-than-air bombers suitable for attacks on London. The chief of the Naval Airship Division, Korvettenkapitän Peter Strasser, came to the conclusion that airship raids were still worth making, but might have taken a different view had he not been misled by false reports of damage done to objectives in Britain. Orders were placed for airships capable of flying at 20,000 feet or more, and a number of existing ships were modified. To make such heights attainable, speed, strength and the comfort of commanders and crews had to be sacrificed to lightness.

Naval airships were sent to attack objectives in Britain on 5 nights between March and September 1917. Most of those which crossed the coast climbed to 16,000 feet or more before doing so. The German meterological service knew little about conditions at such altitudes, and in consequence many ships were blown off course by unpredicted winds. On some occasions instruments froze and crews were partially incapacitated by cold, height-sickness and exhaustion. In these circumstances navigation and target-finding became so difficult that only random bombing was possible for most crews. Although 34 sorties were made on the 5 nights, no important objective was hit and only 24 people were killed or injured by bombing. The British had difficulty in closing with airships that flew so high, but one ship, the newly-commissioned L.48, was brought down in flames on the night of 16/17 June.

Nothing if not persistent, Strasser despatched 11 airships to Britain during the afternoon of 19 October. All reached the English coast by nightfall, but only one flew back to Germany by the orthodox route across the North Sea. Her commander claimed on his return to have bombed two towns in the Midlands from 21,300 feet, but in fact he spent only a short time over the country and there is reason to suspect that he never reached anything like that altitude. The other 10 ships were met by northerly gales at 20,000 feet and blown southwards at high speed. Two returned safely to their bases by way of Holland. Four reached Germany after making long and hazardous flights over England and France, but one of these landed in a wood 200 miles from her base and was damaged beyond repair. Of the remaining 4, one was brought down in flames by French anti-aircraft gunners, another was forced down by French fighters and captured intact, a third made an emergency landing near Sisteron in the French Alps and the fourth was last seen heading south over the Mediterranean after 16 of her crew of 20 had jumped clear and surrendered to the French.

Thus the raid cost the Germans 5 of the 11 ships despatched. Ninety-one inhabitants of Britain were killed or injured, most of them by bombs dropped hurriedly from a ship whose commander found himself unexpectedly over London.

The Naval Airship Division suffered a further setback early in 1918, when 5 ships were destroyed in their sheds at Alhorn, in north-west Germany, by a series of mysterious explosions. Whether these were accidental or caused by sabotage was never established to the satisfaction of all concerned.

Still undaunted, Strasser ordered 4 more raids on Britain between March and August. No important objective was hit in any of the raids, but 74 people were killed or injured by bombing and one woman died of shock when bombs fell near her house. Strasser lost his life in the last raid of all, when the newly-commissioned L.70 was shot down in flames by Major Egbert Cadbury, flying with Captain R. Leckie as gunner and observer in a DH.4 two-seater with a maximum speed of 120 miles an hour and a service ceiling of 22,000 feet.

By that time the German Army's short-lived offensive against Britain with heavier-than-air machines was over, and had cost the Germans heavy losses.

Almost from the beginning of the war, attempts had been made at the Zeppelin factories and elsewhere to develop an alternative to the large rigid airship in the shape of a long-range heavier-than-air machine capable of dropping a substantial bomb-load from a height which would put it out of reach of anti-aircraft guns, and of flying fast enough to present a difficult target to fighters. In 1916 a team led by Karl Rosner of the Gothaer Waggonfabrik designed a large biplane which met most of these requirements. Known in the form in which it went into service in the following year as the Gotha G.IV, this aircraft was 42 feet long, had a wing-span of 75 feet and was armed with 3 machine-guns. Two 260 hp Mercedes engines gave it a maximum speed of approximately 80 miles an hour. Its ceiling with a 300-kilogramme bomb-load was close on 18,000 feet. Although considerably slower than the best contemporary fighters, the G.IV was so well armed that fighters were expected to have some difficulty in dealing with the formations of 20 aircraft or so with which the Germans hoped to go into action in the spring of 1917.

A German strategic bomber unit intended for attacks on England with heavier-than-air machines had been formed in Belgium as early as the first winter of the war, but had moved to Metz when the military authorities were forced to recognize in the following spring that no base from which its aircraft could reach suitable objectives was likely to fall into their hands in the immediate future. After serving in a tactical role at the Battle of the Somme, an offshoot of this unit returned to Belgium in the spring of 1917, was re-equipped with the Gotha G.IV, and became known as the Englandgeschwader, or Bombengeschwader 3.

About 5 pm on 25 May 21 aircraft of Bombengeschwader 3, bound for London, crossed the Essex coast between the estuaries of the Blackwater and the Crouch. When the eastern approaches to London were seen to be covered with dense clouds, the formation turned south over Gravesend. Passing west of Maidstone and Ashford, it returned to Belgium after dropping about 4 tons of bombs near the coast of Kent. Many bombs fell on a camp at Shorncliffe at which Canadian troops were stationed, but a large number struck a crowded thoroughfare near Folkestone harbour where civilians were doing their Whitsun shopping. The 290 people killed or injured included 79 women and 37 children. Some of the Gothas were intercepted by fighters from bases in England or France, but all returned safely except one which came down in the sea and one which crashed on landing. Residents of Folkestone passed a resolution censuring the military authorities and the Government for not warning them that hostile aircraft were approaching.

As a result of this calamity the War Office took steps to speed up the passing of information about movements of hostile aircraft and to station trained observers at 7 lightships off the east coast and at the mouth of the Thames. The Director-General of Military Aeronautics wished also to provide the commander of the air defences with a wireless transmitter so that he could communicate with aircraft in the air. The naval authorities, fearing that such a transmitter would interfere with traffic between the Admiralty and naval units, raised such powerful objections that air raids on Britian were over by the time the transmitter was in service.

On 5 June 22 Gothas approached London from the same direction as on 25 May. Again they turned south well short of their objective, this time dropping bombs on both banks of the Thames at Shoeburyness and Sheerness. Many of the bombs fell harmlessly on waste land or shingle, but 35 soldiers and 12 civilians were killed or injured. One Gotha was brought down in the sea by anti-aircraft fire.

In the light of this experience the Commander-in-Chief, Home Forces, decided to give immediate effect to a new scheme of gunfire planned in March. A reliable method of using fighters to counter raids such as those made on 25 May and 5 June had, however, yet to be devised. Aircraft despatched singly had proved reasonably effective against large rigid airships which came by night, but seemed likely to be almost useless against compact formations of well-armed Gothas.

Shortly before 11 am on Wednesday, 13 June, 18 Gothas crossed the Essex coast at the mouth of the Crouch and set course for London. The weather was fine apart from slight haze. Four Gothas were unable to keep up with the rest. One of these dropped 5 bombs at Margate on its way back to Belgium, 2 bombed Shoeburyness, and the fourth went as far as Greenwich before abandoning its mission. The remaining 14 aircraft flew in diamond formation to the neighbourhood of London Bridge, where they dropped about 4 tons of bombs. Most of the bombs came down within a mile of Liverpool Street Station, but some fell as far away as East Ham, Forest Gate, Islington and Bermondsey. The leader of the formation reported on his return to base that the vast majority had fallen among docks and warehouses, but a count made by the British showed that most of the buildings damaged were houses. Hits were also scored on schools, factories, a church, a town hall, a mission hall and shops. Five hundred and seventy-four people, including 124 women and 144 children, were killed or injured by the bombing and 20 by shells or fragments of shells from anti-aircraft guns. Ninety-two pilots from home defence squadrons, training units and naval squadrons went into the air, but no one was in a position to co-ordinate their efforts and no Gothas were shot down.

A similar raid followed on Saturday, 7 July. About 20 Gothas, again in diamond formation, reached the centre of London and dropped 3 tons of bombs. Extensive damage was done to houses, shops, offices and warehouses; but no objective of major importance was hit, although one bomb fell close to the entrance to the London Docks. Two hundred and forty-four people were killed or injured in London and 6 at Margate, but more than a quarter of these casualties were attributed to anti-aircraft fire. One Gotha was shot down by a fighter and 4 crashed on landing.

The bombing of London in broad daylight on 13 June and 7 July caused intense excitement, almost amounting to hysteria, in governmental and official circles. After the first raid the War Office put forward, and the War Cabinet accepted, a scheme for the expansion of the Royal Flying Corps from 108 to no less than 200 squadrons. After the second raid, the Government set up a two-man ministerial committee to report on the air defences of the United Kingdom and to go into the whole question of the organization and higher direction of the air services. Its members were the Prime Minister, David Lloyd George, and the South African lawyer, politician and part-time soldier Lieutenant-General J. C. Smuts, whom Lloyd George had brought into the War Cabinet.

Whether the appointment of a committee with such wide terms of reference was appropriate is a question that cannot be answered in a sentence. Two daylight raids on London, delivered by a bomber force never much more than forty aircraft strong, would not in themselves have justified a critical examination of the machinery by which the air services were controlled. But Lloyd George had other reasons for regarding such an investigation as opportune. When the Prime Minister's Committee on Air Organization was set up on 11 July, the War Cabinet was on the point of sanctioning an offensive at Passchendaele which not a single member of its War Policy Committee expected to achieve more than a limited success. Lloyd George was much irked by his inability to impose an alternative strategy on the military authorities. He had no faith in the ability of the Chief of the Imperial General Staff and the Commander-in-Chief of the British Expeditionary Force to carry the war on land to a successful conclusion, and a brush with the Admiralty about the introduction of the convoy system had left him almost equally dissatisfied with the First Sea Lord and the Director of Anti-Submarine Warfare. As leader of a precariously balanced Coalition Government, he was not in a position to call for sweeping changes at the War Office and the Admiralty. A Prime Minister so circumscribed could not afford to neglect an opportunity of reforms which might enable him to gain a firmer grip on the national war machine.

The committee presented its first report to the War Cabinet on 19 July. Drawn up by Smuts, it dealt with points which raised no major issue of policy. Smuts recommended that anti-aircraft guns should be used to provide a defensive barrage covering the approaches to London; that three single-seater fighter squadrons, with pilots trained to fight in formation, should be added to the air defences; and that a senior officer with experience of air warfare, responsible to the Commander-in-Chief, Home Forces, should take charge of the whole system.

The post went to Brigadier-General (afterwards Major-General) E. B. Ashmore. An energetic leader and an able organizer, Ashmore had commanded a wing and later an air brigade in France and had also served on the staff of Home Forces. On 6 August he assumed control of the 6 fighter squadrons then at home; of all anti-aircraft guns in the London, Harwich, and Thames and Medway areas, with the addition of certain detached batteries in the Eastern Command and of such mobile guns as might be allotted to him; and of all observer posts east of a line from Grantham to Portsmouth. Almost simultaneously, a scheme for the issue of public air raid warnings to Londoners by the firing of maroons and the display of notices was put into effect for the first time.

Ashmore set up his headquarters at the Horse Guards in

London, where the central control room established in connection with the early-warning system was already functioning. His command was called the London Air Defence Area, but covered much more of the country than the name implied. Provision was made for the establishment of a second air defence headquarters in the north of England should the need arise.

Ashmore's intention was that, when a hostile formation approached London, fighters despatched in response to orders passed by telephone to appropriate airfields should engage it after it had been broken up by anti-aircraft fire. In the event, the Germans made no more daylight attacks on London. After making a few attacks in daylight on more accessible targets such as Harwich, they launched a series of night attacks.

The London Air Defence Area was the prototype of the system of air defence used by the British with conspicuous success in the Second World War. Both systems relied on the detection and tracking of hostile aircraft by a combination of warning devices and direct observation, with the difference that sound locators were used in the rudimentary and radar stations in the developed system. Both systems aimed at bringing all means of active defence under unified control. In both systems, these means included fighter aircraft, anti-aircraft guns, searchlights and barrage balloons.

The use of barrage balloons was first proposed by Ashmore on 5 September 1917, when night attacks on London were the chief danger. The Germans had been using balloon or kite barrages since the spring as an insurance against low-level attacks on certain industrial areas, but Ashmore drew his inspiration from a barrage used by the Italians to defend Venice against attacks by Austrian aircraft. This consisted of 70 balloons which were inflated at the beginning of each moonlight period and left in position until the danger was thought to have receded. Ashmore persuaded the War Office to order 100 similar balloons. He also used balloons of the Caquot type, developed by the French as a counterpart to the Parseval-Sigsfeld kite-balloon and in some respects an improvement on it. By early October the first of a series of aprons, consisting of moored balloons linked by horizontal cables from which weighted wire streamers were suspended, was in operation on the eastern outskirts of London. The number of aprons deployed north and south of the Thames rose by the end of the war to ten. The maximum height attained was of the order of 10,000 feet or so, but balloons capable of raising an apron to 15,000 or even 20,000 feet were thought to be within the bounds of possibility. The streamers could not be relied upon to destroy aircraft which collided with them, but Ashmore was confident that the deterrent effect of the aprons was considerable. At least one bomber is known to have flown through an apron without crashing, but according to a German source the experience was not one which the crew would have wished to undergo a second time.

Between the date of Ashmore's appointment and the early summer of 1918 heavier-than-air machines attacked London or other objectives in the south of England on 2 days and 21 nights, making 284 sorties for the purpose. Gothas provided most of the striking power, but giant bombers still more or less in the experimental stage contributed some 30 sorties. About 53 tons of bombs were dropped and 1,552 people were killed or injured. Twenty-one bombers were destroyed or forced down by the defences, and at least another 25 crashed in Belgium or failed for one reason or another to return safely to their bases. The last raid of the war by heavier-than-air machines, on the night of 19/20 May 1918, cost the Germans 8 of the 43 aircraft despatched. Three were shot down by anti-aircraft guns, 3 succumbed to fighters, 1 made a forced landing in Essex and 1 crashed not far from its base.

These results were a triumph for Ashmore and his team and a complete rebuttal of Baring's dictum that the aeroplane was not a defence against the aeroplane.

Even so, the raids were for some months a source of intense anxiety to the British Government. Tens of thousands of Londoners, chiefly from poor districts where houses tended to be flimsy, flocked whenever they believed a raid was imminent into underground railway stations and the tunnels under the Thames at Woolwich, Greenwich, Blackwall and Rotherhithe. Some families made a habit of trekking from their homes at nightfall even when there was no reason to suspect that the enemy was coming. Large numbers of people took refuge during air raids in police stations or in buildings, otherwise unoccupied at night, which local authorities were compelled by instructions from the Central Government to designate as shelters. Such buildings provided a fair degree of security against bomb splinters, but ministers were haunted by the fear that sooner or later one of them would suffer a direct hit. They also feared that the crowding together of large numbers of people of all ages and both sexes in ill-ventilated stations and tunnels might lead to epidemics and other social evils. Furthermore, experience soon pointed to the danger that scores or even hundreds of people might be crushed in a panic rush to enter such places by steep and narrow ramps or staircases.

Ministers were worried, too, by the actual and potential effects of air raids on war production. Returns from Woolwich Arsenal showed that workers not only tended to miss a shift on nights when London was raided but sometimes to stay away on the following day, and that output declined sharply though only for brief periods on such occasions. At the same time the Government was embarrassed by complaints from various quarters that air raid precautions were inadequate and that the obligation to designate buildings as air raid shelters threw an unacceptable burden on local authorities.

The German air offensive failed, none the less, to make permanent inroads on Britian's capacity to carry on the war. But its failure was not yet apparent when, on 17 August 1917, the Prime Minister's Committee on Air Organization presented its second and final report. Again Smuts was the author, but he consulted Lloyd George, and the influence of the highly imaginitive and volatile Prime Minister is discernible at a number of points in the report.

When the report was written, the War Cabinet had already agreed in principle to a massive increase in the strength of the Royal Flying Corps, and the Government was confident that the necessary aircraft could be found. Problems of procurement and supply had caused a good deal of anxiety in the early stages of the war, when the War Office and the Admiralty were competing for aircraft and especially for the aero-engines which were then the bottleneck. An Air Board, intended to hold the balance between the two ministries but with no executive authority, had been set up in 1916, and early in the following year all concerned had accepted an arrangement by which, at least in theory, the Ministry of Munitions took care of design and procurement and the Air Board decided in consultation with the service ministries how the aircraft produced should be divided between them. These reforms did not end a sometimes bitter rivalry between the Royal Flying Corps and the Royal Naval Air Service, but output rose so sharply in the spring and early summer of 1917 that the Government foresaw no difficulty in meeting the demands of an accelerated programme.

Accordingly, Smuts and Lloyd George took as the point of departure for their study of the future of the air services the assumption that there would soon be enough aircraft to meet all the needs of the Army and the Navy and provide a surplus which could be used as 'an independent means of war operations'. Assuming that the surplus would be so used and that such operations would be conducted by an authority distinct from the War Office and the Admiralty, they went on to ask whether there should then be three air services, or only one. Their answer was that the existence of three air services would lead to chaos. There should be one air service, under an Air Ministry responsible both for allocating units to the Army and the Navy and for independent operations.

Given the premises, this was a logical conclusion. Whether the premises were sound is another matter. Lloyd George and Smuts gave a spurious air of reason to their plea for an independent air force by pointing out at the start that aircraft not needed by the Army or the Navy *could* be used for operations of the kind they had in view. From this springboard of incontrovertible statement they jumped to the conclusion that such operations were desirable or at least inevitable. They also assumed that, in the words of their report, an independent air force would be capable of the 'devastation of enemy lands and destruction of industrial and populous areas on a vast scale'.

There was no warrant for these assumptions in any factual data available to Lloyd George and Smuts when they presented their report. They may have had a good case. Indeed, most people think they did have a good case. But if they had, they never stated it. The Germans had not set up an air force independent of their Army and Navy, but in the summer of 1917 they had been trying for 2½ years to make an impression on the British by using some of their aircraft for purposes not directly linked with the operations of their fleets and armies. They had tried bombing Britain from large rigid airships, of which they were to build well over a hundred between the outbreak of war and the armistice, and had suffered heavy losses without once destroying an objective of major importance or devastating even one small corner of an industrial area or centre of population. They had tried sending heavier-than-air bombers over London in daylight, but had found the results so unsatisfactory that they soon switched to night attacks. Apart from inflicting a good deal of anxiety on the British Government and causing some people to stay away from work during and immediately after raids all the Germans achieved by their bombing of Britain during the First World War was to kill or injure a large number of civilians and a few soldiers and to make themselves almost universally execrated as Huns and baby-killers.

It is true that the British official historian of the war in the air argued when the war was over that the raids served a useful purpose from the German point of view by forcing the British to devote to home defence resources which might otherwise have been used elsewhere. But this argument rests on the assumption that these resources could and would have been more usefully employed in a foreign theatre than at home. That assumption is not necessarily valid. Almost throughout the war the British, like the French and the Germans, gave their commanders on the Western Front large numbers of aircraft and pilots with which to support unprofitable offensives. They would not have gained anything if, by parting with still more aircraft and pilots, they had encouraged their generals to squander even more of their man-power on futile attempts to storm impregnable positions.

In any case, Lloyd George and Smuts did not found their claims on the argument that the measures they proposed would make the war on land easier to win by forcing the enemy to divert men and machines from the Western Front to home defence. The essence of their doctrine was that control of a strategic bomber force would enable the Government to conduct warlike operations independently of the Army and the Navy, and that these might prove decisive. According to them, the day might not be far off when air operations would become 'the principal operations of war', to which 'the older forms of military and naval operations' would perhaps take second place.

It is also true that Lloyd George and Smuts envisaged air attacks of much greater scope than any hitherto attempted. In effect they argued that, because the Germans had killed or injured hundreds of people by making 30–40 bomber sorties over London on 13 June and 7 July, the bombing of industrial areas in Germany by perhaps 10 times as many aircraft might 'form an important factor in bringing about peace'. But British and Germans alike were to find a quarter of a century later that industrial areas were not as easily devastated as Lloyd George supposed, and that not even thousands of bomber sorties could be relied upon to break a nation's will to fight.

On the strength of such arguments, and in face of considerable dissent, the Government formed towards the end of the year an Air Ministry for the purpose of welding the Royal Flying Corps and the Royal Naval Air Service into a unified air force. The post of Secretary of State for Air, declined in gratuitously insulting terms by the millionaire newspaper proprietor Lord Northcliffe, went to Northcliffe's young brother Lord Rothermere, also a newspaper proprietor. Trenchard agreed to become Chief of the Air Staff, although he had never attended the Staff College or served on the General Staff and had little idea of the duties and responsibilities attached to such a post.

Trenchard is universally regarded as an ardent champion – which he afterwards became – of the principle of an air force independent of the Army and the Navy. At the time when he became the first Chief of the Air Staff he held quite different views. Like most army officers of his generation, he regarded the fusion of the Royal Flying Corps and the Royal Naval Air Service as a blunder and the claims made for an independent air force as a possible means of ending the war as a wild exaggeration. He was consoled for his acquiescence in the Government's proposals by the belief that an air force administered by an independent ministry could not endure and that sooner or later air units would return to their parent services.[4]

As a former Director-General of a department of the War Office which supplied the Army with clothing, Rothermere had some knowledge of the machinery of government, but his duties as head of a new ministry were almost as strange to him as those of professional chief of a fighting service which did not yet exist were to Trenchard. A clash between the two men was inevitable and not long delayed. On 19 March, only 13 days before the

Royal Air Force was due to come into existence, Trenchard handed in his resignation.

Its acceptance in the middle of April, a few months after Lloyd George had at last succeeded in ridding himself of an uncooperative Chief of the Imperial General Staff and an almost equally unsatisfactory First Sea Lord, made Trenchard famous. Hitherto he had been known to friends and critics alike as a ruthless fighting soldier of the old school, without much imagination and of limited understanding, but a staunch upholder of aims and methods which Henderson's precept had made othodox. The Government's critics discovered him overnight as one of a trio of brilliant strategists thrust in swift succession into outer darkness because they refused to countenance the Prime Minister's wildcat schemes. A hostile press depicted Lloyd George as sacrificing to his passion for the limelight first the Chief of the Imperial General Staff, Sir William Robertson; next the First Sea Lord, Sir John Jellicoe; and now Trenchard. All, according to one London newspaper, were 'acknowledged masters of their craft'.

The paradoxical sequel was that Trenchard, who in 1917 had regarded the Government's hopes of using an independent air force to hasten the end of the war as evidence that members of the Air Board were 'quite off their heads', was relegated to command of a strategic bomber force intended for the bombing of Germany. By the end of the war 11 squadrons were ready to attack German industrial centres as soon as the Allied Supreme War Council gave the word, and Trenchard had become as ardent an advocate of independent air action as the most enthusiastic of Lloyd George's supporters could have wished.

On 1 April 1918 the Royal Air Force was duly born, with Trenchard as reluctant midwife. Almost simultaneously the American military authorities relieved the Signal Corps of the United States Army of the responsibility for military aviation which it had exercised since the first aeroplanes were bought from the Wright brothers. A vast programme of expansion had been sanctioned in the summer of 1917, but no aircraft of American design suitable for use at the front were available by the spring of 1918, and none appeared in time for any of the 45 first-line squadrons in active employment at the end of the war to be equipped with them. Large numbers of De Havilland DH.4

aircraft intended for use as light bombers were built under licence in the United States and fitted with Liberty engines designed and produced by a consortium of motor-car manufacturers; but the Liberty engine was not suitable for installation in contemporary machines intended for use as scouts and fighters. For these the United States Army had to rely in 1918 not merely on British and French designers but on British and French factories. American airmen had therefore to learn to fly an assortment of unfamiliar machines after their initial training was completed. A dearth of officers qualified by experience and seniority to supervise operational training and deal authoritatively with technical problems contributed to serious delays.

General John Pershing, Commander-in-Chief of the American Expeditionary Force, had never flown and had the reputation of not being particularly sympathetic towards airmen. Nevertheless he recognized the importance of giving his troops adequate air support. He chose as commander of his air component Major-General Mason M. Patrick, an engineer officer of whose all-round ability he had a high opinion. Patrick afterwards confessed that up to that time he had never seen an aeroplane, 'save casually', but he justified Pershing's faith in him by making a bold use of his resources. In August 1918 he concentrated all his first-line squadrons, with units borrowed from the French, in the sector held by the newly-formed United States First Army. He placed the whole under the tactical command of Colonel William Mitchell, an enthusiast who had learned to fly in the winter of 1915–16 and held strong views about air strategy and tactics.

When the Americans passed to the offensive in September, Mitchell seized his opportunity of doing what Trenchard had wished to do at the Battle of the Somme. Like Trenchard, he allotted only a small part of his force to close support of the assault troops. Since, unlike Trenchard, he had only the needs of one army to consider, he was able to use all the rest in a role comparable with that assigned to Trenchard's Headquarters Wing. Tasks assigned to this part of the force included the bombing and machine-gunning of airfields, communications and targets of opportunity as well as air fighting. By retaining direct control of all but the close-support squadrons and despatching his bombers and fighters in relatively large formations, Mitchell succeeded in dominating the air over the battlefield and in making a notable contribution to the land battle by hampering the movements of the enemy's reserves.

The circumstances in which Mitchell was called upon to fight differed so much from those which prevailed during the greater part of the war that the results cannot be taken as a yardstick by which to measure Trenchard's performance at the Somme or the performance of other air commanders responsible for supporting offensives launched in unfavourable conditions. At the Battle of Neuve-Chapelle the British had a chance, which they failed to take, of breaking through a shallow defensive position and reaching open country. All subsequent offensives in the Western Front, up to the time in the late summer of 1918 when the Germans began to crumble, were attempts to storm positions so deep that the defenders were always able to summon reserves before a breakthrough could be completed. Even when the Germans made spectacular advances in the spring and early summer of 1918, the Allies were able to seal off the gaps punched in their lines.

Much thought was given by all the belligerents to the possibility of using air power to turn the scales in favour of the attacker. In Britain Colonel Maurice Hankey, Secretary of the Committee of Imperial Defence and later of the Cabinet, suggested at an early stage of the war that swarms of low-flying aircraft might be used to support attacks by land forces, but aircraft with enough firepower to overwhelm troops in entrenched positions supplemented by concrete pillboxes were not then available. Later, British and French strategists agreed that the all-out offensive by which the Allied and Associated Powers hoped to defeat the Germans in 1919 should include assaults by large formations of tanks with massive air support. They were able to use such methods to a limited extent during their successful advances in the last few months of the war, but the unexpectedly swift collapse of the German armies left a number of questions about the employment of aircraft in support of land forces still unanswered.

One point on which there was no dispute was that experience on all fronts had amply vindicated claims made for the aeroplane as an instrument of reconnaissance. But there was no such unanimity of opinion where other forms of air support for troops were concerned. Many airmen and some soldiers believed that aircraft other than those used for tactical, strategic or artillery reconnaissance, or to keep hostile aircraft at bay, could best contribute to a land battle by attacking objectives beyond the range of field artillery, such as rail centres and ammunition dumps behind the enemy's lines. Others emphasized the difficulty of knocking out such objectives by high-level or medium-level bombing in face of opposition from fighters and anti-aircraft guns. Convinced that the bombing of distant objectives could not in any case exert any immediate effect on the capacity of the enemy's troops to withstand an infantry or tank assault, they argued that aircraft could do far more to help armies by flying low over the battlefield for the purpose of seeking out and destroying targets within range of field guns but none the less left unscathed by artillery bombardments. Regimental officers pointed out that on many occasions during the past 4 years troops trying to storm the enemy's trenches had been met by heavy fire from strongpoints which hours of shelling had failed to knock out.

The issue was further complicated, so far as the British were concerned, by the emphasis laid in the Lloyd George–Smuts memorandum on the bombing of industrial areas and centres of population. Although few people went so far as to say so at the time, it could have been argued in 1918 that, if such methods really could be made effective, then governments might do well to use bombers exclusively for attacks on objectives of that kind and stop using them as dubiously effective substitutes for field, medium and heavy artillery.

Many years later, experience in the Spanish Civil War was to throw new light on these problems. But by that time the leading European powers would already have chosen most of the aircraft with which they were to go to war in 1939. The British, in particular, were to find themselves committed by 1936 to the development of a long-range bomber force which would prove useless for the formation attacks in daylight for which it was intended.

Many other questions relating to the use of air power in war, especially at sea, were left unanswered at the time of the armistice.

German naval airships made many more sorties between 1914 and 1918 for the purpose of reconnoitring the Heligoland Bight and its approaches than were devoted to raids on Britain. Naval airships were also used to reconnoitre the Gulf of Finland and to make a few attacks on objectives behind the Russian lines. But no attempt was made by the German Navy to find out whether its airships could help U-boat commanders and the meterological service by extending their flights to the western approaches to the British Isles, although they were, at any rate in theory, quite capable of doing so. Nor were any of the 40–50 Zeppelin and Schütte-Lanz airships available to the German Army between 1914 and 1917 used to give a new dimension to the war on land by being pressed into service as troop-carriers. A naval airship, the L.57, was modified during construction to enable her to carry supplies to troops in German East Africa, and a second naval airship, the L.59, was similarly modified when the L.57 was wrecked during preparations for a trial flight. The L.59, leaving Jamboli in Bulgaria on 21 November 1917, with 3 tons of medical supplies and 12 tons of weapons, ammunition and spares aboard her, got as far as the Sudan before she was recalled on the ground that the situation of the German troops in East Africa had become hopeless. She returned to Jamboli on 25 November after spending 95 hours in the air and covering well over 4,000 miles.

For various reasons, the German Naval Airship Division's sorties over the Heligoland Bight and its approaches threw only an uncertain light on the fitness of large rigid airships for maritime reconnaissance. More often than not, the weather was the decisive factor. At Nordholz, near Cuxhaven, the Germans built a revolving shed which they made large enough by the early part of 1917 to house their largest airships. Elsewhere, large rigid airships could leave and return to their sheds only in a calm or light airs, or when the wind was blowing from a favourable quarter. Furthermore, visibility had to be fairly good if sorties made for the purpose of spotting hostile warships, or merchant vessels bound for the enemy's ports, were to be worth while. At best, such conditions could be expected on 1 day in 3, and the days on which they occurred were not necessarily those on which the High Command was most in need of information.

There are no grounds for the popular belief that reports from airships averted a disaster to the Germans when they tried to lure the British battle-cruiser squadron into action with the main body of their High Seas Fleet at the Battle of Jutland in the early summer of 1916. One naval airship, the L.11, transmitted a fairly accurate report of the position of the battle-cruiser squadron early on 1 June, but it was more or less nullified by a misleading report transmitted by another naval airship, the L.24. When the Germans made a further attempt, in August of the same year, to bring the enemy's battle-cruisers to action on terms favourable to themselves, the British stole a march on the German Naval Airship Division by putting to sea long before its airships were in position. Later the airships transmitted a good deal of information about the movements of British warships, but not all of it was accurate and a good deal of it was misinterpreted.

For some years after the mishap to the *Mayfly*, the British took little interest in rigid airships. Between 1917 and 1921 they completed about a dozen. Most were copies or adaptions of German designs, but some original work was done for Vickers by H. B. Pratt, who had predicted the failure of the *Mayfly*, and Barnes Wallis. A few of these airships made operational sorties over the North Sea, but they were used mainly for research and experiment. British experiments with mooring masts showed conclusively that large airships could be moored in conditions which made it quite impossible to put them into sheds.

From 1915 until the end of the war the British made considerable use of small non-rigid airships, or blimps, for anti-submarine patrols and convoy escort. Their example was followed by the Americans, the French, and to some extent the Italians, who also used non-rigid or semi-rigid airships to support troops after the Germans and the French had ceased to do so. Encounters between blimps and submarines were so rare that the value of these patrols was hard to judge, but their deterrent effect is generally held to have been considerable. The United States naval authorities thought so highly of blimps that they remained faithful to them after the end of the First World War and continued to use them for convoy escort or off-shore patrols, including radar patrols, until 1961. The Italians made some very good non-rigid and semi-rigid airships during the First World War, and sold a number to foreign powers.

The British considered that the large rigid airships favoured by the Germans for maritime reconnaissance would prove too vulnerable to fire from ships' guns to be suitable for use in naval battles. To scout for their warships they relied mainly on heavier-than-air machines. The Royal Navy made many experiments with seaplane tenders and aircraft carriers to extend the range of its aeroplanes, as did the United States Navy, but had few opportunities of testing their performance in contact with the enemy. An ocean liner adapted to carry 10 aircraft, the *Campania*, was to have accompanied the British Grand Fleet when it put to sea for the Battle of Jutland, but her orders miscarried and she started so late that Admiral Jellicoe, then commanding the Grand Fleet, ordered her to return to Scapa Flow. The small seaplane carrier *Engadine*, with 3 aircraft, accompanied the battle-cruiser squadron, commanded at Jutland by Vice-Admiral Sir David Beatty. One of her aircraft transmitted 3 reports which might have been useful to Beatty if he had received them promptly. As things were, he obtained the information he needed from one of his cruisers. Experience during the First World War convinced the British, as it did the Americans, the Japanese and the French, that aircraft carriers were likely to play an important part in future naval battles, but they were able to reach only tentative conclusions as to the optimum size of such vessels and the kind of aircraft they should carry.

3

THE PERIOD OF DISARMAMENT

In 1916 the United States Government, alarmed by the growing strength of Japan and the long-term implications of the war in Europe, adopted a programme of naval expansion which challenged Britain's command of the sea. When the United States declared war on Germany in the following year President Woodrow Wilson was forced to recognize, however, that nothing like the volume of shipping needed to carry a large expeditionary force across the Atlantic could be found from American resources. He therefore suspended the production of capital ships so that American shipyards could concentrate on the building of destroyers, submarines, and above all merchant vessels suitable for use in wartime as troop transports. Even so, more than half the American troops despatched to Europe in 1918 had to be carried in British ships.

The question of Anglo-American naval rivalry did not, therefore, become acute until the war was almost over. During the negotiations which preceded the granting of an armistice to Germany Colonel E. M. House, who was not only the President's personal envoy but also the accredited representative of the United States Government, pressed the British to renounce the right to search neutral merchant vessels at sea in any future war. They declined to do so, but agreed to discuss the whole question of Anglo-American naval relations at some more convenient time.

At the Preliminary Peace Conference of Paris in 1919, the Americans again raised the question of what was called the Freedom of the Seas. They had it in mind to warn the British that, if they obtained no satisfaction, the United States would not only complete the 1916 capital-ships programme, but might even double it. But the President was not in a position to press the matter. As a result of representations made to him during a visit to the United States while the conference was sitting, he was obliged to ask the Allies to accept substantial amendments to the Covenant of the League of Nations, which was to form an integral part of the Treaty of Versailles. By undertaking to support the President's proposals and to discuss naval armaments after the treaty was signed, the British succeeded in obtaining from Colonel House a written assurance to the effect that the President had no immediate intention of building warships in direct competition with the Royal Navy. House believed that, once the treaty was signed and the League of Nations was in existence, Britain and the United States would be able to settle their differences in the context of a comprehensive scheme of naval disarmament.

Meanwhile they had a common interest in persuading the French to renounce the hope of providing themselves with a strategic frontier on the Rhine by detaching the Rhineland and the Palatinate from Germany. This they did by offering France guarantees against a fresh act of aggression. They were, however, obliged to acquiesce in a more drastic reduction of Germany's armed strength than some members of the British delegation thought desirable. The Germans not only had to content themselves with a small professional army but were compelled to surrender most of their warships, more than 15,000 aeroplanes, about 27,000 aero-engines and all their surviving airships. They were forbidden for 6 months after the restoration of peace to manufacture or import aircraft, aero-engines or their component parts, and from 1922 to 1926 limits were imposed on the size of the aircraft they might build.

These restrictions were fatal to German hopes of reviving and extending commercial airship services immediately after the war. They also had important effects on the subsequent development of civil aviation in all counties. The British rigid airship R.34 flew from Britain to the United States and back only a few weeks after the signing of the Treaty of Versailles; but the first transatlantic flights and the first commericial passenger flights after the war were all made in heavier-than-air machines. In May 1919 Lieutenant-Commander A. C. Read of the United States Navy flew a Curtiss flying boat by stages from Newfoundland to Lisbon; in June the British Captain J. Alcock and Lieutenant A. Whitten Brown made the first direct non-stop flight across the

Atlantic by flying from Newfoundland to Galway in a converted bomber. British, Dutch, French and German firms were all carrying fare-paying passengers or mails between European capitals by the summer. The Zeppelin factories completed in 1924 a 660-foot-long airship for delivery to the United States Navy as part-payment of Germany's war-debt to the United States; but it was not until 2 years later that they were able to resume production on their own account. By that time the aeroplane, although still noisy, inefficient and uncomfortable, had come to be accepted as a reasonably convenient vehicle for fast journeys which could be accomplished in stages of not more than 500 miles or so. The first post-war German airship, the *Graf Zeppelin,* set new standards of comfort, endurance and payload when she did appear, but the heavier-than-air machine had gained too long a start to be easily superseded.

At the end of the First World War British statesmen believed that, although answers had yet to be found to many problems posed by the collapse of the Central Powers and the rise of militant Communism in Russia, they could safely base their long-term plans for their armed forces on the assumption that no great war involving the British Empire would occur for at least ten years. A disarmed Germay seemed unlikely to trouble the peace of Europe for a long time to come. The Americans were thought to be willing to discuss the difficult question of naval armaments on amicable terms. The French were not convinced that the peace settlements had given them the security they deemed their due, but clearly they had more to gain from preventing another war than from starting one. Hence it did not seem to the British unreasonable to aim at reconciling France with Germany and even at persuading her, in the fullness of time, to renounce compulsory military service and come into line with Britain, the new Germany and the United States by relying in time of peace on a small professional army.

Accordingly, as soon as the war was over the British made massive reductions in their naval, military and air budgets, abolished their wartime air defences and reduced their coast defences to a skeleton basis. Contrary to popular belief, it was not because their military leaders lacked foresight, or thought horses more elegant than tanks and aircraft, that they omitted to provide themselves during the post-war years with an up-to-date mechanized army and strong tactical air forces. The General Staff were well aware that armoured formations, supported not merely by reconnaissance aircraft but by bombers and fighters used in a tactical role, were likely to play a crucial part in any future war fought on a European or a global scale; but they were expressly forbidden to prepare for such a war. Their task was to provide an army capable of preserving law and order at home and in a scattered overseas empire, and of mobilizing in an emergency at most two infantry divisions and a cavalry brigade for despatch to any part of the empire where they might be needed.

British hopes of persuading the French to make a major contribution to the general scaling-down of armaments envisaged by the framers of the Treaty of Versailles were soon dashed by the refusal of the United States Senate to ratify the treaty. The defection of the United States meant not only that the League of Nations was deprived of American support but also that the undertakings by which Britain and the United States were to have guaranteed the new frontier between France and Germany became inoperative. The French, alarmed and incensed by the failure of the guarantees, insisted on retaining their large conscript army and a substantial air force to support it. They also formed military alliances with Belgium, Czechoslovakia, Poland, Rumania, and Yugoslavia. Even after Germany had undertaken at Locarno in 1925 to accept her existing frontier in the west as permanent and Britain and Italy had promised to support either France or Germany against an act of unprovoked aggression, they sought a further reinsurance by building along part of their eastern frontier the chain of fortified positions known as the Maginot Line.

A wave of xenophobia, directed chiefly against Britain, swept through the United States after the Senate's repudiation of the Treaty of Versailles. Private citizens demonstrated in favour of Irish Nationalism and against British policy in Ireland; the Secretary of State threatened to stage a demonstration in Congress if Britain did not renounce her long-standing alliance with Japan when it became due for renewal in 1921; the British Ambassador in Washington reported that his wife and children feared for their lives and could not leave the Embassy without police protection. Meanwhile President Wilson, stunned by the frustration of his policies by men whom he had always regarded as his intellectual and moral inferiors, had become a helpless invalid, and Colonel House had ceased to play any part in public affairs.

The Liberal and Conservative statesmen who had joined forces to form Lloyd George's post-war Coalition Government saw little reason to hope that in these circumstances they could reach agreement with the United States Government about naval matters except on prohibitive terms, or that the Americans would consider themselves bound by the guarded promise made by House. They recognized that, in the absence of such an agreement, they must either keep pace with American naval expansion or lose control of the sea and hence the power to protect the trade routes on which the British people depended for the means of existence. At the same time they were extremely reluctant to embark on an arms race with a country which had twice as many inhabitants as the United Kingdom and could raise twice as much money by imposing the same rate of taxation. They sought a way out of their dilemma by setting up a committee to consider whether, by making the best use of air power and of cruisers, destroyers and submarines, Britain could retain her naval supremacy without offering a direct challenge to the Americans by competing with their capital-ship programme. The committee was unable, after interrogating witnesses and studying written submissions, to reach agreement on all points; but the gist of its conclusions was that there was no substitute for the battleship except, in appropriate circumstances, the battle-cruiser.

This was true in the sense that no such substitute existed when the committee submitted its findings in 1921; but in 1921 the British did not expect to become involved in hostilities with a first-class naval power before 1930 at the earliest. By the time they did become involved in such a conflict, the battleship concept was out of date. At the Battle of Midway Island in the summer of 1942 the Japanese Combined Fleet, with 9 battleships and 4 fleet carriers, was defeated by an American Carrier Striking Force which did not include a single battleship or battle-cruiser.

Lloyd George and his colleagues concluded in 1921 that they had no choice but to make the best bargain they could with the Americans. The Japanese alliance was dropped, a truce which led to the partition of Ireland was patched up with the Irish Nationalists, and Britain joined France, Italy, Japan and the United States in accepting, at the Washington Conference in the winter of 1921–22, restrictions on their capital-ship and carrier fleets. Other agreements negotiated at Washington included a Four-Power Treaty by which the British Commonwealth, France, Japan and the United States undertook to respect each other's rights and interests in the Pacific, and a Nine-Power Treaty by which, with one exception, the powers with Far Eastern interests pledged themselves to uphold the sovereignty, rights, interests and integrity of China. The exception was the Soviet Union, which was not represented at the conference since the United States did not recognize the Soviet Government.

The Americans hoped by inducing the powers to accept restrictions on their naval strength to ensure that the Japanese Navy did not become strong enough to present a serious threat to American interests; but they defeated their own object by entering into a supplementary agreement which precluded them from developing a first-class naval base west of the Hawaiian Islands. This meant that, as long as the Naval Treaty and the supplementary agreement remained in force, the Japanese with an inferior fleet would always be better placed to attack American possessions in the western Pacific than the Americans with a superior fleet were to defend them. At the same time, the abrogation of the Anglo-Japanese alliance inflicted on the Japanese a loss of face which materially increased the risk of a conflict between Japan and the Anglo-Saxon powers.

Before they went to Washington, the British had considered the possibility of war with Japan in the light of fears expressed by some Australians that the Japanese might be contemplating an invasion of Australia. They had come to the conclusion that if they did find themselves in a position which involved a serious risk of hostilities with Japan, they could best defend British and Commonwealth interests in India, the Far East and the Antipodes by developing a first-class naval base at Singapore. After the Washington Conference they pressed on with plans for the development of Singapore, but progress was delayed by the reluctance of successive governments to meet the cost of implementing them. It was also delayed by controversies about the choice of site and the nature of the counter-bombardment weapons needed to make the base secure during the period of 3 months or so that was likely to elapse between the outbreak of war and the arrival of a fleet despatched from the United Kingdom. A further complication was that, in order to arrive in fighting trim, a fleet despatched from the United Kingdom would have to refuel on the way. This meant that large reserves of fuel oil, which in turn must be defended against a possible bombardment by the enemy's warships, had to be accumulated at vast expense in Ceylon. The orthodox view was that only fixed defences could provide an effective deterrent, and that these must include long-range guns of large calibre where a bombardment by the enemy's battlefleet might have to be countered. On the other hand, many airmen argued that long-range guns could be replaced by bombers or torpedo-bombers.

The view which ultimately prevailed was that long-range 15-inch, medium-range 9·2-inch, and short-range 6-inch guns were all needed to defend so vital a base as Singapore, but that these could be usefully supplemented by aircraft. Moreover, aircraft would be doubly valuable if the fleet sent to Singapore were not as strong as might be wished, or could not be despatched promptly. However, in the outcome very few aircraft capable of engaging warships were provided. The only aircraft available not merely at Singapore but in the whole of Malaya on the outbreak of war with Japan in 1941 were 24 obsolete torpedo-bombers, 35 light bombers, 72 fighters and 27 reconnaissance machines.

The Americans recognized when the Washington Conference was over that their possessions in the western Pacific would be in jeopardy in the event of war with Japan, but for lack of a first-class naval base west of the Hawaiian Islands they were unable to frame a realistic plan to meet the danger. The plan they did make would stand or fall by the ability of their troops on the spot to hold out without relief in the early stages of a war. Since 3, 4, or – according to a later reckoning – even 9 months might elapse before an expeditionary force supported by the main fleet could fight its way to Manila from Pearl Harbour or the west coast of the United States, the chances of success seemed very slender until the development of bombers capable of striking at the Japanese from bases in the Phillippines made it possible to hope that air power might bridge the gap.

The Americans had intended when the conference was first mooted that it should deal with all aspects of disarmament. The French made it clear that, having been deprived by the defection of the United States of the promised British and American guarantees, they were not prepared to consider any but naval limitations. No attempt was made at Washington to restrict air forces, except that limits were placed on the tonnages of carrier fleets and the displacement of individual carriers. Britain, France, Italy, Japan and the United States agreed that, in principle, no carrier should displace more than 27,000 tons. Since the Americans wished to convert 2 capital ships of their 1916 programme into 33,000-ton carriers each of the signatory powers was, however, allowed to complete 2 carriers of comparable size if it could do so without exceeding its permitted total tonnage.

This concession had far-reaching consequences. The Americans took advantage of it to complete the *Lexington* and the *Saratoga* as large fleet carriers, each with a complement of about 70 aircraft and each, incidentally, displacing about 3,000 tons more than the agreed figure. The Japanese also provided themselves with 36,000-ton carriers, the *Akagi* and the *Kaga*, and these, too, carried about 70 aircraft each. Many Americans regretted the decision which led them to lock up so much of their permitted carrier tonnage in 2 ships, and later both the United States and Japan built lighter carriers. In both countries about 70 aircraft continued, however, to be regarded as the proper complement for a first-class fleet carrier.

The British, on the other hand, based their programmes on the assumption that the optimum displacement for a carrier was well below the legal limit. No British carrier in service on the outbreak of the Second World War displaced more than 23,000 tons, none whose construction or conversion was sanctioned before 1936 carried more than 48 aircraft, and the average number of aircraft carried by the 5 carriers completed before that date and after the end of the First World War was only about 30. Moreover, for many years the Admiralty's responsibility for the choice and design of shipborne aircraft was limited to the formulation of requirements to be met by the Air Ministry. The Lords of the Admiralty, having abolished the post of Fifth Sea Lord and Chief of the Naval Air Service after the creation of the Royal Air Force, were not well placed to keep abreast of technical developments.

Limited financial resources and their natural desire to make the most of the small capacity of their carriers led them to demand multi-purpose aircraft with characteristics not compatible with a first-class performance in any of the roles they were meant to fill. The Americans and the Japanese, with their more spacious carriers, were not exposed to the same temptation to seek compromise solutions. They succeeded well before the outbreak of war in developing efficient shipborne fighters, torpedo-bombers and dive-bombers. The Americans, although they had fewer carriers than the British, also succeeded in training many more pilots for service at sea.

However, the British had no monopoly of error. Not only in Britain but also in the United States and Japan, orthodox naval strategists were long reluctant to admit that well-armed warships – as distinct from the more or less helpless ships used in rare bombing trials – could be sunk by shipborne aircraft, or for that matter by shore-based aircraft. As late as 1939 the only offensive role proposed by the British Admiralty for naval aircraft was the crippling of hostile ships for the purpose of delaying them so that British surface ships could catch them and sink them.[1] Only after the outbreak of war was it generally conceded that torpedo-bombers and dive-bombers were capable not merely of crippling but of sinking even the best-armed battleships and carriers.

In 1921 an Italian officer, General Giulio Douhet, made sweeping claims for air power in a book afterwards translated into English as *The Command of the Air*. He claimed, as Lloyd George and Smuts had done in 1917, that a time might not be far off when air forces would be capable not merely of helping fleets and armies to win battles but of achieving decisive results on their own account. At the same time he shocked many of his readers by asserting that in future wars the battlefield would be 'limited only by the boundaries of the nations at war'. All citizens of belligerent states would become combatants, exposed to attempts on the part of hostile air forces to diminish their output and undermine their will to continue the struggle by bombing their homes, factories and workshops.

Two years later the dictator Benito Mussolini gave the Italian Air Force independent status under its own Ministry. No opportunity of testing Douhet's theories arose as long as

Mussolini remained faithful to his policy of cultivating good relations with France and Britain in order to ensure their support should Germany threaten the independence of Austria; but the Regia Aeronautica established a high reputation for the excellence of its aircraft and the skill of its pilots. In 1926 a Macchi monoplane won the Schneider Trophy race for seaplanes at the impressive speed of 246 miles an hour, and in 1933 General Italo Balbo led a formation of 24 Savoia-Marchetti flying boats from Italy to Chicago and back.

Other notable feats during the late twenties and early thirties included a solo flight from New York to Paris in 1927 by the American Charles A. Lindbergh, and a number of stage-by-stage long-distance flights by the American Wiley Post and the British Alan Cobham, Amy Johnson, Kingsford Smith and others. Long-distance flights in heavier-than-air machines were, however, put in the shade by the non-stop flight from Friedrichshafen to Tokyo made in 1929 by the German rigid airship *Graf Zeppelin*. The 776-foot-long airship, carrying 20 passengers and about a third of a ton of mail in addition to her crew of 41, completed in just over 4 days a journey which would have taken a fortnight by the Trans-Siberian Railway and at least a month by sea.

The French made considerable use of aircraft in their struggle with the rebel chieftain Abd el Krim in Morocco between 1924 and 1926, but their experience threw little or no light on the theory of independent air action outlined by the British in 1918 and afterwards elaborated by Douhet. Their squadrons were used almost entirely for tactical support of troops moving through difficult country in pursuit of an elusive enemy. In these conditions they proved a rather ineffective substitute for cavalry and artillery.

In the United States the doctrine of the strategic air offensive found a passionate advocate in the Brigadier-General William Mitchell who had exercised tactical command of the air force which supported the United States First Army in 1918. After the armistice Mitchell was appointed Assistant Chief of the Army Air Force. When the Department of the Navy allowed a battleship, a cruiser and a destroyer surrendered by the Germans to be used for bombing trials off the mouth of the Chesapeake in the summer of 1921, he organized a bomber force which sank all three ships. Bomber forces under his direction also sank the obsolete American battleship *Alabama* later in the year, and some 2 years later the battleships *Virginia* and *New Jersey*, which the United States had agreed to scrap or sink under the terms of the Washington Naval Treaty. These trials did not prove that warships would be at the mercy of bomber forces in a future war, but they did show that bombers were capable of sinking armoured ships if they could hit them.

During the next year or two Mitchell made himself a thorn in the flesh of his superiors by campaigning for a separate air service. When the airship *Shenandoah* was wrecked in 1925, he delivered himself into their hands by publicly accusing them of falling short of their responsibilities. Found guilty by a court-martial of insubordination, he was suspended from duty for 5 years. The sentence effectively ended his career as a serving officer, but not as a propagandist of air power.

Mitchell was not alone in calling for changes in the organization and control of the armed forces. A committee of the House of Representatives recommended in 1925 the creation not only of an air service independent of the Army and the Navy but also of a department of defence to administer all three services. In the light of these highly controversial proposals President Calvin Coolidge appointed a board under Dwight W. Morrow to report on the whole question of the future of military aviation. On the advice of the board no separate air service was created, but the Army Air Force was renamed the Army Air Corps. A branch of the Department of the Army under an Assistant Secretary was formed to deal with air matters, a senior representative of the air corps joined the General Staff, and a 5-year expansion scheme was sanctioned though not immediately put into effect. These reforms, which left the Navy free to develop its own air service, went some way to meet Mitchell's criticisms. Nevertheless the corps remained almost exclusively concerned with close support of troops until, in the 1930s, the authorities enlarged its scope by charging it with a wide measure of responsibility for air defence at home and abroad and allowing it to develop long-range aircraft suitable for strategic bombing.

In Germany the ban on military aviation imposed by the Treaty of Versailles did not prevent the authorities from preserving the nucleus of an Air Staff within the Ministry of Defence, an organization permitted by treaty. The Germans were able to negotiate with the Soviet Government an agreement by which hundreds of members of their armed forces learned to fly or maintain aircraft of service type at a German flying school on Russian soil. In addition, courses in military aviation were secretly organized at schools established by the German air line, Deutsche Lufthansa. The Ministry of Defence kept in close touch through the Ministry of Transport with Lufthansa and its Chairman, Erhard Milch, a former officer of the flying corps and afterwards Secretary of State for Air. The Ministry of Defence also actively encouraged the development of flying and gliding clubs which attracted thousands of members and which helped to make Germany the most air-minded nation in Europe.

Nor did the restrictions on commercial production in force from 1922 to 1926 prevent the German aircraft industry from making rapid strides. Aircraft manufacturers who opened factories in various parts of Germany between 1920 and 1924 included Hugo Junkers, Ernst Heinkel, Claude Dornier and Heinrich Focke with his partner Georg Wulf. In the following year a brilliant designer of small aircraft, Willy Messerschmitt, acquired the Bavarian Aircraft Works at Augsburg. To escape the attentions of the Allied Control Commission, a number of these pioneers opened factories in Italy, Sweden or Switzerland. Notable contributions to technical progress by German manufacturers and designers during the period of disarmament included the development of advanced thick-wing monoplanes by Junkers, of large flying boats by Dornier, and of fast communications aircraft by Messerschmitt. Soon after the armistice Adolf Rohrbach introduced the principle of stress-skinned construction, afterwards developed by his associate H. A. Wagner and applied in the United States to passenger- and freight-carrying aircraft of revolutionary design and performance. It was also in Germany, at a time when in England A. A. Griffith of the Royal Aircraft Establishment was feeling his way towards the propulsion of aircraft by gas turbine, that A. Lippisch, Fritz von Opel and others made the first experiments with aircraft propelled by rockets.

In Russia, the Communist leaders who seized power in 1917 inherited a few hundred aircraft mostly imported from Britain, France or Italy or built to British, French or Italian designs.

About a third of these were seaplanes; but the chief concern of the Soviet military authorities during the Civil War was to provide tactical support for their land forces. Towards the end of 1919 they came to the conclusion that they could not afford to provide such support except in the most important sectors. That aircraft should be concentrated at the decisive point, not dispersed over a wide front, remained a guiding principle of Soviet air strategy throughout the next quarter of a century and more.

After 10 years of Communist rule the equipment of the Red Air Force included a few machines of Russian design but still consisted largely of foreign aircraft, mostly German or Italian. A Central Institute of Aerodynamics and Hydrostatics and a Military Air Academy had, however, been established before the end of the Civil War. Provision was made in the first Five-Year Plan for Soviet industry, adopted in 1928, for the manufacture of a wide range of all-Russian aircraft. These included naval and military reconnaissance machines, medium bombers, single-seater fighters, and two-seater ground-attack aircraft for use against targets of opportunity on the battlefield. Output was restricted by shortages of skilled labour, machine tools and raw materials and by administrative blunders, but reached about 150–200 aircraft a month by 1932. Russian aero-engine designers continued to draw most of their inspiration from German and French sources, but some original designs for airframes came from a small band of designers among whom Andrei Tupolev was prominent. Progress in the capitalist countries during the next few years was, however, so rapid that most of the aircraft produced in Russia between 1928 and 1932 were soon out of date.

In Britain, Trenchard resumed the post of Chief of the Air Staff in 1919 and continued to hold it until 1929. No longer content that the Royal Air Force should be reabsorbed by the older services, he soon saw that this might happen unless he could hit upon some task which it could perform more cheaply or more efficiently than the Army or the Navy.

One of Trenchard's proposals was that the Air Ministry should replace the Admiralty and the War Office as the authority primarily responsible for defending the United Kingdom against seaborne raids and air raids respectively. Pointing out that the wartime air defences had been swept away, he asked in the context of the second part of this proposal that a few home defence squadrons should be formed to guard against the risk of attacks on London by aircraft of the French Metropolitan Air Force.

Trenchard failed to persuade the Government that, because aircraft as well as warships, local naval defences and coast defence guns could be used against hostile naval forces, an air officer should control the forces so employed. Nor did many people believe that, even if differences of opinion about reparations and Near Eastern problems should lead to strained relations with France, the French would be so foolish as to launch air attacks on Britain at the cost of exposing their ports to a counter-bombardment by British naval forces. The French Metropolitan Air Force was intended not for such a role, but to give tactical support to land forces in the event of trouble with Germany.

Even so, the veteran Conservative statesman Arthur Balfour, whom Lloyd George had made Chairman of a Standing Sub-Committee of the Committee of Imperial Defence, felt bound to point out that post-war economies had created a huge disparity between British and French air striking power. He added that, in the event of war with France, French bombers might rain upon London 'a continuous torrent of high explosives at the rate of 75 tons a day for an indefinite period', and that this might paralyse the War Office and the Admiralty. Scarcely anyone expected war with France, but there was logic in the argument that Britain's capacity to withstand air attack ought to be related to some quantitative standard, and that the air striking power of the only nation whose bombers could reach London was a reasonable standard to adopt.

Probably this argument would not have been decisive had not ministers known that a number of aircraft manufacturers were likely to go out of business in the near future if they received no orders from the Government. Partly as a means of indirectly subsidizing the aircraft industry, partly to improve Britain's negotiating power in the diplomatic sphere, the Government sanctioned in 1922 the creation of a Metropolitan Air Force of 23 squadrons. Trenchard, troubled by recruiting problems, asked for a smaller force, but Lloyd George thought his figure unrealistic.

Trenchard did not assert that the aeroplane was not a defence against the aeroplane, but he still thought attack the best means of defence. Nine of the 23 squadrons were to be equipped with fighters, 14 with bombers.

Soon afterwards Lloyd George, discredited by the failure of his policy of subsidizing the Greeks to fight the Turkish dictator Mustapha Kemal, fell from power. A Conservative Government, led first by Andrew Bonar Law and later by Stanley Baldwin, then took office. The Conservatives, warned by Trenchard that the French were believed to be contemplating additions to an air force already about 300 bombers and 300 fighters strong, increased the planned strength of the British Metropolitan Air Force to a total of 17 fighter and 35 bomber squadrons with a first-line establishment of 598 aircraft. These 52 squadrons were to be supplemented by guns and searchlights which would be provided by the War Office but placed under the operational control of an officer responsible to the Air Ministry. Unpaid civilian volunteers enrolled as special constables were to observe and report the movements of hostile aircraft over the country, and sound locators or other acoustic devices would provide the basis of an early-warning system.

The foundations of a system of what was afterwards called Passive Air Defence were laid in 1924, when the first Labour Government to hold office in Britain set up an Air Raid Precautions Sub-Committee of the Committee of Imperial Defence. Its task was to 'enquire into the question of Air Raid Precautions other than Naval, Military and Air Defences'. The sub-committee did a good deal of useful work, but it relied for its knowledge of the scale of attack that might have to be countered on estimates prepared by the Air Staff at the Air Ministry. These estimates, based almost entirely on experience during the First World War, proved grossly misleading. For example, the Air Staff calculated in 1924 that some 27,000 people might be killed by bombing in London alone during the first month of a future war.[2] Later, when the potential assailant was not France but Germany, they estimated that enough bombs might be dropped daily on Britain in the early stages of a war to kill 66,000 people in the first week.[3] The second of these figures exceeded by a substantial margin the number of civilians killed by bombing in all parts of the United Kingdom during the whole of the Second World War.[4]

The British Government's avowed aim when it adopted the

52-squadron scheme of air defence in the summer of 1923 was to attain parity with the French Metropolitan Air Force as rapidly as possible. In the following November the Secretary of State for Air, Sir Samuel Hoare, warned the Cabinet that the 52 squadrons could not be ready before the end of 1928. In the outcome, a much longer period elapsed before they and the guns and searchlights needed to complete the scheme were forthcoming. The reason was partly that recruits for the Territorial air defence formations needed to man the guns and searchlights were hard to find, partly that successive governments postponed expenditure on the project in the hope that the international agreements to disarm might make it unnecessary. When the Chiefs of Staff, alarmed by events in China, advised the Government in 1932 that the assumption that there would be no great war involving the British Empire for at least 10 years was no longer tenable, about four-fifths of the bomber and fighter squadrons had been formed, but only about one-third of the guns and searchlights needed to bring the air defences to their war establishment could have been deployed and manned in an emergency. Moreover, the speed of aircraft had increased so much since the end of the First World War that a commander responsible for the air defence of London could no longer count on visual and acoustic methods to give him enough warning to enable him to get his fighters into the air before the enemy was overhead. Stanley Baldwin did not foresee in 1932 that an entirely new method of detecting and locating aircraft at long ranges would be discovered within the next few years. 'The bomber', he said in an access of candour which he afterwards regretted, 'will always get through.'

Another of Trenchard's proposals was that aircraft should be used to assist the civil authorities in maintaining law and order in unsettled territories such as parts of the former Ottoman Empire in which the British had assumed responsibilities under mandate from the League of Nations or by treaty. Hitherto a common practice had been to send troops to punish or arrest wrongdoers. This was an unsatisfactory and expensive method. Large numbers of troops had to be maintained in the countries concerned. Strong columns had sometimes to make long marches through wild country, at the risk of clashing with tribesmen who were not amenable to the rule of law, but with whom the authorities did not particularly wish to provoke a conflict. All this cost money, and could lead to unnecessary bloodshed.

A system of air control was introduced in Iraq and Transjordan in 1922, and was afterwards tried elsewhere. Known or suspected malefactors were first called upon to give themselves up and submit to trial. If they refused, they and their neighbours were warned that the village that sheltered them would be bombed on a certain day. The villagers having withdrawn with their portable possessions to a safe distance, a few bombs aimed at selected buildings usually induced them to come to terms. Teams were then flown in to arrest the wanted men, attend to the sick or wounded and relieve the needy.

Since only light bombs which seldom did any damage not easily repairable were used, air control was far less objectionable on moral and ethical grounds than it was sometimes made out to be. Nevertheless it had serious disadvantages for the British. In the first place, the airmen concerned were seldom called upon to do more than make low-level attacks on undefended targets, usually in daylight and often in conditions of perfect visibility. Since countries where air control was practised were for many years the chief training ground for British bomber crews, the result was that officers who rose by 1939 to responsible positions in the Royal Air Force formed a very misleading impression of the tasks the bomber force would face in a European war. Secondly, the Air Ministry's concern with air control put British negotiators at disarmament conferences in an invidious position. The British, it was noticed, were always asking other nations to reduce their armed forces in the interests of all. Yet they themselves not only possessed a powerful navy but insisted, on the pretext that they needed bombers to police undeveloped territories, in maintaining a strategic bomber force which was obviously capable of being used in an offensive role.

4

PRELUDE TO WAR

When the British Government was urged by the Chiefs of Staff in 1932 to abandon the assumption that there would be no great war involving the British Empire for at least 10 years, the world was in the throes of a disastrous slump. A panic on the New York Stock Exchange in 1929 had been followed by the calling in of foreign loans by American investors and a calamitous decline in the volume of international trade. By 1932 markets were clogged with unsold manufactured goods and raw materials, thousands of factories were idle or working below capacity, and scores of millions of people on both sides of the Atlantic were out of work.

Attempts to remedy these evils differed from country to country. In the United States, President Franklin D. Roosevelt sponsored a vast programme of public works as a means of 'priming the pump', but refused to lower tariffs. In Europe a number of Governments tried to stabilize currencies and balance budgets by making cuts in pensions, unemployment benefit and the pay of civil servants and members of the armed forces. Such measures led in Germany to political upheavals which put an end to representative government. In Britain they sparked off a short-lived naval mutiny which alarmed foreign investors so much that the country was forced to abandon the gold standard and the value of the pound fell by a third. In France a Government mindful of Germany's teeming population and vast industrial potential marshalled its diplomatic and financial resources to prevent the Germans from seeking a remedy for economic ills in union with Austria. In Spain, King Alfonso XIII abdicated after the death of the dictator Primo de Rivera, leaving power to fall into the hands of a left-of-centre Government which faced disaster unless it could steer a difficult course between the demands of its Socialist and Anarchist supporters on the one hand and those of the Church, the Army and landowners on the other.

The immediate occasion of the warning given by the British Chiefs of Staff was a crisis in the Far East, precipitated by a clash between Chinese and Japanese troops in Manchuria. The Chiefs of Staff were concerned, however, with the weakness of British arms not merely in the Far East but throughout the world. They asked that provision should be made to meet various defensive commitments, but the Government was not inclined to do much without first seeing what might be accomplished at a full-scale Disarmament Conference which had just assembled under the aegis of the League of Nations at Geneva.

Attempts made during the Disarmament Conference to reconcile the craving of the French for security with the determination of the Germans to throw off the shackles of Versailles were completely unsuccessful so far as proposals to restrict land forces were concerned. Measures intended to prevent or limit the use of air power for purposes of aggression seemed more likely to be accepted, but no one could hit upon a practical means of bringing this about. One proposal was that all bombing from the air should be prohibited, another that the unladen weight of military aircraft should be limited to a maximum calculated to rule out all bombers larger than those suitable for tactical support of troops. The insistence of the British on retaining bombers for use against lawbreakers in undeveloped territories did not help the first of these proposals, but was not a decisive factor. The crux of the difficulty was that there seemed to be no formula, short of a universal agreement to abolish aircraft altogether, by which their misuse could be prevented. Even if all military aircraft were consigned to the scrap-heap, an aggressor would still be able to terrorize his victims by sending bomb-laden civil aircraft across their frontiers.

Early in 1933 Germany acquired, in Adolf Hitler, a leader who seemed all too likely to do just that, should he find himself in such a position. Soon afterwards Japan, offended by criticism of her action in Manchuria and ruled since the previous summer by a non-party Government with militarist tendencies, gave notice of her impending resignation from the League of Nations. A few months later, German officials confessed to the British Air Attaché in Berlin that Germany was already defying her obligations under the Treaty of Versailles by manufacturing military aircraft, building fortfications and stepping up military training. In October Germany ceased to take an active part in the Disarmament Conference and gave notice that she, too, intended to leave the League of Nations.

The conference did not break up until the early summer of 1934, but its failure was apparent long before that time. In November 1933 the British Government, recognizing that British interests in the Far East were threatened by the Sino-Japanese dispute and that obligations accepted by Britain at Locarno might involve her in war with Germany should France become a victim of unprovoked aggression, appointed a Defence Requirements Committee to advise the Cabinet how to meet the 'worse deficiencies' in the national and imperial defences.

The Defence Requirements Committee reported early in 1934 that, although the immediate danger lay in the Far East, the 'ultimate potential enemy' was Germany. There was nothing to show that Germany intended to attack Britain or the British Empire, but she was arming so rapidly that she might be ready for war by 1938 or 1939. Assuming that Hitler might be able to provide himself by that time with a powerful air striking force, the committee recommended that the 52-squadron scheme of air defence should be completed with the least possible delay. The committee also recommended that an expeditionary force of 4 infantry divisions, 1 cavalry division and 1 air defence brigade should be made ready for despatch to the Continent within a month of the outbreak of war. Supported by an air component drawn from the Metropolitan Air Force, these formations would be able to co-operate with Continental armies in securing the Low Countries as a base where British bombers, fighters and observation posts could be deployed in order to ease the problem of defending London against air attacks.

Britain's annual expenditure on her armed forces in recent years had been of the order of £100–£110 million. The measures recommended by the Defence Requirements Committee would cost an additional £71 million, to be spread over the next 5 years. Neville Chamberlain, Chancellor of the Exchequer in a National Government led by the Socialist Ramsay MacDonald, protested that this was more than the nation could afford. The Government then decided to spend rather more on the Air Force but considerably less on the Army than the committee recommended, and to rely largely on an expanded bomber force to convince Hitler that Britain was not prepared to give him a free hand in Europe. These changes would save about £25 million, at the cost of making it impossible to send much more than a token expeditionary force across the Channel in the early stages of a war.

The Germans expected to raise the strength of their Air Force to 48 squadrons by the autumn of 1935 and 114 squadrons by the autumn of 1936. Each squadron was to have 9 or 10 aircraft, or 12 including immediate reserves.

The British were aware in 1934 of these intentions. What they did not know was that, although the Germans succeeded in forming 22 of the first batch of 48 squadrons before the end of the year, these 22 squadrons had only 146 aircraft between them. Nor did the British know until long afterwards that the number of military aircraft suitable for first-line units, including those without engines or otherwise incomplete, at the disposal of the Germans at the end of the year was only 565.

In the light of what they did know, the British adopted in the summer of 1934 a new scheme of air expansion called Scheme A. It was intended to provide by the end of 1938 or early in 1939 a Metropolitan Air Force of 43 bomber, 28 fighter and 13 reconnaissance squadrons, with a first-line establishment of 960 aircraft. These figures did not include some 500 aircraft which would be serving overseas or with the fleet.

This was a poor scheme. It was not due for completion until more than 2 years after the Germans were expected to complete the second stage of their programme, and it made no immediate provision for the stored reserves which would be needed in any but the briefest of wars. Since this could be inferred from published statements, the Germans were almost bound to conclude that the British Government was more interested in making a favourable impression on the general public than in preparing for war.

An attempt to defend the scheme in the House of Commons in November 1934 led Stanley Baldwin into trouble. Rebutting some rather ill-informed criticism from Winston Churchill, Baldwin pointed out that Churchill was wide of the mark in alleging that Germany was already approaching air parity with Britain and that the Luftwaffe would be fully as strong as the

Royal Air Force by the early winter of 1935. When he turned to the more distant future, Baldwin's touch became less sure. By saying ambiguously that he could not look 'more than two years ahead', he gave some of his hearers the impression that he did not expect the Germans to gain the lead before the early winter of 1936 but was not prepared to say what would happen later. There is little doubt that the sense he intended to convey was that he was not prepared to say what the situation towards the end of 1936 would be. Nevertheless he afterwards accepted the other interpretation, apologized for giving the House a false impression and complained that he had been misled.

This misunderstanding had the effect of throwing doubt on the authenticity of the Air Ministry's information about the Luftwaffe's rearmament plans, which in fact was extremely accurate. One result was that not only the Government's critics, but even some ministers, tended for some time thereafter to rely more on unofficial than official estimates of German strength.

This tendency was at least partly responsible for the confusion which arose from a visit to Berlin in the early spring of 1935 by the Foreign Secretary, Sir John Simon, and his henchman Anthony Eden. In the course of a conversation about air armaments, Simon asked Hitler how strong the Luftwaffe was. Hitler replied, 'after a moment's hesitation', that it was already as strong as the Royal Air Force. If Simon and Eden had studied the Air Ministry's figures and believed them, they would have known that this could not be true. As it was, Hitler's claim imparted 'grim foreboding' in Eden's heart.[1]

After Simon's and Eden's return to London, embarrassed German ministers and officials at first denied that Hitler could have made so inaccurate a statement. Later they explained it away by saying that he had intended to make only an approximate camparison. But it was obvious to the British that in any case Scheme A had had no effect on Hitler's plans. Still chasing the will o' the wisp of 'air parity', the Government adopted in the early summer of 1935 an accelerated programme of expansion called Scheme C. This was intended to provide by the spring of 1937 a Metropolitan Air Force of 70 bomber and torpedo-bomber, 35 fighter and 18 reconnaissance squadrons, with a first-line strength of 1,512 aircraft. Nearly half the bomber force would be equipped with aircraft incapable of reaching Berlin, or even the Ruhr, from bases in the United Kingdom, and again no adequate provision was made for stored reserves. An account of the scheme was imparted in confidence to the Germans, but it failed to convince them that the British Government seriously intended to commit the country to war in order to prevent Hitler from accomplishing the aims outlined in his book *Mein Kampf*.

In the meantime air defence exercises in Britain showed that, irrespective of the number of squadrons provided, fighters would stand little chance of intercepting hostile aircraft before they reached London unless the system of air defence was radically overhauled. During the winter of 1934–5 the Government set up an Air Defence Research Committee to consider how this might be done. On the initiative of H. E. Wimperis, Director of Scientific Research at the Air Ministry, the Air Defence Research Committee was supplemented by a Committee for the purpose of investigating particular methods of defence. The distinguished scientist H. T. Tizard, already Chairman of the Government's Aeronautical Research Committee, agreed to serve as a member of the first committee and Chairman of the second.

In preparation for the first meeting of the Committee for the Scientific Survey of Air Defence, Wimperis consulted R. A. Watson Watt of the National Physical Laboratory about the use of electro-magnetic radiations to destroy or damage hostile aircraft. Watson Watt did not believe that this method – the 'death ray' of science fiction – would provide a practical means of inflicting lethal damage. On the other hand, it seemed to him quite possible that approaching aircraft might be detected and located by means of a radio pulse such as he and other investigators had used to detect thunderstorms and to measure the distance from the earth of the Heaviside layer, or ionosphere.

The Committee for the Scientific Survey of Air Defence agreed when it met for the first time on 28 January 1935 that Watson Watt's proposal should be followed up. At the request of Air Marshal Sir Hugh Dowding, Air Member for Research and Development, Watson Watt gave a practical demonstration on 26 February at Weedon, in Northamptonshire. For lack of a suitable pulse transmitter, he used the continuous beam transmission from the British Broadcasting Corporation's short-wave overseas transmitter at Daventry to furnish a visual display on the cathode tube of an improvised radio-location set in a caravan parked about 6 miles away. The pilot of a Heyford bomber from Farnborough was told to make 2 runs in each direction along a 20-mile course calculated to put him above the lateral centre of the beam. As things turned out, he failed to keep precisely above the centre of the beam. Nevertheless the demonstration proved that radio-location was feasible. On 3 of the 4 runs the passage of the aircraft was shown by changes in the display on the cathode tube, and these changes were discernible when the aircraft was up to 8 miles away.

In the light of this experience, arrangements were made for Watson Watt to continue his investigations on behalf of the Air Ministry, and a research establishment was set up in Suffolk. Within six months, experienced users of the equipment could detect aircraft up to 40 miles away. Much longer ranges afterwards became commonplace; but special equipment, not generally available until after the outbreak of the Second World War, was needed to detect aircraft flying below 3,000 feet or so.

Experiments had been made recently in Britain with large acoustic mirrors designed to give audible warning of the approach of hostile aircraft. During the second half of 1935 the Government suspended work on these and sanctioned the construction of the first 5 of 20 radio-location stations intended to cover the eastern and southern approaches to the British Isles everywhere between the Tyne and the Solent.

Up to that time no plans or preparations for air attacks on the United Kingdom had, so far as is known, been made in any country since the end of the First World War. Mussolini was, however, openly assembling forces for a projected invasion of Abyssinia, and there were persistent rumours in diplomatic circles to the effect that Hitler was thinking of sending troops into the demilitarized Rhineland. A pact between France and the Soviet Union, signed in May but still unratified at the end of 1935, might be made the pretext for such a move.

From the end of 1934 British statesmen made many attempts to convince Mussolini that, by attacking Abyssinia in defiance of the Covenant of the League of Nations and of Italy's Treaty of Friendship and Arbitration with that country, he would not only force upholders of the covenant to take action against him but would risk reducing his armed strength in Europe to a level at which he would lose power to intervene should Hitler try, not for the first time, to seize Austria. When these efforts were seen to have failed, the British strongly reinforced their Mediterranean Fleet. By 25 September 1935 they had 7 capital ships and 2 aircraft carriers in the Mediterranean, while the Italians had only 2 and 1 respectively. Fearing that, even so, Mussolini might respond to any attempt to thwart him by attacking their naval bases in the central and eastern Mediterranean, they also strengthened the air defences and local naval defences of Malta and Alexandria and moved bombers to airfields within striking distance of Italian bases in Libya.

Early in October Mussolini duly opened hostilities in Abyssinia. The Italian bomber forces was not confined in the ensuing campaign to a strictly tactical role. Attacks were made on a variety of objectives, in accordance with the theory that wide-spread bombing would impair the enemy's will to fight. Many complaints were made of the bombing of hospitals and open towns and the use of weapons and methods which contravened the letter or the spirit of international agreements. The Italians countered such accusations by replying, in effect, that they were justified in adopting measures which promised to reduce losses on both sides by shortening the war, and that they were dealing with a savage foe whose methods disqualified him from criticizing theirs.

Irrespective of morality or ethics, the operations of the Regia Aeronautica in Abyssinia did not throw much light on the nature of strategic bombing, since the Abyssinians had scarcely any means of defending themselves against air attacks. The ease with which Italian airmen reached and bombed their objectives in such circumstances was no proof that a strategic bomber offensive could be conducted with results satisfactory to the attackers in a European war. The British did, however, draw a negative lesson from their experience of the Abyssinian affair. To be able to strike in case of need at worthwhile objectives in Libya, British bombers in Egypt had to be stationed so far forward that their bases might have been overrun if war had come and Italian troops had crossed the frontier. This experience suggested that the light bombers which figured prominently in Schemes A and C might with advantage be replaced in future air expansion schemes by aircraft of longer range. That consideration played some part in focussing attention in Britain on problems of range and striking power almost at the very moment when the Germans were taking steps to re-equip their bomber force with the not very satisfactory aircraft with which they were to go to war in 1939.

However, the British had other reasons for thinking the time ripe for a review of their bomber force. By the end of the Abyssinian War the British Sydney Camm and Reginald Mitchell and the German Willy Messerschmitt had all designed fast, hard-hitting monoplane fighters to meet requirements formulated in 1934 or earlier. The Hurricane and the Bf.109 (better know as the Me.109) first flew in prototype form in 1935; the Spitfire in 1936. British advocates of strategic bombing reasoned that, to escape destruction by such formidable interceptors, the strategic bombers of the future would need to be even more powerfully armed, and hence still larger and heavier, than the Wellington, Whitley and Hampden heavy bombers which were about to go into production after some 4 years of research and development. In 1936 the Air Ministry, accepting this argument and assuming for the purpose of long-term planning that a strategic air offensive against Germany was a practical operation of war, issued specifications which gave rise to the Short Stirling, the Handley-Page Halifax and the Avro Manchester and Lancaster. The authorities responsible for this act of faith recognized that no comparable aircraft were under development in Germany, but took comfort from the knowledge that they were not alone in believing that the big strategic bomber had a future. The United States Army Air Corps had tested in 1935 a prototype long-range high-altitude bomber built by the firm of Boeing, and had placed a small order for a production version known as the B-17 or Flying Fortress. This much-publicized aircraft, powered by four 1,200-hp Wright Cyclone engines, was afterwards produced in large numbers.

However, the Royal Air Force could not be allowed to mark time until it was equipped throughout with new aircraft, some of which would not be available in quantity before 1942 or 1943. The public had been assured that air parity with Germany was the Government's aim. This pledge had to be honoured, even though commonsense suggested that the number of aircraft the country needed depended not on the number possessed by the potential enemy but on such factors as the size of the area to be defended and on the kind of war the Government meant to fight. Since the Air Staff still maintained that security could be won only by offensive measures, it followed that a numerically strong bomber force must be provided even before the new bombers were ready and even though no one yet knew whether a stratetic air offensive against Germany would be feasible with the aircraft likely to be available during the next few years, or indeed with any aircraft.

Scheme F, drawn up in 1935 and adopted in 1936, was intended to meet this need. It differed from Scheme C in replacing – at least on paper – light by medium bombers, in making substantial provision for stored reserves and in substituting the spring of 1939 for the spring of 1937 as the target date for completion. Its chief defect was that, in order to provide approximately 1,000 bombers with a 225 per cent reserve by the stipulated date, the authorities had to choose aircraft which could be manufactured quickly. Largely for that reason, the Bristol Blenheim and the Fairey Battle were picked as medium bombers suitable for large-scale production under licence by firms new to the aircraft industry. In as much as the first of these, although not fully tested when the first orders were placed and destined to become almost obsolete by the outbreak of war, was in 1936 a promising new aircraft with an impressive performance by the standards of the day, the Air Ministry had no reason to be ashamed of its decision as far as the Blenheim was concerned. The choice of the Battle is harder to defend. Developed from a prototype designed to meet a specification issued in 1932, the Battle had the characteristics of a light rather than medium bomber, and by 1937 was recognized as 'not really capable of being usefully employed in a war against Germany'.*[2]

Soon after the adoption of Scheme F, important changes were made in the organization and system of command of the British Metropolitan Air Force. Hitherto bombers and fighters had been lumped together under one commander. In the summer of 1936 separate Bomber and Fighter Commands were established. In

* Production versions of the Battle were built to modified specifications formulated in 1935 and 1936, but essentially the design dated from 1932.

the following year the Air Ministry accepted an arrangement which restored the Admiralty's control of air squadrons intended for service at sea, and agreed that in time of war the resources of the newly-established Coastal Command, which controlled shore-based reconnaissance squadrons, should be devoted primarily to tasks designated by the Admiralty. These tasks were defined in general terms as 'trade-protection, reconnaissance and co-operation with the Royal Navy'. Despite the lessons of the First World War inadequate provision was, however, made before 1939 for photographic reconnaissance and the interpretation of air photographs.

The creation of a separate Bomber Command and the failure of the air expansion schemes to arrest the growth of the Luftwaffe compelled the Air Staff to frame plans for the bombing of Germany and discuss them with the Commander-in-Chief who would be responsible for their execution should they be put into effect within the next few years. The process led to the alarming discovery that some of the attitudes adopted by airmen in the past bore as little relation to reality as that of a small boy who seeks to increase his importance in the eyes of his parents and friends by boasting that he can drive a racing car.

Since 1922 or earlier, Trenchard and his successors as Chiefs of the Air Staff had maintained that the country must rely primarily on offensive measures for protection against air attacks and that 'to be driven back to relying on defence . . . would be to lose the war'.[3] A joint Planning Sub-Committee of the Chiefs of Staff Committee concluded that if – as the Air Ministry expected – a war with Germany began with heavy air attacks on the United Kingdom, then the bomber force should begin by attacking the Luftwaffe's bases, centres of communication and maintenance depots. To these objectives were afterwards added aircraft factories. If, on the other hand – as the War Office thought more probable – the war began with attacks on France and the Low Countries by Germany's land forces, then the first task for the bomber force should be to attack the communications of the German Army. In either case the bomber force should turn to attacks on German industry as soon as the first phase of the war was over.

Accordingly the Air Ministry communicated to Bomber Command in 1937 a list of no less than 13 air plans which might be put into effect in the event of war. The most important of these were Western Air Plans 1, 4 and 5. The first dealt with attacks on the German air striking force and its ancillaries, the second with attacks on communications, the third with attacks on German industry.

A close examination of Western Air Plan 1 led to the conclusion that, if a determined attempt were made to bomb objectives in Germany at the outset of a war expected to start in 1939, the British medium bomber force was likely to be eliminated in three and a half weeks and the heavy bomber force in seven and a half weeks. Air Chief Marshal Sir Edgar Ludlow-Hewitt, Commander-in-Chief of Bomber Command from the autumn of 1937 until the spring of 1940, doubted whether his bombers would be able to 'penetrate any distance into Germany' unless protected by long-range fighters for which no provision had been made. In any case nothing could be done to carry out the plan from bases in Britain. Since at least a month was expected to elapse after the outbreak of war before the bomber force could be securely established on the far side of the Channel, it followed that Bomber Command could not protect the country against the 'knock-out blow' which the Luftwaffe was thought likely to attempt as soon as hostilities began. Fighters and anti-aircraft guns must be provided not merely as a concession to the insistence of the public on visible and audible means of defence, but as the sole means of averting a calamity which might bring irremediable defeat.

This view chimed with conclusions reached independently of the Air Staff's and Bomber Command's cogitations. Scheme F would provide only 30 fighter squadrons, and the numbers of guns and searchlights needed for air defence at home had been estimated in 1936 at 608 and 2,547 respectively. In 1937 further consideration was given to this question by a committee headed by Air Chief Marshal Dowding in his capacity as Air Office Commander-in-Chief, Fighter Command. The committee recommended that 45 fighter squadrons, 1,264 anti-aircraft guns and 4,700 searchlights should be provided, and that these should be supplemented by some 300 pom-poms for defence against low-flying aircraft, more than 400 barrage balloons of a new pattern designed not merely to deter but to destroy aircraft flying below 5,000 feet or so, and a substantial extension of the area covered by the observation system.

Sir Thomas Inskip, Minister for the Co-Ordination of Defence in the Conservative Government formed by Neville Chamberlain in 1937 and also in the preceding Government, concluded in the light of these recommendations that priority should be given to the manufacture not of bombers but of fighters. By the spring of 1938, when the Government adopted a new scheme of air expansion called Scheme L, he succeeded in imposing this view on his colleagues and in making a convert of Chamberlain's Secretary of State for Air, Sir Kingsley Wood. Scheme L was intended to provide by the spring of 1940 38 fighter and 73 bomber squadrons, as compared with the 30 fighter and 70 bomber and torpedo-bomber squadrons to be provided by the spring of 1939 under Scheme F.

Western Air Plan 4 proved no more acceptable than Western Air Plan 1. The Air Staff, unwilling to see strategic bombers diverted to an army support role, sent the plan to Bomber Command with a gloss which indicated that they did not expect a favourable verdict. The conclusion reached was that attacks on rail targets in Western Germany would absorb practically the entire effort of the bomber force and yield doubtful results at a heavy cost. However, in the light of Hitler's seizure of Bohemia and Moravia in the spring of 1939 the British Government was obliged to defer to the insistence of the French that a substantial expeditionary force should be sent to France within 33 days of the outbreak of war and an advanced striking force of medium bombers be established there. It was then agreed that, in the event of a German invasion of the Low Countries, 'collaboration with the French Army and Air Force in the land battle' should become Bomber Command's primary task 'during any critical phase of the invasion'. No agreement was reached as to the precise form which Bomber Command's contribution should take.

There remained Western Air Plan 5. An advantage of this plan was that it was not designed to counter any particular move by the enemy. Hence there would be no need to put it into effect until the responsible commander was confident that his forces were ready to undertake it.

The plan raised high hopes at Ludlow-Hewitt's headquarters

and elsewhere. The staff of Bomber Command estimated that, given the right conditions, the command could bring the German war machine almost to a standstill in a fortnight, with the expenditure of only 3,000 sorties and the loss of only 176 aircraft, by attacking 19 power-stations and 26 coking-plants in the Ruhr. An Air Targets Sub-Committee of the Government's Industrial Intelligence Committee, on which the fighting services as well as civilian departments were represented, suggested that, alternatively, the industry of the Ruhr might be disrupted by attacks on the Möhne and Sorpe dams.

However, the Air Staff were not satisfied in 1938 that either version of Western Air Plan 5 would be feasible with the resources likely to be available in the following year. Furthermore, the British Government wished, both on general grounds and for fear of provoking reprisals, to restrict bombing to purely military objectives, in the strictest sense of that term, as long as there was any chance of doing so. While the targets envisaged in Western Air Plans 1 and 4 were undoubtedly military objectives, there was an obvious risk that attacks on power-stations, coking-plants or dams might be construed as attacks on the civil population. The Joint Planners pointed out about the time of the Munich crisis that Britain would lose rather than gain by asserting the right to attack industrial targets 'if this involved the right of an enemy to attack London, our supply system and [our] seaborne trade'.[4] The conclusion reached in the light of this submission was that Bomber Command should conserve its strength in the early stages of a war with Germany unless a situation arose in which attacks must be pressed home at almost any cost. Ludlow-Hewitt suggested that heavy bombers too valuable to be risked in daylight over Germany until Britain was stronger in the air might be used in the meantime to drop propaganda leaflets at night.

By the time the Munich crisis was resolved, the Luftwaffe had more than a thousand long-range bombers fit for use and enough fully-trained crews to man about three-quarters of them. No plans had been made for air attacks on the United Kingdom, and it was not until the following year that the Luftwaffe began to assemble data about industrial targets in Britain and to include simulated attacks on British ports and shipping in its training schedules. In the summer of 1939 German aircraft made a number of sorties over the North Sea and the English Channel, and the airship *Graf Zeppelin*, equipped as a flying laboratory, was sent to investigate the radio-location system. Nevertheless the Germans had no thought of attempting the 'knock-out blow' from the air which the British Government feared. The leaders of the Luftwaffe, like their opposite numbers in Britain, Italy and the United States, had been attracted in the past by the arguments adduced for strategic as distinct from tactical bombing, but their doctrines on the eve of the Second World War were strongly influenced by experience in Spain.

German intervention in Spain began in the late summer of 1936, when the National Socialist Government lent General Francisco Franco about 20 Junkers 52 bomber-transport aircraft to carry troops from Spanish Morocco to the mainland. About half a dozen Heinkel 51 biplane fighters provided escort and support. More Heinkel 51 fighters, flown by volunteers, were sent about the end of August, but they were soon outmatched by the Republican Government's more numerous Russian-built and American-built fighters. The Luftwaffe then organized a balanced force of bombers, fighters and reconnaissance aircraft, initially about 200 aircraft strong and commanded by Major-General Hugo Sperrle, to support Franco. Lieutenant-Colonel Wolfram von Richthofen, a cousin of the Manfred von Richthofen who had achieved fame as a fighter pilot in the First World War, went to Spain as Sperrle's Chief of Staff and afterwards succeeded him in command of the force.

In accordance with the theory of 'strategic' bombing prevalent in the Luftwaffe at the time, Sperrle began by using his aircraft to attack Spanish ports with the object of interrupting supplies to the Republican forces. A shortage of heavy artillery soon led Franco to ask him to switch them to direct support of troops outside Madrid. They achieved no great success in a tactical role until the early spring of 1937, when relays of bomb-carrying Heinkel 51 fighters, flying low over the enemy's lines, attacked Republican strongpoints with devastating effect. Almost simultaneously the Republicans scored a notable success on another part of the front by launching a counter-attack at a time when their opponents' aircraft were grounded by wet weather but their own were able to take off from concrete runways.

These object-lessons in the value of tactical air support convinced German officers in Spain that air power, properly applied, could be much more than a *substitute* for artillery. When Sperrle received Junkers 87 and Henschel 123 dive-bombers and Me.109 fighters later in the year, Wolfram von Richthofen stressed the importance of organizing them in flexible close-support formations and of providing forward radio links so that orders based on up-to-the-minute knowledge of the situation could be passed to squadrons on the ground or in the air.

After the end of the Spanish Civil War in the spring of 1939, Richthofen made it his business to convince the authorities that a commander who possessed the means of concentrating massive air power at the right place could make a major contribution to a battle on land by creating favourable conditions for a breakthrough by armoured forces. This view was warmly endorsed by officers who had been sent to gain first-hand experience of the war in Spain before taking up key positions in the training organization at home. These men were well placed to gain a hearing in influential circles and to overcome opposition from extreme advocates of the 'strategic' theory of air warfare. Richthofen did not, in fact, propose that strategic bombing should be renounced, but only that a reasonable proportion of the air forces assigned to a major campaign should consist of units organized and equipped for a tactical role. Nevertheless a natural consequence of the acceptance of his doctrine was that German planners tended after the spring of 1939 to view all operations by land-based aircraft in the context of operations by land forces.

As we have seen, the use of concentrated air power to assist a breakthrough by armoured fighting vehicles had figured prominently in plans made by the British and the French in 1918 for a massive offensive in the following year. Still earlier, far-seeing British strategists such as Hankey had looked forward to the employment of large numbers of low-flying aircraft to support infantry advances. But the reluctance of successive Governments to commit the country to a European war and preoccupation with the doctrine of the strategic air offensive had prevented the British from providing themselves between the wars with a well-found tactical air force. The French, on the other hand, had always regarded their Air Force as primarily an army-support weapon. The re-equipment of their bomber force with modern aircraft during the second half of the 1930s had, however, been seriously hampered by industrial disputes arising largely from the Government's refusal to give active support to the Republican Government in the Spanish Civil War. Consequently their striking power on the eve of the Second World War was very small. Their choice of aircraft, too, was not always lucky. After placing an order in 1938 for dive-bombers comparable with the Junkers 87, they cancelled it on the ground that the prototype was slow and vulnerable. This was a valid criticism both of the French dive-bomber and of its German counterpart; but unfortunately for the French, the low-level medium bomber which they then adopted as their standard tactical bomber proved equally unsatisfactory. The French were better endowed with fighters than bombers, but were hampered by the lack of a dependable means of switching aircraft from sector to sector at short notice.

Largely as a result of economic difficulties aggravated by the Abyssinian War, the Italians, too, were rather weak in the air on the eve of the Second World War. They had no fighter comparable with the Hurricane, the Spitfire and the Me.109, but were working on a jet-propelled monoplane which used a piston engine to operate a ducted fan. This aircraft, the Caproni-Campini, appeared in prototype form in 1940, but its performance was so disappointing that the design was abandoned after a few trial flights. In the BR.20 the Italians had a monoplane medium bomber similar in speed, range and bomb-load to the German Dornier 17 and Heinkel 111, but it was poorly armed and provided little protection for its crew. In general, the output of the Italian aircraft industry was limited in 1939 by shortages of raw materials which Mussolini failed to persuade Hitler to make good. Such limitations made it hard for the Regia Aeronautica to profit by the lessons of the Spanish Civil War.

In Russia the first Five-Year Plan was succeeded by a second, covering the years from 1933 to 1937. A third Five-Year Plan, intended for completion in 1942, was overtaken by events. The second Five-Year Plan brought a substantial expansion of the Soviet aircraft industry, but workmanship was still poor by western European standards, and many complaints were made of incompetence and lack of enthusiasm at the managerial level. The sequel was a series of purges which affected not only industry and the armed forces but the whole of the governmental machine, including the Central Committee of the Communist Party. At least a quarter and perhaps as many as three-quarters of the senior officers of the Red Air Force were shot or dismissed between 1937 and 1939, but most of the leading designers of airframes and aero-engines were spared.

A Soviet air contingent, commanded by a future Chief of Staff of the Red Air Force and staffed by an inordinately large number of its senior officers, gave rather grudging support to the Republican forces in Spain. It was not particularly successful, and began to withdraw before the fighting was over. Convinced by their experience in Spain of the importance of the fighter as a means of clearing the way for tactical bombers, the Russians made strenuous attempts during the next few years to develop an up-to-date monoplane fighter comparable with the Hurricane, the Spitfire and the Me.109.

In the Far East, occasional skirmishes between Japanese and Communist forces in Manchuria or Mongolia made little impact on the Red Air Force until, in 1937, an 'undeclared war' broke out between Japan and Nationalist China. In July the Japanese complained that Chinese soldiers had opened fire on Japanese troops stationed near Peking under the terms of the Boxer Protocol of 1901. Attempts were made by the Japanese Government and the Chinese authorities on the spot to reach a friendly settlement, but both sides strengthened their forces in north China. In addition, Chiang Kai-shek moved strong reinforcements to the neighbourhood of the International Settlement at Shanghai. The Japanese then made additions to the small force of disembarked seamen which they maintained in the International Settlement and earmarked two divisions for despatch to Shanghai in the event of a clash. Fighting began at Shanghai on 13 August. Just over a week later Chiang concluded with the Soviet Government a pact which promised him far-reaching economic and financial support. The Soviet authorities went on to pour supplies into China through Canton and later by an overland route through Russian and Chinese Turkestan. They furnished Chiang with aircraft, technicians and instructors. At the same time they helped to link Chungking with Moscow by inaugurating, in partnership with the Chinese, an air transport service between Alma Ata in Kazakhstan and Hami in Sinkiang.

In the summer of the following year a brush between troops of the Japanese Kwantung Army and Soviet frontier guards on the borders of Manchuria, Korea and the Soviet Maritime Provinces led to a pitched battle in which the Russians claimed that their artillery and aircraft 'turned the Japanese guns into litter and their pillboxes into dust'. The Kwantung Army then withdrew under the terms of a truce, but a more serious clash occurred in the late summer of 1939 near the frontier between Manchuria and the Russian-dominated Mongolian People's Republic. The Russians moved armoured units and air squadrons to the disputed area, and on 20 August inflicted a serious reverse on the Kwantung Army at Khalkhan (or Halkin) Gol. Three days later the Soviet Government concluded with Hitler a pact which caused almost as much alarm in Tokyo as in London and Paris.

5

FROM MUNICH TO NARVIK

The growing conviction of responsible German airmen during and after the Spanish Civil War that co-operation with the German Army was the most valuable contribution they could make to a future war did nothing to diminish the value of the Luftwaffe as a diplomatic weapon. At the time of the Munich crisis in the autumn of 1938 the French had no effective means of defending their capital and centres of production against air attacks. The British, although potentially much stronger, were for the time being almost equally defenceless. Their radio-location system was still far from complete, only 29 fighter squadrons of which all but 5 had obsolete or obsolescent aircraft were fit for active service, and only about a third of the anti-aircraft guns, searchlights and barrage balloons envisaged in current schemes of air defence could be deployed. The knowledge that Germany possessed a powerful bomber force had a profound effect on the minds of British and French statesmen, even in the absence of any evidence that air attacks on Britain and France were included in Hitler's plans.

When German troops moved into Bohemia and Moravia in the following March, about 500 aircraft of the Luftwaffe were used to stage a demonstration over Prague and to carry airborne troops to the heart of the Czech homeland. This open violation of the spirit, if not the letter, of the Munich agreement led even so determined an appeaser as Neville Chamberlain to conclude that Britain could not expect to reach a lasting agreement with Germany as long as the National Socialist Government remained in power. With the object of convincing Hitler that no further act of aggression would be tolerated, the British Government responded to the rape of Czechoslovakia by guaranteeing the territorial integrity of Poland. Similar guarantees were given to

Rumania and – in the light of Italian designs on Albania – to Greece.

The British were too weak in 1939 to mount an air offensive against Germany. They could not disembark troops on German soil or bombard German ports without exposing their ships to attacks by a superior air force, and the troops they proposed to send to France in the event of war would be expected to conform with the orders of a French generalissimo whose plans were essentially defensive. In these circumstances Britain's only hope of giving substantial support to Poland lay in an alliance with Russia. Since the Poles did not wish to become parties to any arrangement which might have the effect of admitting Russian troops to Polish territory, the forging of such an alliance would have been difficult even if partnership with a Communist country had not seemed to many Englishmen an unattractive prospect. The Poles were willing to receive Russian supplies and even to accept Russian help in the air; but whether the Red Air Force, weakened by the recent purges, could make an effective contribution to the defence of Poland seemed rather doubtful. General Sir Edmund Ironside, who visited Warsaw on behalf of the British Government in the summer, warned members of the Cabinet before he left London that Poland was bound to be overrun if attacked in strength. He said when he returned that, although the Poles had excellent troops and were determined to put up a good fight, he had no faith in their strategic plan and feared that their communications would be disrupted by bombing.

In Germany the news that Hitler contemplated an early attack on Poland at the risk of war with France and Britain came as a shock to service chiefs who had not expected to be called upon to fight a major war before 1942. By the end of August the Luftwaffe had a first-line strength of roughly 1,500 bombers, dive-bombers and ground-attack aircraft, about 1,200 fighters, some 800 reconnaissance aircraft (including seaplanes) and approximately 500 transport aircraft. Its reserves (which the British estimated at 5,000 aircraft) amounted to fewer than 1,000 aircraft of all categories. This lack of depth reflected the insistence of Reichsmarschall Herman Göring, Commander-in-Chief of the Luftwaffe and Air Minister, that first-line strength should be increased as rapidly as possible. The more cautious Milch, appointed Inspector-General early in 1939, was still Secretary of State, but for practical purposes his responsibility for framing expansion schemes had passed to Ernst Udet, a former fighter pilot who owed his appointment as Director-General of Equipment to Göring's intervention. Hans Jeschonnek, a 40-year-old soldier and airman who had served under Milch in the early days of the revived Luftwaffe, was Chief of the General Staff.

In principle, all operational units and formations of the Luftwaffe were organized in four air fleets or Luftflotten, numbered 1, 2, 3 and 4. Each Luftflotte commanded such operational formations as were assigned to it, and also a number of administrative formations each responsible for providing operational units in a given area with accommodation, supplies and certain services.

At a conference of senior officers and political chiefs in the second half of August, Hitler broke the news that he intended to settle with Poland in the immediate future 'even at the cost of war'. He met objections founded on Germany's inability to fight a prolonged war on two fronts by assuring his henchmen that France and Britain were in no position to intervene in eastern Europe, and that any economic blockade they might institute would be offset by the pact which Germany was about to conclude with Russia. The essence of his plan was to overwhelm Poland by a lightning campaign and thus confront the western democracies with a situation they could not hope to change except by committing themselves to a long war from which he was convinced they would shrink.

On 23 August the Russo-German pact was signed in Moscow. Hitler gave orders on the same day that the invasion of Poland should begin on 26 August. The British announced on 24 August that they were determined to honour their pledge to the Poles, and Mussolini refused to join a war against France and Britain except on prohibitive terms. Hitler, telling his intimates that he needed time to sort out the political situation, countermanded his order of 23 August, but afterwards decreed that the attack on Poland should begin on 1 September.

Two air fleets were assigned to the campaign in Poland. About 1,600 aircraft strong, they outnumbered the Polish Air Force by more than 3 to 1. Luftflotte 2, based in peacetime on Berlin, was to support advances by the Third and Fourth Armies from East

Prussia and Pomerania; Luftflotte 4, based in peacetime on Vienna, was to support thrusts by the Eighth, Tenth and Fourteenth Armies from Silesia, eastern Moravia and western Slovakia.

Beginning with an elaborate programme of reconnaissance early on 1 September, the 2 air fleets virtually annihilated the Polish Air Force in 2 days by bombing its airfields and forcing units which escaped destruction in the air or on the ground to disperse to isolated landing grounds, where many of them lost touch with their parent formations and could obtain only meagre supplies of fuel and bombs. On the third day the Germans continued their attack on the Polish Air Force by bombing aircraft factories and other objectives in the enemy's rear, but devoted part of their air effort to attacks on pockets of resistance which the first wave of advancing troops had by-passed. Thereafter the 2 air fleets threw their whole weight into support for the land forces. Direct support was given by attacks on strongpoints, gun batteries and troop concentrations; indirect support by the bombing of road and rail communications, barracks, dumps, depots and arms factories. Transport aircraft carried rations, ammunition, fuel and spares to armoured units which had raced forward so fast that their supply columns could not reach them.

By the middle of September the end was almost in sight. On 17 September Russian troops crossed the eastern frontier of Poland and opened fire on Polish troops; that night the Polish Government and Commander-in-Chief sought asylum in Rumania. Nevertheless substantial bodies of Polish troops, including the garrison of Warsaw, continued to hold out in various parts of the country. Hitler decreed for political reasons that the capture of Warsaw should be completed by the end of the month. General Karl von Rundstedt, commanding Army Group South, thereupon ordered the German Eighth Army to invest the city, but not to commit its troops to hand-to-hand fighting in the streets. Surrender was to be enforced by a combination of air attacks and artillery bombardments or, if these failed, by the interruption of supplies of food and water.

On 25 September the Eighth Army's troops advanced to their predetermined siege line under cover of artillery and air attacks. These attacks seemed to the Poles to be aimed at objectives chosen more or less at random; according to the account afterwards given by Rundstedt's Chief of Staff, they were directed in the early stages at outlying forts and other strictly military objectives, and were switched to built-up areas only after aircraft had dropped leaflets warning the inhabitants that the city would be bombed and shelled if the garrison persisted in its refusal to surrender. Heavy air attacks, accompanied by further shelling, were made on 26 September and continued until, towards noon on 27 September, the garrison commander asked for terms. A formal instrument of surrender was signed on the following day.

The bombing of Warsaw caused heavy civilian casualties and aroused great indignation in Allied and neutral countries. To the commanders and staffs of Army Group South and the Eighth Army, the reproaches to which it exposed them seemed unjust and hypocritical. In their view Warsaw was a 'defended place' which could legitimately be bombarded in accordance with the customs and usages of war, which they claimed to have observed. They regarded their artillery and air attacks as regrettable but necessary acts of war carried out, after due warning had been given, in support of siege operations by a commander who was willing to spare the lives of the inhabitants and grant honourable terms to the garrison in return for the surrender of the city. Furthermore they claimed that the sufferings of the inhabitants would have been far greater had the Eighth Army ordered its troops to fight their way into the city instead of investing it.

The bombing of Warsaw apart, the Luftwaffe's performance in Poland made a profound impression on foreign observers. The promptness with which requests from commanders of land forces for air support were met, the speed with which air units were pushed forward to captured airfields, were particularly striking. The British were also impressed by the thoroughness with which the Luftwaffe sought out and destroyed or neutralized the Polish Air Force at the outset of the campaign. They believed that, if their own air force were similarly attacked, the radio-location system and their practice of dispersing aircraft round the perimeters of airfields would save it from being caught and destroyed on the ground, but that aircraft and aero-engine factories in the Midlands and the west of England might prove vulnerable unless special measures were taken to defend them. The Air Ministry's consequent insistence that Air Chief Marshal Dowding should pay special attention to the defence of Sheffield, Coventry, Derby and Bristol did nothing to lighten his responsibility for the defence of London and the south of England, where there were also aircraft factories. Moreover, these anxieties followed closely on new and unexpected demands from the Admiralty for the air defence of merchant shipping and of the main base of the Home Fleet at Scapa Flow.

Problems of air defence at home were further complicated for the British by the despatch to France of the Expeditionary Force and the 10 medium-bomber squadrons which the Air Ministry had undertaken to send across the Channel as an Advanced Air Striking Force. The Expeditionary Force was accompanied by a small Air Component which included 4 squadrons of Hurricane fighters drawn from the Metropolitan Air Force. Dowding, whose needs so far as fighters for home defence were concerned had been assessed shortly before the outbreak of war at 46 squadrons for the main air defence scheme, 4 for the protection of merchant shipping, 2 for the defence of Scapa Flow and 1 for the defence of Northern Ireland, was left on the departure of the Air Component with 35 squadrons to meet all these requirements. At the same time, he had only about one-third of the heavy anti-aircraft guns, three-quarters of the searchlights and fewer than half the barrage balloons to which he was entitled. Furthermore he was under orders to hold 6 of his remaining Hurricane squadrons ready for immediate despatch to the Continent if they were needed there, as assuredly they would be should France or the Low Countries be invaded. Meanwhile the Hurricane squadrons already in France competed with those at home for replacements and spares.

To meet the deficiency, the Air Ministry formed 18 new fighter squadrons during the first 4 months of the war. At the same time Bomber Command was obliged to reduce its first-line strength in order to find aircraft and instructors needed to train crews for the enlarged bomber force the Air Ministry hoped to provide when circumstances permitted. Twenty-three bomber squadrons deemed fit for active operations remained in Britain when the Advanced Air Striking Force had gone. Six of these were Blenheim squadrons, incapable of making any effective contribution to a strategic air offensive against Germany from British bases and intended to supplement the efforts of the Advanced Air

Striking Force should the need arise. The remaining 17 squadrons, which made up the heavy bomber force, mustered about 200 serviceable Hampden, Wellington and Whitley bombers designed to meet requirements first formulated in 1932. Such was the air striking power at the disposal of a nation whose leaders had repeatedly been urged to pin their faith to the bomber as the master-weapon of the future.

Soon after the outbreak of war the British, French and German Governments all expressed their approval of an appeal from President Roosevelt to the belligerents to refrain from unrestricted air warfare. Some British airmen thought that attacks by German aircraft on objectives far from the battlefront in Poland nullified any obligation thus created; but the need to conserve the bomber force strengthened the British Government's determination to limit Bomber Command's activities in the early stages of the war to the dropping of propaganda leaflets and attacks on strictly military objectives which could be bombed without risk to civilian lives and property. In practice this meant that for some months only German warships at sea or in harbours or roadsteads could be attacked.

So far as operations directed against the British were concerned, the Luftwaffe, too, was forbidden to attack built-up areas in the early stages of the war. Its objectives included warships, naval installations, merchant shipping, light vessels and trawlers of the fishing fleet. In addition, seaplanes were used from the early winter of 1939 to supplement the illegal laying of magnetic mines in British coastal waters by submarines and fast surface vessels. On 16 and 17 October Junkers 88 bombers raided naval anchorages in the Firth of Forth and at Scapa Flow, damaging a cruiser and a destroyer and the depot ship *Iron Duke*, but losing 3 aircraft to fighters and anti-aircraft guns. Partly because the air defences of Scapa Flow were incomplete, partly because a German submarine had entered the fleet anchorage and sunk the old battleship *Royal Oak* on 14 October, the Home Fleet withdrew to other bases from October until the following March.

Since Britain lived by her overseas trade and depended largely on coasters to distribute coal to her centres of production, the protection of her merchant fleet was a task of cardinal importance. Immediate responsibility for the defence of shipping against air attacks was, however, divided between a number of authorities, none of them particularly well equipped for the work. Fighter Command could provide some degree of protection for merchant vessels, trawlers and naval auxiliaries near the coast, but continuous escort for convoys moving round it made unacceptable demands on the fighter force and could be provided only in exceptional cases. Coastal Command, whose primary task was maritime reconnaissance, had ready for operational use on the eve of the war 1 squadron of obsolescent torpedo-bombers, 5 squadrons of flying boats, 9 squadrons of Anson general reconnaissance aircraft with an effective radius of action of only 250 miles and 1 squadron of American-built Hudsons superior in all-round performance to the Ansons. Regular reconnaissance patrols over the North Sea were put in hand as soon as war with Germany was seen to be imminent, but on several occasions German warships employed as commerce raiders gained the high seas without detection. The flying boats and general reconnaissance aircraft were not designed to grapple with fast bombers such as the Junkers 88, and the bombs they carried were almost useless against submarines. The Royal Navy had 3 effective aircraft carriers in home waters on the outbreak of war, but they were too valuable to be used for convoy escort except in an emergency, and the performance of most of the aircraft embarked in them left much to be desired. For all these reasons, air power made only limited contributions to the defence of British, Allied and neutral merchant shipping in the early stages of the war.

Attempts by Bomber Command to come to grips with the German fleet proved even more frustrating, and their failure had momentous consequences.

The first attempt was made on the day of Britain's declaration of war on Germany. Fifty-four bombers were sent to attack ships seen in the Heligoland Bight by the crew of an aircraft on reconnaissance, but found no targets.

On the following day 15 Blenheims and 14 Wellingtons were despatched to attack German warships reported to be in Schillig Roads, off Wilhelmshaven, and at Brunsbüttel. The crews of 5 Blenheims and 5 Wellingtons reported on their return to base that they had seen no warships. The remaining Blenheims attacked ships off Wilhelmshaven and in Schillig Roads from heights of the order of 500 feet. The pocket battleship *Admiral*

Scheer was hit by bombs which failed to explode; the cruiser *Emden* suffered minor damage from bomb-splinters and was struck and slightly damaged by one of 5 Blenheims shot down by anti-aircraft fire. The Wellingtons were unsuccessful, although one of them attacked the battle-cruisers *Scharnhorst* and *Gneisenau* at Brunsbüttel. Some of them were engaged by fighters which attacked them from astern and slightly below. Two Wellingtons failed to return, but there was no reason to suppose that they had been shot down by fighters. Nor did the day's events seem to invalidate the theory that bombers flying in close formation for mutual support, as Bombengeschwader 3's Gothas had done when they attacked London in daylight in 1917, had little to fear from fighters. Clearly, most of the losses suffered on 4 September were attributable to the gallantry of the crews of the Blenheims in pressing home their attacks from dangerously low levels in face of accurate anti-aircraft fire.

No further opportunity of inflicting serious damage on the German fleet arose until 3 December. Twenty-four Wellingtons, flying in a formation of 8 sections of 3 aircraft each, were then sent to attack warships near Heligoland. They were met by heavy anti-aircraft fire and 2 Wellingtons were hit, but all returned safely and some damage was thought to have been done to ships which included at least 2 cruisers. Fighters appeared about 10 minutes after Heligoland was first sighted. Again their attacks were delivered from astern. Few, if any, came closer than 350 yards, supposedly because of the deterrent effect of fire from rear guns. Their prompt intervention suggested, however, that early warning of the raid had been received at German fighter bases, possibly from anti-aircraft ships. In fact, a form of radar which gave a fairly good performance at ranges up to 50 or 60 miles had been developed in Germany during the past 4 years.

The results of Bomber Command's next brush with the German air defences were much less encouraging. Twelve Wellingtons, again flying in sections of 3 aircraft each, were sent on 14 December to make an armed reconnaissance of Schillig Roads. Crews were told to drop no bombs unless they could see their targets from 2,000 feet. When they left the English coast they were flying at 1,000 feet, with dense clouds just above them. By the time they approached the target area rain had fallen and the clouds were down to 200 feet. Nevertheless they spent more than half an hour in the neighbourhood. They came under heavy fire from anti-aircraft guns and were also attacked by fighters, at least one of which closed to 250 yards before opening fire. Five Wellingtons failed to return and one crashed on landing. The German fighter force lost 1 aircraft shot down by a Wellington and claimed the destruction of 5 Wellingtons and the probable destruction of a sixth.

The loss of half the bombers despatched was a serious blow to Bomber Command, but whether the aircraft which failed to return had been destroyed by fighters or by anti-aircraft fire was not known to the British. Air Vice-Marshal J. E. A. Baldwin, commander of the bomber group from which the Wellingtons were drawn, compared the raid with the Charge of the Light Brigade, and Ludlow-Hewitt was inclined to agree that the leader of the formation had shown more gallantry than wisdom. But Ludlow-Hewitt's Chief of Staff, Air Commodore N. H. Bottomley, pointed out that there was no proof that any of the Wellingtons had succumbed to fighters. The maintenance of tight formations by aircraft under fire was still, in his opinion, much to be desired.

Ultimately the view that anti-aircraft guns, rather than fighters, must have been responsible for the heavy losses suffered on 14 December was accepted. When 24 Wellingtons were sent to Schillig Roads, Jade Roads and Wilhelmshaven 4 days later, crews were ordered to attack any warships they might see, but only if they could drop their bombs from 10,000 feet or higher. The aircraft were despatched in 4 formations which were to provide mutual support but would otherwise act independently. One aircraft returned prematurely because of engine trouble and was followed, as the result of a misunderstanding, by a second.

The remaining 22 Wellingtons continued towards the target area, flying at 14,000 feet in a cloudless sky. They were engaged south of Heligoland by fighters which broke off their attacks when the Wellingtons came under fire from anti-aircraft guns ashore and afloat. Attacks by fighters were resumed as the Wellingtons left Wilhelmshaven after aiming some bombs at warships there, and continued until the surviving aircraft were 70–80 miles out to sea on the return flight. Some fighters, apparently using the 20-millimetre cannon which formed part of the standard armament of the Me.109 and the Me.110, opened fire at ranges beyond reach of the ·303-inch machine-guns carried by the Wellingtons. Some closed almost to point-blank range. Some attacked from astern, others evaded return fire by attacking from the beam. Some approached in pairs to deliver simultaneous attacks from the starboard and port quarters. Only 10 of the 22 Wellingtons which had reached the target area returned to base.

The British estimated when the action was over that they had destroyed 12 German fighters and seriously damaged approximately the same number. They could not know that the fighter Geschwader primarily concerned reported the loss of only 4 aircraft and damage to another 9, or that it attributed its success partly to the good warning given by a radar station in the Frisians, partly to the compliance of all but a few of its pilots with orders not to attack Wellingtons from astern, and partly to the pertinacity with which the pilots of most of the Wellingtons had stuck to their courses when attacked. What they did know was that half the bombers despatched to an area they could reach without flying any great distance over German territory had failed to return, and that this time there could be no doubt that fighters, not anti-aircraft guns, were responsible for most of their losses. Even though the Wellingtons could, in the course of time, be made less vulnerable by additions to their armament and the provision of self-sealing fuel tanks protected by armour, Bomber Command's chances of ever being in a position to attack the Ruhr in daylight began to seem remote.

In the light of this knowledge, the Air Ministry forbade Bomber Command to attempt any more raids on the lines of those of 14 and 18 December until the armouring of fuel tanks was completed. Nevertheless Ludlow-Hewitt's subordinate commanders and staff did not at once lose faith in the self-defending bomber formation or conclude that all hope of a strategic air offensive against the Ruhr must be renounced. Air Vice-Marshal Baldwin thought that the losses suffered on 18 December were due in part to the failure of some Wellingtons to keep station and that this arose from the tendency of inexperienced pilots to scatter when exposed to anti-aircraft fire. Air Commodore Bottomley wrote as late as 29 December of the inviolability of a tight bomber formation and attributed recent losses to straggling. Air Vice-Marshal A. T. Harris, commander of a bomber group equipped with Hampdens and a former member of the Joint Planning Sub-Committee of the Chiefs of Staff Committee, told Ludlow-Hewitt at a conference on 2 January 1940 that 3 bombers flying in company in daylight were considered by pilots a match for anything as long as they stayed together.

However, on that very day a section of Wellingtons lost 2 of its 3 aircraft in an encounter with Me.110 heavy fighters over the North Sea. Ludlow-Hewitt, after earnest consultation with his subordinates, warned the Air Ministry at the end of the month that a full-scale daylight offensive against the Ruhr might result in losses which would reduce the efficiency of the bomber force by 80 per cent for months to come and deprive it of perhaps half the experienced crews it would need when the new Stirling and Manchester heavy bombers came into service. He suggested that the authorities should consider whether they could find some less suicidal employment for his bombers.

The time might now have seemed ripe for the British to stop chasing the *ignis fatuus* of the strategic air offensive and tackle the problem of providing adequate air support for their land forces. But a mere decision to transform Bomber Command into an army support force would not have solved their problems, even if their airmen had been willing to renounce the doctrines on which they had been nurtured. Experience in Spain had shown that, where serious opposition was to be expected, the key to air superiority over the battlefield was the fighter. Unless supported by large numbers of fighters, which the British could not provide without detriment to the air defences of the United Kingdom, their bombers were likely to prove just as vulnerable in an army support role as in any other.

Ludlow-Hewitt had, indeed, raised before the outbreak of war the question of fighter escort for bombers, but in the context of strategic bombing rather than army support operations. The solution to which his thoughts now turned was the conversion of the greater part of Bomber Command into a night bomber force. He had already decided, at his conference on 2 January, that the Wellingtons of No 3 Group and the Hampdens of No 5 Group should join the Whitleys of No 4 Group in dropping propaganda leaflets so that their crews might gain experience of flying over Germany at night.

Ludlow-Hewitt reached this decision in the light not only of the heavy losses hitherto suffered by the Wellingtons but also of the almost negligible casualties inflicted on the Whitleys. Crews of Whitleys had undergone their share of hardships in consequence of natural hazards, mechanical breakdowns or inability to find their way home; but their reports drew such a reassuring picture of the weakness of the enemy's night air defences that Ludlow-Hewitt could not fail to be attracted by the prospect of enlisting the help of darkness for the great air offensive against the Ruhr which he or his successor was sure to be ordered to deliver when the Air Staff judged that the right moment had come.

The question was whether bomber crews would be able to find their way to their destinations in the dark, locate their targets and bomb them accurately. Commonsense suggested that they would not. The safe return of Whitleys sent to drop leaflets at Frankfurt, Stuttgart, Munich and other German towns did not prove that they had reached those places. Some months before the outbreak of the war the officer then commanding No 3 Group had reported that, in daylight, dead reckoning could not be expected to bring an aircraft flying above cloud much closer to its target than a distance of 50 miles or so. The only scientific aids to navigation available to British bomber crews in the early stages of the war were the astro-sextant and directional radio. Since both called for a high degree of skill on the part of the user and neither could be relied upon for accurate results, the crew of a night bomber could seldom be sure of their position unless they checked it by frequent observation of landmarks. To do this on dark moonless nights in wartime conditions was virtually impossible. A crew might hope, by flying low as they approached a coastline, to pick out a familiar cape or estuary; once they were over hostile territory only self-illuminating objects such as blast-furnaces were visible. In moonlight large rivers, lakes and canals could, as a rule be seen from heights of 12,000 feet or more, but a good deal depended on the weather.

However, although navigation was still largely a matter of observation and although observation threatened to be difficult except in the most favourable conditions, the authorities assumed that somehow or other most night bombers would arrive within 10 miles of their destinations.[1] Whether crews would be able, even if that assumption held good, to find and bomb their targets was another matter. Crews of leaflet-dropping Whitleys reported that in moonlight small towns were visible from heights of the order of 4,000–6,000 feet and that individual buildings could be distinguished from heights up to 3,000–4,000 feet. But the bombing of targets in well-defended areas from such heights as these would scarcely be practical. It seemed to follow that precise bombing of industrial areas at night would have to be confined to self-illuminating objectives, since these alone were likely to be distinguishable from safe heights.

Marshalling yards, although not self-illuminating in the accepted sense, might also, it was thought, be distinguishable from such heights, and steps were taken to ascertain whether this was so. The crews of 2 Whitleys, after reconnoitring marshalling yards at Hamm and Schwerte from relatively low altitudes in January, reported that neither was blacked out and that both could, in their opinion, have been accurately bombed from heights up to 10,000 or 12,000 feet. A further reconnaissance in February by 3 Whitleys provided further evidence. One crew reported, after flying over Bielefeld at 8,000 feet in the light of a three-quarter moon, that the marshalling yards, although only dimly lit, were conspicuous. A second found the Rhine between Duisburg and Cologne 'very distinctive'. The third threw an interesting sidelight on problems of target-finding by getting lost while the first and second pilots were changing seats and failing to locate its position despite a square search at 2,000 feet.

Bomber Command had, however, yet to show that accurate bombing of precisely-located objectives, as distinct from mere reconnaissance, was possible at night. The matter was put to the test on the night of 19 March, when 30 Whitleys and 20 Hampdens were sent to bomb a seaplane base at Hörnum, on the island of Sylt in the Frisians, as a reprisal for a daylight attack by German aircraft on Scapa Flow. The 2 bomber groups concerned were ordered to send only experienced crews and crews with knowledge of the 'particular area' in which the target was situated.

The circumstances were favourable. The moon was 2 days past its first quarter, no deep penetration of German territory was called for, and the seaplane base was not expected to be hard to find. Nevertheless the crews of 2 Whitleys and 3 Hampdens reported on their return to base that they had been unable to locate it. One Whitley and 2 Hampdens returned early with engine trouble, and 1 Whitley failed to return. The remaining 41 aircraft, attacking singly over a period of 6 hours, dropped about 15 tons of bombs from various heights between 1,000 and 10,000 feet. The bomb-aimers of all these aircraft reported that the target was easily recognizable and that they had no difficulty in setting their sights on it. Many direct hits were reported, including hits on hangars and living quarters. Two hangars were described as being left on fire. However, when air photographs taken on 6 April were examined, all buildings appeared to be 'outwardly intact'. Bomber Command, although not aware that the reason was that in fact very little damage had been done, warned the Air Ministry against 'over-optimistic conclusions . . . as to the visibility of objectives at night, and the possibility of identifying them and bombing them accurately'.[2] Nevertheless it was widely assumed at the time that the seaplane base must have been badly knocked about and that the Germans had succeeded in repairing or concealing the damage by the time the photographs were taken.

Soon afterwards Air Marshal C. F. A. Portal, who had succeeded Ludlow-Hewitt on 3 April, received his first directive from the Air Staff. It dealt with the steps to be taken by Bomber Command should the Germans invade the Low Countries or the British Government authorize unrestricted air action without waiting for them to do so. 'The operations of our heavy bombers', Portal was told, 'are to be confined mainly to night action.'[3]

On 9 April Germany ended the twilight war in the west by invading Denmark and Norway. Both sides had made plans to put troops ashore in Norway, the British and the French for the purpose of denying Swedish iron ore to the enemy and securing southern Scandinavia against German or Russian aggression, the Germans in the hope of forestalling the Allies and seizing bases for submarines and aircraft. The Allied plan was, however, to be put into effect only with the assent of the Norwegian Government or if the Germans invaded Norway. Evidence of exceptional German naval activity and a report from a neutral source to the effect that German troops were about to land in Norway were received in London on 6 and 7 April, but the British naval authorities misread the signs in the light of their conviction that an attempt to pass commerce-raiders into the Atlantic was the enemy's most probable course of action. Even when they learned during the late afternoon of 7 April that crews of Bomber Command sent to attack warships reported by the crew of an Anson on reconnaissance to be west of Jutland had seen what appeared to be the greater part of the German fleet heading north-west near the entrance to the Skagerrak, a supposed threat to merchant shipping on the high seas continued to be their chief preoccupation. Measures ordered by the Admiralty disrupted the Allied plan at the very moment when intervention in Norway became appropriate, and the Home Fleet put to sea on a course which left the approaches to the principal Norwegian ports uncovered.[4]

Initially the Germans assigned to the conquest of Norway and Denmark some 6 infantry and mountain divisions, virtually the whole of their effective naval strength and about a quarter of the first-line strength of the Luftwaffe, including nearly all its transport aircraft. Denmark was occupied in face of little more than token resistance after parachutists and airborne infantry had seized 2 airfields in Jutland as bases for operations against Norway. Assault forces were despatched in fast warships to the principal Norwegian ports from Oslo to Narvik. Transport aircraft carried some supplies in addition to parachutists and airborne infantry assigned to the capture of 2 airfields near Oslo and an airfield near Stavanger which figured in Allied plans, but except at Narvik the assault forces depended for their ability to withstand counter-attacks on the early arrival of supplies and follow-up formations which were to be routed through Oslo. The sinking of the cruiser *Blücher* in Oslofjiord by Norwegian coast defence guns nearly wrecked this part of the German plan, but after some delay the city and port were captured with the help of airborne reinforcements. King Haakon and his ministers escaped in the nick of time with the national gold reserves. Kristiansand, Stavanger, Bergen and Trondheim were all captured without great difficulty.

At Narvik about 2,000 troops of a mountain division disembarked early on 9 April from 10 destroyers. Their artillery had been washed overboard by heavy seas during the voyage from Germany, their supply ships failed to arrive and all 10 destroyers were sunk or crippled by the British before they could be refuelled and sent home. An attempt to fly a fresh consignment of mountain guns to an improvised landing ground outside the town was abandoned after 10 heavily-laden aircraft had crashed. Until the third week in April, when the Swedish authorities agreed to receive provisions for transit to Narvik by rail, the troops and the surviving crews of the destroyers depended on such supplies as could be dropped by parachutes, brought by seaplanes or obtained locally. Nevertheless the Allies, hampered by changes of plan and inter-service misunderstandings, did not succeed in driving them from Narvik until the last week in May. Norwegian, Polish, British and French troops then entered the town for the purpose of demolishing any port facilities still intact before the British, the French and the Poles withdrew from the whole of northern Norway in the first and second weeks of June.

Elsewhere the Germans, with all the principal ports and airfields in their hands by the second day, were in a strong position from the outset. The Allies, limited until they managed to reconstruct an abandoned Norwegian airfield near Narvik to bases in Britain and an improvised landing ground in central Norway, could not match the German effort in the air. They recognized that Trondheim was the key to central Norway, but shelved a plan for its recapture by direct assault rather than risk their transports and warships in waters dominated by German aircraft and by Norwegian coast defence guns which might be manned by German crews. In the meantime they sent troops to minor ports north and south of Trondheim in the hope of capturing the port by convergent attacks.

A British force duly landed without opposition at Molde and Åndalsnes, south of Trondheim, but soon found itself committed to attempts to stem the northward advance of German troops from Oslo and cover the retreat of the Norwegians. North of Trondheim, 3 British Territorial battalions without motor transport, field artillery or anti-aircraft guns landed at Namsos, also without opposition. After advancing about half way to Trondheim in company with Norwegian troops they were pushed back about 25 miles by the enemy, but their losses were light and the arrival of well-equipped French mountain troops accompanied by supply ships promised to restore the situation. The decisive factor was an air attack which destroyed warehouses and sheds on the quayside at Namsos and delayed the unloading of transport and anti-aircraft guns brought by the French. In the light of this setback and of reverses suffered by the British and Norwegian forces south of Trondheim, the British and French Governments decided in the last week of April to withdraw their troops from central Norway. About 10,000 British and French troops were safely embarked at the end of April and the beginning of May at Åndalsnes, Molde and Namsos. One British and 1 French destroyer were sunk by bombing during the homeward voyage.

The withdrawal of nearly 25,000 Allied troops from Narvik and its neighbourhood followed in June. The aircraft carriers *Ark Royal* and *Glorious* covered the embarkation. When all the troops had embarked and the *Ark Royal* had withdrawn, 2 British fighter squadrons which had covered the Allied assault on Narvik flew aboard the *Glorious* – a task successfully completed, although none of the pilots had ever landed on a ship before. The *Glorious,* accompanied by 2 destroyers, then set course for home. In addition to the 2 fighter squadrons, which were essentially land-based units unsuitable for use at sea, she carried a number of multi-purpose naval aircraft for her own protection.

Meanwhile the German battle-cruisers *Scharnhorst* and *Gneisenau*, accompanied by the cruiser *Hipper* and 4 destroyers, had left Kiel for the purpose of striking on the night of 8/9 June at the Allied naval base at Harsted, near Narvik. In the light of reports which suggested that the Allies were withdrawing from Narvik, the commander of the force sent the *Hipper* and the destroyers to refuel at Trondheim and began a search for Allied transports and warships in the open sea. During the afternoon of 9 June he came up with the *Glorious* and her attendant destroyers about 280 miles west of Narvik and sank all 3 ships. For reasons which will never be fully known, the *Glorious* had made no use of her aircraft to keep a look-out for hostile warships, and accurate fire from the *Scharnhorst* prevented her from getting them into the air for use as torpedo-bombers once the action began. Severe damage done to the *Scharnhorst* by one of the British destroyers caused the German commander to make for Trondheim without completing his search for the lightly-escorted transports then at sea. Only a few days later a torpedo from a British submarine put the *Gneisenau* out of action for nearly 6 months.

The campaign in Scandinavia provided a striking demonstration of German air power, but it left Germany with no capital ships and only 3 cruisers and 4 destroyers fit for use outside the Baltic. One more cruiser and 4 more destroyers were ready by September. The British, when their naval strength was at a low ebb at the beginning of July, had 4 effective capital ships, 11 cruisers and 80 destroyers in home waters, or 4 effective capital ships, 10 cruisers and 40 destroyers after the deduction of ships assigned to escort duties or other special tasks. When Hitler decided that preparations should be made for a landing in Britain, his planners had therefore to fall back on the hope that air power might redress the balance. The result was that the Luftwaffe became saddled with a task which it was no more capable of performing than the British Bomber Command was of making serious inroads on Germany's industrial capacity.

In the meantime Neville Chamberlain's Government, discredited by its surrender of the initiative in Norway, had fallen from power and Winston Churchill had succeeded Chamberlain as Prime Minister. As First Lord of the Admiralty and Chairman of the Military Co-Ordination Committee in the outgoing Government, Churchill was at least as much responsible as any minister for the muddles and mistakes which put Chamberlain out of office. But his energy, his zeal, his criticisms of Baldwin's and Chamberlain's peacetime leadership, commended him to Socialist statesmen who had witheld their support from his predecessor. Thus he was able to form an all-party Government pledged to win the war no matter what the cost in blood, toil, sweat and tears.

6

THE BATTLE OF FRANCE

Soon after the end of the campaign in Poland, Hitler stressed in an instruction to his service chiefs the importance of capturing bases in the Low Countries from which the Luftwaffe would be able, when the time was ripe, to strike at 'the heart of the British will-to-resist'.[1] According to the Chief of Staff of Army Group South, this was not the first time he had shown that he was prepared, if he thought fit, to divert the Luftwaffe from its army support role. In the course of the campaign he had proposed that Warsaw should be bombed at a time when the army group was not yet ready to enter or besiege the city.[2]

Preparations for an immediate invasion of the Low Countries were carried to an advanced stage in November and again in January, but on each occasion the weather was such that the assault had to be called off. These postponments came as a great relief to the leaders of the Army, who favoured a waiting policy on the ground that Germany's armed forces were not yet ready to try conclusions with the armies of two first-class powers.

The delay gave time for a radical change in strategy. Originally the High Command aimed at seizing a tract of Dutch, Belgian and French territory as a protective belt for the Ruhr and a base for sea and air warfare against Britain. This they planned to do by advancing on a broad front through central Belgium. Critics of the plan objected that it promised no decision. An opening move on the lines of the Schlieffen manoeuvre would not enable Hitler to encircle the whole of the opposing armies, as Schlieffen and the younger Moltke had hoped to do, for the Allied line did not end near Maubeuge as in August 1914; it extended all the way to the sea. An advance through central Belgium might dent or even break the Allied left, but it would not prevent the Allies from forming a new line on the Somme.

After an interview with Lieutenant-General Erich von Manstein, the former Chief of Staff of Army Group South in Poland and Army Group A on the Western Front, Hitler agreed in February that the main thrust should be made not by Army Group B (General Fedor von Bock) on the German right, but by Army Group A (General Karl von Rundstedt) on Bock's left. Rundstedt, with 7 armoured, 3 motorized and 34 infantry divisions under command, was to advance along a line from the Ardennes to Abbeville with the object of cutting off and annihilating the whole of the Allied armies north of that line. Bock, with 28 divisions of which 3 were armoured, was to advance into Holland and Belgium for the purpose of occupying those countries, seizing bases and preventing the Allied armies of the left from escaping to the north and east. Two of his armoured divisions were to be transferred to Rundstedt's command about a week after the launching of the offensive. Seventeen divisions were assigned to Army Group C, in the south, and 45 remained in reserve.

The postponements also gave the Germans time to make useful additions to their armoured strength. By the spring of 1940 their 10 armoured divisions, organized in 4 corps, had some 2,600 tanks, many of them newly manufactured. The French had about 2,400 modern tanks, without counting those contributed by the British, but roughly half were allotted to independent tank battalions. With only 3 armoured divisions formed and 1 forming, they had no armoured counter-attack force comparable with the armoured assault force which the Germans could bring to bear against them.

In the air the Germans had a marked numerical superiority. The Luftwaffe, although still not free from commitments at Narvik, assigned to the campaign in France and the Low Countries about 1,300 long-range bombers, 300–400 dive-bombers, some 1,200 fighters, nearly 650 reconnaissance aircraft, about 470 transport aircraft and some 40–50 gliders. The French had about 150 bombers, some 700 fighters, and 300–400 reconnaissance aircraft fit for use on their Eastern Front. The British had promised, in effect, to use the whole of their bomber force, nominally some 400–500 aircraft strong, to help the Allied armies during any critical phase of an invasion of the Low Countries. They raised the fighter strength of the Air Component of their Expeditionary Force to 10 squadrons when the Germans opened their offensive and later to the equivalent of 16 squadrons, thus contributing some 200–250 fighters exclusive of those based at home but operating over Continental Europe. They also provided enough reconnaissance aircraft to take care of their own sector.

The Allied generalissimo, General Gamelin, had drafted Joffre's order for the Battle of the Marne. Long Chief of Staff of the French Army, he held at the time of the German attack the posts of Chief of Staff for National Defence and Commander-in-Chief, Land Forces. Until recently he had controlled the forces on the North-East Front, which was the only active front outside Norway, through a Deputy Commander, General Alphonse Georges; but in January he persuaded the Government to create for Georges the post of Commander-in-Chief, North-East Front. This change had two important consequences, both unfortunate from the Allied point of view. One was that responsibility for staff work, formerly concentrated at a single headquarters, was henceforth divided between two; the other was that Gamelin, becoming reluctant to give orders to Georges, or even to visit him, for fear of undermining his self-confidence, tended to segregate himself at his command post in the outskirts of Paris and lose touch with events.

The French formed an accurate impression of the German plan in its original form and received good warning of the attacks projected in November and January, but gained no knowledge of the new plan made in February. Gamelin did not at first discount the possibility of an attack through the Ardennes, but eventually he came to the conclusion that the Germans would be unable to bring up their artillery fast enough in that sector to achieve tactical surprise. Putting the bulk of his forces on the left or in and behind the Maginot Line, he left his centre weak in the belief that he would have plenty of time to strengthen it before the Germans could force the crossings of the Meuse if, after all, the unexpected happened. During the winter the British stood in prepared positions along the Belgian frontier, but were ready to move into Belgium when Gamelin gave the word.

The Belgians had renounced their alliance with France after Hitler's remilitarization of the Rhineland, but the French knew as a result of informal exchanges that they intended, if the Germans attacked them, to hold forward positions on the Albert Canal for a limited period and eventually to fall back to a line covering Ghent and Antwerp. After considering various plans and discussing them with the British, Gamelin proposed in November that, if summoned by the Belgians in good time, not only the British Expeditionary Force but also a substantial part of the French armies of the left should move into Belgian territory. The British were to advance to the line of the River Dyle and hold it from Louvain on the left to Wavre on the right, leaving the lower reaches of the river, from Louvain to Antwerp and beyond, to be held by Belgian troops. On the right of the British the French First Army was to advance to the gap between Wavre and the bend of the Meuse at Namur. Further south the French Ninth Army was to swing its left into Belgian territory as far as the line of the Meuse from Namur to the French frontier at Givet. South and south-east of Givet the right-hand corps of the Ninth Army and the whole of the French Second Army, standing on French soil in positions already occupied, would hold the line of the Meuse and the Chiers as far as the terminus of the Maginot Line near Longuyon.

The plan, known as Plan D, was accepted by the Allied Supreme War Council on 17 November with the proviso that it was to be put into effect only if the circumstances were such that the British Expeditionary Force and the French First Army could reasonably expect to reach the line of the Dyle and the 'Gembloux gap' between Wavre and Namur before the enemy arrived in strength. An optional addition to Plan D – the so-called 'Breda alternative' – provided that, in certain circumstances, the French Seventh Army should race forward on the left of the British and try to make contact with Dutch troops in the neighbourhood of Breda.

In the early hours of 10 May 1940 German aircraft ranged far and wide over France and the Low Countries, bombing air bases and destroying aircraft on the ground and in the air. The British and the French escaped catastrophic losses, but the small Belgian and Dutch Air Forces were almost annihilated.

At the same time parachutists and airborne infantry landed at or near key objectives in Belgium and Holland. German troops disguised as civilian workmen or wearing Dutch army greatcoats

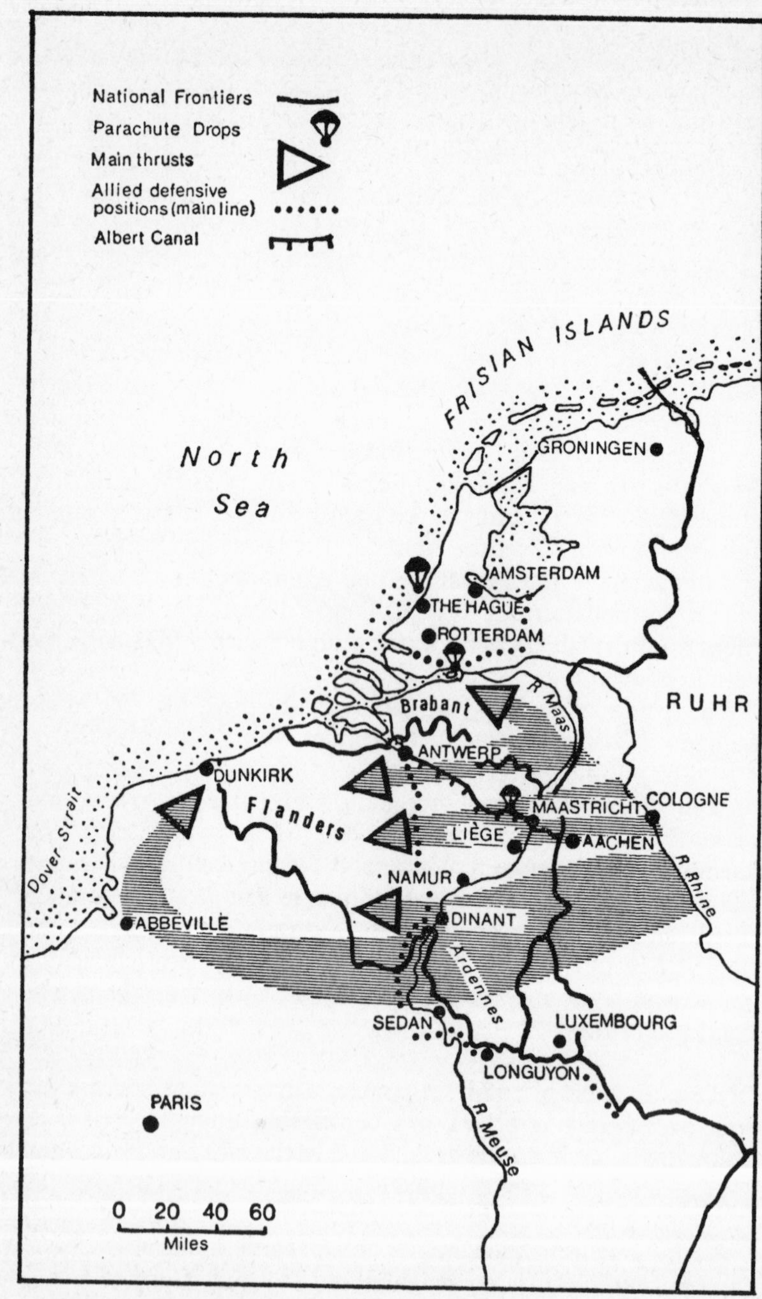

3 The German Offensive in the West, May 1940

and steel helmets had tried earlier to seize bridges in the neighbourhood of Maastricht, but the Dutch military authorities on the spot had succeeded in blowing a number of bridges and had raised the alarm. Parachutists dropped within the perimeter of a crucial Belgian fort at Eben Emael did not capture the fort until the following day, after reinforcements had arrived, but the garrison was distracted from its task of covering neighbouring bridges across the Albert Canal. Three bridges fell into German hands, and only one of them was recaptured by Belgian troops. Thus the forward positions which Gamelin expected the Belgians to hold for at least 4 days were turned on the first day.

At Gamelin's command post at Vincennes, these events were heralded before daybreak by reports from Luxembourg, Brussels and elsewhere of 'suspicious movements' on the German side of the lines. Reports of the bombing of airfields and the arrival of German parachutists in Belgium and Holland followed within the next few hours. About 6.30 am, after the Belgian and Dutch Governments had asked for help, Gamelin decided in consultation with Georges that Plan D and the 'Breda alternative' should be put into effect. The Seventh Army's move to Breda, which proved useless since no Dutch troops were in the neighbourhood, deprived Georges at a crucial stage of 7 of his best divisions.

Contrary to expectations, the advance of the Allied Armies into Belgium was accomplished with little effective interference from the Luftwaffe. By the evening of 14 May the British, with 10 divisions less one temporarily in the Maginot Line, held the line of the Dyle from Wavre to Louvain, with the Belgians on their left. The French First Army, under orders to hold a 22-mile front with 13 divisions at its immediate disposal or under orders to join it, was in contact with the enemy in the 'Gembloux gap' and was fighting well. On its right the 2 corps of the Ninth Army not already on the Meuse when the movement began completed their advance on 13 May.

In the meantime British home-based fighters had helped to cover the embarkation of members of the Dutch Government and royal family and the national reserves of gold and diamonds in ships bound for the United Kingdom, and British demolition parties had destroyed stocks of oil at Dutch refineries to prevent them from falling into German hands. By 13 May Army Group B had a corps under Lieutenant-General Rudolf Schmidt in front of Rotterdam.

The Dutch claimed that Rotterdam was an open city. The German authorities, rejecting this claim on the ground that Dutch troops were actively defending fortified positions in the city or on its outskirts, ordered Schmidt to take the place by assault. Schmidt made provisional arrangements to do so under cover of a dive-bomber attack which would be delivered at 1.30 pm on 14 May unless the garrison promised by 12.30 pm that hostilities should cease forthwith. On learning soon after midday that the ultimatum was likely to be accepted, he despatched a signal postponing the dive-bomber attack. After receiving a non-committal answer from the garrison, he went on to draw up terms of surrender which contained no threats but stipulated that negotiations should be completed by 4.30 pm so that his troops could enter the city by nightfall.

A few minutes before 1.30 pm Rotterdam was approached not by the 90 dive-bombers which Schmidt had asked the Luftwaffe to withhold but by roughly the same number of long-range bombers. There is reason to suppose that these aircraft were sent as the result of a long conversation on the telephone between Göring and the commander of the Luftflotte concerned, but of this there is only presumptive evidence which does not amount to proof.[3] Schmidt gave orders that flares should be lit as a warning to crews not to drop their bombs, but about half the bombers attacked the commercial quarter of the city. Nearly 1,000 civilians were killed, many more were injured, and many buildings were destroyed or damaged. The number of killed and injured was estimated at the time at 30,000. The garrison surrendered about 2 hours later.

This incident caused widespread indignation and resentment in Allied and neutral countries. On 15 May the British Government lifted its ban on the bombing of any but military objectives in the narrowest sense of the term by authorizing Bomber Command to attack objectives east of the Rhine.

By that date the Allies had become painfully aware that the crucial sector of their front in France and Belgium was not the strongly held Gembloux gap but the stretch of the Meuse between the Sambre and the Chiers. When leading elements of Rundstedt's armoured formations reached the right bank of the

Meuse on 12 May, only twelve infantry and garrison divisions of the Second and Ninth Armies, including those on the extreme left which were still closing up to the river, were available to hold the left bank between Namur and the outposts of the Maginot Line, nearly a 100 miles away. The 2 armies also had 4 light cavalry divisions and 2 independent cavalry brigades; but the former were only partly mechanized, and the latter consisted entirely of mounted troops.

However, the demolition on that day of all bridges except a footbridge at Dinant transformed the Meuse, at least for the time being, into an obstacle impassable by tanks. The French did not believe that the Germans would try to cross it in strength before the armoured formations completed the assembly of their artillery. This was expected to take at least four days. German aircraft attacked the Second Army's positions opposite Sedan on 12 May, but were chased away by French fighters. The conclusion reached was that any attempt which the Germans might make to establish a bridgehead on the following day was bound to fail if the French Air Force acted as it had done on 12 May.

That was not the view held by General von Kleist, commander of a group of armoured and motorized formations which included the 19th Panzer Corps (1st, 2nd and 10th Panzer Divisions), the 41st Panzer Corps (6th and 8th Panzer Divisions) and the 14th Motorized Corps of 3 motorized infantry divisions. After telling Hitler's personal representative on 12 May that he would rather cross the Meuse without delay than wait for infantry formations to force the crossings for him, Kleist ordered the 19th and 41st Panzer Corps to pass their assault troops across the river on 13 May at Sedan and Monthermé respectively, and the 14th Motorized Corps to hold itself in readiness to follow the 19th Corps. On Kleist's right the 15th Panzer Corps (5th and 7th Panzer Divisions) was to make a covering attack at Dinant.

The sector about to be attacked by the 19th Panzer Corps (Lieutenant-General Heinz Guderian) was held by the French 55th Division. The left bank of the Meuse was defended by a line of trenches and concrete pillboxes close to the water's edge and a second line of trenches, wired but without pillboxes, at the foot of wooded heights which gave an excellent field of fire for artillery. The 55th Division was short of anti-tank and anti-aircraft guns, but had about 140 field and heavy guns – more than twice the usual allotment for an infantry division – on a front reduced to a width of about 5 miles by the arrival from reserve of the 71st Division, which took over the 55th Division's right-hand sector during the night of 12/13 May. This relief was not an unmixed blessing, since the move was completed too late for the troops relieved to be shifted before daybreak to the positions assigned to them in the 55th Division's new layout. The divisional commander decided, therefore, to wait until the night of 13/14 May before incorporating them in the scheme. Meanwhile they took refuge in woods and the troops already in position were redisposed. The inconvenience resulting from this eleventh-hour change more than offset the benefit conferred on the 55th Division by the contraction of its front.

The 71st Division, too, was not at its best on 13 May. The troops, having served in the neighbourhood throughout the winter, were familiar with the ground they took over from the 55th Division on their left and the 3rd North African Division on their right. But they had not had time to settle into their new positions and were tired after marching 9 miles during the night. Like their neighbours on the left they were not, for the most part, men in the first flower of their youth. The Second Army's best troops had been put further to the right to guard against a turning movement round the northern flank of the Maginot Line. First-class troops did not seem necessary in a sector whose natural defences included an unfordable river 60 yards wide.

The German armoured formations had been promised maximum air support for their attempt to force the crossings of the Meuse. According to Guderian, a prolonged though intermittent air bombardment was substituted at his request for the short, sharp attack which the Luftwaffe at first proposed to deliver in the Sedan sector.

Air attacks in that sector on 13 May began with sporadic bombing of main positions and rear areas. At the same time hundreds of tanks of the 1st and 10th Panzer Divisions assembled beyond the Meuse in full view of the French and within range of their artillery. Some approached the river and opened fire on the loopholes of the 55th Division's pillboxes. The French artillerymen scored some hits, but were sparing of their fire for fear of using up ammunition which might be needed later to support a counter-attack. This proved false economy, for such an opportunity of blunting the enemy's spearheads was never to recur.

The weight and frequency of the air attacks increased towards midday and reached a peak in the early afternoon. For some hours relays of bombers and dive-bombers made repeated attacks on gunposts and infantry positions. No French fighters arrived to chase them away or shoot them down, although the Army and army group commanders had asked earlier in the day for air support. The French suffered only light casualties, since dugouts, pillboxes and trenches gave good protection against anything short of a direct hit; but the crash of bombs and the shriek of dive-bombers were unnerving to men to whom the experience was new.

Between 3.30 and 4 pm, after a brief bombardment by such of Guderian's artillery as had reached him, assault troops of the 1st and 10th Panzer Divisions crossed the Meuse on either side of Sedan in rubber boats. With honourable exceptions the defenders, dazed and cowed by the bombing, did little to prevent them from rushing the first line of trenches and pillboxes.

The 1st Panzers made rapid progress, advancing quickly to the wooded heights on the left bank and descending after nightfall into the valleys beyond. But the 10th Panzers were soon pinned to a small bridgehead by artillery fire from flanking positions, while the 2nd Panzers, whose main body had been delayed by road blocks and broken bridges in the Ardennes, did not succeed in passing its assault troops across the river until the following morning. In any case the troops on the left bank, without supporting arms and only precariously established in unfamiliar country, were not well placed to withstand a determined counter-attack by numerically superior forces with artillery support.

However, within 2 hours of the assault rumours spread through the 55th Division and the corps artillery in its area to the effect that German tanks had already crossed the Meuse. These appear to have originated in statements by artillery observers who reported, correctly but in misleading terms, that the Sedan front had been breached by armoured formations. French infantry and gunners, on foot or in lorries, retreated in wild disorder, some undisguisedly in the grip of mass hysteria, others with the sanction of officers who claimed to have received orders to withdraw but were unable to produce them or to say who had issued them.

By noon on 14 May the 55th Division had ceased to exist. On that day the 71st Division also fell to pieces, although it had not been attacked.

At Monthermé, in the sector held by the right-hand corps of the Ninth Army, aircraft which the commander of the 41st Panzer Corps expected to support his assault on 13 May failed to appear by the time the assault was due. Troops of the 6th Panzer Division managed to cross the Meuse in rubber boats and seize a small area swept by machine-gun and tank-gun fire from the right bank, but could go no further until events elsewhere compelled the whole of the Ninth Army to withdraw.

At Dinant, on the other hand, the 15th Panzer Corps did much more than deliver a mere covering attack. Here the left bank of the Meuse was defended by that part of the Ninth Army which advanced into Belgian territory in accordance with Plan D in order to close up to the river. Leading elements of the 7th Panzer Division (Major-General Erwin Rommel) reached the right bank during the afternoon of 12 May, at a time when the Ninth Army was still moving to positions which the Belgians had not prepared for defence. Rommel's motor-cyclists soon discovered an intact footbridge across a weir, but were prevented from crossing it by an infantry company which had been ordered to guard it pending the arrival of the troops assigned to that part of the front. When these arrived in the late afternoon after a rather leisurely advance, they omitted to go down to the water's edge in accordance with the army commander's orders. The motor-cyclists crossed the bridge unseen under cover of darkness, assembled in battalion strength on the left bank and rushed the neighbouring heights about an hour before daybreak.

Air attacks on the French positions began at dawn. Soon afterwards Rommel's assault troops tried to cross the river in rubber boats at a point immediately north of Dinant, but were stopped by vigorous rifle and machine-gun fire. Later they crossed under covering fire from tanks. With the help of the motor-cyclists already on the left bank, they then established a bridgehead about 3 miles wide by 2 miles deep, which they afterwards extended. The Luftwaffe's efforts did not prevent French tanks and motorized cavalry from counter-attacking with some success on 13 and 14 May, but hampered the movements of the French infantry so much that positions recaptured could not be held.

Furthermore, on 14 May Army Group A redoubled its threat to the Ninth Army's front by passing infantry across the Meuse at points north of Dinant and on either side of Givet.

As a result of strenuous efforts by German engineers, the 19th and 15th Panzer Corps were able to start moving tanks to the left bank of the Meuse in the early hours of 14 May. The commander of the French First Army Group, aware of the crucial importance of preventing them from doing so, had asked as early as 10 pm on 13 May that British and French bombers should be used from dawn on the following day to attack a bridge at Gaulier, in the outskirts of Sedan, which the Germans were known to be reconstructing.

The British, recognizing that the 'crucial phase' specified in their agreement with the French had arrived, were already using their medium bombers in a tactical role. They had suffered fairly heavy losses since 10 May in attacks on German columns in Luxembourg and German-held bridges across the Albert Canal. Eight of the 10 squadrons of the Advanced Air Striking Force still had the obsolescent Battle, and the Blenheims with which the other 2 squadrons and the handful of medium-bomber squadrons at home were equipped were to prove almost as vulnerable as the Battles.

On 14 May British and French bombers, attacking in relays, duly attempted to knock out the Gaulier bridge. The French provided some fighter support, but most of the opposition came from the light anti-aircraft guns with which the German armoured formations were liberally provided. The British, contributing some 90 sorties, lost 40 aircraft, the French about 50. No hits were scored on the Gaulier bridge. Further attempts to halt the German advance on the following day brought the number of sorties flown by the Advanced Air Striking Force since 10 May to roughly 200 and its losses to 73 aircraft. Two days later, a Blenheim squadron lost 11 of its 12 aircraft to German anti-aircraft guns and fighters near the Gembloux gap. The twelfth aircraft was badly damaged.

The use to be made of the British heavy-bomber force should a crisis arise on the Western Front had long been a matter of controversy. The French had always maintained that Bomber Command should be used against German troops, air bases and military communications. The British insisted, both before and after the heavy bombers were found to be unexpectedly vulnerable in daylight, that their proper role was strategic bombing. When the Air Staff gave Air Marshal Portal his first directive as Commander-in-Chief of Bomber Command on 13 April 1940 they told him that, if Germany invaded Belgium or Holland, his attacks should be directed 'in the first instance' against targets in the Ruhr, but added with a kind of artless cunning that this would be done 'in order to cause the maximum dislocation on the lines of a German advance through the Low Countries'.[4] His Hampdens, Wellingtons and Whitleys, less 2 squadrons of Whitleys allocated to the commander of the British air forces in France, were to be used primarily against German oil refineries and synthetic oil plants or, if these could not be identified or attacked with sufficient accuracy, against more easily identifiable targets such as coking-ovens. In addition, 'harassing' attacks were to be made on marshalling yards.

No action could be taken on this directive until, on 15 May, the War Cabinet sanctioned air attacks on objectives east of the Rhine. Arrangements were then made for nearly 100 heavy bombers to be despatched to the Ruhr during the ensuing night. About three-quarters of the crews were given oil targets as their primary objectives. Hampdens, Wellingtons and Whitleys of Nos 3, 4 and 5 Groups flew upwards of 1,500 similar sorties in the course of the next 3 weeks or so. Their losses were not much more than a third as great in proportion to sorties flown as those suffered by Blenheims of No 2 Group which tried to bomb a variety of objectives in daylight.

The Air Staff did not yet know that most British bomber crews were incapable of finding their way to their target areas at night with the means provided. Even so, they can scarcely have believed that Bomber Command's efforts against oil targets and marshalling yards east of the Rhine would seriously impede the progress of German land forces either through the Low Countries or through France. After assembling their armour on the left bank of the Meuse without effective interference from the French, Army Group A's 3 Panzer corps raced westwards through a gap left open by the withdrawal of surviving formations of the Second and Ninth Armies to the flanks. By nightfall on 20 May the 2nd Panzer Division was at Abbeville and one of its tank battalions had reached the Channel coast at Noyelles. On that day, after hearing an impassioned appeal from Air Chief Marshal Dowding and after Dowding had warned the Air Ministry that the 'continued existence of the nation' depended upon 'the Royal Navy and the Fighter Command', the War Cabinet endorsed Churchill's decision that no more fighter squadrons should leave Britain for bases in France, no matter how serious the situation on the far side of the Channel might become. On 19 and 20 May the bulk of the Air Component of the British Expeditionary Force returned to the United Kingdom. Three British fighter squadrons remained in France with the Advanced Air Striking Force.

German air power showed its might when the Luftwaffe's 300 serviceable dive-bombers helped Rundstedt's armour to break through the French defences on the Meuse at points 60 miles apart. Its limitations were shown when the armoured formations were racing to the sea with flanks and rear uncovered. At a time when Hitler was torn between jubilation and premonitions of disaster, the Luftwaffe made strenuous attempts to prevent the Allies from redisposing their forces on either side of Rundstedt's line of advance. Repeated bombing of Allied communications caused some rail cuts and enforced vexatious diversions, but did not prevent the Allied armies from taking up positions from the Sambre to the Scarpe at Arras in the north, from Longuyon and Montmédy along the Aisne and the Somme to the Channel coast in the south. Rail cuts were repaired with 'phenomenal' speed, road convoys were 'kept in motion day and night'. South of the Panzer corridor an exceptionally well-developed network of roads and railways gave the Allies an almost unlimited choice of alternative routes; in the north traffic was so little impeded by the German breakthrough and the attentions of the Luftwaffe that 178 trains ran on the day after Rundstedt's armour reached the coast.[5]

From 17 or 18 May to 22 or 23 May Rundstedt's leading formations were extremely vulnerable to counter-attacks from north and south. As the Panzer divisions advanced, they became separated by increasing gaps from the infantry divisions coming up behind them. Moreover, they and the few motorized infantry divisions which followed them after an interval of 2 or 3 days themselves became increasingly strung out, since troops had to be detached to guard inordinately long flanks. As late as 23 May, when the 19th Panzer Corps on the German left was advancing on Dunkirk, Calais and Boulogne, only 2 divisions of the 14th Motorized Corps were available to defend the right bank of the Somme, in addition to numerous bridgeheads on the left bank, over a distance of 75 miles from Péronne to the sea.

The French High Command recognized that opportunities of scoring a notable success existed, but was unable to seize them. For some days after the break-through on the Meuse, General Georges believed that Rundstedt's armoured formations could be stopped before they reached the sea. He tried to head them off instead of cutting in behind them. Late on 18 May he issued the first order in which he admitted that 'containment' of the enemy's advance might not be possible. At the same time he proposed that on the following day the incomplete 4th Armoured Division (Colonel Charles de Gaulle) should attack northwards from Laon towards Crécy-sur-Serre and that the mechanized cavalry divisions which had covered the First Army's advance to the Gembloux gap should push southwards from the Sensée towards Cambrai and Saint Quentin. When the time came, the cavalry divisions could not move because their tanks had been dispersed among infantry units on the army commander's orders. The 4th Armoured Division reached the strongly-held crossings of the Serre but, unsupported by infantry, could go no further without more covering fire than its own artillery could provide. Nevertheless the division stood firm under attacks by dive-bombers. Thus there is some foundation for the criticism that it was not lack of air power which ruled out effective counter-attacks on 19 May – although the Allies did lack air power – but lack of foresight at the higher levels of command.

Gamelin showed, on the whole, more insight than Georges, but was no more able than he to shape events. As early as 13 May he received the impression that Georges and his staff had allowed the collapse of the Belgian defences on the Albert Canal to blind them to the seriousness of the situation on the Meuse. He found it regrettable that Georges had allowed himself to be caught with no reserves within striking distance of Sedan, learned with astonishment on 14 May that reinforcements were still being sent to the First Army, and was again astonished when he found on the following day that the whole of the Ninth Army was being pulled back. By 18 May he felt that Georges, who was thought never fully to have recovered from wounds inflicted on him at the time of the assassination of King Alexander of Yugoslavia and Louis Barthou in 1934, was physically unequal to his task. Yet he hesitated to replace him and was even reluctant to tell him what to do. On 19 May he gave Georges an 'instruction' which called upon him to launch vigorous counter-attacks from north and south, but in order to spare his feelings prefaced it with soothing words which enabled Georges to declare afterwards that he did not regard it as an order.

Less than 12 hours after signing this instruction, Gamelin was replaced as Chief of Staff for National Defence and Commander-in-Chief, Land Forces, by the veteran General Maxime Weygand. Weygand, assuming effective command on the day when the Germans reached the sea, came to the conclusion that thrusts in both directions along the axis Arras – Bapaume – Péronne would give him a favourable opportunity of restoring contact between the northern and southern groups of armies and of cutting Rundstedt's communications with his forward troops.

On 21 May Weygand travelled by air across the corridor for the purpose of persuading the British to commit their entire force to an advance towards Bapaume from the salient they held at Arras, and the Belgians to make this possible by extending their line and standing in a covering position. After conferring with the King of the Belgians he held a separate conference with the commander of the First Army Group, to whom Georges had delegated the responsibility for liaison with the Allies which Gamelin had entrusted to him. On the way back to his command post after taking leave of Weygand at Ypres, the army group commander was fatally injured in a road accident. He lingered for 2 days without regaining consciousness, and his successor was not formally appointed, or relieved of the full-time appointment he was holding, until late on 25 May.

Almost at the very moment when Weygand began his conference with the Belgians, the British launched an attack towards Bapaume which had been arranged on the previous day. A French infantry corps supported by mechanized cavalry was to have advanced simultaneously from Douai towards Cambrai, but was not ready. Two British light infantry battalions, a battalion of motor-cyclists and 2 tank battalions with 74 tanks were supported on the left by elements of 1 French cavalry division. They inflicted heavy losses on the 7th Panzer Division, captured 400 prisoners and a number of villages from which they afterwards withdrew, and greatly alarmed the 39th (formerly the 15th) Panzer Corps and the German High Command.

The British Commander-in-Chief, Lord Gort, had not been warned in good time of Weygand's arrival. He spent the afternoon with his troops and did not return to his headquarters until 8 pm. Weygand had almost made up his mind to spend the night at Ypres rather than leave without seeing him when he was told that Calais was being bombed. Fearing that his aircraft and its escort might not be able to take off from the neighbouring airfield at Saint Inglevert and that this might prevent him from reaching Paris in time for a conference on the following day if he stayed until the morning, he decided to leave almost at once in a destroyer. Less than 3 hours after his arrival at Ypres he departed without transacting the most important part of the business he had come to do.

In these circumstances, and especially after the failure of the French to advance on 21 May, it was not likely that any Frenchman junior to Weygand would manage to convince Gort that his entire force should be committed to Weygand's plan. Nor could the Belgians safely have relieved the British of the whole of their defensive commitments at a time when both the Belgian Army and the British Expeditionary Force were threatened by Bock's advance through central Belgium. On the other hand, the distance from Arras to the Somme was less than 30 miles. Gort was quite willing to contribute 2 infantry divisions and his tank brigade to an advance on Bapaume and Cambrai in partnership with infantry and mechanized cavalry of the French First Army. In the light of the success achieved by the British on 21 May, it seemed reasonable to assume that such a force would stand a good chance of reaching its objectives. If 'all available forces', including French mechanized cavalry and the newly-arrived and incomplete British 1st Armoured Division, made a simultaneous sortie from the Somme, the corridor might well be breached and at worst the Germans would be given a good fright.

However, before any such plan could be put into effect it would have to be translated into orders on which the various commanders could act and which they would accept. Between the afternoon of 21 May and the night of 25/26 May no such orders could be issued so far as the forces north of the corridor were concerned because no one was competent to issue them. The commander of the French First Army visited Gort's headquarters on 22 May in the hope of concerting plans for an attack on the following day, but he had no authority to tell the Allies what they ought to do. He found that both the British and the Belgians were making tactical withdrawals and that no joint offensive would be possible before 24 May.

On the day of his visit the First Army launched, on a restricted scale, the attack planned for the previous day. One infantry regiment and 2 reconnaissance groups of a mechanized cavalry division were given the task of establishing a small bridgehead beyond the Sensée as the first step towards an advance by the whole division. The infantry regiment reached its objectives without difficulty after skirmishing with German infantry, and the reconnaissance groups went as far as the outskirts of Cambrai. The troops stood firm under air attacks. Nevertheless the army commander, on learning that German reinforcements were reaching the neighbourhood, ordered the whole force to withdraw north of the Sensée and the bridges to be blown behind it.

On the same day the Germans began their drive to the Channel ports and against the western flank of the northern group of Allied armies. By the evening of 23 May German troops were within sight of the outskirts of Béthune. Gort withdrew from the Arras salient that night to escape encirclement, but was still willing to contribute to a counter-attack towards the Somme. The commander of the French First Army now proposed to begin on 26 May by recapturing the bridgehead he had occupied and relinquished on 22 May. On the following day 1 French and 2 British infantry divisions would advance on Péronne and 2 French infantry divisions on Bapaume. French cavalry would cover the flanks.

However, on 25 May Bock began to break into the Belgian positions on the Lys with the obvious intention – confirmed by a captured document – of driving a wedge between the Belgians and the British and cutting Gort's communications with his only remaining port of supply at Dunkirk. On that day Gort made the crucial decision to pull back the 2 divisions he was holding in readiness for a counter-attack and use them in a defensive role near Ypres. The French then agreed that the First Army, the British Expeditionary Force and the Belgian Army should regroup in a large bridgehead covering Dunkirk.

Since the arrival of the Germans at Amiens and Abbeville the British Expeditionary Force had been cut off from its bases in Normandy and Brittany and had been obliged to go on half rations. Gort's Chief of Staff, Lieutenant-General Sir Henry Pownall, had mentioned to the War Office on 19 May the possibility that troops might have to be withdrawn from France by way of Dunkirk and any other ports in the neighbourhood of the Dover Strait which might be open. The Admiralty had begun on the following day to frame a plan to meet a situation which still seemed unlikely to arise. Should Operation Dynamo, as it was called, be put into effect, fighter aircraft would cover the embarkation area from bases in Kent. In the meantime fighters of the Air Component continued, after their withdrawal to the United Kingdom on 19 and 20 May, to support Allied troops in the neighbourhood of Calais, Boulogne and Saint Omer.

The Dunkirk bridgehead was bounded on the west by a line of canals and canalized rivers running inland from Gravelines past Saint Omer and Aire to Béthune. Forward units of Rundstedt's armour approached the Aa canal and Béthune on 23 May, but were delayed by air attacks. Rundstedt gave orders on that day that 'to allow the situation to clarify itself and to keep our forces concentrated' the armoured formations should halt on reaching the canal line. This was an understandable precaution since they had suffered heavy mechanical wastage during the advance from the Meuse and were entering an area in which, according to General von Kleist, the Allies had air superiority.

Hitler arrived at Rundstedt's command post on the following day. After the situation had been explained to him, he agreed that the armoured formations should not go beyond the canal line and is said to have insisted that units which had crossed it should be withdrawn. Army Group A, hitherto intended to play the part of hammer to Army Group B's anvil, was now given the task of preventing the Allied armies from escaping westwards while Army Group B and the Luftwaffe attacked them. Should the Allies try to escape by sea, the Luftwaffe would sink their ships.

The motives which impelled Hitler to adopt this plan and Rundstedt to acquiesce in it or even suggest it have been hotly canvassed, but there is no reason to doubt that Hitler, at any rate, was strongly influenced by the knowledge that he would soon need Rundstedt's armour to complete the discomfiture of the French by attacking the Allied armies south of the Somme. The order forbidding the armoured formations to cross the canal line was afterwards rescinded, but a visit to forward positions on 28 May seems to have convinced General Guderian that the use of tanks inside the Allied bridgehead would entail needless losses.

On the Allied side, the British and the French agreed about 10 am on 26 May that the withdrawal of the First Army, the British Expeditionary Force and the Belgian Army to the bridgehead should be completed during the next 2 nights. Later in the day it became clear that the Belgian Army – soon to surrender unconditionally – was in no state to make an orderly retreat and that its disintegration would expose the British flank and rear. At 6.57 pm the British Admiralty gave the order for Operation Dynamo to begin. About 45,00 men could, it was hoped, be shipped from Dunkirk during the 48 hours which were expected to elapse before embarkation became impossible.

Responsibility for launching air attacks on the bridgehead and interfering with the embarkation and passage of Allied troops was eagerly accepted on behalf of the Luftwaffe by Reichsmarschall Göring. Göring delegated the task to Luftflotte 2, hitherto responsible for supporting Army Group B's advance into Belgium and Holland. At the same time he gave Luftflotte 2 the lion's share of the formations used by Luftflotte 3 since 10 May to support Army Group A's thrust from the Rhineland to the Channel coast. The Luftflotte commander, General Albert Kesselring, afterwards expressed the opinion that the task assigned to his command 'in recognition of its services' could not have been discharged with success even by a fresh air fleet and was manifestly beyond the capacity of units and formations which had been continuously in action or on the move for 3 weeks.

In the last week of May some 550 German single-seater fighters were available for operations from bases in northern France and the Low Countries. The British had some 600 modern single-seater fighters in all parts of the United Kingdom, and roughly a third of these were at the disposal of Air Vice-

Marshal K. R. Park, commanding No 11 Group in the south-eastern counties. A limiting factor on both sides was the number of short-range fighter units which could operate at one time or in swift succession from the relatively few bases within reach of the crucial area. The same factor limited the effort of Kesselring's dive-bombers. His medium bombers, in any case vulnerable unless well supported by fighters, were hampered on a number of occasions during the next few days by clouds which obscured their objectives, and at times by smoke from burning oil tanks.

On 27 May Park's fighters, patrolling at an average strength of 1 squadron, made 287 sorties over north-east France and destroyed ten German aircraft in the immediate neighbourhood of Dunkirk for the loss of 14 of their own. Spitfires were used for the first time over Allied territory. Bombing destroyed a large part of the built-up area of Dunkirk, but the outer harbour remained more or less intact and British and French troops in the bridgehead came to little harm. Nevertheless the outlook seemed by the evening so unpromising that no ships were sent into the harbour during the night and boats were used to lift men from beaches east of the town to waiting naval vessels and auxiliaries. That night the Air Ministry warned Air Chief Marshal Dowding that the following day was likely to be 'the most critical ever experienced by the British Army' and called upon him to provide 'continuous fighter patrols in strength' over the embarkation area 'from first light until darkness'.

In the early hours of 28 May ships were once more ordered to the outer harbour, while others continued to embark troops ferried from the beaches. The beaches were also used for the unloading of supplies of water, food and ammunition. Dowding, mindful of his experience at the Somme and aware that Park's fighters had sometimes been seriously outnumbered on the previous day, disregarded the Air Ministry's demand for continuous cover by allowing Park to despatch his squadrons mostly in pairs at the cost of leaving brief intervals between patrols. At the same time a small addition to Park's strength enabled him to step up his effort to 321 sorties. A marked decline in the Luftwaffe's activity in the afternoon was clearly attributable, at least in part, to poor visibility, but was thought at the time to indicate that Park was gaining the upper hand. At the end of the day the naval authorities expressed their satisfaction with the cover provided, and the demand for continuity was dropped.

The 48 hours during which embarkation was expected to take place had now expired, but the outer harbour was still in use, the bridgehead was still intact, and the beaches were thronged with troops awaiting their turn for embarkation. The Admiralty continued its efforts with a fleet augmented by warships and auxiliaries summoned from bases as far away as Rosyth, Dutch coasters which had escaped to England before the fall of the Netherlands, and large numbers of boats and small craft, including privately-owned yachts and motor-boats, from every river, port and estuary in the south of England. Many of these were manned wholly or partly by civilian volunteers. British and French troops were embarked in equal numbers from the moment when the French military authorities, at first reluctant to allow their troops to depart in British ships, allowed them to go.

On 29 May Park took full advantage of the latitude he was given in consequence of the Air Ministry's latest instructions to his chief. Using up to 4 squadrons at a time to patrol the embarkation area and roadsteads, he did his best to synchronize the arrival of his formations with the ebb and flow of shipping but left intervals of 40–90 minutes between patrols. Three out of 5 large German formations sent to attack shipping in the afternoon were intercepted, but the other two were not. In the course of the day at least 7 ships, including a destroyer, were sunk by bombing, and at least 3, including 2 destroyers, by other means. Many other ships, including 7 destroyers and a sloop, were damaged, most of them by bombs. Nevertheless the number of men who reached England safely was by far the largest hitherto carried in one day.

Still more were carried on the following day, when an overcast sky and a light mist brought a partial respite from bombing, and an even greater number on 31 May in consequence of the arrival of large numbers of small boats which were used to lift men from the beaches. Kesselring's forces resumed heavy air attacks at dawn on 1 June and sank many ships, including one French and three British destroyers, but almost as many men were carried to safety as on the previous day.

At dawn on 2 June it was estimated that some 6,000 British and perhaps ten times as many French troops were still in the bridgehead. In view of the previous day's losses, embarkation was suspended until nightfall, when practically all the remaining British and some 20,000 French troops were successfully embarked. A fresh calculation then showed that the number of French troops still defending the bridgehead was not 40,000 but about 30,000. Between 10.30 pm on 3 June and the early hours of 4 June about 50 warships, naval auxiliaries and small craft entered the harbour and succeeded in embarking all but about 4,000 who were unable to disengage. When the last British ship, the destroyer *Shikari*, left Dunkirk at 3.40 am with 383 troops aboard, the Germans were only 3 miles from the harbour.

The return of the *Shikari* brought the number of British and French troops carried from Dunkirk and its neighbourhood to the United Kingdom since the Germans reached Abbeville on 20 May to nearly 370,000. All except some 27,000 withdrawn before Operation Dynamo began had been rescued in the teeth of the Luftwaffe and under the noses of 2 German army groups. A further 140,000 British troops serving south of the Panzer corridor or on the lines of communication were afterwards withdrawn, with nearly 50,000 Allied troops, through French ports south and west of the Somme.

In the course of Operation Dynamo the British Fighter Command, flying an average of roughly 300 sorties a day over the embarkation area and adjacent waters, lost 106 aircraft and some 80 pilots. The Luftwaffe lost between 26 May and 4 June 156 aircraft, including 5 whose loss was not attributable to hostile action and 19 known to have crashed at places some considerable distance away. The British, believing at the time that 262 German aircraft had been destroyed in the immediate neighbourhood of Dunkirk, somewhat exaggerated Fighter Command's success in its first major conflict with the German fighter force. The fact remained that the Luftwaffe, notwithstanding its numerical superiority and its reputation for ruthless might, had manifestly and incontestably failed to dominate the skies in the crucial area.

(*Above left*) The first military observation baloon: *L'Entreprenante* at the Battle of Fleurus, 26 June 1794

(*Above right*) Man-lifting kites developed by S. F. Cody from the box-kite of Lawrence Hargrave

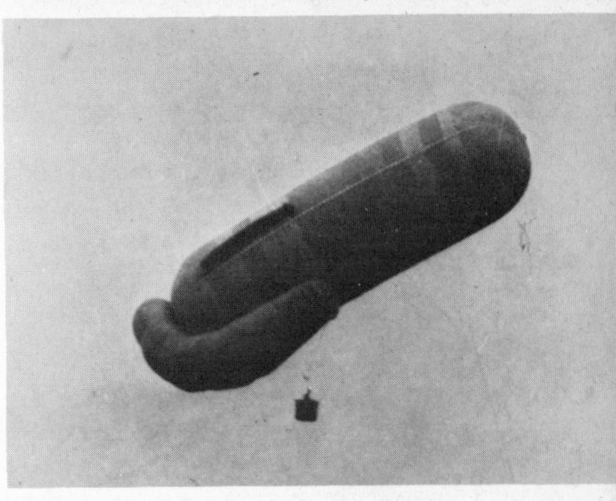

(*Right*) Parseval-Sigsfeld kite-balloon, c. 1900

(*Below*) British barrage balloon, Second World War

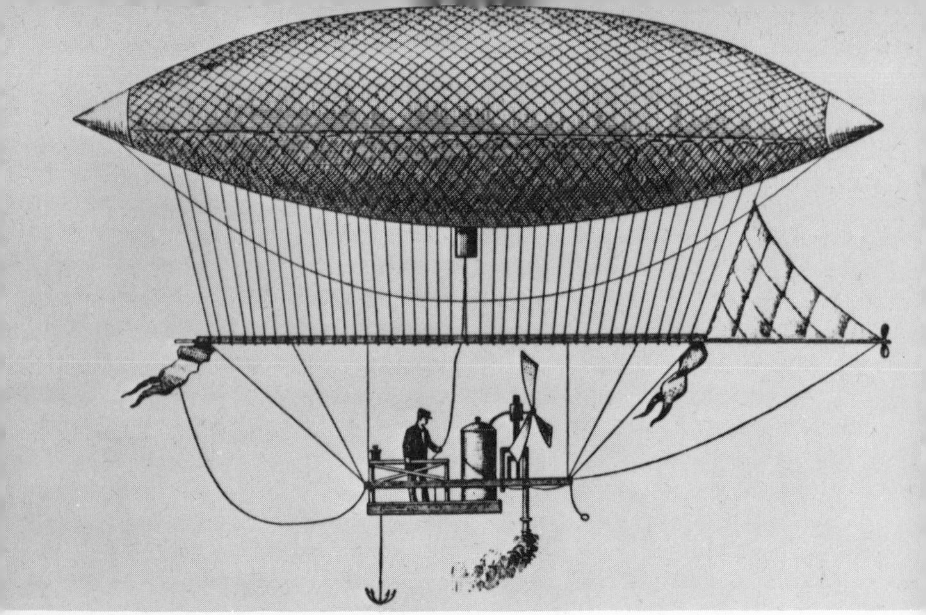

(*Above*) The first successful man-carrying powered aircraft: Henri Giffard's Aerial Steamer of 1852

(*Center*) Lebaudy airship, c. 1902

(*Bottom*) Zeppelin LZ.3 (Z.1) of 1906-7

(*Above*) German naval Zeppelin L.13, c. 1915

(*Right*) United States naval airship *Macon* of 1933

(*Below*) United States naval blimp, post-1940

(*Top*) Clément Ader's *Eole* of 1890

(*Center*) Voisin-Farman of 1907-8

(*Left*) Wilbur and Orville Wright's *Wright A* of 1908

Opposite:

(*Above*) Louis Blériot's *Blériot XI* of 1909

(*Center*) L. Béchereau's *Deperdussin-Monocoque* of 1912-13

(*Bottom*) Igor Sikorsky's *Ilya Mourometz* of 1913-14

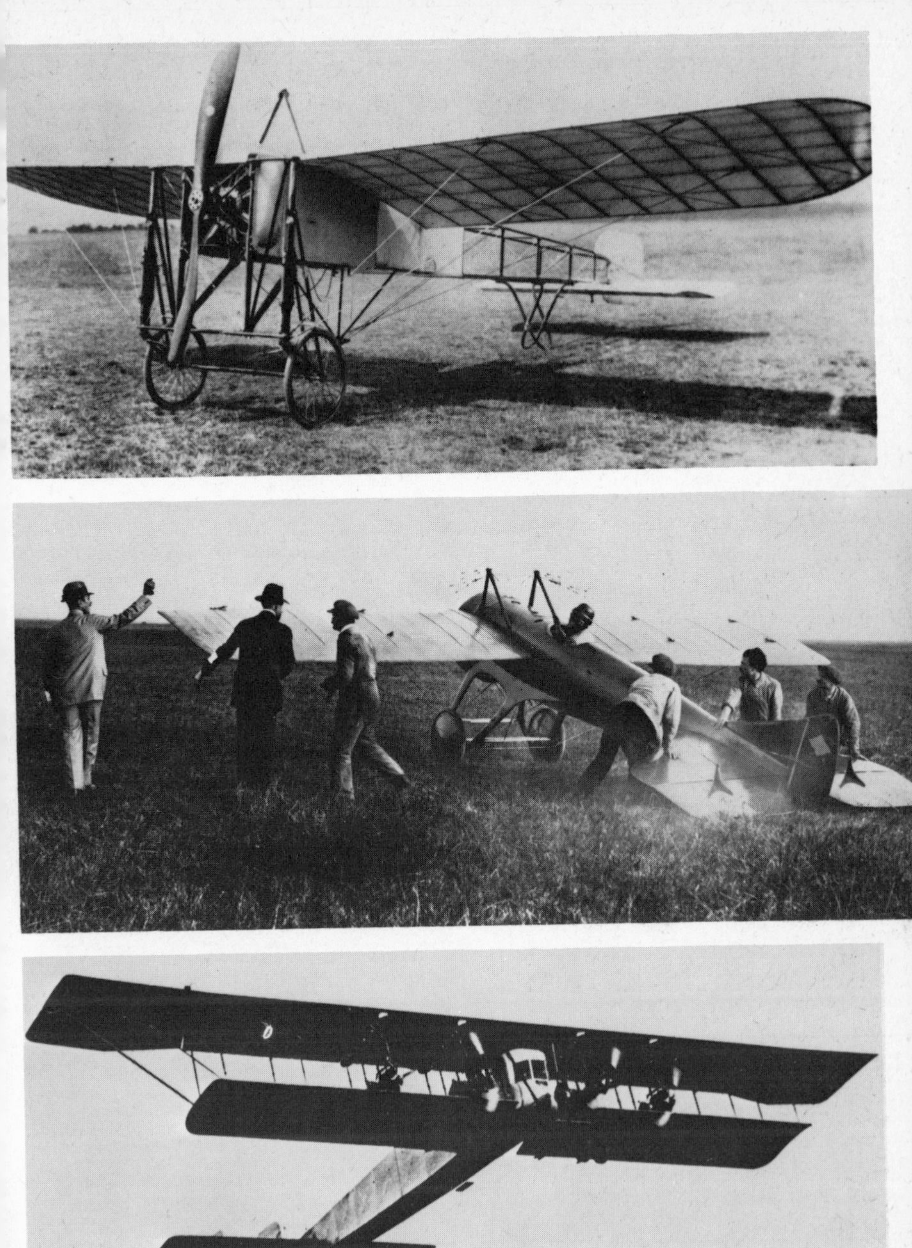

(*Top*) The Royal Aircraft Factory's B.S.1 of 1912
(*Center*) Sopwith Tabloid of 1913
(*Below*) An early fighter: the Fokker E.1 of 1915

(*Above*) Albatros D.XI (German)
(*Center left*) Ansaldso S.V.A.6 (Italian)
(*Center right*) S.P.A.D.VII (French)
(*Bottom*) Bristol F.26 (British)

(*Above*) Hawker Fury, the first military aircraft to exceed 200 mph
(*Center*) Bristol Blenheim, prototype from which the Blenheim Mark I bomber and bomber-reconnaissance aircraft were developed.
(*Bottom*) Polikarpov I-16, Russian monoplane fighter used in the Spanish Civil War

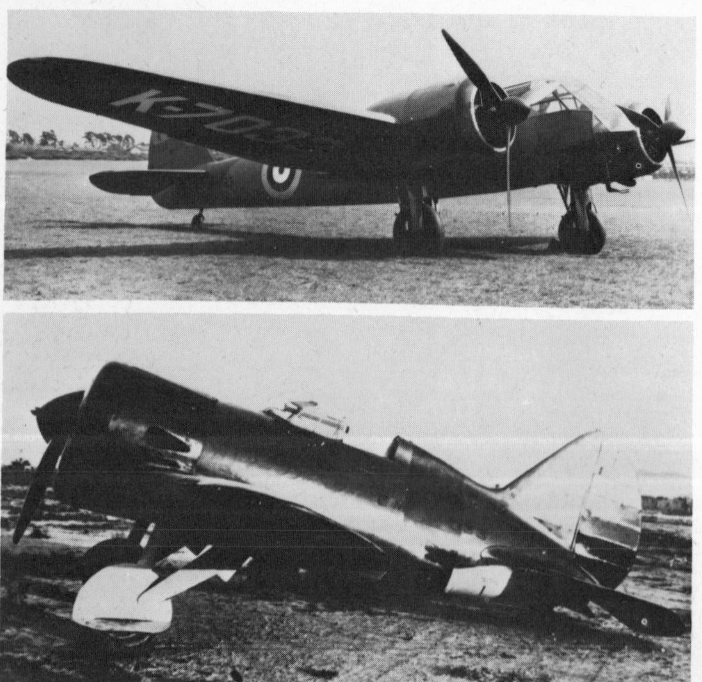

(*Top*) Junkers Ju.87 bomber (German)
(*Above center*) Junkers Ju.88 medium bomber and bomber-reconnaissance aircraft (German)
(*Below center*) Avro Lancaster heavy bomber (British)
(*Below*) Boeing B-17 heavy bomber (U.S.)

(*Above*) Hawker Hurricane (British)
(*Above center*) Supermarine Spitfires (British)
(*Below center*) Bristol Beaufighter (British)
(*Bottom*) Messerschmitt Me. (BF) 109E (German)

(*Top*) Focke-Wulf FW.190 (German)
(*Above center*) Macchi M.C.205 (Italian)
(*Below center*) Republic P-47 (Thunderbolt) (U.S.)
(*Bottom*) Mikoyan and Gurevich MiG-3 (Russian)

(*Above*) Gloster Meteor (British)
(*Center*) Messerschmitt Me.262 (German)
(*Bottom*) Mikoyan and Gurevich MiG-15 (Russian)

(*Top*) North American F-86 (Sabre) (U.S.)
(*Center*) Hawker Hunter (British)
(*Below*) Dassault Super-Mystère B.2 (French)

725
ROYAL NAVY
VL

(*Opposite top*) Lockheed F-104 (Starfighter), U.S. 1,450-mph fighter made under license in a number of countries; photograph shows the first of a batch built in Canada for the Royal Canadian Air Force
(*Opposite center*) BAC Lightning, British fighter and ground-attack aircraft designed to carry two guided missiles at more than twice the speed of sound
(*Opposite bottom*) McDonnell Phantom II, U.S. fighter, ground-attack, and reconnaissance aircraft; interceptor version believed to be the fastest aircraft in service today
(*Above*) English Electric Canberra B.2, fast bomber in service in Britain from 1954 and manufactured under license in the U.S. as the Martin B-57
(*Below*) Boeing B-52A, American multi-jet strategic bomber with provision for refueling in flight

(*Above*) Avro Vulan B.2, British delta-wing bomber in service from 1960

(*Below*) Dassault Mirage IV, French two-seater strategic bomber designed for nuclear bombing

7

THE BATTLE OF BRITAIN

On the eve of Operation Dynamo, the British Chiefs of Staff prepared at the Government's request an estimate of what might happen if France were knocked out of the war and Britain and the British Empire had to fight alone.

This was a task they might have tackled with better prospects of success had they been allowed to postpone it for a week or two. In the third week of May the new administration had been in office so short a time that the beneficial effects of all-party Government on industrial relations and hence on output were only just beginning to be felt. The causes of the French collapse on the Meuse and the failure of the Belgian covering positions on the Albert Canal to delay the Germans even for a day were not yet fully understood. Narvik was still in German hands. No one could yet say whether attempts to extricate the British Expeditionary Force from France would succeed, or what the cost of Operation Dynamo would be if it were tried.

Not surprisingly, the Chiefs of Staff took a gloomier view of the outlook than events were to justify. The withdrawal of Allied forces from Narvik and attempts to withdraw even a small part of the Expeditionary Force by way of Dunkirk were expected to lead to calamitous naval losses. The contributions likely to be made to future German campaigns by airborne forces and so-called Fifth Column activities were somewhat overestimated. The Chiefs of Staff were deeply conscious, too, of the difficulty of replacing both the weapons and vehicles which would have to be left behind if the Expeditionary Force withdrew from Continental Europe under pressure, and the hundreds of aircraft lost or likely to be lost by the time the withdrawal was over. Painfully aware that the home defence divisions had not nearly enough tanks, anti-tank guns and field artillery to deal effectively with a well-found German expeditionary force, they were inclined to underrate the difficulty which the Germans would experience in transporting such a force across an uncommanded sea.

The Chiefs of Staff did, however, recognize that the Germans, precisely because of their naval weakness, were likely to preface any attempt at invasion with heavy air attacks. 'The crux of the whole problem,' they wrote, 'is the air defence of this country.' The most urgent task was, therefore, to find enough fighter aircraft to replace losses and create a substantial stored reserve. This threatened to be extremely difficult. By the end of May about 430 fighters had been lost since 10 May. Output had risen from an average of 132 fighters a month during the first seven months of the war to 256 in April, and the expectation when the Chiefs of Staff drew up their memorandum was that 261 would be delivered in May. Since virtually all these aircraft were needed to replace losses or had gone to form new squadrons, there were practically no reserves at the end of May apart from an immediate reserve equivalent to roughly a third of first-line strength.

The Chiefs of Staff proposed that the Government should tackle the problem by doing its utmost to persuade the United States Government to provide as many aircraft as possible, including fighters 'from stocks now held by the United States Army and Navy'. To adapt American fighters to British needs, train British pilots and mechanics to fly and service them, and organize a constant flow of replacements and spares would, however, have taken many weeks, perhaps even many months. Lord Beaverbrook, the newly-appointed Minister of Aircraft Production, felt sure that the only sound course was to increase the output from British factories. This was done. The Chiefs of Staff expected when they drew up their forecast that 882 fighters would be delivered in May, June and July. In the outcome, 1,267 were delivered. Both the effective strength of the British fighter force and its capacity to withstand losses increased markedly during the summer months. By the second week in August, when Fighter Command found itself committed to a major battle, about 750 fighters were immediately available for active operations, about 350 were undergoing repairs or routine maintenance in squadron or station workshops, and nearly 300 Hurricanes and Spitfires were ready for immediate issue from aircraft storage units to replace losses.

Some anxiety was felt after the return of the Air Component

from France about the supply of trained fighter pilots. In the middle of June Fighter Command had 1,094 pilots towards an establishment of 1,456. On 3 August the Command had 1,434 pilots, and on 10 August 1,396, towards an establishment of 1,588. At no time in August or September did the number fall below 1,377, but it was not until October that the current establishment figure was exceeded.

On the German side, the Luftwaffe used part of its bomber strength in the first few days of June to attack aircraft factories in the outskirts of Paris and oil refineries at Marseilles. Thereafter until the French surrendered some 3 weeks later its chief task was to support drives across and beyond the Somme and the Aisne by Bock's and Rundstedt's army groups. Italy entered the war on 10 June but at first stood on the defensive. Italian troops crossed the French frontier at a number of points in Savoy and the Maritime Alps towards the end of the month, but were unable to push far into French territory.

At the end of June many units of Luftflotten 2 and 3 returned to Germany to rest and re-equip. Little was done to increase the hitting-power of the bomber force in preparation for future campaigns, or to raise the output of military aircraft in general much beyond the figure of 800 aircraft a month attained some 8 or 9 months earlier. German strategists continued to put much faith in the dive-bomber, but only about 400 dive-bombers were available in Luftflotten 2 and 3 in the middle of July, and only about three-quarters of these were fit for immediate use. Moreover, experience had shown that these aircraft, although capable of attacking even small targets such as gunposts and groups of tanks with great precision in favourable circumstances, were extremely vulnerable to attacks by fighters and to fire from the ground.

The Luftwaffe did, however, possess a valuable asset in the shape of a system of radio beams which could be used to guide bombers to their objectives at night or in cloudy weather. In the early summer of 1940 German aircraft made a number of small-scale night attacks on objectives in various parts of the United Kingdom for the purpose of trying out and perfecting the system. These experiments enabled British scientists to detect the beams and devise counter-measures. The British were also helped by indiscreet statements made by prisoners of war, and by other items of intelligence. Dr R. V. Jones, a physicist attached to the Intelligence Branch of the Air Ministry, played a leading part in persuading sceptical colleagues and statesmen that the beams existed and were not a hoax.

In July Hitler made up his mind to prepare for, and if necessary to carry out, an invasion of Britain before comitting himself to the assault on Russia which he also considered in that month.[1] Mussolini offered through his Foreign Minister, Count Ciano, to contribute up to 30 divisions and 10 air squadrons. The offer of Italian land forces was declined, and the Italian bomber, fighter and reconnaissance aircraft for which the Luftwaffe agreed to find bases in Belgium did not arrive until October. In the meantime 13 divisions of the German Army, intended to serve as the first wave of an invasion force, moved by road and rail from various parts of France to the coast facing England, the last of them arriving on 3 August. The German naval authorities, calculating that well over 150 large transports and some 2,000–3,000 or more barges, tugs, trawlers, motor-boats and fishing smacks would have to be assembled between Rotterdam and Le Havre before the first wave could be carried to England, were unable to promise that their preparations would be completed before the third week in September. Göring believed that a month or so of heavy air attacks should suffice to defeat the Royal Air Force. He was therefore content to begin his grand assault on 10 August, although his forces were ready in July. Later the opening date was put back to 13 August. The code-name *Adlertag* was given to the first day of the all-out air offensive.

The essence of the Luftwaffe's plan was that Luftflotten 2 and 3, based respectively in the Low Countries and France east and north of the Seine and in France west of the Seine, were to stike in daylight on 4 successive days at airfields in the south of England. From the second day Luftflotte 5, based in Denmark and Norway, was to supplement their efforts by attacking airfields in the north-eastern counties. By this means the British would, it was hoped, be prevented from keeping up their fighter strength in the south by moving squadrons from the north. Four days of intensive air attacks should, in Göring's estimation, suffice to cripple the air defences south of a line from London to Gloucester. Daylight attacks would be extended after the fourth day to all airfields within reach, and aircraft factories would be bombed both by day and at night. Once the Royal Air Force was knocked out, the whole might of the Luftwaffe would be available to keep British warships from the invasion area, hammer the coast defences and hamper the movement of reserves.

On 10 August Luftflotten 2 and 3 had ready for immediate use

4 The Battle of Britain, Summer 1940

against the United Kingdom 875 long-range bombers, 316 dive-bombers and ground-attack aircraft, 702 single-seater fighters and 227 heavy fighters. Luftflotte 5 had 123 long-range bombers and 34 heavy fighters.* The single-seater fighters were intended to give indirect support to bomber and dive-bomber formations by making offensive sweeps, but could reach only the south-eastern counties. For close escort and for direct or indirect support in more distant areas, commanders of bomber formations were expected to rely on heavy fighters. These were so few that the planning of offensive missions in daylight was extremely difficult.

As a curtain-raiser to the main offensive, Luftflotten 2 and 3 opened in the second week of July a series of attacks on ports and shipping. These were intended to wear down the enemy's fighter force and induce him to thin out his light naval forces in the invasion area. The British responded to them by accelerating the diversion of ocean shipping to west coast ports, changing the organization and timing of their local convoys, and moving to Portsmouth a number of destroyers hitherto based on Dover. They lost 3 destroyers and some 30,000 tons of merchant shipping, but destroyed 286 German aircraft between 10 July and 12 August for the loss of 150 of their own fighters. About 4 million tons of merchant shipping entered or left United Kingdom ports and harbours during the period covered by the attacks.

August 13 began inauspiciously for the Luftwaffe. A last-minute order postponing the start of the offensive was issued in the light of a report which indicated that the weather was likely to improve as the day went on. It reached some recipients too late for aircraft already despatched to be recalled. Some bombers flew to Britain without fighter support, some fighters made aimless sweeps after failing to make rendezvous with the bombers they were to have met. Attempts in the afternoon to complete the programme laid down for *Adlertag* were only slightly more successful. In the course of the day the Luftwaffe made 1,485 sorties and lost 45 aircraft. Fighter Command made 700 sorties and lost 13 aircraft but only 7 pilots. Three airfields as well as docks and

* Reconnaissance aircraft and aircraft not within striking distance of the United Kingdom, or reserved for a purely defensive role, have been excluded from these figures.

warehouses at Southampton were fairly seriously damaged, but none of these was a fighter station. The worst-hit airfield was fit for use again within 10 hours.

The programme scheduled for the second day of the main offensive was postponed until 15 August since clouds covered much of England on 14 August. Scattered raids on 14 August cost the Luftwaffe 19 aircraft. Fighter Command, making some 500 sorties, lost 8 aircraft. A fighter station at Manston, near Ramsgate, was damaged and the Goodwin light vessel, valuable to seamen and airmen on both sides, was sunk.

The role assigned to Luftflotte 5 on 15 August confronted its commander, General Hans-Jürgen Stumpff, with the difficult task of organizing daylight raids by relatively slow Heinkel 111 and faster Junkers 88 bombers on objectives far beyond the reach of single-seater fighters and barely attainable by heavy fighters. Making the best of a bad job, he fitted his few heavy fighters with supplementary fuel tanks at the cost of leaving their dorsal armament unmanned to save weight, assigned them as close escort to the Heinkels, and sent his faster bombers across the North Sea from Denmark without escort or support.

Radar gave the British ample warning of both raids and helped them to destroy 16 of Stumpff's bombers and 7 of his fighters at no cost to themselves. About a dozen Whitleys were destroyed on the ground at a bomber station in Yorkshire, but fighter stations went unscathed. The failure of the British to destroy a higher proportion of Stumpff's force did, however, lend some weight to the criticism that the Hurricane and the Spitfire would have been even more effective interceptor-destroyers than they were had they been armed with 20-millimetre cannon instead of ·303-inch machine-guns. The American-designed Browning machine-gun had been chosen, on expert advice, as the standard armament for British fighters because a fast rate of fire, in which the Browning excelled, was deemed essential if bombers were to be brought down by such short bursts as fighter pilots were expected to be able to fire while they held hostile aircraft in their sights. Hurricanes and Spitfires armed with Hispano-Suiza cannon were under development, but only a few cannon Spitfires and no cannon Hurricanes were in service before the autumn of 1940.

Luftflotten 2 and 3 were more successful but they, too, were heavily punished by the defences. Their contributions brought the Luftwaffe's effort for the day to 1,786 sorties and its losses to 75 aircraft. Fighter Command made nearly 1,000 sorties and lost 34 aircraft. Objectives more or less severely damaged included aircraft factories at Rochester and Croydon and fighter stations at Croydon, West Malling, Middle Wallop, Martlesham, Lympne and Hawkinge. Bomber crews who attacked West Malling reported on their return to base that they had bombed Biggin Hill, while some of those who attacked Croydon believed that the airfield at which they had aimed their bombs was Redhill and others that it was Kenley.

Two more days of comparable activity, on 16 and 18 August, completed the 4-day programme on which Göring had relied to disrupt the air defences south of a line from London to Gloucester. Considerable damage was done to fighter stations at Tangmere, Kenley, Biggin Hill and elsewhere, but the effectiveness of the air defences was so little impaired that Fighter Command flew more sorties on the last of the four days than on the first of them. The Luftwaffe lost 45 aircraft on 16 August and 71 on 18 August, while Fighter Command lost 21 and 27 respectively. Altogether the Luftwaffe lost 258 aircraft between 13 and 18 August. Fighter Command lost 101.

By 19 August, and indeed earlier, it was clear to the leaders of the Luftwaffe that the heavy fighters were incapable of giving effective protection to bombers or dive-bombers. On more than one occasion when attacked by Hurricanes or Spitfires they had formed defensive circles for their own protection and had left the aircraft they were supposed to be escorting to look after themselves. As early as 15 August Göring had provoked dissension by exhorting pilots of single-seater fighters not to content themselves with offensive sweeps but to give direct support to bomber formations. He now ruled that henceforth the primary task of Luftflotten 2 and 3 must be to inflict as much damage as possible on the opposing fighter force, and that only enough bombers should be used to goad the British into action against accompanying single-seater fighters. Luftflotte 5 was to prepare for a night attack on Glasgow and Luftflotte 3, besides continuing its operations in daylight, was to prepare for a night attack on Liverpool. Neither Glasgow nor Liverpool was to be attacked without his express sanction, but such objectives as aircraft factories could and should be attacked at night, and also by day when circumstances were favourable. The Junkers 87 dive-bombers, which had proved extremely vulnerable, were to be withheld until they were needed to support landings in Britain.

On the same day Air Vice-Marshal Park of No. 11 Group warned his controllers and sector commanders against allowing his forces to be drawn into unprofitable encounters with fighters. Their main object must be to engage bombers, and they must send only 'a minimum number of squadrons' to deal with fighters. Should a threat to No. 11 Group's sector stations north of the Thames Estuary catch the group with all its squadrons off the ground, 'engaging enemy mass attacks', the adjacent No. 12 Group must be asked to send squadrons to protect the stations.

The Luftwaffe's intelligence officers believed that the British must have suffered such heavy losses recently that they could have only a few hundred fighters left. They also believed that most of these were concentrated near London and hence could be brought to action by attacks on No. 11 Group's bases, delivered chiefly from airfields in Luftflotte 2's area.

These guesses were wide of the mark. The British had replaced their losses from stored reserves, and these were still a long way from exhaustion. When a new phase of the battle opened on 24 August after a period of cloudy weather with occasional rain, Fighter Command had almost exactly the same number of aircraft fit for immediate use as on 10 August, and the disposition of its forces had changed very little in the meantime. Only about a third of its operational squadrons were stationed in Kent, Surrey, Sussex, Middlesex and Essex.

Even so, it was true that attacks on Park's bases in those counties and in Suffolk were likely to provoke a strong reaction from the British. Moreover, the tactics on which Göring insisted during the next fortnight did have a beneficial effect, from the German point of view, on the ratio between British and German losses. Small bomber formations surrounded by dense clouds of fighters proved more effective than the looser formations previously used. Park's controllers and sector commanders could not, in practice, prevent his pilots from being drawn into encounters with German fighters, no matter how much they might wish to make attacks on bombers their aim. Between 24 August and 6 September the Luftwaffe lost 380 aircraft; but Fighter Command lost 286, and on 4 or 5 days British and German losses were about equal. At the same time, the persistent bombing of Park's sector stations caused him intense anxiety. Cratered runways and perimeter tracks could be quickly repaired. The danger was that efficiency might be impaired where damage to operations rooms and landlines forced sector commanders to fall back on stand-by arrangements.

However, none of this prevented the British from continuing to replace their losses at the cost of depleting but not extinguishing their stored reserves. When the second phase of the battle ended on 6 September, Fighter Command still had approximately the same number of aircraft fit for immediate use as on 10 August, and well over 100 Hurricanes and Spitfires were ready for immediate issue from aircraft storage units. Nor was Fighter Command prevented from making on 6 September more daylight sorties than on any previous day except 30 August.

Conversely, the Luftwaffe was not in a position to replace losses on the scale of those suffered in recent weeks. The result was that, in terms of aircraft fit for immediate use, Luftflotten 2 and 3 had between them on 7 September only 798 long-range bombers, 623 single-seater fighters and 129 heavy fighters. They also had 160 dive-bombers and ground-attack aircraft, but most of these were Junkers 87 dive-bombers which they had been ordered to withhold from the battle until further notice. Luftflotte 5, having parted with its surviving long-range bombers and heavy fighters to Luftflotten 2 and 3, had nothing but a few reconnaissance and mine-laying aircraft and some single-seater fighters for local defence. Moreover, since Hitler's decision for or against invasion must be made by 17 September if landings were to be made before the autumn, the Luftwaffe had only 9 or 10 days in which to gain the stipulated air superiority with forces whose effective strength had declined by some five to six hundred aircraft since its first abortive attempt was made.

In the meantime a new factor, which played a minor but not entirely negligible part in shaping the Luftwaffe's tactics during the next stage of the battle, had come into the reckoning. On the night of 24 August about a dozen German bomber crews out of 170 despatched to various destinations in the United Kingdom were ordered to attack objectives not far from the outskirts of London. These included oil tanks at Thameshaven and aircraft factories at Rochester and Kingston. A few crews dropped bombs on central London in the belief that they were attacking their allotted targets. On the following night the British sent Hampdens and Whitleys to attack industrial targets in Berlin. Heavy attacks on Liverpool by aircraft of Luftflotte 3 followed on the last 4 nights of August. Presumably after consultation with Hitler, who said privately on 30 August that he would like to see London bombed and publicly on 4 September that British cities would be 'exterminated' in retaliation for the bombing of Berlin, the leaders of the Luftwaffe gave a prominent place to industrial targets in London in the list of objectives to be attacked by day and night during a new phase of the struggle for air supremacy due to begin about the end of the first week in September.

The chief reason for the inclusion of such targets among those to be attacked by day was, however, the belief that daylight attacks on London would induce the British to throw in every fighter they had and so enable the Luftwaffe to stage a decisive battle in the air. The bombing of residential areas in order to spread panic was proposed, but Hitler insisted that this was a measure to be adopted only as a last resort. For the present bombs must be aimed at legitimate objectives such as docks, warehouses, factories and power stations.

In London on Saturday 7 September, a committee of experts appointed to study German preparations for invasion presented a report which suggested that such preparations had reached an advanced stage. They pointed out that moon and tide would favour landings in Britain between 8 and 10 September. Air photographs showed that large numbers of barges had arrived recently at Flushing, Ostend, Dunkirk, Calais and ports further west. Long-range bombers were known to have moved from Denmark and Norway to the Low Countries and dive-bombers to be concentrated near the Straits. Finally, four men caught landing from a rowing boat had confessed that they were spies sent to report British troop movements for the benefit of the German Army.

The Chiefs of Staff considered the implications of the report at a meeting in the late afternoon. They came to the conclusion that the military authorities ought to call troops in areas where landings were likely to instant readiness. This they could do by despatching the signal 'Cromwell'; but they would then give the impression that invasion was believed to be imminent, since that was what the signal meant. The headquarters staff of the Home Forces Command reached the same conclusion in the light of an independent study of the same evidence. That evening the signal was despatched, not because the Chiefs of Staff or the staff of Home Forces were entirely convinced that invasion was imminent, but because there was no other practical means of bringing the troops to the required state of readiness. The result was that rumours began almost at once to circulate to the effect that German troops were already landing in Britain, and that a number of unauthorized measures were taken by local commanders or other functionaries. In some areas these included the calling out of the Home Guard and the ringing of church bells.

About 300 bombers of Luftflotte 2, supported by almost every available fighter, flew towards London while the meeting of the Chiefs of Staff was in progress.* Park was not at his headquarters, having been summoned to a conference at Dowding's. Nineteen squadrons of No. 11 Group despatched on the group controller's orders were joined by 4 from adjacent groups. Twenty-one squadrons engaged the enemy, 2 of them twice. Nevertheless few bombers were intercepted before they reached the target area. The Luftwaffe lost 41 aircraft, but 28 British aircraft were destroyed, 16 were badly damaged, and 17 pilots were killed or seriously wounded. About 300 tons of high-explosive and some thousands of small incendiary bombs were dropped. Objectives hit included Woolwich arsenal, Beckton gas works, the Millwall and Commercial docks, West Ham power station and oil tanks at Thameshaven. Bombs also fell near Tilbury, in many parts of London both east and west of Temple Bar, and at places as far apart as Tottenham, Croydon, Crayford (Kent) and Brentwood (Essex).

Casualties were much lighter than the civil defence authorities had been led to expect. Further visits to the London area between nightfall on 7 September and the early hours of 8 September by some 250 bombers brought the weight of high-

* Of the 623 single-seater fighters of Luftflotten 2 and 3 serviceable on 7 September, 533 were assigned to Luftflotte 2. Luftflotte 3's 90 single-seater fighters comprised 27 of a unit stationed in Brittany and 63 of Jagdgeschwader 2. Luftflotte 2 was authorized to call on Jagdgeschwader 2 in case of need, and its units were stationed close to the boundary between the two Luftflotten. Luftflotte 2 controlled all but 22 of the 129 heavy fighters serviceable on 7 September.

explosive aimed at Greater London within 12 hours to 500 tons or more. Even if only half this tonnage fell on London the number of killed and wounded ought, on the basis of calculations made by the Air Staff before the war, to have been about 12,500.[2] In fact, 430 people were killed and about 1,600 seriously injured.[3]

Luftflotte 2 renewed its daylight offensive on 9 September after a quiet day on 8 September. This time some 200 bombers were sent towards London in 2 waves. No. 11 Group put up such a stout defence that only about 90 reached the target area. Few even of these succeeded in bombing their primary targets. The Luftwaffe lost 28 aircraft, Fighter Command 19 aircraft but only 14 pilots. No. 12 Group caused some surprise by sending a wing to take part in combats over London instead of protecting No. 11 Group's stations north of the Thames Estuary as it was asked to do.

In the light of this setback the German naval authorities concluded that the struggle for air supremacy had not yet been won and Hitler that the issue was still in the balance. Confidence in the Luftwaffe was, however, to some extent restored during the next few days. On 11 September about 100 bombers of Luftflotte 2 attacked objectives in and near London and some 30 of Luftflotte 3 attacked an aircraft factory near Southampton. The Luftwaffe lost 25 aircraft and Fighter Command 29. Luftflotte 2's aircraft were again rather ineffectively opposed on 14 September, when each side lost 14 aircraft.

These experiences encouraged Field Marshal Kesselring of Luftflotte 2 to hope that a supreme bid for air superiority might yet put the prize within his grasp. He decided to launch on Sunday 15 September 2 daylight raids on London. Luftflotte 3 agreed to make small-scale diversionary attacks on the Supermarine aircraft factory at Woolston near Southampton and the naval base at Portland.

Kesselring's first raid was made by roughly 100 bombers, the second by a slightly larger number. Recent losses had so depleted his strength that he could make only about 700 fighter sorties to cover both raids, even though he separated them by an interval of 2 hours so that as many aircraft as possible could take part in both. The result was that Park, by twice committing practically all his single-seater fighters and calling on neighbouring groups to contribute the usual reinforcing squadrons, was able on each occasion to match Kesselring's escort and covering forces with approximately equal numbers of British fighters. The bombers distributed their load with little or no attempt at accurate aiming over a dozen or more London boroughs. Luftflotte 3 scored no hits on the Supermarine factory at Woolston and only a few on the naval dockyard at Portland. The Luftwaffe lost 60 aircraft, not 185 as the British believed at the time. Fighter Command lost 26 aircraft but only 13 pilots.

The vigour of the British response to Kesselring's attacks, the failure of so many German aircraft to return and severe damage to many which did return showed conclusively that the British fighter force was still undefeated. Moreover, British bombers had on recent nights attacked concentrations of shipping in the Channel ports with considerably more success than they could count upon when they bombed objectives in Germany. By 14 September 'five steamers had become serious casualties and fifteen barges total losses'.[4] On 17 September Hitler postponed landings in Britain 'until further notice'. On 18 September, after further casualties to barges and other shipping during the preceding night had been reported, he sanctioned the dispersal of transports and naval forces. Thereupon the Naval Staff issued orders to 'stop further assembly of transport units of every kind'.[5]

In theory, revival of the invasion project later in the year remained a possibility with which German planners had to reckon until, on 12 October, Hitler finally renounced any intention of sanctioning landings in 1940. He then directed that, until the spring of 1941, preparations for invasion should be maintained solely as a means of putting political and military pressure on the British. From a practical standpoint, however, the Luftwaffe's failure to dominate the skies over southern England with the resources available in August and early September made it very unlikely that the indispensable air superiority would be attained with those available after 15 September. When Hitler met Mussolini at the Brenner Pass on 4 October he confessed that *Seelöwe*, as the invasion plan was called, could not be carried out in 1940. He attributed this setback to the lack of the 5 consecutive days of fine weather which, according to him, would have given the Luftwaffe all it needed for success. At the same time he admitted that excessive concentration of the invasion fleet had been a mistake and had led to losses.

Göring continued to assert in the meantime that victory over the British fighter force was still possible. He directed on 16 September that bomber formations should be made smaller so that the proportion of fighters to bombers could be increased still further, adding that large formations of bombers and fighters should be used only in perfect weather. The British were not conscious of any immediate respite and were unable to avert damaging attacks on the Bristol Aeroplane Company's factory at Filton on 25 September and the Supermarine factory at Woolston on the following day. They continued, none the less, to inflict fairly heavy losses on the enemy on almost every occasion when he came by day. In the second half of September the Luftwaffe lost 238 aircraft, nearly all in daylight, while Fighter Command lost only about half that number. In the course of the month 467 fighters were delivered to the Royal Air Force, but the effective strength of the British fighter force showed no significant increase and the number of Hurricanes and Spitfires ready for immediate issue from aircraft storage units at the end of the month was only about 160. The supply of pilots continued to cause Air Chief Marshal Dowding intense anxiety. Fighter Command's numerical deficiency fell from 207 pilots on 7 September to 81 on 28 September, but pilots fresh from operational training units were sometimes more of a liability than an asset until they gained experience in first-line squadrons.

In October formations of German fighters, sometimes accompanied by a few bombers or bomb-carrying fighters, made repeated high-altitude sweeps towards and sometimes over London. These tactics were hard to counter. The Me.109 with two-stage supercharger had a better performance at heights above 25,000 feet than any British fighter with the possible exception of new versions of the Hurricane and the Spitfire which were only just coming into service. Moreover, the Observer Corps had difficulty in keeping track of aircraft flying at more than 20,000 feet, especially in cloudy weather. To ensure that incoming formations which might include bombers or fighter-bombers were not missed, Air Vice-Marshal Park had for a time to defy economy by devoting part of his resources to standing patrols. Again his losses were much lighter than the enemy's.

The British regard the Battle of Britain as having begun with the launching of its preliminary phase in July. An analysis by British researchers of German records shows that between 10 July and 31 October units of the Luftwaffe which took part in the battle lost 1,733 aircraft in the course of active operations. British sources give a comparable figure for Fighter Command of 915 aircraft. In addition 200 or more British fighters were too badly damaged to be repairable, but were not total losses in as much as valuable components were recovered from them. Fighter Command lost 414 pilots and 35 other aircrew killed. About 750 British fighters were fit for immediate use at the end of the battle, and roughly 200 Hurricanes and Spitfires were ready for immediate issue from aircraft storage units. The number of pilots in Fighter Command on 2 November exceeded the authorized establishment by 69.[6]

The Regia Aeronautica's contribution to the air offensive against Britain began in the last week of October. By that time some 75 BR.20 bombers, about 100 CR.42 and G.50 fighters and a few reconnaissance aircraft, forming an Italian air corps attached to Luftflotte 2, were stationed at airfields in northern Belgium. The BR.20 was an adequate bomber for night operations, but resembled its British and German counterparts in being highly vulnerable in daylight unless strongly escorted and supported by high-performance fighters. Neither the CR.42 nor the G.50 was particularly suitable for the purpose. The CR.42, a biplane not unlike the obsolescent British Gladiator and only about 20 miles an hour faster, was delightful to fly but carried only 2 machine-guns. Thus it was outclassed not only in performance but also in hitting-power by 8-gun Hurricanes and Spitfires. The G.50, a low-wing monoplane, carried 4 guns, but used substantially the same engine as the CR.42 and was somewhat underpowered. With a maximum speed of 290 miles an hour (at roughly 15,000 feet), it was at least 30 miles an hour slower than the Hurricane Mark I and some 60–80 miles an hour slower than contemporary versions of the Spitfire.

On the night of 25 October 16 Italian bomber crews were ordered to attack Harwich. One aircraft crashed on take-off; 2 ran out of fuel on the return flight and had to be abandoned. Further attacks were made on 4 nights in November, 3 in December and 1 in January. Harwich remained the favourite target, but bombs were also aimed at Ipswich, Lowestoft and Great Yarmouth. Seventy-seven sorties were made between 25 October and 2 January, and some 45 tons of bombs were dropped. The mishaps suffered on the first night were not regarded as operational casualties, and no losses which came within that definition were recorded.

The Regia Aeronautica's first recorded contribution to the daylight battle was made on 29 October, when 15 bombers escorted and supported by 73 CR.42 and G.50 fighters were sent to the neighbourhood of Ramsgate. No British fighters were met, but many aircraft were slightly damaged by anti-aircraft fire, presumably from the airfield at Manston.

On 11 November 40 CR.42 fighters were detailed to provide escort and support for 10 bombers despatched in daylight to Harwich. This task, involving a long flight over water, was an unenviable one for pilots of single-seater fighters stationed at Maldeghem, more than 100 miles in a direct line from the objective. The formation was intercepted by 2 squadrons of Hurricanes. The Italian fighter pilots did their best to protect the bombers and themselves, but their machines were hopelessly outclassed. Three bombers and 3 fighters were shot down. Ten of the surviving fighter pilots made forced landings which slightly damaged their aircraft.

No more daylight raids by escorted bombers were attempted, but fighter sweeps brought the number of offensive sorties made by the Italian fighter force between October and January to 454. A formation of 29 Italian fighters was intercepted by British fighters off the South Foreland on 23 November and lost 2 aircraft. Apart from the fight over Harwich on 11 November, this was the only encounter between British and Italian fighters of which there is incontestable evidence in British and Italian records. No offensive operations were undertaken after January, but Italian fighters continued to make defensive sorties in the neighbourhood of their bases until the Italian air corps was withdrawn in April. During their stay in Belgium, Italian reconnaissance aircraft made 5 sorties classed as offensive, but they seem not to have flown over the United Kingdom.

Towards the end of the Battle of Britain an acute controversy developed between Air Vice-Marshal Park and his neighbour, Air Vice-Marshal T. L. Leigh-Mallory of No. 12 Group. On two occasions in August stations in No. 11 Group's sectors north of the Thames Estuary which No. 12 Group had been asked to guard were bombed. Leigh-Mallory alleged that this was not surprising since No. 11 Group habitually asked for help too late. On a number of subsequent occasions he responded to appeals from Park's controllers not by placing single squadrons over airfields north of the Thames Estuary but by sending a wing of 3, 4 or 5 squadrons, led by the legless pilot Squadron Leader D. R. S. Bader of No. 242 Squadron, to take part in air battles over London. Park thought that the assembly of such large formations was bound to cause delay, and he drew attention to the difficulty of controlling squadrons which came so far south that they risked losing touch with their parent sectors. Leigh-Mallory, brushing these complaints aside, asserted that his big wings were capable of inflicting, and did inflict, enormous losses on the enemy.

German records of the Luftwaffe's losses do not bear out this assertion. There is nothing to show that Leigh-Mallory's wings destroyed, and no reason to suppose that they were likely to destroy, substantially more aircraft than might have been expected to succumb to an equivalent number of squadrons despatched separately. Wings and squadrons did not, in the late summer and autumn of 1940, *fight* as wings and squadrons. As soon as action was joined, they split into pairs of aircraft so that pilots could give each other mutual protection. Hence it made little difference whether squadrons flew to the scene of combat singly or in large formations. What did matter was that enough squadrons should be sent and that they should arrive promptly.

However, in the absence of any objective evidence of German losses the uncorroborated claims made on behalf of No. 12 Group caused a considerable stir. Leigh-Mallory and Bader were given a hearing in high places. Their enthusiastic advocacy of large formations led to some ill-conceived criticism of Park's practice of using his squadrons singly or in pairs, and by implication of Air Chief Marshal Dowding's leadership.

Dowding, when asked by his biographer long after the battle why he allowed the controversy to reach a stage at which it threatened to undermine his authority when he could have nipped it in the bud by calling Park and Leigh-Mallory to order, replied that he did not know until too late how wide and deep was the rift between them. It was not until 24 October that he attempted a reconciliation. He then suggested to Park that, when a heavy attack seemed to be impending, he or his controller should try to warn No. 12 Group, before actually asking for reinforcements, that help was likely to be needed. At the same time he told Leigh-Mallory that his squadrons should not 'normally' be sent beyond the range at which they could receive orders by radio-telephony from their parent stations. Leigh-Mallory must always send at least as much help as Park asked for unless circumstances beyond his control prevented him from doing so, but might send more at his discretion.

By that time the conflict had gone too far to be easily arrested. Until recently it had always been assumed that the air defences existed not merely to inflict losses on the enemy but to prevent him from reaching and bombing his objectives. When Park's sector stations were under constant attack, he had never doubted that he must do everything he could to save them from destruction. The Air Staff had repeatedly drawn Dowding's attention to the importance of defending objectives of a particular class, such as aircraft factories or shipping, and even to the importance of defending objectives of a particular class in a particular locality. At one stage they had gone so far as to urge him to make more use than he wished to do of a particular group of forward bases. Under the influence of Leigh-Mallory's claim that large formations could inflict punitive losses on the enemy, men who believed that they knew better than Dowding and Park how the fighter force should be handled advanced a different theory. When the 'big wing' question was discussed at a meeting at the Air Ministry in November the Deputy Chief of the Air Staff, Air Vice-Marshal W. S. Douglas, showed how far the pendulum had swung by declaring that it did not matter where German aircraft were shot down as long as they were shot down in large numbers. Whether this was a sound axiom was debatable. What was not debatable was that it contradicted one of the principles on which the Battle of Britain had been fought and won.

8

BLITZ AND BLOCKADE

When the leaders of the Luftwaffe decided in the first week of September 1940 that Luftflotte 2's daylight offensive should be switched to London, they committed themselves to the programme of day and night bombing which Hitler had in mind when he announced on 4 September that British cities would be exterminated.

Between dusk on 7 September and dawn on 14 November London was attacked on 67 nights out of 68 by an average of 163 bombers a night. According to the records of the Luftwaffe, nearly 14,000 tons of high-explosive and more than 12,000 incendiary canisters were dropped on London at night during that period. Crews were given precise objectives to aim at, but so seldom succeeded in hitting them that the effect was much the same as if their bombs had been sown broadcast.

By the autumn of 1940 the Luftwaffe had developed three navigational systems based on radio beams. The first, called *Knickebein*, provided bomber crews with a simple navigational aid in the shape of a radio beam which all could follow by using their standard blind-landing equipment. The others, called *X-Gerät* and *Y-Gerät* but known to British intelligence officers as 'Ruffians' and 'Benito', were more sophisticated. *X-Gerät*, or Ruffians, consisted in essence of a main beam crossed by two subsidiary beams laid obliquely across it. The time taken by a specially-equipped bomber to cover the distance between the points of intersection gave its ground-speed and enabled the point at which it should release its bombs if they were to hit the target to be computed. *Y-Gerät*, or Benito, depended on the emission from a ground station of signals automatically re-radiated by a bomber, again specially equipped. The time taken by the signals to travel to and from the aircraft enabled a controller at the ground station to determine its range, and its bearing was given by an auxiliary direction-finding system. The controller could direct the aircraft towards the target and determine the moment at which its bombs should be released.

The Luftwaffe made some use of *Knickebein*, but not of *X-Gerät* or *Y-Gerät*, for its night attacks on London in September, October and early November. However, crews relied to a considerable extent on visual methods, since British countermeasures to *Knickebein* were fairly effective. The loops of the Thames made London comparatively easy to find except on the darkest nights, but nothing like accurate bombing of precise objectives was possible. Damage was widespread and casualties, although they continued to be much lighter than those predicted before the war, bore hardly on the civil population. On the night of 15 October, for example, some 500 tons of high-explosive scattered over a large number of London boroughs killed or seriously injured about 1,300 people. Five of the main railway stations were put temporarily out of action, 3 large water mains were fractured and damage to the Fleet sewer caused its waters to pour into the railway tunnel between Farringdon Street and King's Cross. Many hundreds of fires, including 6 described as 'major' and 9 as 'serious', were reported in the Greater London area.

Repeated air attacks on one of the world's largest and most densely-populated built-up areas completely failed, however, to produce the devastating moral effects foretold by numerous writers on air strategy. Londoners accepted with remarkable equanimity the dangers and discomforts of what they called, more graphically than aptly, the 'Blitz'. Moreover, physical damage failed to halt the machinery of production, distribution and supply. Early in November Churchill reported to the House of Commons that bombing had destroyed or damaged many buildings but had caused only temporary and local interruptions of public utility services. Small physical damage had been done to aircraft production and other forms of war production, although frequent air raid warnings had caused some loss of working time.

The Blitz did, however, bring demands for more effective action against the night bomber than was possible with the means available in 1940. There were still not enough anti-aircraft guns in the United Kingdom to meet the approved scales, but a more serious handicap to the gunners was their dependence on old-fashioned ancillary equipment. Modern gun-laying equipment based on the principle of radio-location was under development, but priority had necessarily been given to devices needed to complete and improve the early-warning system. The same applied to searchlights used in an anti-aircraft role. The night fighter force consisted in September of 6 heavy fighter squadrons equipped with the fighter version of the Blenheim, 2 squadrons of two-seater Defiants which had proved too vulnerable to be used by day, and one half-squadron of Hurricanes which were being used at night as an experiment. The Blenheims carried a form of air-to-air radio-location equipment called A.I., but they were too slow to catch bombers except in the most favourable conditions. The Beaufighters which were to succeed them were just coming into service, but their equipment was not yet working satisfactorily. In any case, A.I. was useless unless the fighter that carried it could be put within 3 miles or so of the target aircraft. Since the Observer Corps could seldom locate hostile aircraft at night with sufficient accuracy to make this possible, little success could be expected until upward-looking radio-location sets suitable for what was called the ground control of interception (G.C.I.) were delivered in substantial numbers. This was not likely to happen before 1941. In the meantime experiments were made in Surrey with G.L. sets developed for gunlaying. These proved reasonably satisfactory when applied to the ground control of fighters, but only a few were available in the autumn and early winter of 1940.

The hope of accelerating progress or discovering a palliative led the Air Council to set up a committee under Marshal of the Royal Air Force Sir John Salmond, a disciple of Trenchard who had served as Chief of the Air Staff from 1930 to 1933, to study problems of night air defence. One of a number of proposals made by the committee was that more use should be made of single-seater aircraft as night fighters. The Deputy Chief of the Air Staff, Air Vice-Marshal Douglas, had already recommended something of the sort, but he confessed after the war that he did so because he was led to believe that a form of A.I. suitable for single-seater fighters would become available in the near future. Air Chief Marshal Dowding, who had a better understanding than Salmond or Douglas of the technical issues involved and who knew that no form of A.I. suitable for single-seater fighters was likely to be perfected for many months, dissented strongly from the proposal. He regarded the use of single-seater fighters without A.I. against night bombers as a 'haphazard' method which could never lead to more than 'an occasional fortunate encounter'. Nevertheless the Air Ministry insisted on his relegating 3 Hurricane squadrons to night fighting.

The Salmond Committee also proposed that the evaluation, or 'filtering', of information from radio-location stations of the early-warning system should be done not at Dowding's headquarters but at the headquarters of fighter groups. Information from new radio-location stations in the south-west and the west was already being dealt with at the headquarters of the recently-established No. 10 Group near Bath and the still more recently established No. 9 Group at Preston. What the committee proposed was not merely that similar arrangements should be made for any further groups that might come into existence, but that the time-honoured method of dealing with information from long-established radio-location stations on the east coast should be changed. The Air Staff endorsed the proposal in the erroneous belief that decentralization would eliminate a link in the chain of communications. In point of fact, the only argument that could be advanced for it was that it would reduce the risk of congestion should the number of stations on the east coast be increased. Dowding thought that the trouble and expense of devolution could not be justified, but again he was overruled. In 1941 separate filter rooms were opened at the headquarters of No. 12 Group (Watnall, near Nottingham), No. 13 Group (Newcastle), No. 14 Group (Inverness) and the new No. 82 Group in Northern Ireland. Filtering for No. 11 Group, whose headquarters were at Uxbridge, continued to be done in the original Command Filter Room at Stanmore until, towards the end of the war, a new No. 11 Group Filter Room was established in premises only a few hundred yards away.

By the early winter of 1940 Air Chief Marshal Dowding had been Air Officer Commander-in-Chief, Fighter Command, for a considerably longer period than a Commander-in-Chief's usual 3-year tour of duty. Having been passed over for the post of Chief of the Air Staff, he stayed on in the knowledge that his appointment was likely to be terminated at short notice when the Air

Ministry found a successor to its liking. Perhaps not surprisingly in view of his refusal to promise early success against the night bomber and his reluctant acceptance of proposals made by the Salmond Committee and the Air Staff, he was relieved of his post with scant ceremony on 25 November. Douglas, the advocate of single-seater aircraft for night fighting and big wings for day fighting, took his place. Three weeks later Leigh-Mallory assumed command of No. 11 Group and Park was relegated to Flying Training Command.

In the meantime Göring decreed that night attacks should be extended to objectives other than London, and in particular to centres of production in the Midlands. London would still be the most important target.

The British received warning of this change of plan from their intelligence sources. Consequently the attack on Coventry made by some 450 bombers on the night of 14 November did not take them altogether by surprise. *X-Gerät* was used operationally for the first time. With its aid the specialist bomber unit Kampfgruppe 100, based in Brittany, dropped incendiary bombs and flares to mark the target for the benefit of the general run of bomber crews. Bright moonlight made the location of precise objectives easier than usual. About 500 tons of high-explosive and some 900 incendiary canisters, dropped over a period of 10 hours, kindled at least 200 fires, cut rail communications with Birmingham, Leamington, Rugby and Nuneaton, and severely damaged 21 important factories. Telephone and power cables and gas and water mains were severed at many points. About 1,400 people were killed or seriously injured.

This highly successful raid might have had serious effects on British war production had it been followed up. As it was, the Luftwaffe did not return in strength to Coventry until the following April. The British took advantage of the respite to bring all fires under control within twelve hours, repair all rail cuts by 21 November and most by 18 November, and shift much valuable plant from damaged factories. Troops and civil defence workers from outside the city helped the local authorities to rehouse the homeless, clear rubble from the streets and restore essential services. Confidence was so soon restored that only about 300 residents of Coventry chose to spend the night of 16 November outside the city, although transport was provided for 10,000.

Production was at a standstill for 24 hours, but was back to normal in less than 2 months.

The Germans followed their raid on Coventry with heavy attacks on other centres of industry and commerce. They applied the term 'major raid' to one in which their crews claimed to have dropped a hundred tons or more of bombs on a given target area or complex of adjacent target areas. London had suffered 57 such raids when they turned their attention to Coventry. Between the nights of 15 November 1940 and 16 May 1941 the Luftwaffe made a further 14 major raids on London, 8 each on Liverpool, Birmingham and Plymouth, 6 on Bristol with Avonmouth and 5 on Glasgow. During the same period 4 major raids were made on Southampton and 3 each on Portsmouth, Hull and Manchester. Coventry had its second and last major raid on the night of 8 April, when roughly 300 tons of high-explosive and 700 incendiary canisters were dropped. Belfast was attacked, according to German claims, by 180 aircraft on the night of 15 April and by 204 on the night of 4 May. Sheffield, Cardiff and Newcastle each suffered 1 major raid. A heavy attack on Nottingham was planned for the night of 8 May, but counter-measures taken by the British led crews sent there to drop their bombs in open country. Nottingham was, however, bombed that night by nearly 100 crews who believed that they were attacking Derby.

Altogether nearly 19,000 tons of bombs were aimed at London in major raids between 7 September and 16 May. Between a quarter and a third of this tonnage was dropped after 14 November. Liverpool (with Birkenhead) and Birmingham were the only other places which attracted more than 1,500 tons of bombs in major raids, but upwards of 2,000 tons were aimed at London, Liverpool, Bristol or Avonmouth, Swansea, Hull, Sheffield, Birmingham, Portsmouth, Cardiff, Nottingham, Southampton, Sunderland, Barrow-in-Furness, Plymouth and Derby in the course of fairly heavy attacks rather arbitrarily classed as minor. Reserves of food, especially animal feeding stuffs and sugar, were heavily depleted by some of the attacks made on London and Liverpool, but such losses could be borne as long as the country's external communications remained open. Losses of oil caused by the bombing of storage tanks were trifling in proportion to stocks accumulated before and since the outbreak of war. In general war production was not seriously affected by the Blitz, although damage to factories, communications and sources of light, heat and power caused much inconvenience and cost the authorities some anxious moments. Among the lessons derived by the British from their experience was the supreme importance of an efficient fire-fighting system.

The Germans lost few aircraft at night to guns and fighters, but the wear and tear imposed by repeated operations was such that by early January more than half the bombers on the strength of Luftflotten 2 and 3 were under repair or undergoing routine maintenance. Thereafter the two Luftflotten devoted a growing share of their effort to the bombing of ports. On 6 February Hitler sanctioned this trend by directing the Luftwaffe to attack 'the most vital British import harbours' and to join the Navy in an offensive against shipping bound for the United Kingdom. He added that aircraft factories and sources of anti-aircraft weapons and ammunition were still to be attacked.

When Hitler's directive was issued, neither the Navy nor the Luftwaffe was particularly well equipped for attacks on ocean trade. At the beginning of February only about 20 U-boats were fit for use in the Atlantic. By July some 60 were available. About 80 bombers, torpedo-bombers and reconnaissance aircraft with crews trained for operations at sea were stationed at bases from the Norwegian Sea to the Bay of Biscay in the spring, nearly twice as many by midsummer. Their scope was, however, rather limited. The only German aircraft capable of covering the approaches to the British Isles as far west as the 20th meridian was the Focke-Wulf 200, originally a transport aircraft but sometimes used during the night air offensive against Britain as a bomber. Between 20 and 30 of these slow-moving and vulnerable machines were available in the spring and summer of 1941, but the number fit for use at one time was never more than 12 and seldom more than 6 or 8. When used at sea they carried bombs, but their primary task was to report the positions of Atlantic convoys for the benefit of U-boat commanders. The duties of the rest of the Luftwaffe's anti-shipping forces in the west included mine-laying in British coastal waters and armed reconnaissance of the North Sea, the English Channel, St George's Channel and the Irish Sea.

The slenderness of their resources did not prevent the

Germans from achieving a remarkable degree of success. In the whole of 1940 they had sunk about $3\frac{1}{2}$ million tons of British, Allied and neutral merchant shipping in the North Atlantic and in United Kingdom waters. In the first half of 1941 they sank more than $3\frac{1}{4}$ million. The higher rate of sinkings was due almost entirely to the more frequent attacks on Atlantic convoys which resulted from effective co-operation between submarines and aircraft.

The British recognized before the end of February that blockade rather than direct interference with production had become the enemy's prior aim. The Chiefs of Staff agreed on 27 February that stronger surface and air escorts must at all costs be provided for Atlantic convoys. On 6 March Churchill summarized in his famous 'Battle of the Atlantic' directive a number of proposals, good or bad, which had already been discussed.

Two problems confronted the British. One was to protect shipping in home waters against attacks by bombers and torpedo-bombers with a relatively short radius of action. The other was to prevent shipping from being sunk on the high seas by U-boats assisted by long-range aircraft, or on rare occasions by long-range aircraft acting independently.

The first problem was relatively simple. The newly-promoted Air Marshal Douglas, with more fighter squadrons than Dowding had ever possessed and with no daylight Battle of Britain to fight, could afford by the spring of 1941 to provide far more lavish cover for local convoys than had hitherto been possible. In February his fighters made 443 daylight sorties for the protection of shipping. In March they made 2,103, in April 7,876, in May 8,287. Attacks in daylight on ships within 40 miles of a fighter station climbed from 41 in February to 89 in March and 124 in April, but fell to 41 again in May and then tailed off to an average of 16 a month during the last 7 months of the year. The volume of merchant shipping sunk in United Kingdom waters fell from well over half a million tons in the first half of 1941 to less than a quarter of a million in the second half. Stronger surface escorts and the better arming of merchant vessels had something to do with these results, but the value of strong fighter protection in daylight was attested by the preference given by the enemy after April to night attacks. These were harder to counter but less effective than attacks in daylight.

The second problem was complicated for the British by a tendency to overestimate both the danger of direct attacks on ocean convoys by long-range aircraft and the ability of the British bomber force to contribute to a reduction of the enemy's striking power. The Government insisted that Bomber Command should attack, if not U-boat bases and airfields where long-range aircraft were stationed, at any rate places where U-boats and long-range aircraft were built. Attempts to carry out this policy had no significant effect on U-boat production and only minor effects on the production of long-range aircraft. Largely or perhaps entirely as a result of Bomber Command's efforts the directors of the Focke-Wulf concern did, however, remove their factories to towns further east than their original quarters at Bremen. The British Admiralty would have liked to see some of the big bombers which were being built for the bombing of Germany transformed into long-range maritime reconnaissance aircraft, but the Air Ministry tenaciously resisted all attempts to divert the big bombers from the purpose to which the Air Staff hoped to put them.

Another proposal was that single-seater fighters carried in modified merchant vessels and launched by catapult should put to sea with ocean convoys for the purpose of shooting down any German long-range aircraft which might venture within reach. This plan was strongly supported by Air Marshal Portal, who had left Bomber Command in October to become Chief of the Air Staff. Fifty merchant vessels of 9,000 tons or so were modified to carry a fighter apiece, and 60 obsolescent Mark I Hurricanes, with pilots and maintenance crews, were set aside to equip them and provide a surplus for training and replacements. In addition the Admiralty equipped an auxiliary aircraft carrier and 4 ocean boarding vessels to carry single-seater fighters. But it was not until 3 August that a naval Hurricane from the ocean boarding vessel *Maplin* destroyed a Focke-Wulf 200 south-west of Cape Clear, and not until 1 November that a Hurricane from the merchant vessel *Empire Foam* chased a similar aircraft into cloud about 650 miles west of the Irish coast. No further interceptions were recorded in 1941 and very few thereafter.

In the meantime the situation was saved by more orthodox means. The arrival of ships ordered on the outbreak of war brought the number of destroyers, escort destroyers, sloops, corvettes, coastguard cutters, trawlers and miscellaneous escort vessels in commission by July to nearly 700. By April the completion of fuelling bases in Iceland enabled escort vessels to accompany ocean convoys as far as 35° West. When destroyers and corvettes operating from bases established by the Royal Canadian Navy in Newfoundland and eastern Canada became available in substantial numbers during the second half of May, surface escort could be given across the full width of the Atlantic. Aircraft armed with depth charges and equipped with air-to-surface vessel radar, supplemented as supplies became available by searchlights of a special pattern developed by Squadron Leader H. de V. Leigh, provided air cover and searched for U-boats in the North and South Atlantic within a radius of 350–400 miles of bases in the west of England, Northern Ireland, the Hebrides, Iceland, Canada, Gibraltar and West Africa. Long-range aircraft extended the radius of action to 600–700 miles, but few such aircraft were available since the Air Ministry was still reluctant to use for maritime reconnaissance aircraft which might one day be needed for the bombing of Germany. As the sequel to a high-level decision which placed Coastal Command under the operational control of the Admiralty with effect from the middle of April it was, however, agreed that all Catalina flying boats for which orders had been placed in the United States should be so used. Growing contributions to the defence of Atlantic shipping were made, too, by the United States Navy as the outcome of Anglo-American staff talks between January and March and President Roosevelt's declaration of a state of unlimited national emergency in May.

These measures brought no startling increase in the number of U-boats destroyed, but they forced U-boat commanders to adopt a variety of expedients in order to survive. Moreover, the Germans did not receive the benefits they might have been expected to derive from the expansion of their U-boat force. Notwithstanding a fourfold increase between January and December in the number of U-boats fit for active operations, the volume of merchant shipping sunk in the North and South Atlantic fell from 1,902,055 tons in the first half of 1941 to 653,561 tons in the second half. This trend was not due merely to the growing preoccupation of the German Navy with other theatres. The volume of merchant shipping sunk in all parts of the world declined from 2,884,307 tons between January and June to 1,444,251 tons between July and December.

As a result of their losses during the early part of the year, and in the light of other considerations, the British reduced their estimate of the volume of imports they could hope to receive in 1941 from 35 million to 31 million tons. The second figure was equivalent to roughly three-fifths of their normal requirements in time of peace. In the outcome they received 30·5 million tons, but reached the end of the year with larger stocks of food and raw materials than they had possessed in the summer of 1940.

To understand how the British, apparently disregarding the lesson they might have been expected to learn from the failure of the Luftwaffe's night air offensive against Britain, came to devote a substantial part of their resources between 1941 and 1945 to attempts to break the spirit of the German people by the bombing of German towns, it is necessary to go back to the night of 24 August 1940, when a few German crews dropped bombs on London in the belief that they were attacking objectives at Kingston, Rochester and Thameshaven.

Churchill, like most Englishmen, regarded this occurrence at the time as an intentional but indiscriminate attack on London. Besides concurring in the decision to bomb Berlin on the following night, he told Air Marshal Portal, then still in command of the bomber force, that he thought Bomber Command 'should henceforth spread its bombs as widely as possible over the cities of Germany'.[1] The idea of indiscriminate bombing did not then appeal to the Air Staff, who still believed that Bomber Command was capable, even at night, of hitting precise objectives such as oil plants. The Prime Minister's hint was, however, not lost on Portal. On 11 September he proposed to the Air Staff that the inhabitants of twenty German towns should be warned by wireless that any indiscriminate attack on a British town would be followed by a similar attack on one or other of those towns. Alternatively, attacks might be made on such a town as Essen, 'the whole of which can for practical purposes be regarded as a military objective', or military objectives in other towns might be attacked in the knowledge that adjacent built-up areas would inevitably be damaged.

The Air Staff showed little enthusiasm for these proposals.

They told Portal on 21 September that disruption of the German oil industry was still the basis of their 'longer term offensive strategy', but that attacks on communications might make an important contribution to the undermining of Germany's economy. At the same time they mentioned other target systems, such as the aircraft industry and the U-boat organization, which might have to be attacked. They did, however, go some way to meet Portal's wishes by conceding that attacks on Berlin, where there were believed to be no targets relevant to their major strategic aims, might be undertaken for the twofold purpose of interfering with industrial activities and harming the civil population.

Subsequent discussion showed that, while the Air Staff regarded harassment of civilians as an inevitable consequence of attacks on military or quasi-military targets in built-up areas and were prepared to tolerate it for that reason, Bomber Command and the Prime Minister had come to regard it as an end in itself. Portal 'believed that the time had come to launch a direct attack on the German people'.[2] His appointment to the crucial post of Chief of the Air Staff in October marked, therefore, at least a temporary renunciation of Britain's traditional policy of *not* fighting a barbarous enemy with his own weapons or according to his own methods.

However, to enunciate a new policy was one thing; to carry it out was another. In the last week of October Air Marshal Sir Richard Peirse, Portal's successor at Bomber Command, was shown the draft of a directive in which the Air Staff proposed to order him to combine attacks on 20 or 30 German towns with the bombing of oil targets and occasional attacks on marshalling yards. Peirse, believing with good reason that comparatively few crews could be relied upon to find a distant target, pointed out that such a wide dispersal of his effort was not likely to yield satisfactory results. The reference to 20 or 30 towns was omitted from the final version of the directive, but Peirse was still asked both to bomb oil targets or other precise objectives and to make 'regular concentrated attacks . . . on objectives in large towns and centres of industry, with the primary aim of causing very heavy material destruction which will demonstrate to the enemy the power and severity of air bombardment and the hardship and dislocation which will result from it'.[3] In addition, he was to bomb objectives in northern Italy, lay mines in German coastal waters, and make occasional attacks on marshalling yards and on shipyards where submarines were built.

Exaggerated and inaccurate reports from informants in Continental Europe of the effects of past attacks on Germany led members of the War Cabinet to believe that this was a realistic programme. Airmen saw in the Luftwaffe's raid on Coventry on the night of 14 November an indication of what the bombing of an industrial centre might accomplish. Even so, there was little support from responsible strategists at the end of 1940 and early in 1941 for the policy of bombing towns for the purpose of undermining what the Air Staff called 'morale'. The Chiefs of Staff recorded, without dissent from Portal, the opinion that Bomber Command should concentrate on disruption of the German oil industry and should not be diverted to other tasks. The vastly experienced Lord Hankey shared that view. The Defence Committee of the War Cabinet, whose *ex officio* Chairman was the Prime Minister, endorsed the report from the Chiefs of Staff, although Churchill himself inclined to the opinion that Bomber Command should 'turn the focus of its attack' to whole German towns and should 'become more ruthless'.[4] Portal, although he had assented to the rambling directive given to Peirse at the end of October, argued in December that the destruction of 17 major oil plants would do immense and possibly fatal harm to Germany's war economy. Bomber Command could, he believed, destroy these targets by making 3,420 sorties against them in 4 months, but would have to make the same number of sorties against oil targets every 4 months thereafter.[5] Nevertheless he continued, with a reservation in favour of attacks on oil targets on all suitable occasions, to give some support to the policy of attacking towns when conditions were such that oil targets could not be attacked with a reasonable prospect of success. He recognized that the bombing of German towns was open to moral and ethical objections, but considered it justified by Germany's past conduct.

However, experience soon suggested that a large town might be the only distant target Bomber Command could hit at night, and that the proportion of crews who could be relied upon to hit even a large town might not be very great. On the night of 7 November 1940 Wellingtons, Hampdens and Blenheims were sent to attack the Krupp arms factory at Essen. The crews of 20 Wellingtons reported on their return that they had attacked the target and had started fires visible for many miles; but with one exception crews of Hampdens and Blenheims, who claimed to have reached the target area between 1 hour and 3–4 hours after the first of the Wellingtons, saw no fires on arrival. Again, on the night of 16 December 134 Wellingtons, Whitleys, Hampdens and Blenheims were despatched to Mannheim to make the first attack on a town as distinct from a military or quasi-military objective. Wellingtons manned by 'the most experienced crews available' were to drop incendiary bombs near the centre of the town and crews which followed were to aim at the fires thus kindled. The crews of 47 Wellingtons, 33 Whitleys, 18 Hampdens and 4 Blenheims reported on their return that they had attacked Mannheim. 'All reports agreed in suggesting that the majority of the bombs had fallen in the target area', and the centre of the town was said to have been left in flames.[6] Photographs taken in daylight on 21 December by a long-range Spitfire of the newly-established Photographic Reconnaissance Unit showed that many bombs had in fact fallen wide and that the attack had 'failed in its primary object'.

A few days later the Photographic Reconnaissance Unit produced photographs of 2 oil plants at Gelsenkirchen which 196 bomber crews claimed to have attacked. These showed that most of the 260 tons of bombs supposedly aimed at the 2 targets had not only failed to hit them but had missed 'by an immeasurable distance'.

A further indication of the inability of most crews to hit precise targets at night came from a raid on Bremen, delivered on the night of 12 March 1941 in response to the Prime Minister's Battle of the Atlantic directive. Fifty-four Wellingtons were to bomb the Focke-Wulf factory and 32 Blenheims to attack the centre of the town. Conditions were described as 'perfect'. The crews of 21 Wellingtons failed to find the factory, although it was near the coast. The remaining 33 crews claimed to have attacked it with 132 high-explosive and 840 incendiary bombs. Air photographs taken after the raid showed that only 12 high-explosive bombs had hit the factory and that a further 28 had fallen within approximately 600 yards of it.

From this and other evidence the authorities concluded that

objectives smaller than whole towns could not be attacked with any prospect of success on dark nights, and that even in the most favourable conditions not more than 3 or 4 bombs out of every 100 aimed at a target the size of an average oil plant were likely to hit it. This calculation was based on the assumption that the average aiming error was 600 yards, but in fact less than a third of the bombs aimed at the Focke-Wulf factory had fallen within that distance of the centre of the target.

During the spring and summer of 1941 Bomber Command continued to despatch aircraft at night to attack a variety of objectives which fell more or less within the framework of the Battle of the Atlantic directive. These raids were undertaken not so much in the expectation that they would make a direct contribution to the battle as in the hope that they might at least do something to hamper war production and interfere with daily life.

Even by that modest standard the results were not very satisfactory. An examination completed in August by a member of the War Cabinet secretariat of more than 600 photographs taken by night bombers during active operations and of operational summaries and other documentary records led to the conclusion that probably not more than 1 in 5 of the crews despatched on night operations in June and July had arrived within 5 miles of their targets. Of crews who claimed to have reached and attacked their targets, probably 1 in 3 had dropped their bombs within an area of 75 square miles round the intended point of aim; but this was true only of all targets lumped together. For targets in Germany as a whole the proportion was probably not more than 1 in 4. For targets in the Ruhr, where industrial haze and a dearth of landmarks made navigation particularly difficult, it was probably not more than 1 in 10.

This analysis made a profound impression on the Prime Minister and his Scientific Adviser, Lord Cherwell. In the light of it the Air Staff were forced to admit that night attacks on precise objectives in Germany were not a practical operation of war with the resources available to Bomber Command in 1941 or those likely to be available for many months to come. Either the night air offensive against Germany must be abandoned, or the bomber force must fall back on attacks on whole towns, since these were the only targets it could hope to hit not merely on dark nights but on any nights.

Abandonment of the air offensive against Germany and diversion of the resources intended for it to some more obviously useful purpose such as maritime reconnaissance or the support of British land and naval forces in the Mediterranean and Middle East was not seriously considered. The Chiefs of Staff insisted that only the bombing of Germany could pave the way for the return of British forces to Continental Europe and enable Britain to impose her will upon the enemy. This left open the possibility of substituting a daylight offensive for a night offensive, but day bombing on a useful scale was ruled out when Portal declared, incorrectly, that a long-range fighter capable of escorting bombers to Germany and back could not be developed.

Thus the destruction of German towns replaced disruption of the German oil industry as Bomber Command's primary aim not because it was regarded as a *better* means of putting pressure on Germany but because disruption of the oil industry was seen in 1941 to be impractical. Furthermore, it would be quite wrong to suppose that the Air Staff conceived the notion that attacks on whole towns might be efficacious only when attacks on precise objectives had to be renounced. The change that occurred in 1941 was that 'area attacks' such as that made on Mannheim in the previous December now took the first instead of the second place.

Nevertheless the priority now given to area bombing involved a radical reconsideration of Bomber Command's future. In September Portal gave his approval to a plan which envisaged the complete destruction of 43 towns with a total population of 15 million. The Directorate of Bomber Operations estimated on the basis of the Luftwaffe's raid on Coventry on the night of 14 November 1940 that one ton of bombs for every 800 inhabitants would have to be dropped in the right place each month for 6 months on end if the required degree of devastation was to be attained. This meant that 18,750 tons of bombs a month for 6 months would be needed to devastate the homes of 15 million people. Assuming that only 1 out of every 4 aircraft despatched would reach the target area and that each aircraft would make 6 sorties a month, the authors of the plan calculated that 4,000 heavy bombers each capable of carrying a 3-ton bomb-load would be needed. Given the 4,000 heavy bombers, Bomber Command would be able to 'break Germany' in 6 months.

Churchill viewed this plan with scepticism. He reminded Portal that the Air Staff had more than once misled British statesmen by grossly exaggerating the effectiveness of bombing. Whether bombing would become a decisive factor in the war against Germany was, he thought, 'very disputable'. Nevertheless he did not challenge the determination of the Air Ministry to expand the home-based bomber force while making what its critics thought was inadequate provision for maritime reconnaissance and the defence of British interests and possessions overseas. The Government, he told Portal, had no intention of departing from the policy of creating a bomber force 'on the largest possible scale'.[7]

A first-line strength of 4,000 bombers could not, however, be attained even in the most favourable circumstances before 1943, and in the outcome nothing like that figure was ever reached.* Moreover, navigational aids still under development would be needed before even 1 in 4 of the crews despatched could be relied upon to locate distant targets. In the meantime Bomber Command had to go on sending crews to targets most of them would never reach, since any severe curtailment of its activities seemed likely to undermine their confidence. Between the beginning of August and the end of October the bomber force made 8,466 operational sorties at night without making much impression on the enemy. Two hundred and sixty-five aircraft failed to return and many were damaged.

These losses caused some concern. The loss of 37 aircraft out of 400 despatched on various missions on the night of 7 November caused still more. The matter was discussed in high quarters, and Air Marshal Peirse received a directive calling on him to conserve his resources in order to build a stong force by the spring. He was, however, assured that no reflection on his handling of the bomber force was intended. Soon afterwards a dispute arose between him and Portal as to whether he had been misled by his weather experts or had disregarded their advice.

* The number of British heavy bombers available for active operations never exceeded about 1,700. As a result of technical developments the *effective* striking-power of the British heavy-bomber force was, however, greater in the closing stages of the war than that assumed for the purpose of the calculation made in 1941. The striking-power of the combined British and American bomber forces in the European theatre of war was, of course, greater still.

After 'all the relevant' papers had been shown to the Prime Minister, then attending an Anglo-American conference at Washington, Peirse followed Park and Dowding into limbo. He was succeeded after an interregnum of some weeks by Air Marshal Harris, the former commander of No. 5 Group. Since leaving No. 5 Group Harris had served briefly as Deputy Chief of the Air Staff before going to Washington as head of a Royal Air Force delegation. During his spell at the Air Ministry he had acquired a reputation as an uninhibited critic of measures which might impede the growth of the bomber force.

Soon after his translation from the Air Ministry to Fighter Command, Air Marshal Douglas declared that he had 'never been very much in favour of the idea of trying to interpose fighter squadrons between enemy bombers and their objective'. He added that he would rather shoot down 50 hostile aircraft after an objective he was defending had been bombed than shoot down 10 before it was attacked. These were rather surprising pronouncements in view of the directives given to his predecessor while Douglas was still a member of the Air Staff.

Douglas also made it clear that he would like No. 11 Group to exploit the proximity of its bases in Kent and Sussex to enemy-held territory by taking the offensive when circumstances allowed. Park had proposed as early as October to send 3-squadron wings on offensive sweeps over the Straits. His successor put forward a more ambitious programme which included sweeps as far afield as Saint Omer, tip-and-run attacks by fighters flying singly or in pairs or fours on targets of opportunity in the departments of the Pas de Calais and the Nord, and occasional raids on objectives in the same area by small numbers of bombers escorted and supported by relatively large numbers of fighters.

An obvious weakness of this programme was that objectives within the radius of action of single-seater fighters which could profitably be attacked were few. The enemy would have only a small area to defend, and a high proportion of any damage the British might hope to do would be repairable by French labour at no cost to Germany's war economy. Douglas and Leigh-Mallory believed, however, that by taking the offensive they could force the enemy to use up his fighters. This was what the Germans, with many more bombers at their disposal than the British could devote to daylight operations in 1941, had tried without success to do in the summer of 1940. An important difference was that, whereas in the summer of 1940 Dowding and Park had been very much concerned to protect sector stations and aircraft factories and prevent the enemy from making accurate daylight attacks on London, it would not matter much to the Germans whether most of the objectives the British now proposed to attack were bombed or not. They indeed could afford, should the opportunity arise, to shoot down 50 hostile aircraft after an objective they were defending had been bombed rather than destroy 10 aircraft earlier.

Tip-and-run raids began on 20 December 1940, when 2 Spitfires from Biggin Hill visited Dieppe and Le Touquet. Both pilots fired at buildings on an airfield and elsewhere, but they saw no German aircraft in the air. Further raids at irregular intervals brought no combats until 12 January, when at least 1 German fighter was inconclusively engaged and 2 British fighters failed to return. Altogether 149 tip-and-run raids were ordered between 20 December and 13 June of the following year. Forty-five were cut short by unsuitable weather. The remaining 102 involved 233 sorties over or near enemy-held territory. Pilots reported seeing German aircraft in flight on 26 occasions. It is now known that the Germans lost fewer aircraft as a result of these operations than the British. A criticism made at the time was that shooting at targets of opportunity in the French countryside and in seaside towns might not seem to Frenchmen a very good way of liberating them from the German yoke. Pilots had orders to attack only German troops or military installations, but were inclined in the excitement of the moment to fire at almost anything that moved.

The first offensive sweep by more than a few aircraft was made on 9 January. Five squadrons in 2 formations swept over the French coast. One formation went as far as Saint Omer. The weather was fine but the ground on the French side of the Straits was covered with snow. No German fighters were seen and no anti-aircraft fire was reported.

The first bomber raid of the series was made on the following day. Six Blenheims of Bomber Command, escorted and covered by 6 squadrons of fighters, aimed bombs at aircraft dispersal pens and stores in wooded country south of Calais. Three squadrons of fighters provided support over the Straits and the French coast from Cap Gris Nez to Dunkirk. A few German fighters were seen and engaged, but no British or German aircraft were shot down. A Hurricane pilot was forced to abandon his aircraft on the return flight and was picked up with a broken leg. Two Spitfire pilots made forced landings, one of them receiving injuries from which he afterwards died. These incidents were a foretaste of the difficulties Fighter Command would experience in pushing its operations to the limit of the radius of action of single-seater fighters.

In the course of the next 5 months aircraft of Bomber Command or Coastal Command accompanied by fighters made 10 similar raids on objectives in the Pas de Calais or the Nord, 14 daylight attacks on shipping and 2 daylight attacks on docks at Cherbourg and Le Havre. Fighters without bombers made offensive sweeps at strengths varying from 14 aircraft to more than 20 squadrons. In all daylight offensive operations between 20 December and 13 June Fighter Command lost 51 pilots. The Luftwaffe lost 40 fighters over France or the Low Countries during the same period, but attributed the loss of only 18 of these aircraft to hostile action. These figures give weight to the subsequent comment of Air Vice-Marshal D. F. Stevenson, whose group provided most of the bombers, that Leigh-Mallory was 'fantastically' wrong if he believed that he could make any serious impression on the Germans by trying to fight the Battle of Britain in reverse.

During the late spring and early summer of 1941 the Luftwaffe moved Luftflotte 2, with practically the whole of its operational formations and units as well as many hitherto under Luftflotte 3, from France and the Low Countries to eastern Europe in preparation for the coming assault on Russia. To conceal these changes spurious orders and reports, purporting to come from formations and units which had already gone, were transmitted by wireless, while units yet to go or destined to remain continued until the night of 16 May to make as many sorties as possible over British cities, sometimes by ordering crews to make 2 or even 3 sorties on 1 night. Luftflotten 3 and 5 were left after midsummer with some 260 bombers, 300 fighters and 60 reconnaissance aircraft in France, Belgium, Holland, Denmark and Norway. About 280 fighters of Luftflotte Reich were deployed in Germany for day and night defence. In the last week of July fewer than half the bombers under Luftflotten 3 and 5 were serviceable.

From the end of March the British Government received a good deal of information which pointed to the likelihood of a German attack on Russia within the next few months. A warning was passed to Stalin, who received it ungraciously. Neither Stalin's attitude nor ideological barriers prevented the Government from wishing, in the national interest, to give Russia all possible aid if she were attacked, but Britain had no means of exerting direct pressure on the Germans except by bombing. On 17 June – 5 days before the Germans opened their attack – the Air Ministry asked the Commanders-in-Chief of the Metropolitan Air Force to consider ways and means of compelling the Luftwaffe to reverse the flow of aircraft from west to east, 'particularly in the event of operations developing against Russia'. The Commanders-in-Chief recommended on 19 June that the daylight offensive should be continued on an increased scale. Attacks by escorted bombers on objectives in the neighbourhood of Lille and Lens should, they suggested, be combined with an offensive against shipping in the Straits and night attacks on objectives in the Ruhr. Such measures would, in their opinion, threaten communications between Germany and France to an extent which might induce the Germans to bring back some of their fighters from eastern Europe.

A new phase of the daylight offensive had in fact begun on 14 June. Between that date and the end of the year escorted bombers made about 90 attacks on objectives in the Pas de Calais and the Nord or at or near Rouen. In addition, more than 100 attacks were made on shipping and dockyards. Fighter-bombers attacked a variety of targets, and fighters without bombs and unaccompanied by bombers made some hundreds of offensive sweeps and tip-and-run attacks. These operations cost Fighter Command 426 pilots killed, missing or known to have been taken prisoner, as compared with 414 killed outright or mortally wounded during the defensive battle between July and October of the previous year. Bomber Command lost 213 aircraft in daylight operations in the whole of 1941, and of these 101 were lost in July and August, when the daylight offensive proposed by the Commanders-in-Chief was at its height. The number of bombers shot down while they were being escorted by fighters was, however, very much smaller than these figures might suggest. Leigh-Mallory estimated that between 14 June and 3 September – after which the scale of attack was reduced in the light of discussions between Douglas and the Air Staff – bomber formations covered by his fighters lost 10 aircraft to anti-aircraft fire and only 4 to German fighters. Air Vice-Marshal Stevenson, his opposite number on the bomber side, put the number of his bombers destroyed by German fighters at 7.

The value of strong fighter support, as distinct from weak support or none, was well shown, albeit in negative fashion, when attacks were made in daylight on the battle-cruisers *Scharnhorst* and *Gneisenau*. At the height of the summer these ships were lying at Brest, where they made tempting targets. Brest was beyond the radius of action of ordinary single-seater fighters, but 5 squadrons of long-range Spitfires with additional fuel tanks would be ready in the second half of July. Five squadrons of fighters would not suffice to give close cover to the 140 or 150 bombers considered necessary to secure a reasonable chance of hitting both ships, and in any case it was doubtful whether the bomber crews could be trained to a standard which would allow so many to fly in one tight formation. Accordingly, it was decided that 3 B-17 (Flying Fortress) bombers should open the attack by flying to Brest at a high altitude but without escort. Eighteen Hampdens escorted by 3 long-range Spitfire squadrons were to follow after an interval of 15 minutes. The arrival of these formations would, it was hoped, induce the enemy to commit the whole of the 30 or 40 fighters believed to be stationed at Brest. At a moment when the enemy's fighters might be expected to have exhausted their fuel and ammunition, 120 bombers without close escort but supported by the rest of the long-range Spitfires would deliver the main attack. At the same time, Blenheim bombers escorted and supported by ordinary single-seater fighters would attack Cherbourg in order to prevent German fighters stationed there from intervening at Brest.

On the eve of the raid the *Scharnhorst* moved to La Pallice, beyond the radius of action of any British fighter. Separate attacks had therefore to be made on Brest and La Pallice. This meant that heavy bombers which were to have taken part in the main attack at Brest had to be diverted to an operation for which no support of any kind could be provided. Other heavy bombers had to be withheld because of technical shortcomings. The number of bombers assigned to the main attack at Brest was thereby reduced from 120 to 78.

Apart from this reduction of strength the attack on Brest was carried out on 24 July more or less as planned. The Fortresses and the Hampdens with their escort were met by some 25–30 fighters. Nevertheless the Germans were not prevented from bringing fighters as well as accurate and intense anti-aircraft fire to bear against the bombers which delivered the main attack. Of the 99 bombers sent to Brest, 11 were shot down and 2 crashed on the way home. The well-supported Blenheims sent to Cherbourg, on the other hand, met little opposition and neither they nor the fighters suffered any losses.

Two attacks were made on the *Scharnhorst* at La Pallice. Of 6 Stirlings despatched late on 23 July, 1 failed to return. The surviving crews reported combats with some half-dozen fighters, supposedly from an operational training unit stationed in the neighbourhood. Fifteen Halifaxes followed on 24 July. Fourteen reached the target area and were met by at least a dozen fighters. All were hit by fire from fighters or anti-aircraft guns, and 5 failed to return. The heavy opposition was thought to have impaired the accuracy of the bombing, but in fact the *Scharnhorst* received 5 direct hits and shipped 3,000 tons of water.

Thus the raids on Brest and La Pallice cost Bomber Command 19 bombers out of 120 despatched. In comparison with losses suffered in repeated night attacks of little or no strategic worth on German towns, this was not too high a price to pay for the infliction of damage which kept the *Scharnhorst* out of action for many months. But the extent of the damage done to the *Scharnhorst* was not known to the British at the time, and to many British airmen the bombing of warships in French harbours seemed a tiresome diversion from what they regarded as the all-important task of bombing Germany. Sir Archibald Sinclair, the Secretary of State for Air, had suggested to Portal in June that a special committee might be appointed to study 'the whole problem of daylight penetration' since, if day bombing was to continue and be extended, more and better long-range fighters and faster bombers or bombers with a higher ceiling would doubtless be needed. None of this was less true after the raids on Brest and La Pallice than before them. But Portal saw no need for any special study of the problem. He did not believe that a long-range fighter capable of holding its own against single-seater interceptor fighters could be developed or that there was any immediate prospect of producing a high-altitude bomber. As for faster bombers, he thought Bomber Command might make some use of the extremely fast Mosquito developed by Geoffrey de Havilland, but he had already rejected an urgent request from Air Marshal Peirse for some of these aircraft and had told Peirse that the Mosquito should be used in the first instance for photographic reconnaissance. Daylight attacks on the interior of Germany would, he thought, be almost impossible until Bomber Command became so strong that it could bear losses comparable with those suffered by the Germans in the Battle of Britain.[8]

Thus day bombing was virtually abandoned in favour of area attacks by night bombers at a time when the moral effects of the attacks hitherto made on Germany could not be accurately assessed and their material effects were admitted by one of the most experienced group commanders in Bomber Command to have been 'definitely disappointing'.[9] The question was whether the fire-raising tactics Bomber Command intended to use in 1942 would improve matters or would lead merely to a vain sacrifice of British and German lives.

American airmen, on the other hand, never doubted that any strategic bombing undertaken by United States forces ought to be done by day and that methods of daylight bombing must be perfected. Within a few weeks of the outbreak of war in Europe American naval and air planners recognized, and the President agreed, that sooner or later the national interest might require that United States forces should be sent to Africa or Europe 'in order to effect the decisive defeat of Germany or Italy or both'. In the autumn of 1940, when the British were seen to be gaining the upper hand in the Battle of Britain, the War Plans Division of the United States Department of the Army recommended that, in the event of simultaneous war with Germany and Japan, Germany should be regarded as the chief adversary and Japan as one to be disposed of later. He and General George C. Marshall, Chief of Staff of the United States Army, agreed that in such circumstances the United States would be obliged to send large land and air forces to Europe or Africa, or both. No one doubted that any strategic bombers included in these forces would be day bombers.

At the Anglo-American conference held at Washington almost immediately after the outbreak of war between Japan and the United States, the 'Germany first' strategy was affirmed on the understanding that it was not to preclude operations designed to secure bases in the Pacific from which an offensive against Japan could eventually be launched. Arrangements were then made for the build-up in Britain of a strategic bomber force of B-17 bombers which would operate from bases in East Anglia. At that time, and for a long time afterwards, the Americans had no more faith than Portal in the long-range fighter. Until they were proved wrong they believed, as the British had believed in 1939, that their bomber formations would be self-defending. By a curious irony it was from an aircraft built in the first place for the British, who did not believe in long-range fighters, that the Americans developed, after a British aero-engine firm had shown the way, the P-51B long-range escort fighter which enabled their bombers to reach distant targets without suffering calamitous losses.

9

AIR POWER IN THE MEDITERRANEAN AND THE MIDDLE EAST, 1940–1945

When the Italian Foreign Minister informed the British Ambassador in Rome on 10 June 1940 that Italy would be at war with the United Kingdom with effect from one minute past midnight, the combined British and French fleets in the Mediterranean were numerically superior to the Italian fleet in warships of every category except submarines. On the other hand, the Regia Aeronautica, although it had passed the peak of its technical development some 4 years earlier and was deficient in spares and reserves of aviation fuel, was in a position to bring greater air strength to bear in the Mediterranean theatre than the British and the French had been able to accumulate in that theatre while they were preoccupied with events elsewhere. As long as the Italians had a fleet in being and access to airfields in Sardinia, Sicily and the Dodecanese they would be well placed to threaten Malta and even Alexandria, make the Sicilian Narrows virtually impassable by Allied merchant shipping, and reinforce and supply their troops in Libya although not those in territories bordering on the Indian Ocean and the Red Sea. The air defences of Malta consisted of 3 Sea Gladiators, 34 heavy and 8 light anti-aircraft guns, 24 searchlights and 1 radar set. There were no British fighters in Egypt, Palestine, Transjordan, Iraq, Aden, British Somaliland, Kenya or the Sudan more modern than the Gladiator, an aircraft slightly inferior in performance to the Italian CR.42.

The collapse of France made matters very much worse from the British point of view. The Italians would have in service by July 6 battleships, 19 cruisers and some 50 destroyers. Admiral Sir Andrew Cunningham, commanding the British Mediterranean Fleet based on Alexandria, had at his disposal 4 battleships, 8 cruisers, 20 destroyers and the 16-year-old carrier *Eagle*, with a maximum speed of 24 knots and a complement of 18 aircraft. A lack of destroyers other than those needed for service with the main fleet meant that practically all other activities had to stop when the main fleet put to sea. Use could no longer be made of airfields in Tunisia, on the African side of the Sicilian Narrows, and only a few shore-based aircraft were available for long-range maritime reconnaissance. A number of airfields and landing strips had been constructed in Egypt and elsewhere since 1939, but the development of well-equipped permanent air bases had been hampered by the difficulty of knowing in what part of the vast area for which the British were responsible such bases were most likely to be needed.

The British considered withdrawing their Mediterranean Fleet from Alexandria to Gibraltar, but soon came to the conclusion that the consequent loss of Malta and annulment of their rights and obligations under their treaty of 1936 with Egypt could not be entertained. The Chiefs of Staff informed all Commanders-in-Chief on 3 July that the intention was that the fleet should remain in the eastern Mediterranean. British bases in Malta and at Alexandria, Haifa and Gibraltar would be defended. Palestine and British possessions in East Africa would be held or, if lost, recaptured. The oil of the Persian Gulf would be safeguarded. Explicit or implicit promises made to the Greeks, the Turks and Arab rulers would be honoured. Most supplies and reinforcements despatched from the United Kingdom would have to go by the long route round the Cape, taking 6 weeks or more to complete the voyage. Aircraft would, however, be disembarked at Takoradi and flown across equatorial Africa to Egypt, some of them carrying light stores. Only on occasions of special urgency would strongly-escorted transports or storeships be sent to Alexandria or Malta by the direct route from Gibraltar.

To supplement 2 surviving Sea Gladiators and 4 Hurricanes which had reached Malta between the Italian declaration of war and the fall of France, the old carrier *Argus* was used at the beginning of August to take 12 Hurricanes to a point from which they could fly to the island. All 12 reached Malta, but 1 was damaged on landing. However, when a further attempt to fly Hurricanes from the *Argus* to Malta was made in November, only 4 out of 12 reached their destination, and these arrived with their fuel tanks almost empty.

Air attacks on Malta began within a few hours of Italy's entry into the war. Between 30 and 40 attacks, the largest by some 60 bombers with fighter escort, were made in June. Seventy civilians out of a population of 270,000 were killed in the course of the month, a floating dock was hit and sunk, and for the time being the British were forced to stop using Malta as a base for submarines. The inhabitants, encouraged by far-reaching measures of passive air defence put in hand by the Governor and military Commander-in-Chief, Lieutenant-General Sir William Dobbie, remained in good heart.

Other tasks which fell to Italian aircraft in the early stages of the war included attacks on warships covering such movements as the passage of the *Argus*, and attempts to sink shipping in the Red Sea by the laying of mines or otherwise. But the Italian Navy, in any case largely preoccupied with the defence of traffic to and from the Dodecanese and Libya, had to compete for the services of the Regia Aeronautica with the Army. In September Marshal Rodolfo Graziani began a cautious advance across the Egyptian frontier with 5 divisions supported by some 300 aircraft. In October Italian forces invaded Greece from Albania. By November so few Italian aircraft were available for the crucial task of barring the Sicilian Narrows to the British that Hitler offered to provide a force for the purpose. Fliegerkorps X, a formation which had played a leading part in the Scandinavian campaign, was ordered in December to leave Norway for the Southern Front. By the middle of January it was established at airfields in Sicily. The tasks assigned to its 190 aircraft included attacks on Malta; but most of its units were essentially anti-shipping units, and both its commander and its Chief of Staff were specialists in operations against shipping.

In the meantime the British Mediterranean Fleet, reinforced by the carrier *Illustrious*, opened a new chapter in naval history by using torpedo-bombers to attack a fleet in harbour. The dropping of torpedoes in shallow water from a low height so that they did not strike the bottom was patiently rehearsed, and reconnaissance aircraft kept watch on the Italian fleet so that a time could be chosen when all 6 battleships were together. Air photographs taken during the afternoon of 11 November showed that 5 of them were berthed in the outer harbour at Taranto and that the sixth was entering it. That night 20 Swordfish aircraft, some drawn from the *Eagle* but all flown from the *Illustrious*, attacked in 2 waves. Two of the aircraft in each wave were detailed to drop flares behind the battleships, others to provide a diversion by flying overhead and dropping bombs. The rest made shallow dives from 4,000 feet or so and released their torpedoes at heights as low as 30 feet. Two Swordfish failed to return. Three of the battleships were disabled. Two of them were out of action for the next 5–6 months; the third never put to sea again. A few hours after the raid all major warships of the Italian battle-fleet still able to steam left Taranto for safer harbours on the west coast of the Italian mainland.

In December the British counter-attacked in Egypt with 2 divisions, supported by roughly 300 aircraft which they were able to assemble only by depleting their air strength at Aden, in the Sudan and at Alexandria. In 2 months they advanced 500 miles, swept the Italians out of Cyrenaica, and captured 130,000 prisoners for the loss of fewer than 2,000 of their own troops killed, wounded or missing.

Well before the British offensive was over, Hitler made up his mind that the Italians must be helped to retain a foothold in North Africa. He also came to the conclusion that the British must be prevented from gaining access to tracts of southern Europe from which the Rumanian oilfields at Ploesti might be bombed, since these were the source from which he expected to draw a substantial part of his supplies until he gained possession of the oilfields of the Caucasus by defeating the Russians. Lieutenant-General Erwin Rommel landed at Tripoli on 12 February 1941 as commander-designate of a corps sent for the purpose of co-operating with the Italians in a 'bold and aggressive' stand near the borders of Tripolitania. In due course Fliegerkorps X was ordered to send some of its aircraft to North Africa for Rommel's benefit. In Europe, Hitler aimed at invading Greece about the first week of April and Russia as soon as possible after the middle of May. The Bulgars undertook to raise no difficulties and the Yugoslavs would, it was hoped, prove equally amenable. However, on 27 March a group of Yugoslav army officers seized power and announced their intention of preventing the country from being dragged in Germany's wake. Thereupon

Hitler declared that Yugoslavia must be 'destroyed'. At the same time he postponed the invasion of Russia until June.

The arrival of Fliegerkorps X profoundly affected the outlook in the Mediterranean theatre. As early as 10 January German bombers and dive-bombers severely damaged the *Illustrious* in the Sicilian Narrows. Between the middle of January and the end of May repeated attacks were made on Malta by German and Italian aircraft. Many buildings were demolished and 375 civilians were killed or seriously injured. The air defences destroyed 60 German and 16 Italian aircraft in the air for the loss of 33 British aircraft in combat, but their reinforcement with Hurricanes brought in carriers or shipped in fast convoys to the island made heavy demands on British naval resources. The mining of the Suez Canal under cover of darkness by German aircraft which refuelled in the Dodecanese also caused the British great anxiety. Not all transports and supply ships could be unloaded and turned round without entering the canal, since wharfage and other facilities at the head of the Red Sea were limited. In any case the canal had to be kept swept, since some shipping was bound to enter it and a disaster which might block it to warships could not be risked.

About the time when Rommel stepped ashore at Tripoli, the Defence Committee of the British War Cabinet ruled that Cyrenaica should be held with minimum forces so that as much help as possible could be sent to Greece. In the light of this ruling General Sir Archibald Wavell, Commander-in-Chief of the land forces in the Middle East, assigned to the defence of Cyrenaica an incompletely trained infantry division and an armoured division whose prior task was to furnish an armoured brigade group for despatch to Greece. Later a brigade of mechanized cavalry without armoured fighting vehicles or supporting arms was added. After a brigade group had been detached from the armoured division little remained of it but a reconnaissance regiment which had only recently exchanged its horses for armoured cars, a weak armoured brigade and an incomplete support group. Both the infantry division and the armoured division were deficient not only in the first-line transport needed to give them tactical mobility but also in the second-line transport needed to carry ammunition and rations to their units. No corps headquarters was interposed between them and the headquarters of the Cyrenaica Command because no corps staff was available after provision had been made for intervention in Greece. The Cyrenaica Command had been formed mainly for the purpose of administering occupied territory and was not organized or equipped to direct a battle of movement by remote control.

Wavell was aware of these shortcomings. He knew he was taking a risk, but believed that a counter-attack was unlikely to be launched before the late spring or early summer and that he and his subordinate commanders and their staffs would have time to bring formations up to strength and make other changes.

Wavell's hold on Cyrenaica was made still more precarious by difficulties of supply. Benghazi, the chief port, had been badly knocked about. When restored to service it proved almost useless in face of air attacks. Seaborne supplies had to be unloaded at ports further back and distributed to depots to which they could be carried by the third-line transport available for the purpose. In these circumstances, and in view of the shortage of second-line transport, not more than one division could be maintained for any length of time in the forward area. Forward positions at Mersa Brega, about midway between Tripoli and Cairo, had therefore to be held by the armoured division alone. For lack of suitable intermediate positions the infantry division withdrew in March to the neighbourhood of Benghazi, about 150 miles to the rear. The mechanized cavalry brigade was still further back. Two squadrons of Hurricanes, 1 squadron of Blenheim bombers and 1 squadron of Lysander army co-operation aircraft were available in Cyrenaica after other commitments had been met. One Hurricane squadron, 2 Blenheim squadrons and 1 squadron of army co-operation aircraft were reserved for service in Greece or elsewhere in the Balkans.

On reaching North Africa Rommel found the Italians preparing to stand on the defensive about 180 miles west of Mersa Brega with 1 incomplete armoured division, 4 infantry divisions with little artillery and such reinforcements as might reach them before they were attacked. A German light division with 70 medium and 80 light tanks began to disembark at Tripoli on 14 February, and a German armoured division was due in May. Very few Italian aircraft were available in Tripolitania, but some 50 dive-bombers, and 20 heavy fighters from Fliegerkorps X arrived in February under a commander authorized to make limited demands on long-range bomber units in Sicily.

By the beginning of March Rommel was satisfied that the British had no immediate intention of advancing on Tripoli. He moved his light division to positions about 25 miles from Mersa Brega and proposed that in May he and the Italians should take the offensive with the object of reoccupying Cyrenaica and afterwards advancing into Egypt, with the Suez Canal as their ultimate objective. The High Command of the German Army responded to Rommel's exposition of this programme by warning him that he could expect no reinforcements apart from the armoured division already promised. His tasks were to guarantee the defence of Tripolitania and to prepare for the capture of Cyrenaica. Whether an attempt to reoccupy Cyrenaica should be made in May must depend on the outcome of a limited offensive which Rommel would not be expected to launch before the armoured division reached him.

Rommel succeeded, however, in persuading Graziani's successor, General Italo Gariboldi, to sanction an early attack by the German light division on the thinly-held British positions at Mersa Brega. Gariboldi stipulated that no advance beyond Mersa Brega should be attempted without his prior sanction.

On 31 March Rommel made 2 attacks on delaying positions held by the support group of the British armoured division. On both occasions the support group held its ground in face of heavy attacks by dive-bombers. Between the 2 attacks the commander of the support group asked that the armoured brigade in rear of his left – which was better equipped to fight than to retreat, since its tanks were badly in need of overhaul – should attack the German right. The divisional commander refused the request on the ground that there were only a few hours of daylight left. After the second attack the support group withdrew a short distance along the road to Benghazi. The armoured brigade conformed with its withdrawal. This movement initiated a retreat which was to cost the brigade disastrous losses resulting from mechanical breakdowns.

On 1 April there was no contact between land forces, but British reconnaissance aircraft reported a big build-up of vehicles in the enemy's rear. On the following day Rommel launched further attacks which left the British uncertain whether he meant to push towards Benghazi or strike across the desert in the general direction of Tobruk and the Egyptian frontier.

Wavell had made it clear before the end of March that he was more interested in safeguarding his forces in Cyrenaica for the sake of the contribution they could make to the defence of Egypt than in retaining territory, and was not prepared to risk defeat in order to hold Benghazi. Nevertheless he found it hard to believe at the beginning of April that Rommel was ready for more than a limited offensive. He concluded that Benghazi was the enemy's most probable objective and that he would be playing into Rommel's hands if he made no serious attempt to defend the place. On 2 April he flew to the headquarters of the Cyrenaica Command to discuss matters on the spot. While he was there a signal was received in which the commander of the armoured division asked to be allowed to keep his whole force together even at the cost of leaving the road to Benghazi uncovered. Wavell insisted that the road should be defended, even though this might mean that the armoured brigade and the support group would have to retreat by different routes.

In the outcome Rommel could not be prevented from reaching Benghazi. Moreover, by disregarding Gariboldi's protests and making a bold use of Italian as well as German units he was able not only to advance along the coast road but also to fan out to the east. The British armoured brigade, which might have counter-attacked with some prospect of success had it been allowed to do so during the first day or two, when it still had most of its tanks and could call on the support group, was so weakened by mechanical breakdowns and difficulties of supply that it fell to pieces without ever having been used in the offensive role for which it was intended. Within a fortnight the British were driven out of practically the whole of Cyrenaica except Tobruk, which they succeeded in holding as a bastion on Rommel's flank. Before withdrawing from Benghazi they managed, however, to carry out such effective demolitions that roughly half the supplies consigned to Rommel during the next few months had to be unloaded at Tripoli, 1,000 miles from his forward troops. After twice failing to take Tobruk by assault in April and May, he settled down to reorganize his forces and await reinforcements.

For the British the most serious consequence of the retreat from Cyrenaica was the loss of airfields at which they had hoped, when enough aircraft arrived from the United Kingdom by way of Takoradi, to establish strong forces for the defence of their shipping in the central Mediterranean and attacks on Axis convoys. The frustration of these hopes led the Government to put considerable pressure on Wavell and his successor, General Sir Claude Auchinleck, to launch a fresh offensive with the least possible delay.

When Italy entered the war in the summer of 1940, Mussolini announced that he had no designs on Greece or other Balkan states. Within a few weeks the Italian press and radio began to accuse the Greeks of breaches of neutrality. In August the Italian civil and military authorities in Albania outlined proposals for the invasion of Greece from Albanian territory; in September the number of Italian divisions in Albania rose from 5 to 9. As the sequel to discussions between Mussolini and his service chiefs, the Italian Foreign Minister, Count Ciano, informed the Greek Government at 3 am on 28 October that Italian troops would begin to cross the frontier 3 hours later.

In the light of the Italian ultimatum and its rejection by the Greeks, the British decided to give effect to a project, previously discussed, for the establishment of a naval fuelling base at Suda Bay in Crete and to send a few bombers, fighters and anti-aircraft guns to the Greek mainland. In November they agreed to assume responsibility for the defence of Crete so that the Greek garrison could be used against the Italians. Their decision to offer more substantial help at the cost of weakening their hold on Egypt and Cyrenaica was made during the winter and was formally accepted by the Greek Government on 22 February 1941.

In the autumn of 1940 the Greeks had some 16 divisions in all parts of the country, but only 3 of these and part of a fourth were on a war footing when hostilities began. About a third of their army was reserved for the defence of eastern Macedonia and could not be used elsewhere unless the benevolent neutrality of Bulgaria could be assumed. They had no tanks, few anti-tank or anti-artillery guns and little transport. Since most of their 160 military aircraft were of French or Polish manufacture, replacements and spares were virtually unobtainable. Much heartened by the arrival of British aircraft, they none the less succeeded in halting the Italians and throwing them back to a defensive front in Albanian territory. This was not altogether surprising, since the Italian plan of campaign was based on the assumption that little or no resistance would be met. Even so, the inability of a relatively well-equipped Italian army with substantial air support to reach any of its objectives after a confident ultimatum had been delivered dealt a severe blow to Mussolini's self-esteem.

During the winter of 1940–1 the Italians raised the strength of their land forces in Albania to the equivalent of 28 divisions. On 9 March they launched an attack on a 20-mile front under cover of an intense artillery bombardment and with support from roughly 130 bombers and fighters stationed in Albania. About 190 aircraft based in Italy were at call. The Greeks had only a few aircraft still fit for use, but the British provided a squadron of Gladiators, a squadron of Blenheim bombers and a few Hurricanes, Wellingtons and Blenheim fighters. In addition, British naval aircraft attacked Italian shipping in Albanian waters and sank at least 4 ships. A British expeditionary force commanded by Lieutenant-General Sir Henry Maitland Wilson was about to disembark in Greece under the terms of an Anglo-Greek agreement, but this was intended for use against the Germans.

Again the Italians were unsuccessful. Notwithstanding their marked superiority in the air their offensive began to lose its momentum about the middle of March and petered out some 10 days later. By that time 14 Greek divisions, forming the bulk of the Greek Army, were deployed on the Albanian front. They had fought well but were very tired. Whether the Germans could be prevented from overrunning Greece would depend, therefore, on the effectiveness of the British contribution.

By 1 April the German Twelfth Army was ready to invade Greece as soon as the High Command ordered it to do so. Hitler's decision to attack Yugoslavia as well as Greece made little difference to the timetable. As a result of preparations made during the autumn and winter there was ample accommodation at airfields in Rumania and Bulgaria not only for the 500 or 600 aircraft of the Luftwaffe already there but also for reinforcements which could be quickly brought from France, Germany and Sicily.

On 6 April Germany declared war on both countries. The Luftwaffe was used to attack Belgrade and the port of Piraeus, where a hit on a British ship whose cargo included 250 tons of high-explosive had devastating effects; but its chief task during the first few days was to give direct support to the land forces in Yugoslavia. In this it succeeded so well that by 8 April leading elements of the Twelfth Army were at Prilep, barely 30 miles from the Greek frontier.

The plan on which the British and the Greeks had agreed was that the equivalent of 4 British or British-controlled divisions, assisted by 3 weak and incomplete Greek divisions, were to hold a line some 70 miles long between Katerini, on the Aegean, and a point on the Yugoslav frontier north-west of Edessa. In eastern Macedonia, 3 immobile Greek divisions and some fortress troops, facing north and north-east, were to hold a line from the coast east of Kavalla to a point west of the junction between the frontiers of Greece, Bulgaria and Yugoslavia.

This was not a plan which held out much prospect of success. The line to be held in eastern Macedonia provided some good defensive positions, but it was more than 120 miles long and was weak near its western extremity, opposite Salonika. The position for which the British were to assume responsibility was based on strong natural features interspersed with gaps inadequately prepared for defence. Moreover, an enemy who succeeded in reaching Prilep could turn it by continuing along a relatively easy route and entering Greek territory between Monastir and Florina. However, the British accepted the plan since the only alternative was to allow Greece to be overrun without a struggle.

In the outcome, the main defensive position was turned while the British were still deploying. The British had therefore to withdraw their left to a position south of Florina. This move left them with an open flank which could have been made secure only if the right of the Greek forces in Albania had been swiftly withdrawn to fill the gap. The Greek Commander-in-Chief, understandably reluctant to withdraw troops which had held their positions with conspicuous success, waited too long before giving the order. In any case the Greek Army, largely dependent on ox-drawn wagons for its transport, was not equipped to travel fast. For the British and the Greeks the campaign became a race to escape encirclement by an enemy with almost overwhelming air superiority. In general the British were much better provided with transport than the Germans, whose infantry divisions still relied on horse-drawn transport; but the Twelfth Army's forces included mountain divisions better suited to conditions in Greece than were British formations trained and equipped for a campaign in the Western Desert of Egypt. On 21 April the Greek Government informed the British Ambassador, Sir Michael Palairet, that the Greek Army could no longer fight successfully and that the British expeditionary force would, in the opinion of the King and his constitutional advisers, be able to do more for the common cause by withdrawing to fight another day than by staying to be defeated.

Between 24 April and 1 May about 50,000 British, British Commonwealth and Allied troops departed from the mainland of Greece under the protection of the Royal Navy. Originally the majority were to have gone straight to Egypt, but eventually it was decided that more than half should be carried in the first instance only as far as Crete so that transports could return quickly to pick up another load and escort vessels would have only a short distance to go. The troops had to be embarked at night in order to escape the attentions of the Luftwaffe, and most of them had to be lifted from beaches because the port of Piraeus had become almost unusable in consequence of the explosion there. Practically all heavy equipment, including about 8,000 lorries, had to be left behind. Two British destroyers and 4 transports were sunk by bombing. The campaign on the Greek mainland cost the British about 12,000 casualties, or roughly a fifth of their force, but many sick or wounded afterwards rejoined their units. The conclusion drawn by the British military authorities was that British and Commonwealth troops were well able to stand up to the Germans, but must have strong air support if they were to hold their own in future campaigns.

In the middle of April the Luftwaffe proposed an airborne invasion of Crete. About 500 transport aircraft and 72 gliders were available to carry some 13,000 troops of an airborne corps, supplemented by troops drawn from 2 mountain divisions and other details. In addition, small parties were to be despatched by sea with equipment and supplies. Fliegerkorps VIII, with roughly 500 first-line aircraft ready for immediate use, was to provide air support.

Hitler gave his approval less than 24 hours after the beginning of the British withdrawal from the mainland. The Luftwaffe, helped by an improvement in the weather, prepared airfields in Greece and the Aegean with commendable speed, but its knowledge of conditions in Crete was faulty. The strength of the garrison was underestimated and areas which in fact were strongly held were believed to be clear of the enemy. The Cretans, traditionally patriotic and well disposed towards the British, were thought likely to co-operate with German troops.

On the side of the defenders, the situation in May was that little had been done to prepare the island for defence since the arrival of the British in the previous November. Until January the only dangers which had seemed to threaten Crete were bombardment by Italian warships, seaborne landings by Italian troops and attacks by Italian bombers from the Dodecanese. In recent months the threat of German intervention had become apparent, but priority had gone to the mainland and to Egypt and Cyrenaica. As late as 18 April Churchill placed the defence of Crete last in a list of tasks which included withdrawal from the Greek mainland and the protection of ships carrying equipment and supplies to Tobruk.[1] About 32,000 British and some 10,000 Greek troops were available after the withdrawal had been completed and men unfit to fight had been sent to Egypt, but the arrival of relatively large numbers of men who had no place in the original scheme of defence was not an unmixed advantage. Only 32 heavy and 36 light anti-aircraft guns and 24 searchlights were deployed for the defence of Suda Bay, Canea and other vital points in an island 160 miles long with poor communications and a population of 400,000. An airfield at Heraklion and landing grounds at Retimo and Maleme, all on the north coast, had been developed as forward bases for aircraft from Egypt, 300 miles away, but they were so vulnerable to bombing that on 19 May the few surviving aircraft of the small fighter force hitherto stationed in Crete were sent away.

The Germans launched their airborne assault on 20 May after nearly a week of softening-up attacks. Many parachutists landed in the midst of the defences and were killed or captured in the first few minutes. Others fell clear of defended areas but were unable to reach the points at which they had been told to rally. Unit commanders who did succeed in gathering their men about them wondered how long they would be able to survive without supplies which might or might not arrive later in the day or on the following day and to which they might or might not be able to gain access.

The essence of the German plan was that Heraklion, Retimo and Maleme should be captured promptly so that transport aircraft bringing mountain troops with supporting arms could land there by the second day. At first light on 21 May Heraklion and Retimo were still firmly in British hands. At Maleme, where the defences were confused by the arrival of large numbers of parachutists at widely separated points, the landing ground was in dispute. During the morning the Germans made so little progress that they faced the possible loss of their entire airborne corps. The situation was saved by the arrival in the afternoon of a mountain regiment carried in transport aircraft which landed under artillery fire. Canea was captured on 27 May by a parachute battalion which had received no rations at all during its first 5 days in Crete. The British managed, with great difficulty, to withdraw about 18,000 of their troops, leaving nearly 12,000 in the enemy's hands. They lost 3,479 soldiers and 2,011 seamen killed or wounded, the Germans about 6,000 airmen and soldiers killed, wounded or missing.

To the Germans the undertaking seemed, when it was over, to have been so hazardous that tentative plans for airborne expeditions to Cyprus and thence to Egypt were not pursued, and no further landings on a comparable scale were attempted. Outside Germany the capture of Crete by airborne troops alone made a powerful impression. Both the British and the Americans developed airborne divisions and used them with mixed results in the later stages of the war. The Russians used airborne brigades and studied the problem of grouping them in airborne divisions. At the same time experience in Crete strengthened the conviction of the British that they could not hope to meet the Germans on level terms either in Africa or in Europe until their troops had much more powerful air support than had been provided in the past.

In the light of this consideration the British viewed with dismay the slow growth of their first-line strength in the Middle East. About 220,000 troops, some 13,000 airmen and some 6,000 seamen were carried to Egyptian ports from the United Kingdom, Australia, New Zealand, India and South Africa in the first 7 months of 1941. During the same period large numbers of aircraft were shipped to Takoradi, while others flew directly or by way of Gibraltar to Malta and either stayed there or went on to Egypt. But the rate at which brigades, divisions and air squadrons could be trained, equipped and made fit for an offensive role depended on many factors besides the despatch of men and machines. In the case of the Air Force, these included the speed with which aircraft sent in crates, sometimes without essential items of equipment, could be assembled, flown 4,000 miles across equatorial Africa, taken up by operational units, and where necessary modified to suit local conditions.

Towards the end of April the authorities in London decided that a bold attempt should be made to rush much-needed equipment to their forces in the Western Desert. For the first time since the Luftwaffe advertised its arrival in Sicily by damaging the *Illustrious*, a fast convoy was sent from Gibraltar to Alexandria by the Mediterranean route. Five ships carrying tanks and aircraft were detached from a large convoy bound for the Cape and Suez. Heavily escorted, they passed through the Straits of Gibraltar during the night of 5/6 May and reached the entrance to the Sicilian Narrows at dusk on 8 May. One ship, carrying 57 tanks and 10 Hurricanes, caught fire and blew up after 2 mines had exploded near her. Thick weather, rare in the central Mediterranean in May, helped the rest to reach Alexandria safely on 12 May.

Wavell promised that the greater part of the 238 tanks and 43 Hurricanes thus delivered should be devoted to an attempt to relieve Tobruk. His offensive, launched on 15 June, was unsuccessful. Of the 2 armoured brigades which played the leading parts, one was equipped with slow and vulnerable infantry tanks, the other with cruiser tanks which were faster but mechanically unreliable. The 2 brigades had no time before the battle to rehearse their roles together or with the infantry. Some crews who had not handled a tank since February had barely a fortnight in which to accustom themselves to vehicles new to them. The British, with 200 serviceable aircraft to roughly the same number of German and Italian, were not outmatched in the air, and indeed made many more sorties than the enemy. The fact remains that, having started their offensive on 15 June with roughly 190 tanks, they had only 39 still fit to fight when they called it off on 17 June. A significant feature of the battle was the good use made by Rommel of his anti-tank guns.

A few weeks later Wavell handed over his command to Auchinleck and took Auchinleck's place as Commander-in-Chief in India. Auchinleck soon made it clear that he was not prepared to take the offensive until he was satisfied that his troops were ready, and that this was not likely to happen before November. A new Eighth Army commanded by General Sir Alan Cunningham, who had distinguished himself in East Africa but had no experience of desert warfare and had never commanded an armoured force, would then launch an offensive designed to relieve Tobruk and defeat the enemy's armoured forces in Cyrenaica. Air Marshal A. W. Tedder, who had succeeded Air Chief Marshal Sir Arthur Longmore in command of the air forces in the Middle East, formed a Western Desert Air Force for the purpose of supporting the Eighth Army. While awaiting the start of the offensive Tedder's forces made many attacks on Tripoli, Benghazi, airfields and ports of embarkation in Sicily and Italy, and supply dumps in the enemy's forward area. These caused the Axis leaders a good deal of anxiety, but did not prevent them from preparing to assault Tobruk at almost exactly the moment when Cunningham proposed to advance to its relief. By mid-November Rommel's resources included 2 German armoured divisions, with some 240 tanks, in addition to his light division and 5 Italian infantry divisions. An Italian mobile corps of 1 armoured and 1 motorized division completed the force under the command of Rommel's immediate superior, General Ettore Bastico. The Italian armoured division had about 150 medium tanks of Italian design and manufacture; roughly the same number of Italian light tanks were divided between the armoured division and non-armoured divisions. Bastico could call on some 340 serviceable aircraft of the Luftwaffe and the Regia Aeronautica stationed in Cyrenaica. Much larger numbers of German and Italian aircraft were stationed in Tripolitania, Sicily and elsewhere, but the limiting factor was the quantity of fuel available at bases within reach of the forward area. In November this barely sufficed for the aircraft already in Cyrenaica.

By the same date General Cunningham had under his command a powerful mechanized army of 6 divisions and 6 independent brigades or brigade groups, with nearly 750 tanks. In addition, about 500 tanks in transit or in workshops constituted a reserve on which he would be able to draw to replace losses. In general, his tanks were less well armed and less robust than their German counterparts, and his 2-pounder anti-tank guns were inferior in range and striking power to the 50-millimetre and 88-millimetre guns with which Bastico's 3 German divisions were equipped.

In the air the British had the advantage. With more than 600 serviceable aircraft in Egypt and Malta, they could reconnoitre freely and maintain a heavy scale of attack on the enemy's system of supply and forward installations. The German Me.109F single-seater fighter was, however, considerably faster than any British fighter yet in service in the Western Desert. In the past the British had had no counterpart to the German Junkers 87 dive-bomber, and experience had shown that medium bombers could seldom deal effectively with tanks. In the coming battle Tedder proposed to remedy this shortcoming by using bomb-carrying Hurricanes to make low-level attacks on battlefield targets. In the light of the unsatisfactory outcome of the June offensive, he had set up an elaborate organization to deal with requests for air support. He retained the right to decide for himself how his forces should be used to meet competing demands, but impressed upon all concerned the importance of ensuring that the Army lacked nothing the Air Force could provide.

Cunningham opened his offensive on 18 November by thrusting the main body of his armour across the frontier well south of Bardia. His intention was to decide in the light of the enemy's response whether he could best bring the German armour to battle by continuing towards Tobruk or by wheeling back to the north and east. Rommel had flown to Rome on 14 November to confer with the Italian High Command. Incomplete reports of Cunningham's movements which reached him when he returned on 18 November convinced him that the British were attempting no more than a reconnaissance in force and that dispositions made with a view to his coming attack on Tobruk need not be changed. The result was that Cunningham, with a crucial decision to make at the end of the first 24 hours, found himself no better able to judge on the second day than on the first how the enemy would respond to his advance. A series of inconclusive engagements left him at the end of the third day with the greater part of his armoured force split into 3 widely-separated formations, each with about half as many tanks as Rommel could bring to bear against it if the two German armoured divisions stayed together. Of the 477 tanks which had crossed the frontier on 18 November, well over 100 had succumbed by the evening of 20 November to mechanical breakdowns or had been disabled by the enemy. Cunningham's 13th Corps, which had stayed in the frontier area with orders to pin down the enemy's forces there, had about 130 tanks not included in the 477; the force still locked up at Tobruk about the same number. The question which was to cause Cunningham intense anxiety during the next few days was whether his major armoured formations were still strong enough to knock out the enemy's.

Most of Bastico's aircraft were grounded on waterlogged airfields during the first few days, and at no stage did they intervene decisively. Nevertheless the British soon ceased to derive as much benefit as might have been expected from their air superiority. In a battle of movement fought over a vast area there was no 'bomb-line' beyond which any troops or vehicles seen could be assumed to belong to the enemy. Single vehicles or groups of vehicles which might equally well be British, German or Italian were likely to appear from any direction at any moment throughout the hours of daylight, and no vehicle could be safely attacked unless it was positively identified as hostile. The wide range of vehicles used by all 3 armies, the frequent use of captured equipment, the clouds of dust stirred up by any movement in the desert – all these made identification difficult, especially for the pilot of a low-flying fighter-bomber whose field of vision in a downward direction was at best extremely limited. Moreover, where a tank battle was in progress it sometimes happened that, even though tanks belonging to one side could be clearly distinguished from those belonging to the other, the sides were so closely intermingled that airmen dared not intervene for fear that a bomb aimed at a German tank might hit a British one.

An aspect of the desert particularly troublesome to airmen was the scarcity of natural features which could be easily recognized, described and located on a map. For lack of such landmarks fighter pilots and bomber crews were often unable to say exactly where they were when they witnessed some occurrence which seemed worth reporting. At the outset of the battle the British had only 3 squadrons of aircraft specifically assigned to tactical reconnaissance, while on the Axis side of the lines conditions on the ground were so bad that for the first few days the Luftwaffe and the Regia Aeronautica could scarcely reconnoitre at all.

For these and other reasons, commanders on both sides had to fight the battle without always knowing where the enemy was or in what direction he was moving. Cunningham did not always know even where his own forces were, how many tanks they had or how they had fared during the past 24 hours. This was not because his formations and units did not try to send full and accurate reports, but because the means of doing so did not always exist. Wireless transmitters broke down, or transmitted messages which could not be received and understood because they were jammed by the enemy or made unintelligible by atmospherics. The Axis forces were also troubled by such frustrations, but in general German transmitters were more reliable than those possessed by the British in 1941.

On 20 November Rommel at last admitted that the British must be assumed to have launched a major offensive, but his assessment of the situation was still wide of the mark. He believed that the British 4th Armoured Brigade, which had more than 100 tanks left after losing about 50 in 2 encounters with the 15th Panzer Division, was a spent force.

On the same day Cunningham, either because he believed that victory was within his grasp or because he feared that it would elude him unless he staged a diversion of some kind, agreed with his subordinate commanders that the garrison of Tobruk should begin on the following day a sortie which, according to the original plan, was to have been attempted only after the enemy's armour had been brought to battle and defeated.

The outcome was a series of confused engagements which seriously depleted Cunningham's armoured strength in the forward area. On 23 November he asked Auchinleck to visit his headquarters. When Auchinleck arrived from Cairo by air, Cunningham told him that he no longer had the superiority in armour on which his plan was based. He asked whether he should continue the offensive at the risk of losing all his fast tanks, or break it off while he still had some left for the defence of Egypt.

In the meantime the 13th Corps was fighting well in the

frontier area, and Rommel was thinking of moving his armour eastwards to relieve his hard-pressed forces there as soon as it was free to go. Auchinleck told Cunningham that he must continue to attack the enemy relentlessly, 'using all your resources even to the last tank'.[2] Two days later he decided to relieve Cunningham of his command. He was satisfied with Cunningham's conduct of the battle up to 23 November and with the steps he had taken to carry out the instructions given to him on that day, but felt that a commander who had begun to think in terms of defence could not be expected to carry the offensive to its end. Major-General N. M. Ritchie, hitherto Deputy Chief of the General Staff at Auchinleck's headquarters, assumed command of the Eighth Army on the following day. Ritchie was not qualified by experience or seniority for command of an army. He was chosen because it seemed to Auchinleck essential that the post should be filled without delay by an energetic officer who knew the plan and was conversant with his views.

After midday on 24 November Rommel ordered the 15th and 21st Panzer Divisions to the frontier area. This move put the 2 divisions out of easy reach of German and Italian single-seater fighters, created formidable problems of supply and cost Rommel at least 30 tanks. Above all, it gave the British time to reorganize and refit. Cunningham had told Auchinleck on 23 November that he estimated that he had only 44 serviceable tanks left and that the enemy had 120. When the 15th and 21st Panzer Divisions returned from the frontier area to the neighbourhood of Tobruk on 27 and 28 November, they had 74 tanks between them, while the British 4th and 22nd Armoured Brigades had 122.

Barely a week later Rommel and Bastico had ceased to think of taking Tobruk and were forced to consider whether they should withdraw from the whole of Cyrenaica or only part of it. Within 6 weeks they were back in the positions from which Rommel had launched his offensive 9 months earlier. During their advance the British found hundreds of wrecked German and Italian aircraft at airfields and landing grounds and on scrap-heaps. Since November the German and Italian land forces had suffered more than twice as many casualties as the British. During the past 9 weeks British aircraft based in Egypt and Malta had made nearly 12,000 sorties in direct or indirect support of the Eight Army. Some sorties had been wasted, some bombs supposedly aimed at the enemy had fallen on British troops. On some occasions squadrons had stood by for hours awaiting calls to action which never came. Despite such lapses co-operation between land and air forces had, on the whole, been not merely good but far better than previous experience had led army officers to expect. No British army had ever in the past received such powerful air support. The Western Desert Air Force, commanded by Air Vice-Marshal A. Coningham, became the model on which future British tactical air forces were based.

Having defeated the enemy's forces in Cyrenaica but not destroyed them, Auchinleck faced much the same problems early in 1942 as had confronted Wavell nearly 12 months earlier. Limitations of supply and the need to relieve tired and depleted formations compelled him to break off the pursuit in the middle of January and stand on the defensive with one incomplete armoured division and one infantry brigade group in the forward area and one infantry division far to the rear. Squadrons of the Western Desert Air Force within reach of the front were roughly 450 aircraft strong, but only about 280 aircraft were immediately available for operations.

On 5 January a convoy reached Tripoli carrying 54 German tanks, with crews, a supply of fuel and other stores. By the third week of the month Rommel had at his disposal 10 weak German and Italian divisions, with a fighting strength equivalent to that of 3 full-scale divisions and equipped with 84 German and 89 Italian tanks. Sandstorms which hampered air reconnaissance helped him to concentrate his forces in the forward area without detection. On 21 January he launched a surprise attack supported by some 300 German and Italian aircraft. Largely because heavy rain on the previous night had turned a crucial airfield into a quagmire, the British were heavily outmatched in the air. On the second day Rommel turned the line on which they had intended to stand should they be driven from their covering positions. Thus the airfields of western Cyrenaica, after remaining in the hands of the British just long enough for some much-needed supplies to be carried to Malta in January, fell once more into the possession of the Germans and the Italians.

In January the commander and staff of Luftflotte 2, withdrawn from the Russian front, took charge of operations by the

Luftwaffe in the Mediterranean theatre. Fliegerkorps II, also withdrawn from the Russian front, then became responsible for units in the central Mediterranean, Fliegerkorps X for operations further east. At the same time the Axis air forces opened a new series of heavy attacks on Malta, with the object of making the island useless as a base for naval and air operations against their supply routes. Malta was heavily bombed during the passage of the convoy which reached Tripoli on 5 January. More than 600 tons of bombs were aimed at the island in January, more than 1,000 in February. By the middle of March about as many German aircraft were stationed in Sicily as at the height of the earlier offensive against Malta in 1941.

Strenuous attempts by the British to meet this new threat began in March. Some 30 Spitfires flew to Malta from the *Eagle* on various dates in that month, but most of them were soon destroyed on the ground or in the air. In April the American carrier *Wasp* brought another 47. All but one flew safely to their destination from a point about 45 miles north-east of Algiers, but these too were soon knocked out by bombing or in combat.

In May the British, again helped by the Americans, made a further attempt to build up the island's air defences. On 9 May 64 Spitfires brought by the *Wasp* and the *Eagle* flew to Malta from a point about 60 miles off the African coast; on 18 May the *Eagle* brought another 17. This time maintenance crews were standing ready to remove the long-range tanks from the Spitfires as soon as they came to a standstill, and pilots were waiting to take them into the air before the enemy, warned by radar of their arrival, could send bombers to catch them on the ground. These measures were successful in as much as they were followed by a marked increase in the effectiveness of the air defences, but they came too late to prevent the Axis powers from sending valuable cargoes to North Africa in ships which the British could not sink. In April alone the German and Italian forces in Cyrenaica and Tripolitania received nearly 50,000 tons of fuel and more than 100,000 tons of other military stores.

During the spring and early summer the commanders of the land forces on both sides prepared to take the offensive at the opportune moment. Auchinleck steadfastly refused to be hurried, but the Government made it clear to him in May that, unless he was prepared to make way for a successor, he must do something to regain the airfields of western Cyrenaica by midsummer, since otherwise Malta might be starved out. By the time this ultimatum was digested, there was reason to believe that Rommel might be ready to attack first.

The positions occupied by the Eighth Army's forward troops at Gazala consisted of a series of wired 'boxes', each garrisoned by a brigade group with its own artillery and enough supplies to last about a week. Some of the boxes were contiguous, others were separated by wide gaps. They were covered by minefields extending from the coast west of Gazala to Bir Hacheim, about 40 miles to the south. These positions were intended not to present an impregnable front to an attacker but to force him to accept battle on unfavourable terms. The front could be turned by an enemy willing to make a wide sweep through the desert at the risk of outrunning his supplies. Alternatively, it could be penetrated by one equipped to clear a passage through minefields in one or other of the gaps between the boxes. In either case the assailant would have to run the gauntlet of the Eighth Army's 2 armoured divisions in order to reach Tobruk.

Auchinleck strongly advised Ritchie to concentrate the 2 armoured divisions in a central position well back from the front, where their 500 tanks could be supported by the field artillery and anti-tank guns of an entire armoured corps. But the relations between the two men had become not unlike those between Gamelin and Georges in 1940. Auchinleck was unwilling to deprive the army commander of the right to dispose his forces as he thought best. He was also unwilling to assume direct command of the Eighth Army and relegate Ritchie to a subordinate position or send him back to Cairo. Ritchie wished to hold the 3 mobile brigades of one of his armoured divisions ready to meet the enemy's armour at an early stage should Rommel turn his flank. He did not, therefore, concentrate both armoured divisions in the position pointed out by Auchinleck.

Even so, Ritchie seemed *likely* to be able to deal with almost any situation that could arise. He had nearly 1,000 tanks at his disposal, including reserves, while Rommel had fewer than 600. Auchinleck believed, too, that Ritchie could count on powerful air support. As things turned out, only about 190 of the Western Desert Air Force's 320 aircraft were serviceable on the eve of the battle, while the Germans and the Italians were thought by the

British to have about 400 serviceable aircraft in North Africa and in fact had 497. The Luftwaffe and the Regia Aeronautica also had more serviceable aircraft than the British in the theatre as a whole.[3]

Rommel opened his attack on 26 May. During the night he took the bulk of his armour round the British flank, and early on the following day he disrupted the armoured division which Ritchie had placed in his path. The 2 armoured brigades of Ritchie's other armoured division then counter-attacked, at first separately but afterwards together. The situation soon became so confused that British bomber crews and fighter-bomber pilots had difficulty in finding targets they could safely attack. The 2 German armoured divisions lost about a third of their tanks by nightfall on 27 May, and by that time one of them was already short of fuel and ammunition. The British had no problems of supply, but their freedom of manoeuvre was restricted by the need to defend huge stocks which they had accumulated in preparation for the offensive they were to have launched in June.

Rommel, using his artillery and anti-tank weapons to hold off the enemy, then concentrated his mobile formations east of the minefield and proceeded to open a passage through it as a line of supply and possible escape route. Despite Auchinleck's belief that the British were 'definitely superior in the air', dive-bombers gave Rommel powerful support. A poorly co-ordinated counter-attack on 5 June was unsuccessful and cost the British heavy losses in tanks and men. A week later Rommel, with roughly 200 tanks, attacked the remnant of Ritchie's armour, defeated it in a 2-day battle and drove it from the battlefield.

Ritchie responded to this calamity by withdrawing 2 infantry divisions to the Egyptian frontier. Auchinleck sent his Chief of the General Staff, Lieutenant-General T. W. Corbett, to Ritchie's headquarters with orders to insist that Ritchie should not abandon Tobruk but should rally his forces for a defensive battle in a position which would enable him to use his surviving tanks under cover of artillery fire from high ground. The interview was unsatisfactory, Tobruk fell on 21 June, and on 25 June Auchinleck relieved Ritchie of his command and assumed direct control of the Eighth Army. He went on to make a fighting retreat to a partly prepared position at El Alamein, where he could stand with his right on the sea and his left on the impassable Qattara depression 40 miles to the south.

The Axis leaders had intended to follow the capture of Tobruk by landing seaborne and airborne forces in Malta. Rommel begged to be allowed to continue his advance, and Hitler and Mussolini agreed that he should do so. This last-minute change of plan sowed confusion in the rear. The 2 German armoured divisions reached the Alamein–Qattara position at the end of June with only 55 serviceable tanks between them. They were short of water, had received only intermittent help from the Luftwaffe and the Regia Aeronautica since leaving Tobruk, and could not have moved at all without captured fuel. Meanwhile the British had been making strenuous attempts to provide the Eighth Army with stronger air support, even at the cost of withdrawing aircraft from training units. In terms of aircraft fit for immediate use, they succeeded in raising the effective strength of the Western Desert Air Force to some 460 aircraft by the last week in June. The corresponding figure for the German and Italian Air Forces in North Africa fell by the same date to roughly 420 aircraft. Thus the British managed at the crucial moment to attain local air superiority, although the Germans and the Italians still had more serviceable aircraft in the theatre as a whole. Furthermore, by the end of the month the British were once more able to use Malta as a base for attacks on Axis convoys.

Rommel could not fail to recognize on reaching the Alamein–Qattara position that he would stand no chance of taking it with any forces likely to be at his disposal in the near future if he gave the British time to recover from the strain of the past few days. Without pausing to make a thorough reconnaissance he committed his well-nigh exhausted troops to a series of attempts to cut through the Eighth Army's forward positions and reach the coast road east of El Alamein. Repeated air attacks, heavy artillery fire and difficulties of supply made this a hopeless undertaking. After losing more than half his tanks on 1 and 2 July and making virtually no progress on 3 July, Rommel reported that the strength of his divisions was down to 1,200–1,500 men apiece and that he expected to have to remain on the defensive for at least a fortnight. In a later report he complained that the Royal Air Force was destroying his vehicles at the rate of 30 a day. He asked for more air protection for his troops and their supplies and more air attacks on the enemy's communications.

The battle afterwards called First Alamein left the British and the Axis forces still facing each other in positions which could not be turned. Repeated attempts by Auchinleck during the next few weeks to clear a path with his infantry by which his armour might debouch into open country and annihilate the enemy showed that the problem of opening and exploiting a gap in a continuous front had not changed as much since the First World War as might have been expected. No matter how well the infantry might fight or how effectively it might be supported by artillery and air bombardments, the difficulty of co-ordinating the movements of follow-up formations with those of the forward troops in circumstances never predictable when the assault was launched was still the governing factor. At the end of July Auchinleck told his corps commanders to rest and reorganize their troops and prepare to meet the attack which he thought Rommel might deliver before the arrival of reinforcements allowed the Eighth Army to launch a fresh offensive.

Auchinleck's tentative plan for the defensive battle was to allow the enemy to penetrate the southern part of his front, draw him towards a belt of high ground called the Alam el Halfa ridge and there use a combination of armour, field artillery and anti-tank guns to destroy him. In essence, these were the tactics he had wished Ritchie to use at Gazala.

First Alamein was a turning-point in the Second World War, but its significance was obscured at the time by Auchinleck's inability to smash the remnant of Rommel's force. Churchill was so far from understanding its importance that he afterwards described the month of July as one in which he was 'without a gleam of military success'.[4] Early in August he flew to Cairo, where he was joined by General Sir Alan Brooke, Chief of the Imperial General Staff. Churchill's faith in Auchinleck had barely survived the loss of Tobruk. It was undermined during his stay in Egypt by complaints of poor co-ordination between the Eighth Army's infantry and its armour. Churchill was also seriously displeased when General Corbett warned him, on the authority of his tank expert, that some 300 tanks which President Roosevelt had agreed to send to Egypt could not be made battleworthy until 2 or 3 weeks after their arrival. He and Brooke agreed that changes must be made. Auchinleck was replaced as Commander-in-Chief of the land forces in the Middle East by General the Hon. Sir Harold Alexander, who was to have commanded British and American troops soon to disembark in North-West Africa under the Supreme Command of General Dwight D. Eisenhower. Lieutenant-General B. L. Montgomery, a brilliant lecturer on strategy and tactics, was chosen to take Alexander's place, Lieutenant-General W. H. E. Gott to command the Eighth Army. But Gott, a seasoned campaigner with a wide experience of desert warfare, was killed on 7 August when an aircraft in which he was travelling on leave to Cairo was forced down by 2 German fighters and destroyed on the ground. Montgomery was then appointed in his stead. Command of Eisenhower's land forces went to Lieutenant-General K. A. N. Anderson. In the outcome, however, Anderson was responsible in the early stages of the campaign in North-West Africa only for the British component of Eisenhower's force.

Corbett, too, was relieved of his post. Ironically, he was succeeded as Chief of the General Staff of the land forces in the Middle East by the officer whose warning about the time needed to make newly-arrived tanks battleworthy had so displeased Churchill when it reached him at second hand. No changes were made in the command of the air forces. The consensus of opinion in the circles in which Churchill moved was that co-operation between land and air had become much better in recent months but that there was still room for improvement.

Alexander and Montgomery soon agreed that no major offensive would be possible before late October. Montgomery wished to open his attack by moonlight, and he could not be ready in time for the September moon. Adopting the substance of Auchinleck's tentative plan for the defensive battle which he expected to have to fight in the meantime, he disposed the greater part of his infantry in considerable depth behind the northern part of his front and placed an infantry division and an armoured brigade in prepared positions on and near the Alam el Halfa ridge. If the enemy came by the southern route, as there was reason to believe he meant to do, light mobile formations and armoured brigades would delay his advance, but would make it their business to lead him to the ridge.

Rommel fell ill in August, but agreed to remain at his post

under medical supervision until a successor could be found. He also agreed to launch an offensive at the end of the month. His plan was that practically the whole of his mobile forces, with 200 good and some 250 less good tanks, should pass through the enemy's front in the lightly-held southern sector during the night of 30 August. Difficulties of supply and scant reserves of fuel would prevent them from making any wide turning movement round the Alam el Halfa ridge. They were to deploy south of the ridge at 6 am on 31 August and try to reach the coast road east of El Alamein by the shortest route.

This plan was very unlikely to succeed. Rommel could not tell how much the British knew of his intentions, but his course of action was predictable since the southern sector was the only part of their front he could hope to breach. His mobile formations would have to make their way at night across a wide tract of unreconnoitred country behind the enemy's lines. Even if they succeeded in avoiding minefields whose precise location was not known, they were sure to be attacked when daylight revealed their presence. The British had well over 700 tanks. Their anti-tank guns now included 6-pounders capable of stopping the strongest German tank at ranges up to three-quarters of a mile. Rommel had praised the Eighth Army's artillery in July and had noted that it was being strengthened.

In the air there was approximate numerical equality between the two sides. The Luftwaffe and the Regia Aeronautica had some 450 aircraft immediately available for operations in the forward area, the Western Desert Air Force about 400. The Me.109F was faster than all save a small proportion of Coningham's fighters, but the British were better provided than the Germans or the Italians with fuel and bombs. In the second half of August German and Italian fighters did their best to keep British aircraft at arm's length, but Coningham succeeded in sending his tactical reconnaissance aircraft over the enemy's lines by escorting them with 2 or 3 squadrons of fighters at a time. Rommel was seen to be strengthening the southern part of his front, and the assembly of his mobile forces on 30 August was noted and reported.

In recent months the crews of 2 naval air squadrons lent to Tedder had made themselves experts in flying over the desert at night and locating and illuminating targets for the benefit of night bombers. Their Albacore aircraft, designed as torpedo-bombers, were very slow, but this and the good downward view they provided made them particularly suitable for the purpose. As darkness fell on 30 August, Wellington bombers accompanied by flare-dropping Albacores attacked German and Italian troop concentrations. Further attacks during the night made the progress of the mobile formations desperately slow. At 9 am the 2 German armoured divisions were still far from the positions they should have reached 3 hours earlier. Rommel, too ill to leave his truck, thought of countermanding the offensive. On reflection he decided to allow the attack to go forward, but postponed it until noon and shifted its axis slightly to the west. Further delayed by a sandstorm which had the compensating advantage of hampering Coningham's aircraft, one of the armoured divisions reached the start-line about 1 pm, the other an hour later. Neither succeeded in getting past the Alam el Halfa ridge, and at dusk the attack was called off.

Repeated bombing during the ensuing night cost the German armoured divisions heavy losses and imposed a tremendous strain on officers and men. The 15th Panzer Division made some progress on 1 September, but Rommel announced at noon that he saw no hope of getting enough fuel forward to continue the advance as far as the coast road and that he proposed to go over to the defensive where he stood. On the following day he ordered the mobile formations to withdraw gradually to the western edge of the enemy's minefields. Montgomery gave an augmented infantry division the task of cutting off the enemy's retreat by closing gaps in the minefields, but the divisional commander did not receive the order to move until after the withdrawal had begun, and the attempt was unsuccessful.

The Battle of Alam el Halfa was the last fought between British and Axis forces in the Western Desert of Egypt in which air superiority was in dispute. By October the British, with some 530 aircraft immediately available for army support as compared with roughly 150 German and some 200 Italian, were able to dominate the skies to an extent which prevented the enemy from hampering, or even observing, the build-up of their forces for the great offensive due towards the end of the month. They also had a superiority of roughly 2 to 1 in men, more than 2 to 1 in tanks, and more than 3 to 1 in anti-tank guns. The failure of

Montgomery's first attempt to shatter the enemy's defences between 23 and 26 October was due not to any lack of air power or firepower but to the inherent difficulty of a frontal assault on unturnable positions defended in depth and underestimation of the time needed to clear minefields amidst the din of battle.

At the beginning of November Montgomery launched a fresh assault, again with powerful air support. This time he managed to batter a way through the enemy's defences, but his pursuit was very slow. Rommel, who had returned from sick leave to resume command when his successor died of heart failure at the beginning of the battle, succeeded in extricating a good many of his troops but lost nearly all his tanks. The British took some 30,000 prisoners and much booty.

Rommel's force, led until March by Rommel himself, then made a long retreat through the Western Desert of Egypt, Cyrenaica and Tripolitania to Tunisia. After crossing the frontier it stood at Mareth in positions prepared by the French before the war. Montgomery, after failing to take the Mareth line by a frontal assault, succeeded with massive air support in turning it and penetrating the enemy's flank and rear through a narrow defile. Elaborate precautions were taken to ensure that fighter-bomber pilots and bomber crews attacked the right objectives at the right time and did not bomb British troops.

On 8 November 1942 British and American troops went ashore in Morocco and Algeria for the purpose of gaining control of the whole of French North Africa 'and if necessary Spanish Morocco'. Carrier-borne aircraft and aircraft from Gibraltar covered the arrival and disembarkation of the troops. French forces on the spot offered much more than token resistance in some places, but Allied aircraft were able to land on a number of airfields in Algeria on the first day.

At the planning stage the British and American authorities had agreed, after long debate, that the initial landings should be confined to places near Casablanca, Oran and Algiers. The planners recognized that this might make it impossible for the Allies to occupy Tunis and Bizerta before German or Italian forces arrived there and that crucial air bases on the African side of the Sicilian Narrows might therefore fall into the wrong hands. But the Allies lacked the means of establishing more than three lodgement areas. They were not prepared to forego landings in Morocco and thus lose a chance of seizing Casablanca at an early stage as a port of entry for supplies and reinforcements from the United States.

Within 24 hours of the arrival of Allied forces in Algeria and Morocco, German and Italian bombers, dive-bombers, fighters and transport aircraft landed on airfields in Tunisia. By the end of November some 17,000 combatant troops, including part of a German armoured division with about 50 tanks, were carried to the neighbourhood of Tunis and Bizerta in transport aircraft or by sea. Nearly twice as many arrived in December. On the Allied side, a limited flow of shipping, a lack of transport and poor communications in the forward area made the build-up very slow. Before long General Anderson's highly-mechanized but incomplete and inexperienced force was immobilized by torrents of rain which made forward landing grounds unusable and problems of supply more intractable than ever. The Allies had to reconcile themselves to the knowledge that the part of French North Africa most vital to them would not be occupied without a stiff fight and was not likely to fall into their hands before the spring or early summer of 1943.

When Rommel finally left Africa in March, the force he had brought from Egypt went under the command of General Jürgen von Arnim, already commanding the troops carried to Tunisia by air and sea since November. Similarly, when Montgomery crossed the Tunisian frontier in pursuit of Rommel, his Eighth Army and Anderson's First Army were welded into an army group under the command of the British General Alexander. The Allies had already agreed to form a Mediterranean Air Command which put American as well as British air forces in the Mediterranean theatre under Tedder's control.

On 7 April Hitler and Mussolini met at a castle near Salzburg. They agreed that a bridgehead in Tunisia must be retained at all costs in order to make it difficult for the Allies to gain a foothold in southern Europe. Whether such a bridgehead could in fact be held was another matter. The Luftwaffe, weakened by heavy wastage in Africa and on the Russian front, was so short of long-range bombers that it had lost the power to strike effectively at British warships in the Sicilian Narrows. Nor could it do much for the Italian fleet, whose lack of carriers forced it to rely on shore-based aircraft for air cover. The Allied Mediterranean Air Force, with a first-line strength of more than 3,200 aircraft, could put at least 1,500 aircraft into the air at one time from bases in North-West Africa and Malta alone. The Luftwaffe had some 500 serviceable aircraft in the whole of the Mediterranean theatre; the Regia Aeronautica could find for service outside metropolitan Italy at most about 450. The crucial factor was the ability of the Axis powers to supply their forces in Tunisia by air.

Nine days after the meeting between Hitler and Mussolini, Alexander ordered his armies to destroy or capture the enemy's forces in Tunisia. The First Army, on the left, was to advance directly on Tunis and Bizerta. The Eighth Army was to contain the enemy on the right and push from the base of the Cap Bon peninsula towards the Gulf of Tunis.

Under pressure from both armies, General von Arnim had no choice but to fall back until he could retreat no further. His last chance of salvation disappeared when Alexander's forces overran airfields used by fighters to cover the arrival of transport aircraft. Thereafter the authorities at home could neither supply his army nor withdraw it. For him there could be no Dunkirk. On 7 May leading elements of the First Army entered Tunis and Bizerta. Wholesale surrenders during the next week brought the number of prisoners taken by the First and Eighth Armies in Tunisia to roughly a quarter of a million. On 13 May Alexander signalled to London that the Allies were 'masters of the North African shores'.

At the close of the Tunisian campaign the Allies had in North Africa some forty British, British-controlled, American and American-equipped French divisions, with powerful air support and backed by a strong, well-balanced British fleet. Troops and stores from the United States could be shipped at least as safely to North Africa as to the United Kingdom. The Germans felt so sure that the Allies would not miss a chance of gaining a foothold in the Balkans that, although they were still desperately short of long-range bombers, they moved well over 400 aircraft (mostly single-seater fighters) to the central and eastern Mediterranean from western Europe and the Eastern Front. But the British and the Americans had agreed in 1942 that their main effort against Germany should be made in north-west Europe, and they were unwilling to reverse their decision even when it became clear that no invasion of north-west Europe would be possible before the spring or early summer of 1944. The case for a landing in the Balkans in 1943 and an advance to the Danube basin made no appeal to the Americans, and the British did not care to press the matter at the risk of putting Anglo-American relations in jeopardy. Like Haig and Robertson in 1917, the United States Chiefs of Staff were determined that the enemy should be attacked where he was likely to be strongest, and found it hard to believe that anyone who advocated a different course was not actuated by sinister motives.

The Allies did, however, agree that Sicily should be invaded and that first the small fortified islands of Pantellaria and Lampedusa should be seized. The garrisons of Pantellaria and Lampedusa surrendered to small landing parties on 11 and 12 June respectively after both islands had been subjected to heavy naval and air bombardments. More than 4 weeks then elapsed before the Allies put ashore on beaches in Sicily about 115,000 British and nearly 70,000 American troops brought from ports of embarkation as far apart as the Clyde, Alexandria, Port Said, Tripoli, Sfax, Tunis, Bizerta, Malta, Algiers and Oran. Naval covering and support forces included 6 British battleships. Air support was provided by naval aircraft from 2 British carriers and shore-based aircraft from Malta, Gozo, Pantellaria and Tunisia. Allied air power proved, however, a very uncertain weapon. Between 3 and 16 August the Germans withdrew from Sicily to the Italian mainland about 40,000 men, 94 guns, nearly 10,000 vehicles including 47 tanks, and large quantities of ammunition and other stores. The Italians withdrew about 62,000 men, 41 guns and 227 vehicles. The Allies failed to interfere effectively with these movements, and indeed were scarcely aware until the withdrawals were almost over that they had begun.

The invasion of Sicily began on 10 July. On 24 July the Fascist Grand Council in Rome passed a resolution unfavourable to Mussolini. On the following day he was placed under arrest. His successor, Marshal Pietro Badoglio, announced his intention of continuing the war in partnership with Germany, but was suspected almost from the start of seeking an opportunity of coming to terms with the Allies. On 15 August emissaries despatched by Badoglio to Madrid approached representatives of the Allied Governments. Agreement was reached on 3 September, but it was decided that no public announcement should be made until the Allies were ready to put substantial forces ashore on the Italian mainland for the purpose, amongst others, of protecting the Italians against reprisals by the Germans.

Troops of the Eighth Army landed unopposed at Reggio on 3 September, but landings in the Gulf of Salerno on which the Allies relied to secure Naples were not due until 9 September. The news that Italy had concluded an armistice with the Allies was broadcast from London late on 8 September. German troops promptly surprised and disarmed all units of the Italian Army and the Regia Aeronautica within reach, but could not prevent the Italian battlefleet from leaving Spezia for Malta in accordance with the terms of the armistice agreement. German bombers from the south of France, using FX.1400 wireless-controlled bombs, attacked the fleet on passage and sank the battleship *Roma*. Altogether some 90 Italian warships, including 5 battleships, passed into Allied control.

In the interests of surprise, the landings in the Gulf of Salerno were made without preliminary naval and air bombardments. This innovation nearly proved disastrous. Short-range fighters from escort carriers and long-range fighters from Sicily covered the landings, but they could not hold off counter-attacks by elements of 4 German divisions south of Naples, nor could they prevent German aircraft, some of them equipped with the FX.1400 bomb, from repeatedly attacking warships and merchantmen off Salerno.

Naval and air bombardments which followed the landings did something to restore the situation, but it was not until the second half of September, when the troops put ashore at Salerno made contact with the Eighth Army, that the Germans began to withdraw. Alexander's forces then attained their immediate aims by capturing Naples and a group of airfields near Foggia from which long-range bombers would be able to attack objectives which could be reached only with great difficulty by the British and American bomber forces in the United Kingdom.

Meanwhile the Germans hastened to strengthen their forces not only in Italy but also in the Balkans. To Hitler it seemed clear that the Allies would not have gone to the trouble of establishing themselves in southern Italy unless they meant to present a direct threat to his sources of raw materials in Rumania and Hungary by crossing the Adriatic. Much to his astonishment, they confined themselves to a painstaking advance across the grain of the country towards northern Italy.

By the end of 1943 Britain and the United States commanded immensely powerful naval and air forces. Since the beginning of July their ships and aircraft had sunk well over 100 German submarines; their merchant shipping losses in all parts of the world had fallen from well over 2 million tons in the first half of the year to just over a million tons in the second. In the course of the year their shipyards and factories had produced some 18,500 assault craft of all categories. Germany was the enemy they had undertaken to defeat before they tried to defeat Japan, and their troops in Italy were the only British and American troops in contact with the German Army. Yet the Mediterranean theatre had fallen so low in the scale of priorities that Alexander was sometimes hard put to find the means of continuing his offensive.

Early in 1944 he succeeded, after a long wrangle, in obtaining enough assault craft to land troops behind the enemy's lines. On 22 and 23 January some 50,000 British and American troops, with 5,000 vehicles, were put ashore at Anzio, less than 40 miles from Rome. As at Salerno, preliminary naval and air bombardments were omitted in the interests of surprise, but this time positive steps were taken to give the impression that landings were to be made elsewhere. Almost complete surprise was, in fact achieved at Anzio, but the commander of the landing force failed to seize his opportunity of pushing inland without delay. Rome was not captured until 4 June, 2 days before British and American seaborne and airborne forces landed in Normandy. The Germans then withdrew to a strong defensive line from Pisa on the Ligurian Sea to Pesaro on the Adriatic. As the sequel to a long controversy between the British and United States Governments and Chiefs of Staff, Allied troops landed in the south of France in August under cover of naval and air bombardments. In October advantage was taken of Hitler's decision to withdraw from Greece, Crete and the Aegean to put Allied forces into Greece and occupy Athens. More troops had to be sent to Greece later in the year to deal with disturbances which culminated in civil war. Alexander, with forces weakened by these diversions, made slow progress on the Italian mainland, and it was not until the war in Europe was almost over that he brought his campaign to a successful conclusion by accepting the unconditional surrender of all the enemy's forces on the Southern Front. Whether the massive naval and air power at the command of the Allies would have enabled him to turn the enemy's lines and advance on Vienna had he been allowed to concentrate his forces for the purpose remained at the end of the war an unanswered question.

10

GERMANY AND RUSSIA, 1939–1945

The dismemberment of Poland in 1939 brought the Soviet Union substantial territorial gains and added some 13 million Poles to her population. It also had the less desirable effect of giving her a common frontier with Germany and making the strongly fortified Stalin line, near the former Polish frontier, almost useless. The Soviet authorities recognized that sooner or later new defensive positions would have to be installed on the Russian side of the demarcation line in central Poland, but they did not regard this as an urgent task. They attached more importance to the consolidation of their influence in the Balkans and the Baltic states than to fixed defences whose value was debatable. Until the summer of 1940 they believed, too, that Germany's armed forces were likely to have plenty to do in western Europe until 1941 or later.

The Soviet Government had no great difficulty in persuading Esthonia, Latvia and Lithuania to accept pacts of mutual assistance which gave Russia the right to establish naval, military and air bases in all three countries. When Finland refused towards the end of 1939 to grant them similar facilities, the Russians picked a quarrel with her and declared war on her.

Since the Finns had only a tiny air force, the Russians expected their air power to give them a big advantage. Their opening offensive was, however, a disastrous failure. In the early winter of 1939 mobile columns were sent across the frontier, and an attempt was made to drop some thousands of parachutists at vulnerable points behind the Finnish lines. Only a few of the parachutists were dropped in the right places, many were picked off by snipers as they were descending or were killed or captured soon after they had landed, and only a small proportion of the survivors reached the supplies that were dropped for them. With few exceptions, the Russian mobile columns were cut off and annihilated by troops trained and equipped to move rapidly across snow-covered country. Russian aircraft were able to fly over Finnish territory almost with impunity, but few of the objectives they succeeded in damaging had any military value. The Mannerheim line, a system of steel and concrete fortifications constructed by the Finns across the Karelian isthmus, proved impregnable until, in the following February, the Russians combined a massive artillery and infantry assault with a turning movement across a frozen inlet of the sea. On 12 March, after the Russians had reached the Viipuri–Helsinki road, the Finns signed a treaty which transferred small tracts of Finnish territory to the Soviet Union and gave the Russians the right to establish a naval base on the northern side of the Gulf of Finland.

The Russians admitted after the Russo-Finnish war that it had cost them more than 206,000 casualties. Since this figure exceeded the entire strength of the Finnish Army on the outbreak of war, their chances of survival should they be attacked by German forces comparable with those used against the British and the French in 1940 seemed fairly slender. In the early summer of 1941 the opinion expressed in diplomatic circles in Moscow, as reported by the British Ambassador, Sir Stafford Cripps, was that the German Army could beat the Red Army in 3 or 4 weeks.[1] Military experts in London and Washington did not take quite such a gloomy view of the Red Army's chances, but thought it unlikely that the Russians would be able to hold out for more than a few months without British and American support. Stalin himself admitted about a month after the Germans opened their offensive that the situation was tense. Later he added that the Soviet Union would be either defeated or crippled unless the Western Allies sent him arms and raw materials and opened a 'second front'.

The Germans launched their invasion on 22 June with roughly the same number of divisions as they had used on the Western Front in 1940, and with fewer than 3,000 aircraft to support divergent advances by 3 army groups on Leningrad, Moscow and the Donetz basin. According to the Soviet official history, the Red Army was caught with its major formations scattered over a wide area and had only 1,475 modern tanks, manned largely by inexperienced crews. As the result of a spectacular expansion of the Soviet aircraft industry in recent years, the Russians had plenty of aircraft, but the vast majority of those in service in 1941 were obsolete or obsolescent. They had no radar and no navigational aids comparable with those used by the Germans against Britain. The construction of a large number of airfields within easy reach of the new frontier had been ordered, but so few were ready that all short-range fighters available for use against the Germans had to be concentrated at a limited number of bases where they could not be adequately dispersed for lack of space. Ground-to-air and air-to-ground communications were rudimentary by British and German standards. The Red Air Force was deficient not only in up-to-date long-range bombers capable of carrying a big bomb-load, but also in the long-range transport aircraft to which the rulers of a vast country with poor surface communications might have been expected to give a high

5 The German Invasion of Russia, 1941

priority. 'Strategic' bombing in the British sense was almost entirely ruled out by a dearth of suitable aircraft, and was not encouraged by a system which allocated air formations more or less permanently to armies or groups of armies. Apart from reserves controlled by the central authorities, formations not so allocated included units assigned to the Navy and a small metropolitan fighter force for home defence.

In accordance with their more flexible system, the Germans distributed the 2,800 aircraft available for the attack on Russia between 3 air fleets which were not placed unreservedly at the disposal of the Army or army group commanders, and whose strength and composition could be varied to suit changing circumstances. Luftflotte 2 received at least 1,500 aircraft to support an advance on Moscow by 50 divisions of Army Group Centre; Luftflotte 1 about half that number to support a thrust by 29 divisions of Army Group North through the Baltic states, with Leningrad as its ultimate objective. Army Group North was, however, to be reinforced on the thirtieth day at the expense of Army Group Centre. Army Group South, with 42 divisions supplemented by a group of German, Hungarian, Italian and Rumanian divisions moving on its right, was to advance to Kiev and beyond with support from Luftflotte 4, initially some 500–550 aircraft strong. In addition, aircraft of Luftflotte 5, afterwards used to attack Allied convoys bringing supplies to Russia, would be available to support a push towards Murmansk. German intelligence officers estimated the first-line strength of the Red Air Force at 7,500 aircraft in European Russia and some 3,000 in the Far East, but believed that the qualitative superiority of the Luftwaffe would far outweigh its numerical inferiority.

Broadly, the tasks assigned to the Luftwaffe at the outset of the campaign were first to paralyse the Red Air Force, secondly to support the land forces by attacking a variety of objectives on and beyond the battlefield and by reconnoitring widely and in great depth. Additional tasks for Luftflotte 1 were to immobilize the Soviet Baltic Fleet and disrupt sea communications between Russia and the Baltic states by laying mines and attacking warships and merchant shipping. With the possible exception of Luftflotte 2, none of the Luftflotten had the means of providing bomber or dive-bomber support on the scale to which the German Army had become accustomed in Poland and in France and the Low Countries, but all except Luftflotte 5 were fairly generously equipped with tactical and long-range reconnaissance aircraft.

Despite unmistakable signs that an offensive was imminent, the Soviet authorities refused up to the time when the Germans crossed the demarcation line in strength to allow their troops to send patrols into enemy-held territory or to open fire on German aircraft. Many units of the Red Army, receiving no warning from their parent formations or the High Command that they were about to be attacked or that their positions might be turned, were overwhelmed or by-passed in the first few hours. Estimates of the number of Russian aircraft destroyed in the opening phase vary from 800 in the first 24 hours to 1,200 by noon on the first day.

Army Group Centre, with the strongest force and the most powerful air support, made good progress and met no serious check until after it had passed Smolensk. Army Group North, not so well provided with tactical air support since Luftflotte 1 had much to do with limited resources, began well but ran into trouble when its leading troops were still 100 miles or more from Leningrad. Army Group South, delayed by unfavourable weather and setbacks to the armies on its right, had yet to reach Kiev in the middle of July.

On 19 July, 2 days before Army Group North was due according to the original programme to be reinforced, the Supreme Command directed Army Group Centre to use its armour to clear up the situation on its flanks before continuing its advance on Moscow. This order gave rise to a long and bitter controversy between Hitler and his service chiefs. The leaders of the Army, arguing that Moscow was not only the Soviet capital but also the chief centre of communications in European Russia and that the enemy would use his best troops to defend it, regarded Army Group Centre's offensive as the key to victory over the Red Army. Hitler maintained that success depended on crippling the enemy's war economy by capturing or investing Leningrad, occupying the Ukraine and the Donetz basin and seizing Rostov. He believed that in this way he could, at one and the same time, deprive the enemy of the wheat and oil of southern Russia and put himself in a position to replenish his own granaries and reserves of oil at the enemy's expense.

The controversy dragged on throughout the summer. It was

not until 21 August that Hitler ruled in terms which brooked no denial that 'the most important aim before the onset of winter' was not the capture of Moscow but the conquest of southern Russia. He then insisted that the greater part of Army Group Centre's armour, led by the redoubtable General Guderian and covered by more than 500 aircraft of Luftflotte 2, should strike southwards at an angle of 90° to the axis of the advance on Moscow. Army Group South, by-passing Kiev, was to send its armour northwards to meet Guderian at a point between Kiev and Kharkov.

This manoeuvre was carried out with brilliant success during the last weeks of summer. The 2 armoured forces met on 16 September at Lokhvitsa, more than 100 miles east of Kiev. Well over half a million Soviet troops were trapped in a huge pocket between the Dnieper and the Desna.*

This feat of arms brought Hitler little nearer to a solution of his problems. The Red Army had suffered terrible losses but was still undefeated. Army Group South was still 300 miles from Rostov, Army Group Centre more than 200 miles from Moscow. Army Group North was at the gates of Leningrad, but the city was destined never to fall into German hands. Moreover, even if Army Group South did capture Rostov, Hitler was wrong in thinking that its loss would deprive the Russians of the oil of the Caucasus. They would still be able to draw supplies through Astrakhan and Saratov. No provision had been made when the invasion was launched for a winter campaign. Little had been done before or since that time to equip the Luftwaffe for prolonged siege operations. German aircraft factories were still turning out the bombers of 1939, and were not producing enough even of those to replace current losses.

Conversely, the Russians, recovering from a bad start, were preparing themselves for total war. On 3 July Stalin announced a 'scorched earth' policy. Not a loaf of bread or a pint of oil, not a locomotive or a truck, not a head of cattle or a bushel of wheat, was to be left to fall into the hands of the enemy at places from

* The fate of the 527,044 officers and other ranks of the Red Army admitted by Soviet official historians to have been encircled remains mysterious. According to the Russians, not more than a third were captured. The Germans claimed 665,000 prisoners. Presumably their figure included men captured outside the pocket.

which the Red Army was forced to retreat. Between July and November more than 1,500 industrial undertakings of national importance moved from Leningrad, Moscow, the Ukraine, the Donetz basin and other vulnerable areas to the banks of the Volga, the Urals, Siberia, Kazakhstan or central Asia. In response to urgent pleas from Stalin, the British Government promised in July to give the Soviet Union all possible material and economic help. A convoy carrying crated and uncrated aircraft left Reykjavik on 21 August and reached Archangel in September after 48 Hurricanes had flown from the old carrier *Argus* to Murmansk. While the convoy was at sea the British agreed to send Stalin 5,000 tons of aluminium at the earliest possible moment and 2,000 tons a month thereafter, and to find half the 400 aircraft and 500 tanks a month for which he asked. When the United States government confessed itself unable to find more than a proportion of the rest even by drawing on allocations promised to Britain, the British undertook to make up the deficiency at the cost of delaying the expansion of their forces at home and in the Middle East. At a conference in Moscow in September the Russians were told that their requirements for tanks and aircraft would be fully met. In addition, Britain and the British Empire would provide the Soviet Union with a wide range of raw materials and the United States would supply a variety of manufactured goods. The British also promised 250 Bren gun carriers a month for an indefinite period, the Americans some scout cars and anti-aircraft and anti-tank guns.*

The effects of the German invasion on the Soviet economy were none the less not far short of disastrous. Industrial output fell in the second half of 1941 by about a half. At the end of the year the authorities reported serious shortages not only of raw materials, weapons and ammunition but also of grain and sugar.

At the end of September Army Group Centre, with all but a few of the armoured divisions hitherto distributed between the three army groups under command and supported by some 1,300 aircraft of Luftflotte 2, launched a new series of thrusts towards

* According to the Soviet Commissariat of Foreign Trade, the Soviet Union received from Britain, the British Empire and the United States between 1941 and the summer of 1944 5,480 British or Canadian and 3,734 American tanks and 5,800 British and 6,430 American aircraft, in addition to many thousands of motor vehicles and large quantities of ammunition.

Moscow from the west and south-west. Spectacular advances during the first few days alarmed the Soviet authorities so much that they replaced the veteran Marshal T. S. Timoshenko as commander on the Central Front by General G. K. Zhukov, brought up reinforcements from central Asia and the Far East, and on 12 October began to prepare their capital for a siege. On 19 October, after the diplomatic corps and many government agencies had withdrawn to Kuibyshev on the Middle Volga, a state of emergency was proclaimed and warnings were issued to the effect that looters and 'deviationists' would be shot.

In the second half of October rain, sleet and snow turned roads to rivers of mud and slush and made tracks and field paths impassable. In some places the Germans were unable to supply their forward troops except by air. At the end of the month they came to the conclusion that their only sound course was to pause, regroup and wait for a hard frost. A withdrawal to winter quarters followed by a renewed offensive in the spring was considered but not approved.

The respite gave the Russians an opportunity of taking stock of the situation and tidying up their dispositions. By the middle of November about half the peacetime population of 4 million had left Moscow. Good progress had been made with schemes of active and passive air defence based on British experience in the winter of 1940–1. Innovations familiar to Londoners included balloon barrages and fire-fighting teams on the British model. Fresh troops to bolster the Central Front were beginning to arrive in substantial numbers from the Far East and were posted to strategic positions well behind the front.

When the Germans resumed their offensive after a fortnight's intermission, they found that the advantage in the air had passed to the Russians. In order to provide air cover for the advancing troops, commanders of air formations pushed their short-range fighter and dive-bomber units as far forward as they could, even at the cost of stretching their communications to the limit. In some cases their zeal defeated its purpose. The Red Air Force, working from permanent bases with runways kept free of snow and ice, could put fighters as well as bombers into the air at times when German fighter pilots had to be forbidden to take off for fear that landings on rough, icebound airfields might damage their machines to an extent which units with few spares and limited facilities for repairs could not afford. Medium bombers could reach the battlefield from less hazardous airfields in the rear, but without fighter escort and support they could not hold their own against Russian fighters.

Despite a consequent lack of continuous air cover, the Germans succeeded at the beginning of December in establishing a small bridgehead east of the Volga Canal at Dmitrov, about 40 miles north of Moscow. Late on 2 December elements of the German Fourth Army made contact with the outer ring of the defences of Moscow in the western suburbs, but they were soon brought to a standstill by a combination of atrocious weather, exhaustion, approaching darkness and determined opposition. On the German right armoured elements invested Tula on the following day and pushed their spearheads still further to the east, but after a few hours a local counter-attack restored communications between Tula and Moscow.

Forty-eight hours later Zhukov opened a counter-offensive which ended any immediate threat to Moscow and soon developed into a series of convergent thrusts towards Smolensk from points as far apart as Lake Ilmen in the north and Yelets in the south. Hitler, always reluctant to give ground, forbade a general retreat to a relatively secure front covering Smolensk. He insisted on retaining so many salients that the length of the line held by his troops when the spring thaw brought the Russians to a halt was out of all proportion to the size and importance of the area they were defending. In the meantime they suffered appalling hardships. Handicapped by unsuitable clothing and equipment not designed to work in sub-zero temperatures, they depended for their supplies on a sparse network of roads supplemented by railways not of standard gauge. The engines of tracked and wheeled vehicles could not be relied upon to start unless they were warmed up every few hours throughout the day and night. In the coldest weather weapons not made to withstand the Russian winter tended to jam or become almost impossible to load. Fuel for mechanically-propelled vehicles was scarce, but was so often used to light fires in defiance of orders to the contrary that no commander could be sure that his units in fact possessed the stocks they were supposed to hold. Frost-bite and general debility induced by exposure to intense cold caused heavy wastage and lowered the efficiency even of men not on the sick list. By Christmas the German Army's casualties since 22 June were estimated at three-quarters of a million.

In some ways the effects of the winter campaign on the Luftwaffe were still more calamitous, largely because many units were already in poor shape when the winter campaign began. Between June and October units serving on the Russian front made an effort equivalent to 1 sortie every 2 days by every aircraft they possessed, including aircraft under repair or otherwise unserviceable. Luftflotte 2's units were then called upon to make, in exceptionally difficult conditions, a supreme attempt to support Army Group Centre's advance to Moscow and its subsequent retreat. Repeated bombing of British cities from French, Belgian and Dutch airfields in the winter of 1940–1 had reduced Luftflotten 2 and 3 to such a state that only about half their bombers remained serviceable. In the winter of 1941–2 repeated operations from Russian airfields in support of Army Group Centre and against Moscow reduced Luftflotte 2 to a still worse plight. Some units were left by the end of 1941 with fewer than a third of their aircraft serviceable, some became so depleted of aircraft and crews that they had to be disbanded.

The effects on the long-range bomber force of wastage suffered on the Russian front at a time when the Luftwaffe was heavily engaged in the Mediterranean theatre were particularly disastrous. In September 1939 the Luftwaffe had possessed 1,213 long-range bombers of which 1,104 were serviceable. At the end of 1941 it had, in all theatres, 918 such aircraft of which only 383 were serviceable. At the end of the following March, when Zhukov's offensive had spent its force and Rommel had driven the British from the greater part of Cyrenaica, there were 977 long-range bombers, of which 480 were serviceable, on all fronts.

Dive-bomber and ground-attack units, too, were heavily depleted by simultaneous operations on the Russian front and in the Mediterranean theatre. Their strength declined from 384 aircraft in September 1939 to 256 at the end of 1941, the number of aircraft serviceable from 267 to 132.

In the light of such figures the authorities were forced to admit that the Luftwaffe had lost the power to provide air support for the armies in Russia on the scale hitherto regarded as normal. When the headquarters of Luftflotte 2, accompanied by

Fliegerkorps II and its constituent units, moved to Sicily early in 1942, there remained on all parts of the Russian front about 1,750 serviceable and unserviceable aircraft of all first-line categories. By withdrawing and re-equipping units in rotation, the authorities succeeded by midsummer in assembling on the main front in Russia about 2,500 aircraft, of which not more than three-quarters were serviceable. In addition, some 200–300 aircraft of Luftflotte 5 were available for operations on the Murmansk front and against Allied shipping in Arctic waters. Of the 2,500 aircraft on the main front, about 1,500 were allotted to Luftflotte 4 to support offensives in the south on which Hitler relied to give him a decisive success before his troops were overtaken by another Russian winter. Fewer than 400 aircraft, of which not more than 280 were serviceable, remained to support holding operations in the Leningrad sector after some 600 had been allotted to the Central Front.

In the meantime Hitler had fallen out with the High Command of the German Army and assumed direct control of its operations. He divided the land forces in southern Russia into two army groups, designated A and B. His plan for the summer of 1942 was that Army Group A, after securing its flank in the Crimea, should advance on Stalingrad by way of Rostov. At the same time Army Group B was to encircle the whole of the Russian forces in the bend of the Don by crossing the river at Voronezh and approaching Stalingrad from the north. The garrison of Stalingrad would then be either forced to surrender, or rendered powerless by investment and bombardment. Once that was done, Army Group A was to move into the Caucasus and capture its oil wells, refineries and pipelines. Eventually forces based on the Caucasus might advance to the head of the Persian Gulf and sweep through the Levant to meet Rommel in North Africa.

About 600 of Luftflotte 4's aircraft were used to support the preliminary offensive in the Crimea. Repeated air attacks made little impression on the fortifications of Sebastopol, but early in July the fortress succumbed to an infantry assault supported by a massive artillery bombardment.

Meanwhile the Russians launched a spoiling attack in the Kharkov sector. Aircraft of Luftflotte 4 diverted from the Crimea supported counter-attacks which encircled 3 Soviet armies but threatened to delay the advance on Voronezh. Hitler, encouraged by Army Group B's success at Kharkov and a rapid advance by Army Group A to Rostov, then decreed that, in order to save time, Army Group A should move into the Caucasus and seize Tuapse, the Armavir–Maikop plateau and Grozny without waiting to join Army Group B in capturing or masking Stalingrad. Army Group B, instead of making a wide sweep east of the Don after capturing Voronezh, was to advance on Voronezh and Stalingrad along separate axes and form a defensive front along the line of the river between those places.

From the German point of view the consequences of this change of plan proved disastrous. Army Group A, wheeling into the Caucasus from Rostov, exposed to any Russian forces which might approach from the direction of Stalingrad or the Kalmuk Steppes an attenuated flank protected only by 1 motorized division of Army Group B at Yelista, some 80 miles to the north. Army Group B, with 1 weak and 2 good German armies and 4 armies composed of Hungarian, Italian and Rumanian troops, was compelled to disperse its numerous and ill-assorted formations over so large an area that effective co-ordination of their movements from a single headquarters was not to be expected. Moreover, all supplies not only for Army Group A but also for Army Group B's forces in the Stalingrad sector had to pass through a bottleneck at Rostov, and all rail-borne supplies for the whole of both army groups had either to cross the Dnieper by a single bridge at Dnepropetrovsk or to be unloaded and reloaded at Zaporozhe, where the only railway bridge had been destroyed by the Russians in 1941 and was not repaired until 1943.

So wide a dispersal confronted not only the general and administrative staffs of both army groups but also Luftflotte 4 with formidable problems. In the early stages of its advance towards the Caucasus from Rostov Army Group A made such rapid progress that little help from short-range tactical support units was needed, or could have been provided without greater administrative inconvenience. Luftflotte 4 provided indirect support by attacking centres of communication in the Caucasus and Transcaucasia, Black Sea ports as far south as Georgia, and shipping in the Caspian and the lower Volga. Rail centres between Moscow and Stalingrad were also attacked in the interests of both army groups.

Such widely scattered attacks could have little immediate effect on the army group's progress. The Army Group Commander, Field Marshal Wilhelm List, had no great difficulty in thrusting his spearheads to Armavir and Maikop and in occupying Nalchik in the Kabardino. He failed, however, to reach Tuapse, and his troops advancing on Grozny were brought to a halt when they reached a position prepared by the Russians at Mozdok in the eastern foothills of the Caucasus. List observed that he might have been able to reach Grozny had he been allowed to concentrate on one objective at a time, and was promptly dismissed for saying so.

Short-range aircraft were then moved to bases within 130 miles of the battlefront, but an attempt to turn the Mozdok position with their help was so decisively defeated as to convince even Hitler that Grozny could not be reached before the winter. He decided that Army Group A should not attempt a hazardous withdrawal through the Rostov bottleneck, but should hold on to its gains at Maikop and go over to the defensive in the hope that the outlook might improve in 1943.

Operations in the Caucasus absorbed about a third of Luftflotte 4's resources. Roughly 1,000 aircraft were devoted to direct and indirect support of Army Group B.

Not more than 600 or 700 of these aircraft were, however, serviceable at one time. These would have been of little value had they been evenly spread over Army Group B's 300-mile front. Accordingly, Luftflotte 4 used all the available tactical-support aircraft first to support the army group's advance on Voronezh, next to support its advance to the Middle Don. Finally, all aircraft not urgently needed in the Caucasus gave direct or indirect support to an assault on Stalingrad.

The Russians, recognizing that the whole of their communications south of Moscow were in jeopardy, decided that Voronezh must be defended to the last. They succeeded in holding the crossings of the Don, and after the departure of Luftflotte 4's tactical-support units launched a counter-attack which the Germans repelled with difficulty.

In the sector between Voronezh and Stalingrad, the Russians withdrew in good order to the left bank of the Don and retained a bridgehead on the right bank at Kletskaya, about seventy miles north-west of Stalingrad. Later they established a second bridgehead further upstream at Serafimovich. The Germans and their allies, encouraged by their relatively easy capture of Rostov to believe that the enemy was in full retreat and unlikely to stage a comeback, were content in most places to close up to the right bank of the river and to make no serious attempt to cross it.

In the second half of August General Friedrich Paulus, commanding the German Sixth Army and with the Fourth Panzer Army temporarily under command, launched a major assault on Stalingrad. By the second week in September his troops stood on the right bank of the Volga at points on either side of Stalingrad and had repelled a counter-attack from the north. In the meantime Luftflotte 4's bombers had reduced much of the built-up area of the town to a waste of rubble bristling with Russian snipers and small parties of infantrymen armed with grenades and automatic weapons. The Russians still held the left bank of the Volga, and they also held a bridgehead about 7 miles wide on the right bank downstream from Stalingrad. Until the middle of November, when the river became jammed with ice-floes, they were able to ferry nightly to the part of Stalingrad they still held enough supplies and reinforcements to ensure that the Germans were kept busy. At the same time they concentrated powerful counter-attack forces in and behind their bridgeheads across the Volga south of Stalingrad and across the Don at Kletskaya and Serafimovich.

According to Soviet sources, the strength of these counter-attack forces rose by the third week in November to more than a million men with some 900 tanks. The Sixth Army's intelligence officers reported the arrival of fresh troops in and behind the enemy's bridgeheads, and they estimated about the middle of November that there were 8 Russian armies on the Don-Volga front. Their warnings did not, however, make much impact on the High Command. Army Group B asked in October for 2 additional divisions for use against the Kletskaya bridgehead, but was told that reinforcements on so generous a scale could not be found.

At 4 am on 19 November about 800 guns and mortars massed in the Kletskaya and Serafimovich bridgeheads began a heavy bombardment of positions held by the Rumanian Third Army and the left of the German Sixth Army. Four hours later Russian armoured formations debouched from the bridgeheads. According to German eye-witnesses the Rumanians fought bravely, but they had no heavy artillery and no long-range anti-tank guns. Snow had begun to fall at midnight, the cold was intense and visibility was poor. The Rumanian Third Army was quickly overwhelmed, and an attempt by an armoured corps of one weak German and one partly-trained Rumanian division to restore the situation was unsuccessful. By 23 November the Russians were across the Sixth Army's rear communications and roughly a quarter of a million German and Rumanian troops were caught in a pocket from which most of them were never to escape.

Hitler, unwilling that the Sixth Army should try to reopen its communications at the risk of losing its hold on Stalingrad, ordered General Paulus to stand firm. Paulus was promised, on Göring's authority, 500 tons of airborne supplies a day. About 200 transport aircraft were available for the purpose, and these were supplemented by some 90 aircraft from long-range bomber units. In favourable conditions the 200–225 sorties a day needed to deliver the stipulated tonnage might not have been beyond the capacity of such a force, but conditions in Army Group B's area were far from favourable. Appalling weather, inadequate facilities for repair and maintenance, and lack of fighter cover all made the task of the air transport units extremely difficult. Between the last week in November and the first week in January about 100 tons of supplies a day were delivered. On 10 January the Russians captured the only airfield at Stalingrad on which transport aircraft could land safely. Thereafter most, and eventually all, supplies had to be dropped, not landed, and deliveries fell off sharply.

In December Field Marshal Erich von Manstein, commanding the newly-formed Army Group Don, began an attempt to relieve Stalingrad by advancing from Kotelnikovo, 100 miles to the south-west, with 200 tanks, 3,000 tons of supplies and a fleet of tractors with which he hoped to extract some of the Sixth Army's field guns. In theory Army Group Don included the Sixth Army in addition to surviving elements of the Fourth Panzer Army and the Rumanian Third and Fourth Armies. In practice, Manstein could not prevent Hitler from giving direct orders to Paulus by means of a wireless transmitter which linked the Supreme Command with a liaison officer inside the Stalingrad pocket.

At nightfall on 19 December forward elements of Manstein's force reached a point within 30 miles of the Sixth Army's nearest troops. At 6 pm that evening Manstein ordered Paulus to break out of the pocket and make contact with his troops. Paulus refused to do so, pleading that he needed time to redispose his troops, that they were hungry and exhausted, and that he had only enough fuel to take his tanks about two-thirds of the distance they would have to cover. On 27 December Manstein was forced to withdraw from his forward positions, and on 2 February the last of the German troops at Stalingrad laid down their arms.

From that date until the end of the war in Europe, the Russians were always able to concentrate more aircraft than their opponents on any part of the front they deemed decisive. At Kursk in the summer of 1943 the Germans launched a major offensive in the hope of dealing the Red Army a blow which would cripple it for months to come. Of the 2,000 German aircraft on the whole of the Russian front from Murmansk to the Sea of Azov, about half were used to support attacks on two relatively narrow fronts by 17 armoured and 10 infantry divisions with some 2,500 tanks. Despite an effort which rose at the height of the assault to nearly 3,000 sorties a day, the Luftwaffe failed to attain air superiority over the battlefield, and the offensive failed at a heavy cost. Thereafter British and American air attacks on Germany forced the leaders of the Luftwaffe to give more and more of their attention to defensive measures. By the end of 1944 only a third of Germany's air strength was deployed on the Eastern Front, nearly four-fifths of the Luftwaffe's first-line aircraft were fighters, and the Red Air Force outnumbered the German air forces with which it was in contact by 5 or 6 to 1.

11

AIR POWER AND THE WAR IN THE FAR EAST AND THE PACIFIC, 1941–1943

When the Japanese began in 1933 to modernize and reorganize their army, they made no departure from their existing policy of maintaining separate air forces to support their naval and land forces. No strategic bombing on the lines contemplated by the British was envisaged, and no bomber force independent of the Army and the Navy was created.

By 1941 the Japanese Army had at its immediate disposal some 1,500 aircraft organized in 5 air divisions. Each air division was made up of 2 or 3 air brigades. An air brigade consisted as a rule of either 3 or 4 air regiments, each of 3 squadrons. The authorized establishment of a fighter squadron was 16 aircraft; bomber and reconnaissance squadrons had from 9 to 12 aircraft each. The strength of an air regiment varied, therefore, between 27 and 48 aircraft, while that of an air brigade might be as high as 120 aircraft but was more often in the region of 90–100, while that of an air division was of the order of 275–350 aircraft.

The only major air formations at the disposal of the Japanese Navy in 1941 were the First and Eleventh Air Fleets and the 24th Air Flotilla. The First Air Fleet consisted of 5 large squadrons divided between the fleet carriers *Akagi, Kaga, Shokaku, Zuikaku, Soryu* and *Hiryu* (about 70 aircraft each) and the light fleet carriers *Zuiho, Shoho, Ryujo* and *Hosho*. The *Hosho* carried 21 aircraft and the other light fleet carriers 31 each, but the *Shoho* was not due for completion until early in 1942.

The Eleventh Air Fleet was composed of the 21st, 22nd and 23rd Air Flotillas, based towards the end of 1941 in Formosa and southern Indo-China. All its aircraft, of which it had about 500, were shore-based in the sense that they operated from bases ashore, but some of them were flying boats. About 60 aircraft of the 24th Air Flotilla were based in the mandated islands in the Pacific north of the equator.

Naval air units not organized in major formations provided about 200 aircraft embarked in seaplane carriers, seaplane tenders and miscellaneous warships not assigned to fleet carrier or light fleet carrier squadrons, and also about 200 seaplanes and flying boats for maritime reconnaissance from shore bases. A number of naval aircraft not included in the foregoing figures were assigned to home defence.

Early in 1941 the Japanese Naval and General Staffs began work on tentative plans for war with Britain, the Netherlands and the United States. When economic sanctions imposed in the following summer threatened them with extinction of their stocks of oil and other raw materials, they redoubled their efforts in order to be ready, should the need arise, to strike before the north-east monsoon in the South China Sea and winter gales in the North Pacific reached their full force. They aimed at seizing the rich sources of oil, rubber, tin and bauxite in Indonesia and South-East Asia as soon as possible should they be compelled to go to war, but the Army could spare only 11 divisions and some 700 aircraft for offensive purposes after allotting 40 divisions and 800 aircraft to the defence of Japan, Korea, Manchuria and occupied China. They concluded that they could not afford to advance to the Netherlands East Indies without first protecting their flanks by defeating the British and American forces in Malaya and the Philippines, eliminating the British garrison of Hong Kong, and seizing British Borneo.

The army air forces available for these tasks belonged to the 3rd and 5th Air Divisions. The land forces available after one division had been placed in reserve were organized and disposed as follows:

Fourteenth Army (Rynkyu Islands, Formosa, Palau)
16th Division
48th Division
Fifteenth Army (Indo-China)
33rd Division
55th Division
Sixteenth Army (Formosa and Palau)
2nd Division

Twenty-Third Army (South China)
38th Division
Twenty-Fifth Army (Indo-China, Hainan, Canton)
Imperial Guards Division
5th Division
18th Division
56th Division

The tasks allotted to these formations and supporting air formations are summarized below.

Stage One

a. Twenty-Third Army, supported by some 80 bombers, fighters and reconnaissance aircraft detached from 5th Air Division, to seize Hong Kong.

b. Fourteenth Army to invade the Philippines. Eleventh Air Fleet (less 22nd Air Flotilla) and 5th Air Division (less detached elements) to make preliminary attacks and provide cover and support.

c. Fifteenth Army, temporarily assisted by Imperial Guards Division from Twenty-Fifth Army, to invade Siam. Support to be provided by detached elements of 5th Air Division.

d. Twenty-Fifth Army to invade Malaya and provide detachment for invasion of British Borneo. Cover and support to be provided by 3rd Air Division and 22nd Air Flotilla.

e. One regiment of 55th Division, detached from Fifteenth Army, to join naval landing parties in seizing Guam, Wake, and objectives in the Bismarck archipelago and New Guinea. Cover and support to be provided, as far as possible, by 24th Air Flotilla.

Stage Two

a. Fifteenth Army to invade southern Burma from Siam. Support to be provided by 5th Air Division, including elements transferred from Philippines after capture of Manila.

b. Sixteenth Army to occupy Dutch Borneo, Celebes, Amboina, Timor, southern Sumatra and Java after reinforcement by 38th Division and 48th Division from Hong Kong and the Philippines. Air cover and support to be provided by elements of First and Eleventh Air Fleets.

c. Twenty-Fifth Army to invade northern Sumatra from Malaya.

Major naval units at the disposal of the Japanese included, in addition to their 6 large and 4 light fleet carriers, 10 battleships already in commission and 1 about to be commissioned, 36 cruisers, 113 destroyers and 63 submarines. The British, the Dutch and the Americans had in the Far East and the South-West Pacific 2 capital ships, 15 cruisers, 30 or more destroyers and about 40 submarines, but these ships had not been welded into an integrated fleet. British, Dutch and American officers had, however, met to exchange views and information. The United States Pacific Fleet of 9 battleships, 3 aircraft carriers, 21 cruisers, 67 destroyers and 27 submarines based on Pearl Harbour was too far away to intercept Japanese forces approaching the Philippines or Malaya. The Americans had no first-class naval base in or near the crucial area, and attempts by the British to persuade them to send the whole or part of the Pacific Fleet to Singapore had failed.

Both the British and the Americans, therefore, were badly placed in the latter part of 1941 to defend their interests and possessions in South-East Asia and the South-West Pacific. The Americans hoped to assemble in the Philippines by the following spring about 100 B-17 bombers which could be used to strike at Japanese forces in Formosa or at an invasion fleet on passage, but only some 30–40 of these aircraft were delivered by the time the Japanese were ready for war. Similarly, the British looked forward to the spring of 1942 as the time by which they could expect to have at Singapore a strong, well-balanced fleet of 7 or more capital ships, 1 aircraft carrier, 10 cruisers and some 24 destroyers. They hoped that in the meantime the battleship *Prince of Wales* and the battle-cruiser *Repulse*, recently despatched to Singapore against the better judgement of the Admiralty, might have some deterrent effect on the Japanese and that, if the worst came to the worst, they might be able to sink or damage Japanese warships and transports in the South China Sea by sending aircraft based in Malaya to attack them. Only 35 light bombers and 24 obsolete torpedo-bombers were, however, available for the purpose at the crucial time.

When the possibility of an armed conflict between Japan and the Western Powers was discussed in Tokyo in 1940 Admiral

Isoruku Yamamoto, Commander-in-Chief of the Combined Fleet, described as 'outrageous' the foreign policy which could lead to such an outcome. He predicted that Japan would have cause to regret any action which involved her in war with the United States and added that any such action might well result in her being stabbed in the back by Russia. The Emperor Hirohito pointed out that the results of naval exercises in which war with the United States was simulated did not suggest that Japan was likely to gain the upper hand in such a conflict.

However, her chances would, of course, be very much improved if the United States Pacific Fleet could be put out of action on the outbreak of hostilities by a surprise attack like that which had crippled the Russian Far Eastern Fleet in 1904. The British success against the Italians at Taranto in 1940 suggested a way in which this might be done. On Yamamoto's orders, naval airmen studied the problem of using torpedo-bombers and high-level bombers to attack the American battlefleet in shallow water at Pearl Harbour. A war-game at the Naval Academy in Tokyo in September 1941 suggested that the attempt might cost Japan two carriers, but this did not seem too high a price to pay. Practical trials were conducted with the help of a miniature mock-up of Pearl Harbour constructed at a secluded base, and experiments were made with armour-piercing bombs fitted with special fins and torpedoes to which wooden stabilizers were attached.

On 7 November Vice-Admiral Chuichi Nagumo assumed command of a striking force consisting of the 1st Division of the 3rd Battle Squadron (2 battleships), the 1st, 2nd and 5th Carrier Squadrons (*Akagi, Kaga, Soryu, Hiryu, Shokaku* and *Zuikaku*, with 432 aircraft), the 8th Cruiser Squadron (2 heavy cruisers), and the 1st Destroyer Flotilla (1 light cruiser and 16 destroyers). On 26 November the force, less 7 destroyers of the 1st Destroyer Flotilla not required, left Hitokappu Wan, in the Kurile Islands, with orders to steam through waters far from the usual shipping routes to a point about 275 miles north of Pearl Harbour. It was accompanied during the first part of the voyage by 8 tankers, and 3 submarines moved ahead of it and on its flanks. Arrangements were made to recall the force should negotiations still in progress in Washington be successful. Unless recalled, or aware that his force had been detected, Nagumo was to send his bombers and torpedo-bombers early on Sunday 7 December to attack the

American battlefleet and airfields on the adjacent island of Oahu. By that time 20–30 long-range submarines not under his command would have taken up positions between 8½ and 100 miles west of Pearl Harbour. Their tasks were to report movements of shipping into and out of the harbour, attack any warships that might emerge when the bombing was over, and send 5 midget submarines into the harbour to attack targets of opportunity.

Japan's formal decision to go to war was made on 1 December, some days after the American Secretary of State, Cordell Hull, had dropped a bombshell in Washington by breaking off negotiations for an interim settlement of outstanding questions and presenting proposals for a permanent settlement on terms which no Japanese Government could have accepted. On the following day Nagumo received a signal which told him that he would be expected to carry out the operation as planned unless he had reason to believe that surprise had been lost. The Japanese Foreign Minister, Shigenori Togo, intended to break off diplomatic relations with the United States before the attack was delivered, but he failed, partly because he was misled by the Naval Staff and partly because he underestimated the time needed by the staff of the Japanese Embassy in Washington to decode and paraphrase a long message, to issue the necessary instructions in time. The result was that the Japanese Ambassador, Admiral Kichisaburo Nomura, was unable to deliver the message until roughly an hour and a half after the attack had begun.

Besides providing the Navy with its only first-class base west of the Continental United States, Oahu was of considerable military importance as a place of assembly for troops and air squadrons intended for service in the Philippines. The Army was responsible for the air defence of the island in general, the Navy for the defence of the navy yard and for maritime reconnaissance. The naval Commander-in-Chief and the Commanding General had been warned in a joint report by their air force commanders that a raid by carrier-borne aircraft was the most probable form of attack on Oahu.[1] They knew, too, that war might come at any moment. However, in the light of indications that the Japanese were preparing for a southward drive from Indo-China, hostilities seemed more likely to begin with an invasion of Malaya or the

Philippines than with trouble in the central Pacific. When the Commanding General learned in the last week of November that the authorities in Washington expected the Japanese to make 'an aggressive move' within the next few days he refrained, correctly but as things turned out unfortunately, from passing this highly secret information to his air force commander. The air defences of Oahu were organized on a training basis, the radar information centre at the Army's administrative headquarters was not continuously manned. Of more than 30 flying boats available to the navy for maritime reconnaissance, only 3 were on patrol in the early hours of 7 December. None of them went near Nagumo's carriers.

However, the authorities did have some reason to suspect before the bombs began to fall that 7 December might not turn out to be an ordinary Sunday. The wake made by the periscope of 1 of the Japanese midget submarines was seen from a minesweeper 2 miles off the entrance to the harbour about 3 hours before sunrise. A destroyer and a flying boat attacked the same or another midget submarine with depth charges and gunfire just as the sun was rising, but nearly an hour then elapsed before the significance of these events was understood ashore.

Nagumo reached his launching area at first light. He decided to use 353 of his aircraft to attack objectives afloat and ashore and 39 for a defensive patrol in the neighbourhood of his ships. Forty aircraft described as not fully operational were held in reserve. A first wave of 40 torpedo-bombers, 51 dive-bombers, 49 high-level bombers and 43 fighters took off immediately and approached the north coast of Oahu about 7.40 am. Some aircraft flew straight across the island to attack airfields, others made a sweep to starboard in order to approach Pearl Harbour from the south-west.

Until recently army radar stations dotted about Oahu and using mobile equipment had maintained daily watches from 7 am until 4 pm. In the last week of November it had been arranged that watches should be maintained every day from 4 am until 7 am and that, except on Sundays, operators should then train for another 4 hours before knocking off for the day.

At 6.45 am on 7 December two enlisted men in charge of a station at Opana, near the northernmost extremity of the island, detected a single aircraft approaching at a fairly high speed. This was a seaplane sent ahead of the first wave of Nagumo's striking force, but was assumed by Lieutenant Kermit Tyler, the inexperienced officer on duty at the radar information centre, to be a friendly aircraft. Fifteen minutes later Tyler released the watch in accordance with his instructions, although he himself was not due to go off duty until 8 am.

The two men at Opana, Privates Joseph Lockard and George Elliott, continued to watch the set while awaiting the truck that was to take them to breakfast. At 7.20 am they saw by far the largest echo they had even seen. They were unable to pass this information through the usual channels, since there was no one at the other end of their direct line to the information centre; but they succeeded, with some difficulty, in persuading a telephone operator to connect them with Lieutenant Tyler. They told him that they estimated that 50 or more aircraft were approaching from the north at 180 miles an hour. Tyler, who knew that 2 American carriers were at sea and that roughly a dozen bombers on a delivery flight were expected from the mainland, assured them that any aircraft they might have detected must be American.

The result was that the arrival of Nagumo's first wave took the fighter and anti-aircraft artillery defences completely by surprise. No fighters were in the air to meet the enemy, and most of the aircraft on the island were parked in uncamouflaged positions in the open. Only 1 ship out of 70 warships and 24 auxiliaries at Pearl Harbour was under way. Few anti-aircraft guns ashore or afloat were fully manned, and even those which were could not be fired until ammunition was fetched from depots or extracted from locked boxes.

The leading aircraft of the first wave reached Pearl Harbour about 7.55 am. A second wave of 80 dive-bombers, 54 high-level bombers and 36 fighters arrived about three-quarters of an hour later. In 2 hours Nagumo sank or crippled all 8 of the battleships at Pearl Harbour and 10 other warships or auxiliaries, destroyed or damaged 349 American aircraft and killed or wounded 3,581 American sailors, soldiers and marines for the loss of 29 of his own aircraft. The Japanese also lost all 5 of their midget submarines and 1 ocean-going submarine. About 100 civilians, most of them employed by the Army or the Navy, were killed or injured. Very few bombs fell elsewhere than at naval or military installations, but defective or incorrectly-fused shells from anti-aircraft guns did about half a million dollars' worth of damage in the built-up area of Honolulu.

This was the most impressive feat of airmanship the world had yet seen. By omitting to destroy or seriously damage the navy yard Nagumo failed, even so, to make his success as complete as it might have been. Of the 8 battleships sunk or crippled, only 1 became a total loss. Six rejoined the fleet after being repaired and, where necessary, refloated. One was sold for scrap. One battleship and all 3 carriers of the Pacific Fleet escaped the holocaust by being elsewhere at the time. Thus the Americans were left not only with an almost unimpaired naval base in the central Pacific but also with the nucleus of a carrier force which they soon made even more powerful than the enemy's.

Landings in northern Malaya began about the same time as the attack on Pearl Harbour or perhaps a little earlier; landings in southern Siam and attacks by land and air forces on Hong Kong a few hours later. Landings in British Borneo – defended only by 1 infantry battalion and a few native troops and armed police with practically no naval or air support except that provided by a small Coastal Marine Service and a few aircraft from far-off airfields – were made on 16 and 24 December.

To defend the island of Hong Kong and some hundreds of square miles of the mainland separated from it by a narrow channel, the British had 6 battalions of Regular troops and 6 companies of the Hong Kong Volunteer Defence Corps. These were supported by 28 medium and mountain guns, supplemented by coast defence and beach defence guns in fixed positions. For naval and air support they relied on 1 destroyer, 8 motor torpedo boats, a few gunboats and miscellaneous patrol vessels and 5 obsolete or unsuitable aircraft. The Japanese 38th Division had a superiority of roughly 3 to 2 in infantry and was well supplied with mountain and field artillery, but the crucial factor was the air support provided by the regiment of light bombers, squadron and a half of heavy bombers, and squadron each of fighters and reconnaissance aircraft contributed by the 5th Air Division. Air attacks destroyed all 5 of the British aircraft on the first day. The British completed by the morning of the sixth day an orderly withdrawal to the island, but they had to leave their pack animals behind because the vessels intended to carry them had been sunk. A combination of air and artillery bombardments during the next few days started uncontrollable fires, damaged at least 1 water main beyond repair, reduced the naval strength of the British to 2 gunboats and a few torpedo boats, knocked out pillboxes and searchlight posts and cut landlines.

After failing to cross the channel between the mainland and the island on 15 December, the Japanese succeeded in doing so on the night of 18 December under cover of smoke from a paint factory and oil tanks set alight by bombing. With 9 battalions ashore by the evening of 23 December and complete command of the air, the Japanese soon reduced the defenders to such straits that on 25 December the Governor, Sir Mark Young, surrendered the Crown Colony without conditions to Lieutenant-General T. Sakai of the Twenty-Third Army. A small force cut off in the southern part of the island held out until the early hours of the following day.

In Malaya the British had 31 battalions organized in 3 divisions, 2 reserve brigade groups, 2 fortress brigades and 1 detached battalion. Only 1 corps of 2 divisions was, however, available to meet an attack from the north after other commitments had been met. Moreover, the defence of airfields in remote areas with poor communications would immobilize almost an entire division of that corps. Only 158 aircraft, including the torpedo-bombers and light bombers already mentioned, were available to support the land forces, reconnoitre the South China Sea, and strike at an invasion force. The Japanese Twenty-Fifth Army, supported by an entire air division and a naval air flotilla, would have almost overwhelming air superiority from the outset.

The British recognized that the key to a successful invasion of Malaya from the north was possession of the Siamese ports of Singora and Patani. If circumstances permitted, the main body of the one division which was all the British could spare would move into Siam to deny Singora to the enemy or block the road connecting Singora with the trunk road leading through Malaya to Singapore. A smaller force would advance a short distance into Siamese territory to block the road from Patani at a position called The Ledge. Should circumstances not permit an advance to Singora, the main body would stand athwart the trunk road in a partially prepared position at Jitra, about 18 miles south of the

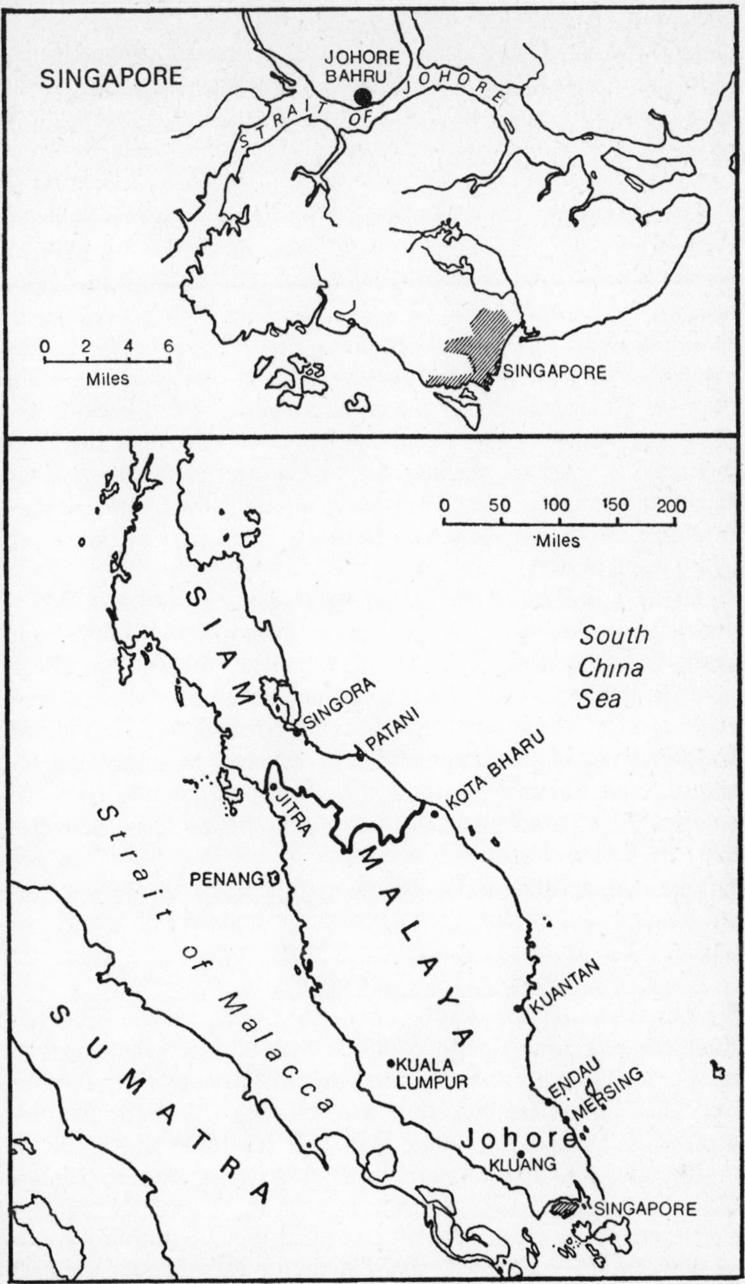

6 Malaya, 1941

frontier. In that case the smaller force would still need to advance to The Ledge in order to prevent the enemy from outflanking the Jitra position and gaining access to the trunk road at a point south of it.

The onus of deciding whether to order an advance to Singora rested upon Air Chief Marshal Sir Robert Brooke-Popham, Commander-in-Chief of the land and air forces in Malaya, Burma, Hong Kong and British Borneo. Brooke-Popham hoped until the eleventh hour to be able to authorize the move, but he hesitated so long for fear of affronting neutral opinion by sending troops far into Siamese territory without an invitation from the Siamese Government that in the end he had to fall back on the Jitra alternative. Less understandably, he also withheld the inescapable order for the advance to The Ledge so long that the Japanese got there first. The result was that the commander of the force at Jitra was haunted almost from the start by the fear of being outflanked.

About 1 am on 8 December, 3 transports accompanied by warships anchored off Kota Bharu, in northern Malaya, and began disembarking troops of the Japanese 56th Infantry Regiment in landing craft.* The moon had risen and the skies were clearing after heavy rain. Air Vice-Marshal C. W. H. Pulford, Brooke-Popham's air commander in Malaya, promptly ordered 'all available aircraft' to attack the transports, landing craft and troops. Later he arranged for a full-scale attack to be delivered soon after dawn.

Less than an hour and a half later, Japanese transports arrived off Singora and Patani. By sunrise large numbers of troops had disembarked at both places with little opposition from the Siamese. Air Vice-Marshal Pulford, having committed most of his bombers and torpedo-bombers to attacks on the relatively small force at Kota Bharu, could do little to intervene. Furthermore, attacks on his airfields in northern Malaya by aircraft based in Indo-China soon cost him heavy losses. By nightfall on 9 December he had lost more than half his force and could no longer afford to use forward airfields in north-eastern Malaya whose defence was the primary task of the troops stationed in

* 1 am on 8 December at Kota Bharu corresponds to 5.30 pm on 7 December by Greenwich Mean Time. The time in Washington was 12.30 pm on 7 December.

that neighbourhood. Throughout the rest of the campaign in Malaya the British could reckon on being outnumbered in the air by at least 5 to 1 and often by 10 to 1.

An unpromising start did not deter Admiral Sir Tom Phillips, commanding the British Eastern Fleet, from taking his weak battlefleet to sea at 5.35 pm on 8 December with the intention of smashing the Japanese forces off the coast between Kota Bharu and Singora. He made it clear before he left that he counted on receiving strong fighter support when he reached his destination. In view of Pulford's decision to withdraw from airfields in north-eastern Malaya Phillips had, however, to be told in a signal despatched early on 9 December that fighter support could not be provided as far north as Singora. Nevertheless he continued on his course until, at 8.15 pm, he saw that Japanese aircraft were shadowing him. Concluding that surprise had been lost and that he would gain nothing by running his head into a noose, he reluctantly turned back for Singapore.

During the early part of the ensuing night persistent rumours circulated in Malaya to the effect that Japanese troops had landed or were landing at Kuantan, nearly 200 miles further south than Kota Bharu. One consequence was that Phillips received about midnight a signal which caused him to set course for Kuantan, apparently in the belief that the originator of the signal would assume that he was going there and arrange for fighters to meet him. No Japanese troops had in fact landed at Kuantan, and Phillips found nothing of interest there. Nor was he met by fighters. A squadron of fighters was, however, held ready to go to his aid, if summoned, from an airfield less than an hour's flying time away.

Phillips had not moved far from Kuantan when, at 10.20 am on 10 December, a Japanese aircraft approached his flagship. For reasons which will never be known, he did not report that he was being shadowed or ask for help. Had he done so, the fighters standing by for the purpose could almost certainly have reached him in time to drive away the aircraft of the 22nd Air Flotilla which began to attack him about an hour later. As it was, repeated attacks by torpedo-bombers and high-level bombers sank both his capital ships. Destroyers which had accompanied him from Singapore picked up 2,081 survivors, but Admiral

Phillips was among the 840 officers and ratings who lost their lives.

Thus the Japanese gained by the exercise of their air power freedom to disembark and concentrate their forces for the invasion of Malaya without effective interference from the enemy. At the same time the British were compelled by their lack of air power to stake their hopes of retaining the use of Singapore as a port of entry for reinforcements and supplies on attempts to keep the Japanese at arm's length. Once driven by the fear of encirclement from Jitra, they could not afford to disengage, retreat to southern Malaya, and regroup for a decisive battle. In order to deny to the enemy airfields which would put Singapore within easy reach of his medium-range and short-range aircraft, they had to fight a series of delaying actions which frittered away their strength and disheartened their troops.

At President Roosevelt's urgent request, the British General Wavell reluctantly accepted early in 1942 responsibility for a so-called American-British-Dutch Area extending from Burma to the Moluccas and from Luzon to the Cocos Islands. Operations in so vast an area could not be effectively controlled from a single headquarters, but Wavell was willing to do his best to patch up the situation in the hope that by the spring he might be strong enough in the air to take the offensive. His interventions in Malaya were unsuccessful. In effect, the British lost the battle for Singapore when the relatively junior officer to whom the defence of Johore was entrusted adopted a disposition which invited the Japanese to cut through his left and turn his main position on the trunk road.

On 31 January the British withdrew the last of their troops to the island of Singapore. The Japanese commander, Lieutenant-General T. Yamashita, had fewer infantry battalions in the forward area than the British had in Singapore, but he was well provided with guns and mortars and could count on receiving about ten times as much air support as the enemy. By the end of the first week in February he was in a position to bring observed fire to bear on 3 of the 4 airfields on the island and had captured all or most of the posts on the mainland which were the basis of the enemy's early-warning system. The Johore Strait, less than a mile wide at most points, was fringed in many places by mangrove swamps which would prevent the defenders from gaining a clear view of the surface of the water.

Yamashita opened his assault with prolonged artillery and air bombardments which cut all landline communications in the forward area of the threatened sector. Troops defending the beaches on which the Japanese began to land under cover of darkness on 8 February were unable, therefore, to receive orders from the rear. Having been warned against disclosing their positions to the enemy by using their searchlights before they were ordered to do so, they forfeited an important advantage by not using them at all. In the confusion which followed, parties of Japanese infiltrated their positions. Attempts by troops who found themselves by-passed to make their way at night to pre-selected rallying points led to still worse confusion. The brigadier responsible for the sector in dispute had to renounce a counter-attack and withdraw to a defensive position some miles from the coast.

This was a serious setback for the British. Their scheme of defence was based on the assumption that the enemy could not be prevented from coming ashore. Since the island was too small for a battle of manoeuvre, it followed that local commanders must act resolutely to prevent him from pushing inland. That did not seem on 9 February to be what was happening.

Lieutenant-General A. E. Percival, commanding the land forces in Malaya, decided later in the day that, if the worst came to the worst, he would not retreat to the east of the island but would fall back to a line covering the town of Singapore. As the result of a misunderstanding, some of his troops withdrew to that line long before he intended them to do so. The built-up area of Singapore thus became a legitimate target for Japanese aircraft and artillery. Bombing and shelling killed or injured large numbers of civilians, blocked streets with rubble and fractured water mains at many points. On 14 February the municipal authorities reported that more than half the water which ought to be reaching consumers was running to waste and that supplies were not expected to last more than another 48 hours. In the light of still gloomier reports on the following day Percival agreed with Yamashita that his troops should lay down their arms in return for a promise on Yamashita's part to protect the civil population. Yamashita thus carried to a triumphant conclusion a campaign which brought him 130,000 prisoners and much booty at the cost of fewer than 10,000 casualties to his own troops.

Air power also served the Japanese well in the Philippines. General Douglas MacArthur, commanding the land and army air forces there, received news of the disaster at Pearl Harbour about 4 am on 8 December.* Official confirmation which arrived from Washington about 90 minutes later was followed at first light by an attack by aircraft from the *Ryujo* on a seaplane tender anchored off Davao. According to plan, MacArthur's bombers were to have attacked Japanese airfields in Formosa immediately after the outbreak of hostilities, but the attack was postponed until the afternoon in order to give time for a preliminary reconnaissance. In the meantime little or nothing was done to disperse bombers and fighters parked on MacArthur's airfields in Luzon. About 200 aircraft of the Eleventh Air Fleet which arrived soon after midday destroyed nearly 100 American aircraft on the ground and others in the air for the loss of only 7 of their own machines. Although the air defences of Luzon included an early-warning system based on radar, only 1 squadron of fighters was in the air when the enemy arrived. All but 2 of its aircraft were destroyed.

This calamity reduced MacArthur's air forces in the whole of the Philippines to some 17 bombers and fewer than 40 fighters, not all of them undamaged or fully serviceable. MacArthur's naval colleague Admiral Thomas C. Hart, commanding the United States Asiatic Fleet of 3 cruisers, 13 destroyers and 29 submarines, had some 32 flying boats for maritime reconnaissance.†

On 10 December the Eleventh Air Fleet returned to deal with the naval base at Cavite and other objectives in the neighbourhood of Manila Bay. About 100 fighters escorted and supported some 50–60 bombers. Three-quarters of an hour's warning given by radar enabled MacArthur's air force commander to put up practically all his surviving fighters, but the Eleventh Air Fleet's fighters outnumbered them by nearly 3 to 1. Bombing started uncontrollable fires in the navy yard and destroyed the entire reserve stock of torpedoes for Hart's submarines.

* i.e., about 3 pm on 7 December by central Pacific time.

† On 8 December 2 of Hart's cruisers, 4 of his destroyers and all his submarines were at Manila Bay. The third cruiser and 5 destroyers were at Tarakan in Borneo. The remaining 4 destroyers, which Hart had agreed to lend to Admiral Phillips, were on passage to Singapore.

Two days later Japanese naval fighters shadowed American flying boats returning from a search for Japanese carriers, followed them to their moorings and attacked them on the water. Hart then withdrew his surviving flying boats to Java.

Thus by the evening of 12 December the Japanese had complete control of the approaches to the Philippines in the air and on the surface of the water. Except in so far as their submarines might sink an occasional Japanese ship, the Americans could neither prevent the enemy from disembarking troops and supplies at will, nor reinforce and supply their own army.

In the second half of December MacArthur withdrew 14 surviving heavy bombers to Port Darwin, in Australia, and ordered his troops to make a fighting retreat to the Bataan peninsula, at the entrance to Manila Bay. On 11 March he handed over his command to Major-General Jonathan M. Wainwright and left, on orders from Washington, for Australia. On the night of 8 April Wainwright withdrew with the small part of his force which could be embarked before daylight to the island fortress of Corregidor, garrisoned by the United States 4th Marine Regiment. On 6 May he surrendered Corregidor and all surviving forces in the Philippines to Yamashita, who had assumed command of the Fourteenth Army.

Where command of the air eluded them the Japanese did not find the going so easy. A first attempt to capture Wake Island, more than 600 miles from the nearest Japanese airfield and only lightly attacked by the 24th Air Flotilla, was unsuccessful. Before making a second and successful attempt to put troops ashore they used aircraft from the *Soryu* and the *Hiryu* to bomb the island for many days in succession.

Both the Japanese and the Western Allies recognized that the key to possession of the Indonesian archipelago was control of the Java Sea, the Makassar Strait, the Flores Sea, the Banda Sea and the Molucca Passage. The naval forces available to the Allies to dispute control of these waters with the enemy when Wavell assumed command of the American-British-Dutch Area comprised 9 American, British and Dutch cruisers, some 25 American, British and Dutch destroyers, and some 40 American and Dutch submarines. With the exception of the submarines, most of these ships had to be used to protect convoys bringing reinforcements and supplies. The Japanese had already occupied key positions in British Borneo, and on 11 January they seized Tarakan in Dutch Borneo and Menado and Kema in northern Celebes. By developing air bases at those places they soon put themselves in a position to dominate the Molucca Passage and the Makassar Strait and to push southwards to Kendari in southern Celebes and Balikpapan in south-eastern Borneo. Amboina, captured between 31 January and 4 February, gave them control of the Banda Sea and put their aircraft within striking distance of Timor.

On the western flank, 2 troop-carrying convoys escorted and supported by cruisers, destroyers and a light aircraft carrier left Camranh Bay, in Indo-China, in the second week of February for southern Sumatra. Wavell ordered Rear-Admiral K. W. F. M. Doorman of the Royal Netherlands Navy to attack the convoys when they arrived off the coast of Sumatra, but lack of fighter cover forced Doorman to turn back in face of repeated air attacks. By the end of the month the Japanese were in possession of all points of strategic importance throughout southern Sumatra. Airborne troops, already used at Menado, contributed to the invasion of southern Sumatra by capturing oil installations at Palembang.

The Japanese had given some thought to a possible invasion of Australia, but had come to the conclusion that they could not find the troops and shipping needed for the purpose. Many Australians believed, however, that invasion was imminent when, on 19 February, some 200 Japanese aircraft attacked Port Darwin. About 150 of these aircraft came from 4 of Nagumo's carriers, the rest from Kendari. Twelve ships in the harbour were sunk, much damage was done ashore, and about 500 people were killed or injured. The Japanese lost 5 aircraft.

On 21 February the Combined Chiefs of Staff proposed to Wavell that, since Java was likely to be invaded in the near future, he and his staff should withdraw at his discretion from the headquarters he had established there. Wavell recommended that his headquarters should be dissolved. Jonkheer Dr van Starkenborgh Stachouwer, Governor-General of the Netherlands East Indies, then assumed command of all Allied forces in his area. These included 8 cruisers, 12 destroyers, 32 submarines still fit for sea and some 80–90 serviceable aircraft. In addition to some 40,000 partly trained volunteers, 12 Dutch and 2 Australian infantry battalions, with British, Dutch and American supporting arms, were available for the defence of Java.

In effect, the battle for Java was lost when on 27 February Admiral Doorman, with 5 cruisers and 9 destroyers, was defeated by a Japanese escort and covering force of 4 cruisers and 14 destroyers, under Rear-Admiral T. Takagi, while attempting to close with transports bringing an invasion force. No air striking forces were employed on either side, but reconnaissance aircraft helped Takagi to keep track of Doorman's movements. Doorman, who had no spotter aircraft, went down with his flagship. Japanese troops began to disembark in Java on 1 March. The Governor-General agreed on 8 March to capitulate to the Commander-in-Chief of the Japanese Sixteenth Army, and a formal instrument of surrender was signed on 12 March. On the same day Japanese troops landed without opposition in northern Sumatra.

On the outbreak of war with Japan the British had only 1 squadron of fighters, and no bombers, in the whole of Burma. They had, however, provided the country with a good network of airfields and Rangoon with an efficient early-warning system based on radar.

The Americans had formed while still at peace 3 squadrons of fighters, manned by volunteers, for the defence of the Burma Road in Chinese territory. When Burma was threatened one of these was, with Chiang Kai-shek's permission, stationed near Rangoon. The others were stationed at Kunming, in the Chinese province of Yunnan.

In the first few days of war the Japanese Fifteenth Army overran Siam and seized a British airfield at Victoria Point, in the extreme south of Lower Burma. Bombers of the 5th Air Division began a series of raids on Rangoon in the third week of December, but they were so stoutly opposed by the British and American fighter squadrons that the divisional commander ruled in January that attacks should be made only at night. On 19 January a battalion of the Japanese 55th Division seized a second airfield at Tavoy. The British then withdrew from an indefensible position at Mergui. All 3 of the airfields prepared by the British in the most southerly part of Burma thus fell into the enemy's hands within 6 weeks of the outbreak of hostilities.

The 5th Air Division's attacks caused many Burmese inhabitants of Rangoon to take refuge in the jungle and many Indians employed at the docks to start walking towards India along jungle tracks. Labour became hard to find, and the care of refugees with no means of subsistence became a major task for the civil and military authorities.

The Fifteenth Army had orders to concentrate the 33rd and 55th Divisions at Raheng, in eastern Siam, and hold them ready to advance on Rangoon by way of Moulmein as soon as the campaign in Malaya was known to be going well. There was no road from Raheng to Moulmein, but jungle tracks in the frontier area were improved by Siamese labourers under the direction of Japanese engineers. Later in the war the Japanese tried to improve communications between Siam and Lower Burma by putting British, Dutch, Australian and a few American prisoners of war and Burmese and Malayan conscripts to work on the notorious 'Burma railway'.

For his advance on Moulmein Lieutenant-General S. Iida, commanding the Fifteenth Army, had 12 infantry battalions supported by some 200–300 aircraft of the 5th Air Division based on the 3 Burmese airfields he had captured and on airfields in Siam. To move and supply about 35,000 combatant and non-combatant troops he had fewer than 600 lorries, about 700 horses and some 50 troop-carrying vehicles. He was opposed by 10 infantry or rifle battalions of the 17th Indian Division, mostly under strength and not fully trained. The British had some 60–70 serviceable aircraft to support their troops and defend Rangoon.

The commander of the 17th Indian Division, Major-General J. G. Smyth, V.C., considered that his best course was to concentrate his inexperienced troops near the estuary of the Sittang, east of Rangoon. His immediate superior, backed by Wavell, insisted that he should try to hold or delay the enemy at Moulmein and afterwards at a series of intermediate positions. Smyth made a skilful fighting retreat to the east bank of the Sittang, but his troops were heavily attacked towards the end of it by Japanese aircraft and were also bombed by their own side. On reaching the Sittang he was overtaken by disaster. As the result of an error of judgement aggravated by a misunderstanding, the bridge by which his troops were to have crossed the river was demolished when only a third of them were across. Many of the troops left on the wrong side found ways of crossing the river and eventually rejoined their units, but for the time being the 17th Indian Division ceased to be an effective fighting force.

The Japanese crossed the Sittang in strength on 3 March. They entered Rangoon on 8 March to find that the British had gone and that half the native population had taken to the jungle. The reorganized 17th Indian Division, the 1st Burma Division and the newly-arrived 7th Armoured Brigade, accompanied by many thousands of refugees, then completed the longest retreat in British military history by marching along jungle tracks to India.

With Rangoon in their hands the Japanese were able to raise the strength of their land forces in Burma to 4 and eventually to 10 divisions. By the end of April they also had in Burma more than 400 aircraft of the 5th Air Division. Early in April they sent Nagumo's carrier force into the Indian Ocean with orders to attack British naval bases in Ceylon. The British Eastern Fleet, now comprising 1 small and 2 large carriers, 5 battleships, 7 cruisers and some 16 destroyers, was in fact using a base in the Maldive Islands of whose existence Nagumo was unaware. He withdrew on 9 April after damaging shore installations at Colombo and Trincomalee, sinking 1 smaller carrier, 2 cruisers, 2 destroyers, 1 corvette and 6 merchant vessels. He also destroyed 39 British aircraft for the loss of 6 of his own. Vice-Admiral J. Ozawa, commanding a separate striking force of 1 light carrier, 6 cruisers and some 10 destroyers, sank about 90,000 tons of merchant shipping off the coast of Madras and dropped bombs at two places on land. Thereafter the British used Kilindini in Kenya as a base for their slower warships and the Maldive Islands as a forward base.

The Japanese occupation of Burma made the Burma Road unusable as a means of sending supplies to Chiang Kai-shek. The Americans organized an air lift across the foothills of the Himalayas from Dinjan, near the frontier between India and Upper Burma, to Kunming and Chungking. At the same time the British embarked on a vast programme of airfield construction in Bengal and Assam. They also accumulated large quantities of military supplies for an eventual advance into Burma.

Burma is a huge country, larger than France and Belgium put together. Much of it is densely forested. To keep watch on the whole of it and also maintain an inviolable front from the Bay of Bengal to the Himalayas was a task beyond the power of the Japanese. At no time in 1942 or 1943 were the British able to amass, or to extract from the Combined Chiefs of Staff, the resources needed for the massive advance to Rangoon by land or sea which they would have liked to undertake. They soon found, however, that small parties of parachutists could be dropped without great difficulty behind the enemy's lines, that aircraft could even land on improvised landing strips in a country occupied by the enemy and take off again, that the Japanese front could be penetrated by men on foot accompanied by pack animals. Moreover, where roads and railways were few, where movement across the surface of the earth was made difficult by dense forests, unbridged rivers and high mountains, the problem of supplying by air not merely small parties of troops behind the enemy's lines but whole armies assumed vast importance. In the forests of Burma and Assam, the transport aircraft was the key to mobility.

For the British Burma was never a 'forgotten front'. As long as the Japanese made no serious attempt to invade India, however, the Combined Chiefs of Staff were not likely to give a high priority to a theatre in which such attempts as were made to push the enemy back proved unrewarding. The framing of an agreed strategy for the forces in South-East Asia was made difficult, too, by conflicts of opinion between the British and the Americans as to whether the Allies should aim primarily at restoring land communications with Chungking, recapturing Rangoon or increasing the scope of the air lift to China either in the interests of Chiang Kai-shek's armies or in those of an American bomber force established in that country for the purpose of attacking Japanese shipping.

Conversely, there could be no doubt in 1942 of the importance of countering Japanese threats to Allied communications between Australia and the United States. By the end of March the Japanese held a string of bases in northern New Guinea, the Bismarck archipelago and the northern Solomons. A raid on Tokyo in April by American bombers from the carrier *Hornet* convinced them that they ought to do their best to destroy what remained of the United States Pacific Fleet before trying to push much further south. Expeditions to Tulagi in the British Solomon Islands Protectorate and Port Moresby in southern New Guinea were, however, not countermanded.

The essence of the Japanese plan was that 1 transport screened by 2 destroyers was to put a naval landing party ashore at Tulagi. Eleven transports screened by 6 destroyers, supported by 2 light cruisers and a seaplane tender and covered by the *Shoho*, with an escort of 4 cruisers and a destroyer, were to enter the Coral Sea and make for Port Moresby. A carrier striking force consisting of the *Zuikaku* and the *Shokaku*, accompanied by 2 cruisers and 6 destroyers, was to deal with any warships sent by the Allies to intercept the Port Moresby invasion force, and was also to send aircraft to attack airfields in Australia.

Admiral Chester W. Nimitz, the new Commander-in-Chief of the United States Pacific Fleet, learned from his intelligence sources that a large Japanese convoy was likely to enter the Coral Sea about the beginning of May. He assembled under Rear-Admiral F. J. Fletcher a task force consisting of the carriers *Yorktown* and *Lexington*, 8 cruisers, 13 destroyers and a tanker. The *Yorktown* and the *Lexington* carried 141 aircraft, the *Zuikaku* and the *Shokaku* carried 125, and the *Shoho* carried 21.

The Battle of the Coral Sea, fought on 7 and 8 May, was the first naval battle in which all losses on both sides were inflicted by aircraft from ships which never came close enough to the enemy to use their guns. The Americans lost the *Lexington* but sank the *Shoho* and damaged the *Shokaku*, and the Japanese withdrew without disembarking any troops at Port Moresby or reaching the position from which their carriers were to have launched attacks on Australian airfields.

An expedition intended to bring the United States Pacific Fleet to action and destroy it followed at the end of May and the beginning of June. Admiral Yamamoto's plan was to lure the Americans into a trap by sending small forces to occupy islands in the western Aleutians under cover of attacks on the eastern Aleutians by aircraft from a light carrier force. A strong battleship force was then to take up a position between Pearl Harbour and the western Aleutians and engage any American warships moving in either direction. While the enemy was thus preoccupied, transports covered by battleships, cruisers, destroyers and the

Zuiho were to disembark about 5,000 troops on Midway Island, more than 1,000 miles north-west of Pearl Harbour. About 270 aircraft from the *Akagi, Kaga, Hiryu* and *Soryu* were to make preliminary attacks on the island. Finally, any American airships not already sunk were to be finished off by aircraft from the carriers and by the main battlefleet.

Nimitz received good warning of an impending offensive in the central Pacific. He formed two task forces, one consisting of the *Yorktown*, 2 cruisers and 6 destroyers under Fletcher, the other of the *Enterprise*, the *Hornet*, 6 cruisers and 9 destroyers under Rear-Admiral R. A. Spruance. Together they formed a Carrier Striking Force under Fletcher's command. The 201 aircraft of Fletcher's carrier force would be supplemented by roughly 120 shore-based bombers, fighters and reconnaissance aircraft from Midway Island.

On orders from Nimitz, intensive air searches of the approaches to Midway Island began on 30 May. About 9 am on 3 June the pilot of a Catalina flying boat duly spotted the invasion force about 700 miles west of its objective. Fletcher, rightly judging in the light of reports which reached him later in the day that Nagumo's carrier force had yet to appear and was likely to come from the north-west, set a course that evening which he hoped would put him within striking distance of Nagumo by the following morning. Nagumo in fact arrived at sunrise on 4 June at his launching position 240 miles north-west of Midway Island. By the time he was spotted by an American reconnaissance aircraft, he had sent 72 bombers and 36 fighters to attack the island, retaining 93 bombers armed with torpedoes and armour-piercing bombs to deal with any American warships that might appear. Later he decided to use these aircraft for a further attack on the island, but cancelled the order when he learned from one of his spotter aircraft that American ships which included at least 1 carrier were closing with him. He had just completed the recovery of the aircraft despatched at sunrise and begun to refuel and rearm them when he found himself under attack by aircraft from all 3 of the American carriers. By midday the *Akagi*, the *Kaga* and the *Soryu* had all succumbed to accurate attacks by dive-bombers. Aircraft from the *Hiryu* disabled the *Yorktown*, but the *Hiryu* was then put out of action by dive-bombers from the *Enterprise*. Yamamoto, on learning that Nagumo had lost all

4 of his carriers with their entire complement of aircraft, ordered a general retirement.

Encouraged by success, the United States Joint Chiefs of Staff agreed on 2 July that Nimitz should drive the Japanese from Tulagi and establish a foothold in the southern Solomons as a first step towards recapture of the northern Solomons, the Bismarck archipelago and eastern New Guinea by forces to be controlled by MacArthur. On learning a few days later that Japanese engineers from Tulagi were building an airfield on the neighbouring island of Guadalcanal, they came to the conclusion that the Japanese must be expelled from Guadalcanal as well as Tulagi and the adjacent islets of Gavutu and Tanambogo.

Soon afterwards Japanese troops from the Bismarck archipelago disembarked at Buna in northern New Guinea as the prelude to an overland advance on Port Moresby. Australian troops under MacArthur's control brought them to a standstill 32 miles from Port Moresby in September, and eventually they were driven back with catastrophic losses to Buna. In the meantime some of the aircraft which MacArthur had intended to use to help Nimitz had to be used to support, and sometimes to supply, his troops in New Guinea.

The expedition to Guadalcanal and Tulagi was the first seaborne expedition to enemy-held territory undertaken by United States forces since 1898. The gist of the plan was that some 19,000 officers and men of the United States Marine Corps, with their equipment and supplies, were to be carried to the southern Solomons in one lift by 23 transports escorted and supported by 8 cruisers and 15 destroyers. Such air support as could be given from bases 600 miles and more away was to be provided by nearly 300 aircraft stationed in New Caledonia, the New Hebrides, Fiji, Samoa and Tongatabu, and by those of MacArthur's aircraft in Australia and New Guinea which he could make available for the purpose. The landings were to be covered by carrier-borne aircraft from the *Saratoga, Enterprise* and *Wasp,* which would form with the battleship *North Carolina* and attendant cruisers and destroyers an air support force commanded by Admiral Fletcher. Fletcher was also to command the entire enterprise.

The transports, with their accompanying warships, reached Iron Bottom Sound, between Guadalcanal and Tulagi, without opposition on 7 August. The marines who went ashore on Tulagi and the neighbouring islets were opposed by some 1,500 Japanese who resisted almost to the last man but were soon overpowered. Those who went ashore on Guadalcanal expected to have to deal with some 5,000 of the enemy. In fact there were fewer than 2,500 Japanese on the island, and only about 600 of these were fighting troops. They withdrew to another part of the island, allowing about 11,000 marines to stream ashore on the first day without opposition. The marines occupied the unfinished airfield on 8 August but omitted to seize the neighbouring Mount Austen, which they were to have taken on the first day.

Japanese aircraft arrived from the Bismarck archipelago within the first few hours to attack the transports, but were driven off by fighters from Fletcher's carriers after scoring one hit on a destroyer. A larger formation which came on 8 August set fire to a transport and damaged a second destroyer, but lost 19 aircraft out of 43. Fletcher lost 21 of his 99 fighters on the 2 days.

That evening Fletcher sent a signal to the Commander-in-Chief of the South Pacific Area, suggesting that he should withdraw the air support force on the ground that he had lost too many fighters, might be attacked by large numbers of bombers and torpedo-bombers, and was running short of fuel. He then made off to the south-east without waiting for a reply. His unfortunate subordinate, Rear-Admiral Richmond K. Turner, who had protested when Fletcher told him earlier that he proposed to withdraw the air support force after 48 hours, was thus left after only 36 hours to complete the unloading of equipment and supplies without benefit of fighter cover.

During the ensuing night a scratch force of 7 Japanese cruisers and 1 destroyer arrived from the Bismarck archipelago to make a surprise attack on the transports. The Japanese commander did not succeed in reaching them, but sank or disabled 4 cruisers. Turner continued to unload equipment and supplies until 4 pm on the following day. He then withdrew the transports and all the surviving warships.

Turner's departure left the marines with rations for a month and about half their allotment of ammunition. They had no radar, no coast defence guns and none of the heavy equipment they were to have used to complete the airfield and erect permanent buildings. Nor had they any aircraft until, on 20 August, a converted merchant vessel brought a first instalment of 19 fighters and 12 dive-bombers.

By that time the Japanese had begun to reinforce their garrison under cover of darkness. The sequel was a long struggle for control of the approaches to Guadalcanal, in which the Americans were forced to take far greater risks than they would have incurred had their carriers stayed until the marines were firmly established ashore with all their equipment and supplies.

Meanwhile the marines remained pinned to a beachhead about 7 miles wide and 2½ miles deep. On 15 October, after naval and air bombardments had destroyed more than half their aircraft and nearly all their reserves of fuel, Admiral Nimitz observed that control of the sea in the neighbourhood of the southern Solomons appeared to have been lost. He added that the situation, although critical, was not hopeless. Substantial reinforcements, including about 130 naval aircraft, were then moved to the South Pacific from other areas. Early in 1943, after the Americans had made the prodigious effort needed to relieve the marines first put ashore and raise the strength of their garrison to some 50,000 men, the Japanese withdrew to the islands of the New Georgia group in the central Solomons. By that time the struggle for Guadalcanal had cost the Americans and their Allies 2 large fleet carriers, 8 cruisers and 14 destroyers. The Japanese had lost 2 battleships, 1 light carrier, 4 cruisers, 11 destroyers and 6 submarines.

12

THE STRATEGY OF DESTRUCTION

When Roosevelt and Churchill, with their service advisers, met at Casablanca early in 1943 to consider how the war might be brought to a successful conclusion, there could be no doubt about the importance of air power as a means of support for fleets and armies. On every front, from Trondheim to Guadalcanal, on which British or American had been in contact with German or Japanese forces, air support had proved a crucial factor.

What contribution, if any, 'strategic' air operations could make to the winning of the war was not so easy to determine. In 1942 the British Bomber Command had aimed 45,000 tons of bombs at a variety of targets, including centres of production and population in Germany. The results were so hard to assess that the Chief of the Air Staff, Sir Charles Portal, had great difficulty in forecasting the effects of future air offensives. He was 'thrown back upon the old method of taking the German offensive against Britain in 1940 and 1941 as the yardstick'.[1]

However, at Casablanca the Chief of Staff of the United States Army, General George C. Marshall, pressed for an Anglo-American invasion of northern Europe. His British counterpart, Sir Alan Brooke, insisted that no such invasion was likely to succeed if it were launched before 'visible cracks' appeared in Germany's 'armed structure'. The outcome of a long debate was that the Combined Chiefs of Staff accepted the proposition that strategic air offensives by the British at night and the Americans in daylight might be a means of producing such cracks. The British and American heavy bomber forces in the United Kingdom were to aim under Portal's direction at 'the progressive destruction and dislocation of the German military, industrial and economic system, and the undermining of the morale of the German people to a point where their capacity for armed resistance is fatally weakened'.[2]

Just how these aims were to be attained remained a matter of controversy. Air Chief Marshal Sir Arthur Harris of the British Bomber Command was determined to continue the 'area attacks' which had begun before he took up his appointment. He had no faith in 'panacea mongers' who claimed that the destruction of objectives of a particular class, such as oil plants, might be decisive. Lieutenant-General Ira C. Eaker of the United States Eighth Air Force shared the conviction of his superiors in Washington that it was 'better to cause a high degree of destruction in a few really essential industries than to cause a small degree of destruction in many industries'; he also believed that it was 'possible to conduct precise pattern bombing operations against selected precision targets from altitudes of 20,000 to 30,000 feet in the face of anti-aircraft artillery and fighter defenses'. Any directive acceptable to both men which took into account conflicting opinions as to which industries were 'really essential' was bound to be framed in such broad terms as to be susceptible to almost any interpretation its recipients cared to put upon it. The directive approved by the Combined Chiefs of Staff at Casablanca on 21 January 1943 invited the commanders to attack German submarine construction yards, the German aircraft industry, 'transportation', oil plants and 'other targets in enemy war industry', in that order of priority, but reminded them that they must also attack U-boat bases in western France and might be called upon from time to time to attack objectives in northern Italy and warships at sea. In practice, they tended to attack those objectives which they wished to attack and deemed their forces capable of attacking.

At the beginning of 1943 Harris still had only about 500 serviceable first-line aircraft. It was only by calling on operational training units as well as first-line units that he had been able to make as many as between 630 and 1,046 sorties a night on 4 nights in the previous summer. By March he had more than 900 modern heavy bombers and some 50–60 fast Mosquito bombers used as a pathfinder force. By the end of January all but a few of his aircraft were fitted with the navigational aid known as Gee, and other navigational aids known as Oboe and H2S were in service on a limited scale.

Gee, introduced experimentally in the summer of 1941 and on a large scale in the spring of 1942 but based on proposals made in

1938, was a device which enabled the crew of a bomber to receive pulse transmissions from 3 ground stations and calculate their position with an accuracy of half a mile to 5 miles at ranges up to 300–400 miles. The transmissions were easily jammed and the system was not accurate enough for blind bombing, but it helped many crews who might otherwise have become hopelessly lost to return safely to their bases.

Oboe was a blind-bombing system developed after observation of the use made by the Germans of navigational beams in 1940. It was used operationally in a rudimentary form towards the end of 1941 and introduced as Oboe Mark I about 12 months later. The essence of the system was that 2 ground stations tracked a specially-equipped aircraft and determined the precise moment at which it should release its bombs. Whether the bombs hit the target depended not only upon the accuracy of calculations made by the staffs of the ground stations but also upon the skill with which the aircraft was flown. The maximum range at which the system could be used depended upon the height at which the aircraft flew; for an aircraft flying at 28,000 feet it was 270 miles. The transmissions could be jammed and were sometimes unintentionally masked by transmissions made for or on behalf of Bomber Command for other purposes, but no effective interference by the enemy was experienced before the late summer of 1943. Apart from its limited range a disadvantage of the system was that only a limited number of aircraft – originally one for each pair of stations – could be controlled at a time. Its use was therefore restricted to pathfinder aircraft carrying marker bombs.

H2S was a navigational aid and blind-bombing device which owed its origin to early experiments with air-to-air and air-to-surface radar, but it was not used operationally until 1943. It did not rely on transmissions from ground stations. The bomber carried a downward-looking radar transmitter and a receiver which presented the crew with a radar picture of what lay beneath them. Land could be distinguished from water and built-up areas from open country, but the image of a town on the cathode-ray tube of the receiver did not necessarily resemble its shape on a map. Except in the most favourable conditions the equipment called for a good deal of skill and experience on the part of the user. Serious disadvantages of H2S were that its transmissions could easily be picked up by the enemy and that its adoption jeopardized the secrecy of the current version of the air-to-surface vessel radar used by aircraft of Coastal Command to detect submarines. In the light of experiments with equipment taken from a bomber which came down near Rotterdam in March, Professor L. Brandt developed *Naxos*, a form of radar which warned U-boat commanders of the approach of aircraft equipped with the latest type of ASV and enabled night fighters to home on the British bomber stream though not on individual aircraft. A later development, *Korfu*, gave the Germans the means of detecting H2S transmissions from bombers parked at their bases in England and tracking a stream of bombers led by H2S-equipped aircraft the whole way to the target.

Bomber Command's effort showed a marked upward trend in February, but Harris dated the beginning of what he called the Battle of the Ruhr from the night of 5 March, when some 400 bombers despatched to Essen were led by pathfinders which dropped markers blindly on the strength of Oboe indications. The point of aim was the Krupp arms factory. Photographs taken during the raid seemed to indicate that roughly 150 crews had dropped their bombs within 3 miles of it, and the centre of Essen was seen on photographs taken in daylight on 7 and 8 March to have been severely damaged.

Further attacks on the same lines were made on the nights of 12 March and 3 April. Essen was also attacked on the nights of 30 April and 27 May, when 305 and 518 aircraft respectively were despatched. On those 2 nights cloudy weather forced the pathfinders to lay sky markers instead of dropping markers on the ground, and the bombing was not well concentrated. Ninety-two bombers failed to return from the 5 raids and 334 were damaged. The damage done to Essen caused the German authorities some anxiety, but the extent to which Germany's 'armed structure' was weakened by the raids remains hard to determine.

According to the definition adopted by British official historians, the Battle of the Ruhr lasted from the night of 5 March to the night of 13 July. Only about half Bomber Command's major raids during that period were aimed at the Ruhr. Either on account of the exigencies of the weather or for other reasons, attacks were made on German towns as far apart as Kiel and Rostock in the north, Stettin and Berlin in the east, Nuremberg, Munich and Stuttgart in the south, and Aachen in the west. Pilsen in Czechoslovakia, Turin and Spezia in Italy, and Lorient and Saint Nazaire in western France were also attacked. Many of these places were outside the range of Oboe and had to be attacked with the help of H2S. The results were often unsatisfactory, and casualties were heavy. About 18,000 sorties were made in 43 major raids during the period covered by the Battle of the Ruhr. Eight hundred and seventy-two aircraft failed to return and 2,126 were damaged, some of them beyond repair.

General Eaker was not in a position to make any such effort in the first half of 1943. Nor was he yet aware of the difficulty of the task before him. When members of his staff arrived in Britain in the spring and summer of 1942, they told British officers that they did not fear the German fighter force 'because we shall send long-range fighters to protect our bombers'. The P-38 (Lightning) fighters intended for the purpose were, however, soon moved to North-West Africa. Later P-47 (Thunderbolt) fighters and again some Lightnings were provided, but neither of these aircraft was capable of accompanying bombers to Bavaria or Brandenburg and back. Portal learned from an American source before the end of 1942 that 'the policy of escorting the bombers with fighters had been abandoned and the bombers would in future be responsible for their own defence on long-distance raids'.[3]

Whether the bombers would, in fact, be able to defend themselves on long-distance raids was debatable, but at any rate it was clear that they would stand no chance of success unless they flew in large, compact formations. Eaker estimated that he would have to despatch at least 300 bombers at a time to distant targets. He calculated that he would need a first-line strength of at least 800 bombers to sustain such an effort for any length of time. Taking wastage into account, he put his minimum requirement at 944 bombers by the summer of 1943, 1,192 by the autumn, 1,746 by the end of the year and 2,702 by the spring of 1944. He believed that with such resources he could, in partnership with the British Bomber Command, reduce Germany's output of submarines by 89 per cent, of bombers by 65 per cent, of fighters by 43 per cent, of ball-bearings by 76 per cent and of synthetic rubber by 50 per cent. In addition, serious harm could, he thought, be done to the German Army by attacks on the sources of its vehicles.

However, for a long time deliveries of American heavy

bombers to the United Kingdom were so slow that Eaker's minimum requirement seemed very unlikely to be met. The Eighth Air Force began active operations on 17 August 1942 with a raid on Rouen by 12 bombers. Between that date and the end of the year Eaker's bombers made 957 sorties against targets within reach of British or American fighters. His first attack on a target in Germany was a raid on Wilhelmshaven on 27 January 1943 by 91 bombers. During the first half of 1943 he made no attacks which involved long flights over hostile territory. Even so, his losses were not inconsiderable. Of 115 aircraft sent on 17 April to attack the Focke-Wulf factory at Bremen, 16 were destroyed and 44 damaged. Altogether the Eighth Air Force made some 4,500 bomber sorties between January and June. About 3,800 crews were reckoned to have reached their objectives, some 250 aircraft were lost and some 1,300 damaged.

A summit conference at Washington in May gave the Combined Chiefs of Staff an opportunity of revising their directive for the combined bomber offensive in the light of recent events. They had recognized at Casablanca that operations by the Eighth Air Force might become impossible if the enemy made substantial additions to his day fighter force. They had therefore put attacks on the German aircraft industry second only to the offensive against submarine construction yards, which they then regarded as the most important task of all. At Washington they noted that, while merchant shipping losses were beginning to decline, the strength of the German day and night fighter forces was increasing. They concluded that failure to arrest this tendency might be fatal to the interests not merely of the Eighth Air Force but of the British Bomber Command as well. On 10 June Harris was formally advised in a letter which became known as the 'Pointblank directive' that the Combined Chiefs had decided that 'first priority in the operation of British and American bombers based in the United Kingdom' must go to attacks on the enemy's fighter forces and the industries on which they depended. Eaker was given as an 'intermediate' task of 'primary importance' reduction of the enemy's fighter strength. Harris was to continue to aim at the general disorganization of German industry, but to pay special attention to places associated with the airframe, aero-engine and ball-bearing industries and the destruction of aircraft repair depots and storage parks and of 'enemy fighters in the air and on the ground'. A Combined Operational Planning Committee was to help the two commanders and their staffs to co-ordinate their operations and choose targets.

The opening of the combined bomber offensive did not come as a surprise to the German Air Ministry. Almost from the moment when the United States entered the war its agents had predicted a big build-up of American bombers in the United Kingdom. Udet's suicide towards the end of 1941, when his shortcomings as an organizer of production became manifest, enabled the more perspicacious Milch to reassert his grip on a department long out of his control. Notwithstanding Hitler's insistence that priority should go to offensive weapons and Göring's reluctance to thwart him, Milch succeeded with the help of the newly-appointed Minister for Weapons and Munitions, Albert Speer, in putting through in 1942 a reorganization designed to increase the output of fighters. New single-seaters with turbojet engines were under development, but the Focke-Wulf 190 and the latest version of the Me.109 seemed unlikely to be surpassed by any British or American fighter for some time to come. For lack of a more obviously suitable addition to the night fighter force, a heavy-fighter version of the Junkers 88 bomber was put into production and proved remarkably successful. The big Heinkel 177 bomber, designed to fill a conspicuous gap in the Luftwaffe's armoury, was already in bad odour, and the Junkers 288 was destined never to go into service. The Luftwaffe would have to depend for its hitting power on bombers admittedly out of date and on the FZG.76 pilotless aircraft whose development and production Milch authorized in the summer of 1942 on the strength of an oral description and a rough sketch by Dr Fritz Gosslau of Argus Motorenwerke.

By the time the Allies launched their combined bomber offensive these reforms had begun to bear fruit. The strength of the German day fighter and night fighter forces, which had fallen at the end of 1941 to 1,387 aircraft, rose in the first 6 months of 1943 from 1,961 aircraft to 2,817. At the end of June some 1,300 of these aircraft were stationed on the Western Front. The Luftwaffe had some 1,600 bombers in all theatres, but only about 1,000 of them were serviceable and only 828 bomber crews were described in its records as 'fully operational'. In the whole of 1942 and the first half of 1943 only about 60 night attacks on

Britain by more than a few aircraft at a time had been attempted, and only on 16 nights had more than 100 tons of bombs been dropped. Except when lightly defended targets such as cathedral cities or holiday resorts were attacked – as in the 'Baedeker raids' of 1942 – the results had, on the whole, been extremely poor.

So far as the British Bomber Command was concerned the Pointblank directive was somewhat unrealistic. German aircraft factories were widely dispersed, and some of them were in open country or in small, remote towns which Sir Arthur Harris was unlikely to regard as suitable targets for area bombing. Repair depots and storage parks were still less likely to attract him. He could not be made to attack objectives to which he could legitimately object on tactical grounds, and his crews were not likely to have many opportunities of destroying German fighters in the air. On the other hand, they might hope to reduce the effectiveness of the night air defences, at least for a time, by using the device called Window. This consisted of strips of metallized paper which could be dropped in large quantities to confuse the enemy's radar. Its adoption had long been deferred for fear that the enemy might retaliate in kind, but the Air Staff were aware before the end of 1942 that the Germans were familiar with the underlying principle of Window and hence were already in a position to use such a device if they wished to do so. Ministerial objections were withdrawn after Portal pointed out on 15 July that the German bomber force was 'weak, badly trained and fully extended'.[4]

Window made its début on the night of 24 July, when Bomber Command delivered the first of a series of massive attacks on Hamburg. Hamburg was beyond the range of Oboe, but its proximity to a coastline and river of distinctive shape made it easily identifiable by crews using H2S. The German fighter controllers were thrown into confusion on the first night by the masking of their upward-looking radar by Window, but they afterwards developed a method of directing pilots towards the bomber stream which did not depend upon radar indications. In 4 attacks on the nights of 24, 27 and 29 July and 2 August, Bomber Command made 3,095 sorties and dropped nearly 9,000 tons of bombs. Eighty-six bombers failed to return and 174 were damaged. Attacks by 235 bombers of the Eighth Air Force were made in daylight on 25 and 26 July. At least 43,000 inhabitants of

Hamburg out of a population of roughly a million and a half are believed to have been killed, industrial output was halved for about a month, and the labour force was reduced for the rest of the war by about a tenth.

On the night of 17 August Bomber Command despatched 597 aircraft to Peenemünde, an experimental station off the Pomeranian coast at which the Germans were suspected of developing a novel weapon which might be either a long-range rocket or a pilotless aircraft. Both the German Army and the Luftwaffe had experimental establishments at Peenemünde, and work was in fact being done there both on the A-4 long-range rocket and on the FZG.76. Forty bombers failed to return, considerable damage was done to buildings and 735 people were killed. Among these were some scientists and technicians and a substantial number of impressed foreign workers. In the interests of security, most trials of the A-4 rocket were made thereafter at an SS camp at Blizna in Galicia. The result was that agents of the exiled Polish Government were able to pick up fragments of rockets and send them to London. At the same time, although not solely in consequence of the raid, a plan for large-scale assembly of the A-4 at Peenemünde, Friedrichshafen and Wiener Neustadt was abandoned and the work was transferred to an underground factory near Nordhausen in the Harz Mountains.

Bomber Command's operations during the next few months were widely dispersed. In addition to Hamburg and Peenemünde, targets bombed in the course of 33 major attacks on German towns between 24 July and 18 November included Berlin, Bochum, Bremen, Düsseldorf, Essen, Frankfurt, Hagen, Hanover, Kassel, Leipzig, Leverkusen, Mannheim with Ludwigshafen, München-Gladbach, Munich, Nuremberg, Remscheid and Stuttgart. Raids were also made on Milan, Turin, Genoa, Modane and Montluçon, amongst other places outside Germany.

In the course of the 33 major attacks on German towns Bomber Command made about 17,000 sorties and lost 695 aircraft. Another 1,123 aircraft were damaged. There is nothing to show that the attacks did anything to lessen the determination of the German people or their leaders to continue the war. Their effect on industrial output cannot be accurately assessed, since it is impossible to know what would have happened had no attacks been made; but according to the best evidence available Germany produced in 1943 not only many more military aircraft than in 1942 but also many more armoured fighting vehicles, field guns, large-calibre anti-tank guns and rifles. She also produced more lorries, light cars, vans and motor-cycles, many more heavy anti-aircraft guns, more machine-guns and more submarines.

At the beginning of July the outlook for the Eighth Air Force was still unpromising. Eaker was more than 200 bombers short of his target figure for 1 July and likely to be more than 300 short of the figure for 1 October. Nevertheless attacks on distant objectives could not be delayed much longer if such objectives were to be attacked at all before the days became too short. Among those which seemed to cry out for attention were the Messerschmitt factory at Regensburg, on the Danube, and 3 factories at Schweinfurt, a town of some 60,000 inhabitants near Würzburg where more than half the ball bearings used in Germany were made.

On 17 August Eaker despatched 146 bombers with orders to attack Regensburg and fly on to Algeria. On the assumption that this raid would draw up and exhaust the enemy's fighters, 230 bombers despatched to Schweinfurt were to follow after a brief interval.

The bombers bound for Regensburg were accompanied as far as the German frontier by Thunderbolts, which then turned back. The bombers were promptly set upon by German fighters, and 24 were lost. The bombers bound for Schweinfurt were prevented by unfavourable weather from taking off punctually, with the result that the German fighters had plenty of time to refuel and rearm. Thirty-six bombers, making 60 out of the 376 despatched to both places, were lost. In addition, more than 100 were damaged. Serious damage was, however, done to 1 of the 3 main factories at Schweinfurt.

A further attack on 14 October did still greater damage, but the effect on Germany's 'armed structure' was almost negligible. An enquiry initiated by Speer revealed huge stocks of ball bearings held not by manufacturers but by consumers. By redistributing these where necessary, and by making other adjustments, the authorities were able to ensure that production of weapons, vehicles and engines vital to the war effort was not affected.

As on previous occasions, the Thunderbolts escorting the

bombers turned back in the neighbourhood of Aachen. Sixty bombers out of 291 were lost and 17 damaged beyond repair. Another 121 were less seriously damaged.

This experience convinced even the most resolute that the self-defending bomber formation was a myth and that attacks in daylight on distant targets must be renounced, at least for the time being. In effect, Eaker's attempt to carry out the Pointblank directive had thus to be suspended at the very moment when he found himself in a position to put 600 or 700 bombers into the air at one time. The strength of the enemy's day and night fighter forces had declined somewhat since the summer, but the German aircraft industry had produced in the 7 months since the directive was issued many more fighters than in the whole of 1942 and about twice as many as in the whole of 1941.

The question was whether the Americans could find an escort fighter which might enable them to continue their attacks in daylight, or would have to go over to night attacks as the British had done.

Aircraft mentioned as possible long-range escort fighters when the matter was discussed at a high level in the summer of 1943 included the P-47, the P-38 and the P-51, or Mustang.

At that time P-47 fighters accompanying B-17 bombers from the United Kingdom usually went about as far as the frontier between Belgium or Holland and Germany, and then turned back. The P-38 could go rather further, but it was mechanically unreliable and had the minor disadvantage of a distinctive shape which made it instantly recognizable by the enemy.

The P-51 in its original form, with Allison V-1170 engine, made no appeal to the United States Army Air Corps and only a limited appeal to the British for whom it was built. However, the firm of Rolls-Royce, impressed by its high speed at altitudes up to 5,000 feet, made experiments with a version powered by a British-built Merlin engine. The outcome was the P-51B, powered by a Merlin engine built by Packard under licence. This remarkable aircraft had a maximum speed of 455 miles an hour at 30,000 feet and, when fitted with suitable drop-tanks, could accompany bombers to Berlin and beyond.

It was not until after the Schweinfurt disaster in October that orders were given for the delivery of substantial numbers of P-51Bs to the Eighth Air Force, and not until the following February that Eaker's successor, Major-General J. H. Doolittle, was able to use them on a large scale. In the meantime strong pressure was put on Harris to attack objectives, such as Schweinfurt in particular, which the Eighth Air Force could reach only at a prohibitive cost. Harris was extremely reluctant to attack Schweinfurt, not only on tactical grounds but also because he did not believe that even the complete destruction of its ball-bearing factories would have the almost magical effects predicted by British and American experts. He pointed out that people had been saying for years that the Möhne and Eder dams were vital to Germany's war economy. A team led by Wing Commander Guy Gibson had breached both dams in the previous May with the help of a bomb specially designed by Dr Barnes Wallis for the purpose, but Germany's war economy seemed unaffected.

Having weakened his case by mingling tactical with strategic objections, Harris was unable in the end to withstand a direct order to attack Schweinfurt; but he managed to spin out his disobedience so long that the matter became one of principle rather than expediency. On 24 February the Eighth Air Force despatched 266 bombers to attack Schweinfurt in daylight. Harris despatched 734 aircraft to attack the town that night. By that time about a third of the plant from the main ball-bearing factories had been removed to factories elsewhere. Great damage was done by the 2 attacks, but 'it was not a shortage of ball bearings which caused Germany to lose the war'.[5]

By the early part of 1944 Britain and the United States commanded powerful means of imposing their will on Germany and Japan. There were, however, serious shortcomings in the system by which they sought to ensure that their strength was used to the best advantage. In theory, the Combined Chiefs of Staff were responsible for framing strategic plans for all theatres in the light of decisions made by their political masters at summit conferences. In practice, they could do little in their corporate capacity to influence events in the Pacific theatre and could exercise, at best, no more than a loose control over the disposal of American merchant shipping and naval resources and American-built assault craft.

These limitations had important effects on preparations for Overlord, as the projected invasion of northern Europe was called. It was not until late in 1943, when the decision was made to postpone landings in Normandy from the beginning of the following May to the beginning of June, that plans could be based on the assumption that enough assault craft to give more than a doubtful prospect of success would be forthcoming. Furthermore, it was not until April that the Supreme Commander for Overlord, General Eisenhower, learned that the Chief of the United States Naval Staff, Admiral King, had agreed to contribute some American warships to the bombardment force. Eventually Eisenhower succeeded in assembling more than 4,000 assault vessels, of which about a quarter were drawn from resources allocated to the United States, and some 1,200 combatant vessels of which the Americans contributed about 200. About 5,000 British and roughly the same number of American aircraft, apart from transport aircraft and gliders, would be available to provide direct and indirect support.

Roughly a third of these aircraft were heavy bombers. The failure of the heavy bomber forces to attain the aims of the Pointblank directive by the time the preliminary phase of Overlord was due cast doubt on their ability to make a useful contribution to Overlord; but it did not prevent Air Chief Marshal Harris from claiming in December that area attacks by his Lancaster bombers alone should suffice to bring Germany to the point of surrender by 1 April and thus make Overlord unnecessary.

This claim, which recalled Göring's attitude to Sealion, seemed to Harris's immediate superiors so far-fetched that they were led to question the whole basis of his advocacy of area bombing and to override more resolutely than they might otherwise have done his objections to a night attack on Schweinfurt. Meanwhile Harris had embarked on what he called the Battle of Berlin. Between the nights of 18 November 1943 and 24 March 1944 he devoted more than 9,000 sorties to 16 major raids on Berlin and more than 11,000 sorties to major raids on a dozen other German towns. About 14,000 of these 20,000 sorties were made by Lancasters, and 681 Lancasters failed to return. Altogether 1,047 bombers were lost in the 35 raids, and 1,682 were damaged. A still higher rate of loss was incurred on the night of 30 March, when 795 aircraft were despatched to Nuremberg and 106 were destroyed or damaged beyond repair. Photographs taken during the raid suggested that very few of the bombers sent to Nuremberg reached the target, and in general the attacks delivered between November and March fell well below the standard of concentration achieved in attacks on Essen and Hamburg in the previous spring and summer. Not only the relative ineffectiveness of these raids but also the high rate of loss were rightly attributed at the time to the growing strength and skill of the German night fighter force. The big, heavily-laden British bombers were easily outpaced and outmanoeuvred by fighters, and even crews whose aircraft were not damaged found the going hard and accurate bombing difficult. A contributory factor was the comparative uselessness of H2S over a large, homogenous built-up area such as Berlin.

In November 1943 the Allies formed the United States Fifteenth Air Force in Italy for the purpose of attacking objectives in southern Europe and forcing the enemy to distribute his fighters more widely. From 1 January 1944 the Eighth and Fifteenth Air Forces together formed the United States Strategic Air Forces in Europe, under the command of General Carl Spaatz. Portal retained the responsibility for directing the combined bomber offensive which had been conferred upon him at Casablanca. The Combined Chiefs of Staff and the United States Air Staff rather than Portal were, however, chiefly responsible for the wording of a new directive given to the commanders of the heavy bomber forces on 17 February. This omitted the customary reference to 'the morale of the German people' and called upon Spaatz and Harris to make depletion of the Luftwaffe their primary aim. They were to attack first objectives associated with the production of airframes and airframe components for the German fighter forces and German or German-controlled ball-bearing factories, secondly 'installations supporting German fighter air forces'. Launching sites for pilotless aircraft, which the Germans had begun to construct in northern France in the previous October, were lumped with Berlin and other industrial areas as objectives to be attacked only when the weather was unsuitable for attacks on primary objectives.

Attacks on the launching sites had in fact begun some 2 months earlier. In December the Eighth Air Force attacked 24 sites of a kind called by the British 'ski sites'; the British Bomber Command attacked 5. Twenty-three were attacked by tactical bombers of the United States Ninth Air Force and the British

Second Tactical Air Force. As a result of these attacks the Germans abandoned work on the sites, except as a blind, and built newer and simpler sites afterwards known to the Allies as 'modified sites'. The modified sites were mentioned in agents' reports as early as February, but little was known about them in London until April. By that time the bomber forces were pre-occupied with other tasks. Partly for that reason, partly because the importance of the new sites was underestimated and because they made poor targets, no attacks were made on them before they went into action, apart from one experimental attack in May.

Portal did not believe when the new directive was issued that the American strategic air forces would be able to reach more than a few of their objectives. Neither he nor Spaatz foresaw in February the extent to which the P-51B would transform the situation. When its potentialities were fully understood and exploited, American bombers and fighters were able to roam far and wide over Europe. Their activities did not prevent the Germans from producing the huge total of 36,000 aircraft of first-line type in 1944, but the Luftwaffe suffered heavy wastage and its strength rose during the year by only a few hundred aircraft. How far its inability to profit by a vastly increased input of new and repaired aircraft was attributable to losses inflicted by the Americans the record does not clearly show.*

A considerable effort had also to be devoted between the beginning of 1944 and the launching of Overlord to attempts to delay the introduction of pilotless aircraft and the still mysterious long-range rocket. Further attacks on ski sites brought the weight of bombs aimed at such sites since early December to more than 23,000 tons. In addition, more than 8,000 tons of bombs were aimed at sites whose purpose was unknown but which agents described as having some connection with 'secret weapons'.

* According to a survey made by the British after the war, the Luftwaffe received 43,312 new or repaired aircraft of first-line type in 1944 and lost 20,010 destroyed or missing and 14,147 damaged. Thus there ought to have been a surplus of 9,155 aircraft after losses were made good; yet the strengths of first-line and operational training units appear to have risen during the year by only 745 aircraft. Questions to which there seem to be no satisfactory answers are first what proportion of the huge wastage revealed by these figures was attributable to the Pointblank offensive, secondly why many units were below establishment at the end of the year although plenty of aircraft ought to have been available to bring them up to strength.

Meanwhile a question which called imperatively for an answer was how the Allies should use their air power to save their forces due to disembark in Normandy in June from being overwhelmed by counter-attacks after they had landed. An air commander with a staff had been appointed to study such questions as long ago as the late summer of 1943. Since a big fighter battle was expected at that time to develop over the beaches and the lodgement area, the choice fell on Air Chief Marshal Sir Trafford Leigh-Mallory, who had succeeded Douglas at Fighter Command. Leigh-Mallory produced a plan which envisaged a preliminary air bombardment of rail targets in France and Belgium for the purpose of bringing about a state of affairs in which tactical bombers would be able to prevent the enemy from moving reinforcements to the invasion area.

This plan called for co-operation from the heavy bomber forces. Spaatz and Harris, however, were obviously unwilling to accept orders from Leigh-Mallory. After prolonged negotiation it was arranged that Tedder, who was to act as Deputy Supreme Commander, should direct the operations of heavy bomber forces to be put at Eisenhower's disposal for a limited period.

The transportation plan, as it was called, was not accepted without a great deal of controversy. Churchill objected to it as likely to cause heavy casualties among French and Belgian civilians. Spaatz thought the Allies ought to aim primarily at establishing air superiority and that they were most likely to gain it by attacking oil plants since these, in his opinion, were objectives which the enemy would take good care to defend and whose destruction would be disastrous for him. Nevertheless he accepted, after some debate, the argument that the transportation plan must come first in point of time. Harris, on the other hand, at first flatly refused to be diverted from area attacks on German towns. He argued that most of his crews were notoriously incapable of hitting small, precise targets and implied that in any case a bomb not dropped on Germany was a bomb wasted.

By the early part of 1944 Portal was becoming increasingly sceptical of the effectiveness of area bombing. He was also becoming increasingly reluctant to defer to Harris. He arranged that Bomber Command should be directed to make experimental attacks by moonlight on specified targets in France in order to 'obtain experience of the effects of night attack on airfields, communications centres and ammunition dumps'. Attacks on a number of marshalling yards in March were so outstandingly successful that Harris could no longer claim that the part allotted to him in the transportation plan was beyond the capacity of his force. In the outcome, Bomber Command aimed some 42,000 tons of bombs at rail targets, mostly in France, during the preliminary phase of Overlord which ended early in June. The United States Eighth Air Force aimed about 24,000 tons of bombs at such targets during the same period. On the eve of the landings, Bomber Command aimed some 5,000 tons of bombs at coast defence batteries on the French coast.

By the time their troops went ashore in Normandy on 6 June, the Allies had complete control of the air over the invasion area and its approaches. Neither the commander of the German naval forces in the English Channel and the Bay of Biscay nor the veteran Field Marshal von Rundstedt, commanding the troops in France and the Low Countries, received any warning from the Luftwaffe on 5 June or during the ensuing night that an Allied invasion force was at sea. The few bombers, fighters and reconnaissance aircraft stationed in northern France, Belgium and Holland were enormously outnumbered. Substantial numbers of day and night fighters were deployed for the defence of the German homeland, but they made little or no contribution to events elsewhere until more than 6 months after the Allies had established themselves on French soil.

About a week after D-day the Germans opened an attack on London with pilotless aircraft, soon called by the British flying bombs. A few flying bombs were aimed at other targets, and after a week or two some were launched from aircraft. The missiles, gaining speed as they crossed the Channel and reaching a maximum of 400 miles an hour or so as they approached the target, were vulnerable to fighters and anti-aircraft guns; but the guns had to be redeployed and furnished with the latest ancillary equipment before they became fully effective. In the meantime the Allied bomber forces devoted a big effort to countermeasures. Between the middle of June and the end of August they aimed about 74,000 tons of bombs at targets associated with the flying bomb, about 8,000 tons at targets associated with the long-range rocket. A great many bombs were wasted on ski sites and other objectives no longer of any value to the enemy. The most rewarding targets were underground storage depots, which could be isolated by the judicious placing of big bombs.

Command of the air enabled Harris to use his bombers in daylight on some occasions. It also enabled the Allies to use heavy bombers against battlefield targets, not always with satisfactory results. Massive bombardments by large numbers of heavy bombers, even when accurate, tended to cover the battlefield with clouds of dust and smoke which hampered tactical bombers and fighter-bombers. Troops who saw perhaps 1,000 heavy bombers fly over the lines to attack the enemy's positions tended, too, to expect little opposition and to be disheartened when artillery posts and strongpoints were found to be intact.

After breaking out of their lodgement area in Normandy in August, the Allies advanced rapidly into Belgium and towards the Franco-German frontier. Their air power failed to prevent large numbers of German troops with some or all of their heavy equipment from escaping across the Seine, and they omitted on reaching Antwerp to gain control of the seaward approaches to the port by establishing themselves beyond the Scheldt. Eisenhower refused on logistic grounds to sanction an immediate thrust towards the Ruhr by some 20–40 divisions, but agreed to an attempt by 1 corps of 3 divisions to break into the North German Plain with the help of 3 airborne divisions which were to seize 9 bridges over 3 major rivers and 5 minor waterways. The attempt failed not for lack of air power but because the British 1st Airborne Division, intentionally dropped about 7 miles from its objective, was unable to seize a crucial bridge across the Lower Rhine at Arnhem and hold it while the 30th Corps came forward from Eindhoven on a front so narrow that the slightest hold-up might be disastrous. Attempts by Eisenhower's troops further south to push towards the Middle and Upper Rhine between Aachen and Nancy were also unsuccessful.

On 8 September the Germans launched the first of some 1,400 A-4 rockets aimed at the United Kingdom from improvised sites in Holland between that date and 27 March 1945. All save 40–50 were aimed at London, but only 517 reached the London Civil Defence Region, a vast area extending to the suburbs and beyond. In addition, large numbers of A-4 rockets were aimed during the next few months at Antwerp and a few at other Belgian or French towns. Antwerp was also the target for flying bombs launched after the beginning of September from sites in Germany. Finally, well over 1,000 flying bombs aimed at London and some 50 aimed at Manchester were launched from aircraft between the middle of September and the following January, and in March 275 flying bombs of a new long-range pattern were aimed at London from sites near Rotterdam.

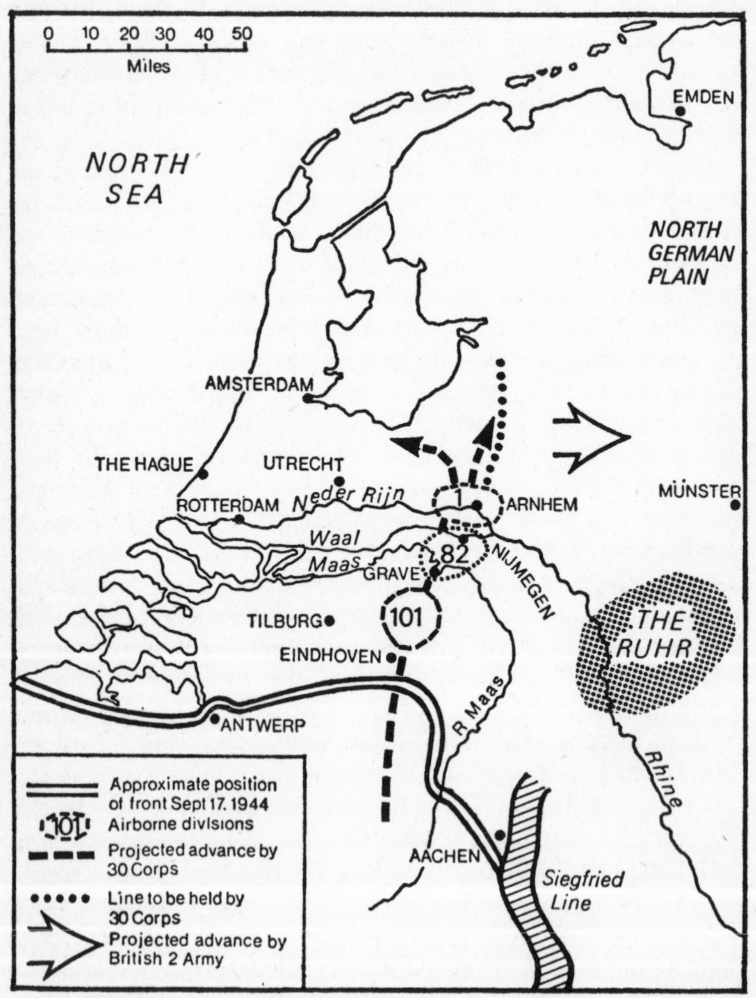

7 Arnhem

Guns and fighters dealt so successfully with flying bombs aimed at London between September and March that only 79 reached the London Civil Defence Region. The A-4 rocket, despite its inaccuracy and a tendency to burst in the air, proved a far more dangerous weapon. Covering the distance from western Holland to London in less than 5 minutes and approaching the target at 2,200–2,500 miles an hour, it confronted the air defences with formidable problems. Clearly, no fighter conceived or conceivable could intercept it. The use of anti-aircraft guns to place a curtain of shell fragments at a given point on the course of an approaching rocket, as predicted by radar, was proposed; but the Chiefs of Staff refused to sanction a trial on the ground that the chances of success were too slender to justify a volume of fire which might alarm the public and would be difficult to explain away.

Active counter-measures to the A-4 were limited, therefore, to attacks by bombers or fighter-bombers on launching sites, storage sites, launching troops and their vehicles, and links in the system of supply. These measures, which could have been stepped up if the scale of attack had increased, had some effect on the enemy's rate of fire but were never decisive. The effects of the general Allied air offensive against communications were, however, such that it is doubtful whether the Germans could substantially have increased the flow of missiles to the forward area even if ample supplies had been available. Thus the A-4 rocket, although it could be regarded to some extent as a substitute for the strategic bomber, was not a substitute for air power. Even if the Germans had been able to produce in bomb-proof factories enough missiles and fuel for a major offensive, to mount such an offensive in 1944 or 1945 they would still have needed air power to protect the launching troops and their communications.

In 1944 the British and the Germans introduced almost simultaneously to active service the Gloster Meteor twin-jet single-seater fighter and the twin-jet Me.262, which first appeared as a fighter although Hitler would have preferred to use it exclusively as a light bomber. The Me.262, with a ceiling of 40,000 feet and a maximum speed of 525 miles an hour, was some 45 miles an hour faster than the Meteor. Despite the introduction of this and other remarkable aircraft, the Luftwaffe was in such low water by the end of the year that it was only by choosing a season when Allied aircraft were likely to be grounded by bad weather that the German Army could expect to counter-attack with any prospect of success. This factor was largely responsible for the timing of the offensive in the Ardennes by which Hitler hoped to drive a wedge through the Allied armies and recapture Antwerp and Brussels. Its launching on 16 December caught Eisenhower unprepared, but the tide is generally reckoned to have begun to turn when the 2nd Panzer Division came to a standstill before Dinant on 23 December. Lack of air support was, of course, only one of the German Army's troubles, but it is a fact that 23 December was the first day since 12 December on which the weather was good enough for Allied aircraft to take the air in strength.

On 1 January about 800 German fighters, many of them drawn from Luftflotte Reich, made a desperate attempt to reduce Allied air superiority by opening fire with machine-guns and cannon on a large number of airfields. They destroyed about 130 aircraft, but 200 German fighters failed to return. Thereafter the Germans were slowly pushed back, in appalling weather, more or less to the line they had held on 16 December.

In the meantime General Eaker did not relinquish his belief – which proved correct – that oil was the Achilles' heel of the German economy. As early as April 1944 the Fifteenth Air Force delivered a series of attacks on the Rumanian oil installations at Ploesti. The Eighth Air Force, although largely preoccupied with other tasks, followed up these attacks on 12 May by sending 935 bombers to attack 5 oil targets in Germany. By the middle of the following month Eisenhower, Tedder, Spaatz and Harris had come to an informal agreement to regard oil plants as suitable objectives for heavy bombers not required for attacks on flying-bomb or long-range rocket targets or for tactical bombing, and Harris had to all appearances sealed the bargain by sending 294 aircraft to attack an oil plant at Gelsenkirchen on the night of 12 June. Further attacks on oil plants by aircraft of Bomber Command followed during the next few weeks, although most of these were made by only a few bombers at a time.

On 31 July the Joint Intelligence Sub-Committee of the British Chiefs of Staff reported that Germany was likely to crack by the end of the year if her land forces continued to be heavily engaged on 3 fronts and if continued air attacks prevented her from repairing damaged oil installations. This report was doubly welcome since Britain's manpower and economy were becoming so stretched that she might be unable, should the war in Europe be prolonged beyond the end of 1944, to make the major contribution to the war against Japan which seemed necessary to preserve her status as a first-class power.

When Eisenhower announced on 6 September that few, if any, further attacks on rail targets in France would be needed the way seemed clear, therefore, for a 'final and overwhelming' air offensive which might with advantage be directed against oil targets. Alternatively, the enemy might be paralysed by far-reaching attacks on rail targets in Germany, or Berlin might be heavily bombed for the purpose of enforcing surrender before conditions became so chaotic that the Allies could not hope to find an acceptable government to replace the National Socialist regime.

A week later Portal persuaded the Combined Chiefs of Staff to agree that, subject to Eisenhower's right to call for such direct support as his armies might need, control of the strategic bomber forces should revert to him and his American counterpart, General H. H. Arnold. Representatives of the British Air Staff and Allied Supreme Hearquarters (SHAEF) agreed on the same day that priority for the strategic bomber forces should go to oil targets. A directive in that sense was sent to Harris on 25 September.

But Harris continued to pay far more attention to area attacks than to selective bombing. About 66 per cent of his effort in October was devoted to general area attacks, about 6 per cent to attacks on oil plants. The proportion devoted to oil plants in November was higher, but was still only about a quarter of the total. In letters written to Portal in December he made it clear that he had no faith in the oil plan. He added that he would carry out his part in it to the 'utmost' if he were ordered to do so, but this was scarcely reassuring since his utmost was what he claimed to have done in the case of attacks on the ball-bearing industry. Nevertheless Portal came to the conclusion that it was better to go on with a commander-in-chief with whom he could not see eye-to-eye than to make a change when success was almost in sight.

Thus it was without Harris's approval, and indeed against his wishes, that the Allies continued with a policy afterwards described by Harris as backing an outsider which happened to win. Between the beginning and the end of 1944 Germany's production and imports of finished oil products declined by approximately two-thirds. Early in 1945 air-launched flying bombs ceased to approach the United Kingdom not, indeed, because there was no more fuel for flying bombs but because there was none for the aircraft that launched them.

Bomber Command continued to make area attacks on German towns, some associated with the oil industry or other industries of strategic interest and some not obviously so, until in April Portal ruled in effect that no more should be made. A much-criticized decision to attack Dresden some 3 months before the end of the war in Europe was, however, not made by Harris. Proposals for a devastating attack or series of attacks on some big town other than Berlin, to be made as a means of hastening the end of the war should the National Socialist regime show signs of collapse, had been put forward in the previous August. The project then lapsed until January, when its revival as a means of helping the Russians was discussed. The Russians, it was said, might be materially assisted by the devastation of a town immediately behind the front they were attacking. At the same time such a move might serve to demonstrate both to the Russians and to the Germans the reality of the Grand Alliance and the importance attached to it by the Western Allies. The outcome of exchanges between the Prime Minister, the Secretary of State for Air, Harris and members of the Air Staff was that Churchill peremptorily asked on 26 January to be told whether the Air Ministry agreed that 'Berlin, and doubtless other large cities in East Germany' should be 'considered especially attractive targets'.[6] Harris was then instructed, and Spaatz was asked, to put Berlin, Leipzig, Dresden 'and associated cities where heavy attack will cause great confusion' second only to synthetic oil plants as targets for heavy bombers operating from the United Kingdom.

The Russians do not appear to have asked specifically for an attack on Dresden when the matter was discussed with them at Yalta in February, but they did ask in the early stages of the conference that communications should be attacked in order to prevent the Germans from moving troops eastwards from the

Western Front and Italy, and in particular that Berlin and Leipzig should be 'paralysed'. Later they made it clear that they would not welcome attacks on objectives east of a line from Berlin through Dresden and Vienna to Zagreb and implied that they no longer attached the same importance to the co-operation of the British and American strategic bomber forces.

However, no new directive reflecting the discussions at Yalta was given by the Air Staff to Harris or by Spaatz to the Eighth Air Force. The Eighth Air Force had already, on 3 February, made a heavy attack on Berlin. On the night of 13/14 February more than 800 aircraft of Bomber Command were sent to make a devastating attack on Dresden; the Eighth Air Force followed with heavy attacks on 14 and 15 February and 2 March. On 17 February and later, statements appeared in the press to the effect that the Allies had, for the first time, adopted a policy of 'deliberate terror bombing' in order to hasten Hitler's doom. These statements were misleading in as much as there was nothing new about area bombing. What was new about Bomber Command's raid on Dresden was that it was the first attack undertaken for the avowed purpose of helping the Red Army. A fair comment might have been that the Red Army no longer seemed to need such help and that the raid had the appearance of having been undertaken not so much to help the Russians as to impress them.

In the war with Japan the Western Allies faced problems radically different from those posed by the war with Germany. Germany was a highly industrialized country, occupying a central position in Europe and able during the greater part of the war to draw not only on her own resources but also on those of occupied or satellite countries for large quantities of raw materials which did not have to come to her by sea. Japan, a group of islands poor in natural resources, depended on imports for most raw materials and for much of her food. That situation was not materially altered by her seizure of Malaya, Indonesia and the Philippines, since those of their products which were needed in Japan had still to be carried there in ships. She could not hope to win a long war against two such highly industrialized nations as Britain and the United States. When she went to war, she gambled on the hope that, by presenting them with a *fait accompli*, she could induce them to recognize her claim to a special position in South-East

Asia rather than go to the trouble of expelling her by force from territories inhabited mainly by Asiatic peoples.

The carrying capacity of the Japanese merchant fleet on the outbreak of war was just under 6 million tons. This barely sufficed to meet peacetime needs. Newly-built ships and ships captured or requisitioned during the next 13 months added the best part of 2 million tons, but these additions were more than offset by the loss of nearly 3 million tons torpedoed by Allied submarines or sunk by Allied aircraft. Japan was thus left at the end of 1943 with less than 5 million tons of merchant shipping to meet requirements swollen by the demands of war. By that time, and indeed by the early summer of that year, the Japanese were outnumbered in major warships of every class except heavy and light cruisers by a remodelled United States Pacific Fleet. By the end of the year the Americans and their Allies also had such strong land and air forces in the central Pacific, Australasia and the South Sea Islands that their biggest problem was not so much to build up their strength as to discover how they could best bring it to bear against an enemy who held life cheap.

Some western strategists argued that in these circumstances the Americans could safely rely on an expanded fleet of submarines to win the war for them by sinking Japanese merchant shipping faster than it could be replaced. A weakness of this argument was that the rate at which the Japanese might be able to replace their losses when they became fully aware of the risks they were running could not be foreseen. Whether opposed landings in the Japanese homeland would be necessary remained almost until the end of the war a controversial question; but it seemed clear that in any case the Allies would be well advised to seize bases from which Japan could be invaded if the need arose. The step-by-step advances in the central and south-west Pacific to which they committed themselves were not, however, undertaken solely with that end in view. The Combined Chiefs of Staff, and the United States Chiefs of Staff in particular, were also concerned to capture both bases from which a heavier weight of air attack could be brought to bear against Japanese shipping, and bases from which the Japanese homeland could be bombed.

Between 1941 and 1944 the American firm of Boeing developed with remarkable speed the B-29, a long-range bomber capable of flying to Tokyo and back from bases in the Marianas or from Chengtu in the Chinese province of Szechwan. Since the Marianas were still in Japanese hands in 1943, the British agreed towards the end of that year that 4 or 5 airfields near Calcutta should be made ready to receive 1 or 2 wings of B-29s which would be based there when they were not operating from forward bases at Chengtu. Pending the introduction of the B-29, American bombers based in China could attack Japanese shipping off the Chinese coast but could not reach Japan. An important aim of Allied diplomacy in 1943 and the early part of 1944 was, therefore, to obtain from the Soviet Government the use of bases which would bring the Japanese homeland within reach of existing bombers.

Stalin promised on 2 February 1944 that the Americans would be allowed to establish bases for up to 1,000 bombers in the Russian Maritime Provinces after the Soviet Union declared war on Japan. The Russians then built 6 or 7 new airfields near Vladivostok. They went on to propose that the Americans, besides sending a strategic air force of their own to Russia in due course, should provide the Red Air Force with 540 heavy bombers and train Soviet airmen to use them. At the Yalta Conference early in the following year, however, the Russians abandoned this project. They also withdrew their implied promise of bases in the southern part of the Maritime Provinces and offered the use of airfields much further north, in the neighbourhood of Komsomolsk and Nikolaevsk.

In the meantime the Americans, profiting by their experience at Guadalcanal and the growing strength of their forces on land and sea and in the air, pushed steadily towards their objectives in the central and south-west Pacific with massive support from carrier-borne and shore-based aircraft. These operations were regarded as mere preliminaries to the full-scale offensive against Japan which the Allies had agreed to launch when Germany was defeated.

The first attack by American aircraft on the Japanese homeland since the famous carrier raid of 1942 was made on 15 June 1944 when 65 B-29s of the 58th Bomber Wing, based near Calcutta, were despatched from Chengtu. They aimed about 120 tons of bombs at a steelworks and did a good deal of damage to a neighbouring industrial area. Further attacks on objectives in Japan and Japanese-occupied China and Manchuria followed in

July and August. All fuel, bombs and spares delivered to Chengtu had, however, to be carried by air. This proved so uneconomical that early in 1945 the United States Chiefs of Staff directed that the 58th Wing should concentrate at Calcutta and the Chengtu bases be closed down. Meanwhile the Americans had captured the Marianas after a tremendous struggle, including preliminary air battles between Japanese land-based naval aircraft and American carrier-borne aircraft. The 58th Wing made a number of attacks on objectives in South-East Asia before joining the 73rd Wing in the Marianas in April.

The significance of these events from the point of view of the air defence of Japan was not lost on the Japanese. On learning in 1943 that the Americans were developing a new long-range bomber and that airfields with particularly long runways were being built near Calcutta and in China, they initiated measures which raised the numbers of fighters and anti-aircraft guns deployed for the defence of the homeland to some 750 and 600 respectively by the summer of 1944. Within 10 days of the fall of Saipan in the Marianas and 5 weeks of the first raid by bombers from Chengtu, the militarist Government of General Kideki Tojo was forced to resign in favour of one dedicated to the task of carrying on the war as best it could while seeking the way to a negotiated peace.

The first raid by aircraft from the Marianas did not, therefore, take the Japanese by surprise. On 24 November 1944 111 B-29s of the 73rd Bomber Wing were despatched from Saipan with orders to bomb an aircraft factory and the docks at Tokyo. More wings followed within the next few months and were posted to Guam and Tinian.

Attempts by aircraft from the Marianas to bomb precisely-defined objectives in Japan in daylight were, however, not much more successful than those made by aircraft from Chengtu. Apart from having to run the gauntlet of the defences, crews were often hampered by clouds which made target-finding and accurate bombing difficult or impossible. By the early part of 1945 only one of 9 aircraft factories scheduled by the United States Chiefs of Staff for destruction had suffered major damage. Meanwhile the Japanese were able, by stepping up output and by drawing on units driven from their outlying possessions, to make substantial progress towards a target of 5,000 aircraft of all types based at home by the end of March.

The Americans, following the example of the Germans and the British, then turned to night attacks by aircraft carrying a relatively small proportion of high-explosive bombs and a high proportion of incendiaries. The effects were devastating. According to the account given by the Japanese after the war, one night's bombing in March alone destroyed more than a quarter of a million houses, killed some 80,000 people and left a million people homeless.

Early in April a new Japanese Government was formed, in which Shigenori Togo accepted the post of Foreign Minister with the intention of persuading the Soviet Government to mediate between Japan and the Western Powers. Since Stalin had made up his mind to attack Japan about 3 months after the end of the war in Europe, it was not surprising that Togo made slow progress. Nevertheless the United States Government was aware by July that the Japanese wished to make peace, but were anxious to preserve the monarchy and reluctant to accept unconditional surrender. At the same time, the tenacity with which Japanese troops had defended the islands of Iwo Jima and Okinawa in recent months gave the Allies reason to believe that an invasion of the Japanese homeland might cost as many as a million American and British casualties. In these circumstances they decided to usher in the nuclear age by dropping on Japan the 2 atomic bombs at their disposal.

13

AIR POWER IN THE NUCLEAR AGE

The origin of the atomic bomb can be traced to the early experiments of the English-domiciled New Zealander Sir Ernest Rutherford or, less remotely, to the experimental splitting of the atom by two of his disciples in 1932. By that date Rutherford had already warned the Secretary of the Committee of Imperial Defence, Sir Maurice Hankey, of the strategic implications of atomic power.

In 1938 Otto Hahn of Berlin split the nucleus of the uranium atom. Subsequent study of the theory of nuclear fission suggested that enormous power might be released by a chain reaction, but the mass of crude uranium needed to produce such a reaction was shown by Rudolf Peierls, a German-born physicist domiciled in Britain, to be so great that the manufacture of an atomic bomb light enough to be carried in an aircraft seemed impossible.

Soon after the outbreak of the Second World War Peierls made in association with Otto Frisch, the nephew of a former collaborator of Otto Hahn, a fresh calculation based on the assumption that the isotype uranium 235 could be isolated from crude uranium. This led to the conclusion that production of an atomic bomb would be feasible if a method of isolating uranium 235 in adequate quantities could be devised. A method proposed by Franz Simon, a German-born physicist who had lived in Britain since 1933, seemed so promising that the British Government decided in 1941 to establish a pilot plant for the production of nuclear explosives in north Wales. A full-scale plant would be established later in Canada.

In the United States a group of refugee scientists tried in 1939 to interest President Roosevelt, through Albert Einstein, in developing nuclear weapons in order to forestall Hitler. At that time the American authorities were more interested in the industrial than the military aspect of nuclear research. As a result of disclosures made by the British it was, however, agreed between Roosevelt and Churchill on 20 June 1942 that the development of nuclear weapons should be carried out in the United States and Canada as a joint Anglo-American enterprise, on the understanding that neither country was to use such a weapon against a third party without the consent of the other. At Churchill's request, this agreement was formally recorded at a summit conference at Quebec in the following year.

The production of uranium 235 on a useful scale proved more difficult than either the British or the Americans expected, but enough was produced by the summer of 1945 to make a uranium bomb. In addition, an experimental bomb and a bomb suitable for warlike purposes were made from the artificial element plutonium. The British Government learned as early as March that 'a weapon' was likely to be ready by the late summer, and later that the Americans proposed, if the British agreed, to use it against the Japanese some time in August. The British reply to these soundings was to the effect that the matter was one which the President and the Prime Minister might wish to discuss at a summit conference to be held at Potsdam in July.

On 16 July, after the British and American delegations had reached Potsdam but before the formal opening of the conference, the experimental version of the plutonium bomb was successfully exploded in New Mexico. Neither Churchill nor Roosevelt's successor, President Harry S. Truman, seems to have remarked at the time that this experiment threw only an uncertain light on the probable behaviour of the uranium bomb which the Americans proposed to use first.

In the course of separate conversations with Churchill and Truman at Potsdam, Stalin mentioned the overtures made by the Japanese and added that the Soviet Government had taken no action upon them. Since the American authorities had intercepted and deciphered Togo's instructions to the Japanese Ambassador in Moscow, this disclosure cannot have come as a surprise to Truman. He was understood by Churchill to agree that in the circumstances the Allies might be well advised to stretch a point in favour of the Japanese by not insisting too rigidly on unconditional surrender. After consulting Churchill, he told Stalin that the Western Allies had a new weapon of extraordinary power, but did not say that it was an atomic bomb.

No decision had yet been made to use the bomb. Truman and Churchill agreed that, before it was used, the Japanese should be given an opportunity of surrendering in the light of an assurance that the Allies had no intention of enslaving them, destroying their nationhood or permanently occupying their country. They were also to be told that the Allies were willing to grant them access to raw materials and eventually to world markets.

A declaration in these terms was issued on 26 July, after the draft had been approved by Chiang Kai-shek. It contained no reference to the future status of the Emperor, although Truman had been strongly advised by the veteran Secretary of War, Harry L. Stimson, to reassure the Japanese on that point.

The declaration was not conveyed to the Japanese Government through a neutral intermediary, in accordance with orthodox diplomatic practice. It was merely broadcast by radio. The Japanese authorities learned of it from their monitoring service. They decided to await the results of the approach they had asked the Soviet Government to make to the Allies on their behalf before replying to it.

Since their silence was taken to mean that they did not wish to surrender on the terms proposed, the uranium bomb was dropped early on 6 August on the crowded city of Hiroshima from a B-29 flying at 30,000 feet. About 80,000 people were killed instantly, and many afterwards died lingering deaths from the effects of radiation.

Even in face of this disaster, the Japanese did not at once give in. It was not until the early hours of 10 August that they decided to send to Washington, by way of Berne, an offer to surrender on the understanding that the monarchy would not be abolished. By that time a second B-29 had dropped the plutonium bomb on Nagasaki, and the Soviet Union had declared war on Japan with effect from the morning of 9 August. The Russians were thus able to claim the substantial territorial concessions at the expense of Japan and China to which they were entitled under the terms of an agreement with the Western Powers if they entered the war against Japan within 3 months of the end of the war in Europe.

The effect of these concessions was to restore to Russia the favourable position in the Far East of which she had been forcibly deprived by the Japanese some 40 years earlier. Almost simultaneously, the Russians greatly strengthened their position in Europe by establishing virtual hegemony over Poland, Rumania, Czechoslovakia, Hungary and a substantial part of Germany. At first the Western Powers were to some extent consoled for these setbacks by the belief that they had established a commanding lead over the Soviet Union in the field of nuclear weaponry. They were to learn by 1949 that in fact the Russians were not far behind them, and in some respects might even be ahead of them.

At the end of the Second World War the long-standing controversy between advocates and opponents of so-called strategic bombing was still unsettled. Students of war who questioned the utility of the strategic bomber could and did point out when the war was over that the Anglo-American strategic air offensive had not shaken Germany's determination to continue the struggle as long as her armed forces were still capable of fighting, or prevented her from greatly increasing her output of aircraft and armoured fighting vehicles during the last 2 years of the war in Europe. Selective attacks on Japanese aircraft factories had been conspicuously unsuccessful. The long-range bomber, according to its detractors, had in general proved so inherently inaccurate and unsatisfactory a weapon that only the development of ancillary devices, culminating in the atomic bomb, had enabled the belligerents to go on using it.

To this their opponents replied that a combination of selective and area attacks had completely disrupted Germany's synthetic oil industry, that there was no knowing how many aircraft and armoured fighting vehicles the Germans might have produced during the last 2 years of the war in Europe if their cities and factories had not been bombed, and that area bombing had proved highly effective when applied to Japan. Mistakes and miscalculations had been made in the early stages of the Allied bomber offensive, but these had been put right. As for the atomic bomb, it was not a desperate expedient, born of the need to compensate for the inherent inaccuracy of the long-range bomber, but merely the outcome of an ineluctable process by which offensive weapons became progressively more destructive. The Hiroshima bomb had not, in point of fact, done noticeably more damage than might have been produced by one night of high-explosive and incendiary bombing, but far more powerful nuclear bombs were sure to be forthcoming. These would make air power so potent a weapon in the hands of their possessors that all that was needed to secure a tranquil future for the capitalist world was to ensure that only the right people used them.

Even for men convinced that they knew which were the right people, this was more easily said than done. A *Pax americana* founded on exclusive access to nuclear weapons was never a practical possibility. The British already knew how to make atomic bombs; others could learn to do so. Pyotr Kapitza, a citizen of the Soviet Union, had been considered by Rutherford his most promising pupil. The best the Americans could hope to do when their monopoly of nuclear bombs came to an end was to remain a step ahead of the Russians in the development of the means of delivery and perhaps in the evolution of methods of defence.

At the end of the Second World War, some British strategists predicted that within 10 years the strategic bomber would be superseded by a family of ballistic missiles developed from the German A-4 rocket. The Americans showed their faith in rocketry to the extent of engaging the services of Dr Wernher von Braun, a pioneer of the A-4, but they continued to develop the long-range bomber, set up a strategic bomber force independent of the Army and the Navy, and spent large sums on the acquisition and development of bases from which long-range bombers would be able to reach worthwhile objectives in the event of war with Russia. In addition, hundreds of millions of dollars were sunk in an abortive project called Navaho, which envisaged the delivery of nuclear bombs by long-range pilotless aircraft remotely derived from the German FZG.76.

As was only to be expected, such projects were vehemently opposed by army officers on the ground that both the manned and the pilotless bomber were doomed to early obsolescence. Critics of the Government's programmes did not claim that the long-range ballistic missiles they favoured were inherently more accurate than bombers. Their chief objection to the bomber was that it could be easily brought down by short-range missiles, not necessarily fitted with nuclear warheads. They also complained that the Government's preoccupation with the deterrent effect of nuclear bombing tended to divert attention from other elements of a balanced strategy. Among these were large, long-range transport aircraft which would enable the army to retain its mobility even in face of nuclear attack. Only when such aircraft were available in substantial numbers would it be possible to move large bodies of troops rapidly to an active front after keeping them safely dispersed until the last moment.

In point of fact, the authorities at whom these criticisms were aimed did begin soon after the Second World War to develop a troop-carrying transport aircraft designed to carry a 10-ton load 1,000 miles, deliver it by parachute and return to base without stopping to refuel. About the same time, the United States Army introduced all-metal gliders developed from the plywood or fabric-covered gliders used to supplement powered transport aircraft in 1944 and 1945. Experiments with all-metal gliders fitted with engines to boost their performance led to the adoption of short-take-off-and-landing aircraft designed to deliver heavy equipment to forward areas.

Vertical take-off-and-landing aircraft were adopted for military use as the sequel to trials by the United States Army in 1946 of helicopters designed by the Russian-born Igor Sikorsky and developed by him in the United States. Experience in Korea a few years later showed that they were far less vulnerable than might have been expected.

The useful lift of a heavier-than-air aircraft is, however, very small in relation to the weight and complexity of the structure. To lift really heavy loads, or to move large numbers of troops in 1 sortie, it would be necessary to re-introduce the large rigid airship. The construction of 30-million-cubic-foot helium-filled airships, capable of moving hundreds of tons of equipment or stores, or an equivalent number of troops, over long or short distances would be quite feasible, but the initial cost would be fairly high and they would need expert handling. Such aircraft would be too vulnerable to be employed in a tactical role, but could be used to increase the strategic mobility of land forces normally stationed at bases remote from places to which they might have to be rushed in an emergency.

Transport aircraft played a crucial part in the first round of the Cold War between the Western Powers and Communist Russia. In 1948 Belgium, Britain, France, Luxembourg and the Netherlands formed a defensive alliance and the United States Government received authority from the Senate to associate itself with such arrangements where it judged that American interests were involved. The Soviet authorities responded to this move by cutting surface communications between Berlin and the British, French and American occupation zones in West Germany and offering the inhabitants of West Berlin food and fuel if they would accept incorporation in the Russian sphere of influence. The Western Powers advised the inhabitants to turn a deaf ear to these proposals, supplied West Berlin by air, and ultimately succeeded in forcing the Russians to reopen surface communications.

The Western Powers then welded their occupation zones into the West German Federal Republic, and the European democracies committed themselves by the North Atlantic Treaty of 1949 to a military alliance with the United States. In the following year the signatory powers agreed that West German troops should take part in the defence of western Europe, but before effect could be given to this decision the British had to overcome objections from the French by promising to station troops and a tactical air force in Continental Europe until the end of the millennium.

The next round of the Cold War was fought in Korea, a rugged peninsula extending southwards from Manchuria and bounded on east and west by the Sea of Japan and the Yellow Sea.

During the Second World War the Governments of Britain, the United States, the Soviet Union and the Nationalist China of Chiang Kai-shek had agreed that Korea should become a free and independent sovereign state as soon after the end of the war as she was ready to stand on her own feet. Five years after the defeat of Japan, Chiang was an exile from the Chinese mainland and Korea was so far from being free and independent that she was split in two. North of the 38th parallel, the Russians had set up a Democratic People's Republic of Korea under a Korean-born former officer of their army of occupation, Kim Il Sung. South of it a commission of the United Nations, intervening at the request of the United States, had established a Republic of Korea under a Princeton-educated Korean politician, Syngman Rhee. Both Governments claimed jurisdiction over the whole of Korea, and relations between them were such that trade between the 2 parts of the country had come to a complete standstill.

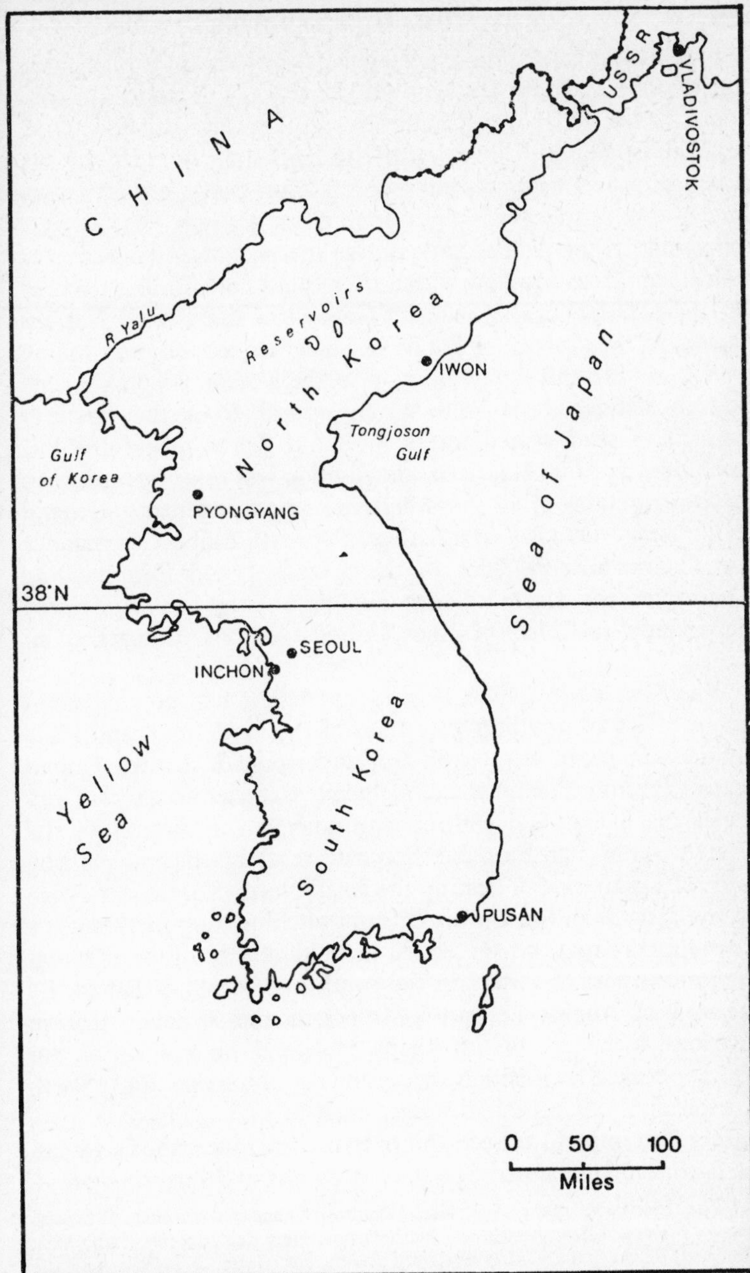
CHINA
USSR
VLADIVOSTOK
R Yalu
Reservoirs
North Korea
IWON
Sea of Japan
Tongjoson
Gulf
Gulf
of Korea
PYONGYANG
38°N
SEOUL
INCHON
South Korea
Yellow
Sea
PUSAN
0 50 100
Miles

8 Korea

At 4 am by local time on 25 June 1950 the Korean People's Army, supported by Russian-built tanks and aircraft, invaded South Korea and began to advance rapidly towards the capital, Seoul. The South Korean Army, trained and equipped by the Americans but without tanks, aircraft or heavy artillery, was driven back with heavy losses. Seoul fell on 28 June.

Inevitably, the Americans took the invasion of South Korea as a challenge from Moscow which they could not afford to decline. On their initiative, the Security Council of the United Nations passed, in the absence of the Soviet delegate, a resolution calling for a cease-fire and the withdrawal of the Korean People's Army. Sixteen nations responded to an appeal from the Security Council to send armed forces to South Korea to enforce this resolution, but the American contribution was much greater than the contributions of all the other nations put together.* General of the Army Douglas MacArthur, Supreme Allied Commander and Commander-in-Chief in the Far East and Commanding General of the United States Far East Army, was appointed Commander-in-Chief of the United Nations Command in Korea.

When the Korean War began, MacArthur had no combatant troops of his own within 300 miles of the battlefront, and his 4 divisions in Japan were weak and undertrained. But the United States Seventh Fleet, which included a carrier force, was put under his operational control, and some 1,200 aircraft of the United States Far East Air Force were at his disposal. Using some of his aircraft to destroy the small North Korean Air Force on the ground and in the air before switching most of them to a close-support role, he succeeded in holding a bridgehead round the crucial port of Pusan, in the south-east corner of Korea. By the end of August he had 3 American and 5 South Korean divisions, with some British troops, to defend the bridgehead, but attacks near the junction between his American and South Korean divisions repeatedly threatened to split his front in two.

In an attempt to reduce the pressure on MacArthur's forces, 98 B-29 bombers aimed 850 tons of bombs in 26 minutes on 16

* The 16 nations were Australia, Belgium, Canada, Colombia, Ethiopia, France, Greece, Luxembourg, the Netherlands, New Zealand, the Philippines, Thailand, Turkey, the Union of South Africa, the United Kingdom and the United States. Denmark, India, Italy, Norway and Sweden sent medical units but no combatant troops, warships or military or naval aircraft.

August at an area measuring about 7 miles by 3 in which North Korean troops were believed to be assembling. This revival of the carpet bombing attempted by British and American bombers during the Overlord campaign in 1944 had little or no apparent effect on the enemy, and American historians were unable to find positive evidence when the war was over that it had killed even a single North Korean soldier.

During the battle for the Pusan bridgehead, American aircraft made the first of a series of major attempts to cut the enemy's communications by attacking bridges and road and rail centres in his rear. This form of attack, too, was based on experience in Europe during the Second World War. In the light of hindsight, it seems obvious that attempts at interdiction were not likely to have decisive effects on an army which did not depend upon mechanical transport and whose divisions needed only about 50 tons of supplies a day, as compared with 300 tons or more for a European or American division. This was not, however, apparent at the time. The result was that, throughout the Korean War, the demands of the United Nations troops for close support in the form of attacks on objectives within 50 yards to 10 miles of the front line conflicted with a persistent belief among airmen that attacks on rear communications were more rewarding. The fact remains that, without the help given by the United States Fifth Air Force, MacArthur's American and South Korean troops would almost certainly have been unable to hold the bridgehead during a crucial period in August and early September.

At the same time, the widespread belief that an army without air support could not take the offensive against one supported by bombers and fighters was utterly contradicted by the determination with which the Korean People's Army pressed home its attacks after all but a handful of its supporting aircraft had been destroyed. Americans who had predicted in June that the North Koreans would fold up as soon as the Fifth Air Force went into action were proved completely wrong.

The next phase of the war began on 15 September, when United States marines carried in American, British, British Commonwealth, French and Dutch vessels landed behind the enemy's lines at Inchon, on the Kimpo peninsula less than 20 miles from Seoul. This outflanking movement, launched by MacArthur against the advice of most of his subordinate commanders, was brilliantly successful. In hazardous conditions, but with powerful naval and air support, the marines established themselves ashore by dusk on the first day at a cost of only 196 casualties. By the end of the month Syngman Rhee was back in his capital and the Korean People's Army was in full retreat behind the 38th parallel after losing two-thirds of its strength. The lustre of MacArthur's victory was, however, dimmed in the eyes of some beholders by the sight of the appalling devastation wrought by his supporting aircraft and artillery.

For all practical purposes, the aims of the Security Council had now been attained. However, MacArthur had been authorized by the American Joint Chiefs of Staff on the day of the landings at Inchon to make plans for the occupation of North Korea if the Chinese or the Russians did not intervene, and on 7 October the General Assembly of the United Nations passed a resolution calling for the unification of Korea and its transformation into a sovereign state. At a conference at Wake Island 8 days later, MacArthur assured President Truman that there was virtually no risk of Chinese or Russian intervention and that the Chinese 'had no air force'.

Meanwhile MacArthur's forces crossed the 38th parallel, despite a warning from the Chinese Foreign Minister, Chou En-lai, that Communist China would intervene in Korea if they did so. On 19 October they captured Pyongyang, the capital of North Korea. A week later they were attacked by Chinese Communist forces close to the Manchurian frontier and at points well south of it.

From 1 November the Chinese were supported by Russian-built MiG-15 fighters and fighter-bombers. On 26 November they opened a series of counter-offensives which carried them early in the New Year to Seoul. By 24 January 1951 the United States Eighth Army stood 40 miles south of Seoul after completing the longest retreat in American military history.

Thereafter until the end of the war, the United States and her allies aimed not at defeating the enemy, but at forcing him back to the 38th parallel and inflicting on him such losses and setbacks as might induce him to agree to a cease-fire. MacArthur, dissenting from this policy and calling for the destruction of China's capacity to wage war by air and naval attacks on her industry, was dismissed in the spring of 1951 and replaced by Lieutenant-General Matthew B. Ridgway.

In the following summer, after Ridgway had repelled a fresh offensive and the Chinese had been duly driven beyond the 38th parallel, the Soviet delegate to the Security Council of the United Nations proposed in a broadcast speech that the belligerents in Korea should discuss a cease-fire and an armistice. Negotiations began on 10 July and continued, with intermissions, until the summer of 1953. On 27 July 1953 an armistice was at last signed and the war was over.

During the last 2 years of the war the United Nations had therefore to find some way of using their air power that was consistent with their new policy of limited war, or 'containment', yet compatible with their aim of putting pressure on the enemy to make peace.

By the time the policy of containment was initiated, American heavy bombers had knocked out most industrial targets in North Korea without noticeably affecting the enemy's capacity to carry on the war. Since attacks on industrial targets in China were ruled out on political grounds, the choice of methods and objectives was limited.

A few weeks before the negotiations began, the United States Far East Air Force launched a massive interdiction programme whose object was to isolate and paralyse the Chinese armies in the field and thus bring the Communist negotiators to the conference table in a suitable frame of mind. Attacks by day and night on road and rail systems, including bridges, embankments, tunnels, cuttings and other potential bottlenecks were continued for 12 months, but the enemy was not prevented from bringing up enough supplies to maintain his troops in static positions, and the effect on the peace talks was negligible. In addition, many attacks were made in the late summer and early autumn of 1951 on the enemy's fighter airfields, but these brought such heavy losses that attacks in daylight had to be suspended. The Americans succeeded, by continuing their attacks at night with the aid of sophisticated navigational equipment, in doing a good deal of damage to the airfields, but were powerless to arrest a build-up which gave Communist China the third strongest air force in the world.

In the summer of 1952 the Americans turned to attacks on the

North Korean hydro-electric system, which supplied current not only to North Korea but also to some industrial undertakings in Manchuria. In terms of damage done, the attacks were spectacularly successful, but they had no noticeable effect on the enemy's willingness to make peace. Similarly, attacks on factories, barracks and airfields at and near Pyongyang did immense damage but brought peace no nearer.

Meanwhile fear and hatred of Communism in the United States were increased by the discovery that western scientists did not have the commanding lead in the field of nuclear weaponry which had long been considered their prerogative. By 1949 the Russians were known to have made and tested an atomic bomb. President Truman was urged to sanction the development of thermonuclear weapons more destructive by far than any uranium or plutonium bomb, but in view of the unanimous opinion of the Government's Atomic Energy Commission that they would be inordinately expensive and that their introduction would lower the moral standing of the United States, he declined to do so until, early in 1950, he learned that Klaus Fuchs, a German-born nuclear physicist employed by the British, had made important disclosures to agents of the Soviet Government. He then authorized an emergency programme for the development and production of such weapons. An experimental bomb was tested in 1952 at Eniwetok in the Marshall Islands, but it weighed 65 tons and was far too large to be carried in an aircraft.

The President's decision to add thermonuclear weapons to the nation's armoury did not save his party from falling into disrepute as a result of his failure to obtain a decision in Korea. Throughout 1952, with elections looming, leading Democrats inside and outside the administration were accused by their critics not merely of wishing to live with Communism rather than destroy it, but of showing favour to men suspected of seeing some merit in Communist ideals. At the same time, many Americans complained that the full employment and all-round material prosperity of which the Democrats boasted had been bought with bloodshed in a war which the Government was incapable of winning. Elected by a record number of votes at a moment when peace seemed as far off as ever, the Republican presidential candidate, General Eisenhower, prepared to take up office in the knowledge that he could count on firm support from a country and a Congress which had reacted strongly against 20 years of Democratic rule.

Eisenhower chose as his Secretary of State John Foster Dulles, a God-fearing New England lawyer with a long experience of public affairs and a profound distrust of foreigners. Dulles believed that Truman had acted rightly in supporting the Koreans against invasion from the north, but he also believed that the Korean War would never have occurred if 'the Communists' had been warned in advance that an invasion of South Korea would be resisted by American forces. His view was that the only effective way of stopping potential aggressors was to convince them that they risked being subjected to retaliatory blows so damaging that aggression would not be profitable.

Even before his inauguration, Eisenhower let it be known that, although he did not hope or expect to win the war in Korea and would aim at an honourable truce, he meant to make it clear to the North Koreans and their backers that, if they insisted on prolonging the negotiations begun in 1951, he would think it his duty to 'enlarge the war' by striking at the Chinese both in Korea and elsewhere. The use of atomic bombs was not expressly mentioned in this context, but Eisenhower was known to agree with Dulles that the threat of nuclear attack was a diplomatic weapon he should not hesitate to use.

On 13 May 1953 American bombers began a series of successful attacks on irrigation dams which supplied water for the North Korean rice crop, and whose destruction flooded roads and railways. Soon afterwards General Mark Clark, Ridgway's successor, received his brief for a fresh round of negotiations, due to begin on 25 May. He was told that, if the North Koreans proved unforthcoming, he was to break off the talks and carry on the war 'in new ways never yet tried in Korea'. Almost simultaneously, a hint was conveyed to the Chinese to the effect that failure to reach agreement might lead to an extension of the war in their direction, and that disagreeable surprises might be in store for them.

Less than a fortnight after the new series of talks began, the negotiators reached agreement in principle. Although doubtless due in part to the bombing of the North Korean dams, this outcome was generally regarded in the United States as a triumph for the new administration's policy of firmness backed by implicit or explicit threats of nuclear attack.

On 8 August, only 12 days after the signing of the armistice, the Russians announced in Moscow that they had learned how to make thermonuclear bombs. This was confirmed on 12 August, when monitoring devices recorded a thermonuclear explosion in Soviet territory. Reliance on the deterrent effect of long-range bombers carrying nuclear bombs continued, none the less, to be the essence of the defensive strategy of the Western Powers until progress in rocketry led to the gradual replacement of the manned bomber by more sophisticated and more highly automated weapons systems.

The next few years saw a nuclear arms race which was bound to lead to either a catastrophe of unprecedented magnitude or a stalemate. In the spring of 1956 a senior officer of the United States Army told a Congressional Committee that a nuclear assault on Russia by the Strategic Air Command of the United States Air Force might be expected to result in 'several hundred million' deaths and that these would not be confined to inhabitants of the Soviet Union but might extend to areas as far east or west as the Philippines or western Europe, according to the direction in which the wind was blowing at the time. Since comparable casualties could doubtless be expected to result from a nuclear assault on the United States by Russian bombers, it seemed reasonable to assume that, at least for the time being, neither side would be eager to provoke an all-out conflict.

There remained the danger that either the United States or the Soviet Union might at some future time gain so clear a lead in offensive or defensive weapons, or in both, that her statesmen would think it advisable to stake everything on a preventative war before the pendulum swung in the opposite direction. During the lifetime of the Eisenhower administration there seemed to be some grounds for the belief that the Russians might gain such a lead in the field of medium-range ballistic missiles. In 1955 Lieutenant-General Walter Dornberger, for more than 10 years the German Army's leading authority on large rockets, expressed the opinion that the Russians had already produced large numbers of missiles capable of reaching objectives in western Europe from the Soviet Union or from countries accessible to Russian troops. He added that, in his estimation, the Russians were not likely to be behind the Americans in providing themselves with missiles of the Polaris type which could be fired from submarines.

In the meantime the foreign policy of the United States was strongly influenced by demands from her service chiefs for access to bases from which virtually all parts of the Soviet Union could be reconnoitred, and if necessary attacked by manned aircraft. Just as the need to maintain their sea power throughout the world had led the British to conclude treaties in the middle of the nineteenth century with foreign potentates of almost every creed and colour, so in the middle of the twentieth the need to maintain their air power on a global scale was one of a number of motives which impelled the Americans to enter, directly or indirectly, into far-reaching alliances from which their forebears would have recoiled.

Ironically, the Suez crisis of 1956, which strained relations between the United States and Britain almost to breaking point, had its origin in an alliance intended to serve the interests of the United States, although she was not a party to it. This was the Baghdad Pact, concluded between Britain, Iran, Iraq, Pakistan and Turkey at the prompting of John Foster Dulles. The pact caused so much resentment in Egypt that Dulles and the British were moved to placate the Egyptian dictator, Gamal Abdul Nasser, by offering to finance a long-dormant project for the construction of a dam above the existing Nile dam at Aswan. It was the brusque and undiplomatic withdrawal by Dulles of this offer which led Nasser, in a fit of anger, to seize the Suez Canal and express the hope that the Americans would 'choke to death on their fury'. This in turn led to an attempt by the British and the French to wrest the canal from him under cover of an Israeli attack on Egypt.

In the context of a history of air power, the most interesting feature of the Suez affair is the ease with which the British, the French and the Israelis gained complete control of the air over Egypt by using their bombers and fighters in a tactical role to support an Israeli advance into the Sinai peninsula and British and French airborne landings in the Canal Zone. The Egyptian Air Force was virtually annihilated in 48 hours. In another 48 the British, the French and the Israelis could have conquered the whole of Egypt.

At the height of the Suez crisis, the Soviet authorities threatened to use long-range ballistic missiles against the British and the French unless they withdrew their troops from Egypt. What action they could in fact have taken is hard to say. Many reports were received in the west about the time of the crisis of the building of missile sites in various parts of the Soviet Union, but so far as is known it was not until the early summer of 1957 that the Russians succeeded in launching a missile with a range of more than 1,000 miles. In the following August they claimed to have launched within the past few days a missile of much longer range. This was described by the Soviet leader Nikolai Khrushchev as 'a super-long-distance intercontinental multi-stage ballistic missile', and was said to have landed in the target area after covering an immense but unspecified distance and reaching an unprecedented height.

At that time the Americans were hoping to put into orbit before the end of the following year a small spacecraft, or unmanned satellite, weighing about 20 lbs. In the light of Khrushchev's claim, some of their experts predicted that the Russians would launch a satellite within 30 days. Nevertheless the launching of the satellite Sputnik I on 4 October came as a great shock to most Americans. The authorities responded to it by hastening the launching of the American satellite, but their attempt to put it into orbit in December was unsuccessful.

British and American experts agreed that the launching of Sputnik I was proof that the Russians had reached a stage at which they were capable of making and launching inter-continental ballistic missiles. Whether they had yet produced such missiles in substantial numbers was another matter.

The outcome was a contest in which the United States and the Soviet Union vied with each other in developing offensive missiles of extreme range and providing themselves with the means of defence against such missiles. At the same time they competed with each other in launching spacecraft for peaceful purposes. On the plea that satellites were a military necessity, the Kennedy administration in the United States was able to sanction much interesting work whose true justification was that it served the relatively harmless purpose of satisfying human curiosity, although some of it also had practical applications in such fields as meteorology, communications and strategic reconnaissance. A beneficial effect of the American and Russian space programmes was that the launching of satellites which could be tracked by observers in many countries fostered friendly exchanges between Russian and western scientists.

The risk of an unsought nuclear holocaust was also reduced by the knowledge that, with the coming of the missile age, disaster might result from nothing more than the premature pressing of a button in consequence of an administrative blunder. Especially after the Cuban crisis of 1962, in which the United States came perilously close to making war on the Russians in order to prevent them from establishing missile bases in the Caribbean, the masters of the White House and the Kremlin recognized that it behoved them not only to keep a tight rein on their subordinates, but also to provide themselves with the means of instant communication in a crisis. The Cuban crisis also helped, by giving the British an opportunity of tendering advice which was well received in Washington, to repair some of the damage done to Anglo-American relations by the Suez affair.

The high cost of medium-range and intercontinental ballistic missiles and of the early-warning and tracking systems needed to counter them was, however, a serious disadvantage from the point of view of statesmen concerned to maintain living standards and balance budgets. Notwithstanding all that had been said and written immediately after the First World War about the eventual replacement of manned aircraft by ballistic missiles, the cost of these new weapons and weapons systems was added to that of air forces which had still to be maintained for tactical purposes, even if they were no longer needed to the same extent as formerly for long-range strategic reconnaissance and bombing.

Air power in the shape of bombers, fighters and reconnaissance and transport aircraft continued, too, to seem indispensable to nations which could not afford, or which did not need, to provide themselves with the paraphernalia of intercontinental rocketry. In the Six Day War in the Middle East in 1967, Israeli air power was a crucial, even a decisive factor. The Israelis owed their superiority in the air not, as was widely believed in Arab countries, to help given to them by foreign air forces, for in fact such help was not forthcoming. They owed it to thorough preparation, a sound choice of targets, careful briefing, an organization which enabled them to refuel and rearm their aircraft in 10

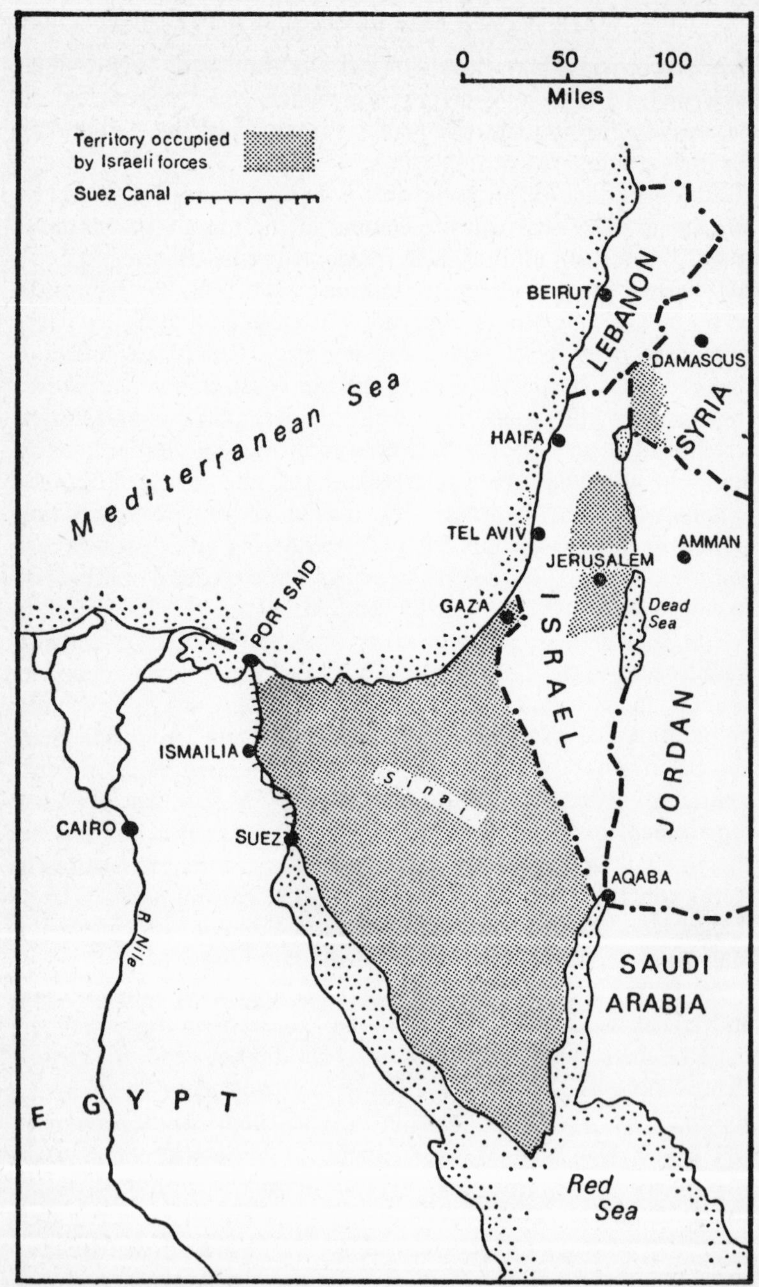

9 The Six Day War, 1967

minutes or less, and the skill and pertinacity of well-trained airmen. In 3 hours on 5 June, the Israeli Air Force destroyed nearly 300 Egyptian aircraft on the ground and in the air and virtually annihilated the Egyptian Air Force. Many of these aircraft were destroyed in pre-emptive attacks on 17 airfields. The Jordanian Air Force was wiped out with almost contemptuous ease. The Israelis thus gained freedom to send their aircraft at will over hostile territory in support of their advancing columns.

In contrast to Israeli experience in the Six Day War, possession of the world's strongest air force did not enable the Americans to impose their will on the enemy in the long-drawn war in Vietnam to which they committed themselves after escaping with difficulty from their involvement in Korea. Despite all their efforts, the problem of finding targets or target systems worth attacking proved even more intractable in Vietnam than in Korea, where the Americans did at least gain some benefit from the bombing of the North Korean irrigation dams. In Vietnam the ruthless bombing of objectives assumed to be valuable to the enemy served to devastate the country without, so far as is known at present, having much effect on the peace negotiations to which, as in Korea, the Americans were obliged to have recourse in order to extricate themselves from an intolerable commitment. When Captain Baden-Powell declared in 1908 that air power would control the fate of nations, he can scarcely have foreseen the immense difficulty the nations would experience in learning to use and control that power.

NOTES

CHAPTER 2

1 H. A. Jones, *History of the Great War: The War in the Air*, II, p. 199.
2 Ibid., Appendix VIII.
3 Ibid., Appendix IX.
4 Robert Blake (Editor), *The Private Papers of Douglas Haig*, pp. 252, 273, 280.

CHAPTER 3

1 Captain S. W. Roskill, *History of the Second World War: The War at Sea*, I, p. 32.
2 T. H. O'Brien, *History of the Second World War: Civil Defence*, pp. 15–16.
3 Ibid., pp. 92–3, 95–6.
4 Ibid., p. 678.

CHAPTER 4

1 Earl of Avon, *Facing the Dictators*, p. 141.
2 Sir Charles Webster and Noble Frankland, *History of the Second World War: The Strategic Air Offensive against Germany*, I, p. 73.
3 Ibid., pp. 54–5, 62–4, 74–5.
4 Ibid., p. 99.

CHAPTER 5

1 Webster and Frankland, op. cit., I, pp. 205, 209.
2 Ibid., p. 211.
3 Ibid., p. 212; IV, pp. 109–10.
4 Roskill, op. cit., I, pp. 158–60 and Map 14.

CHAPTER 6

1 Webster and Frankland, op. cit., I, pp. 136–7n.
2 Field-Marshall Erich von Manstein, *Lost Victories*, p. 59.
3 J. R. M. Butler, *History of the Second World War: Grand Strategy*, II, pp. 569–70.
4 Webster and Frankland, op. cit., IV, p. 110.
5 Colonel A. Goutard, *The Battle of France*, 1940, pp. 193, 199, 206–7.

CHAPTER 7

1 Ronald Wheatley, *Operation Sea Lion*, pp. 29–51.
2 T. H. O'Brien, op. cit., pp. 15–16, 144.
3 Ibid., p. 388.
4 Wheatley, op. cit., p. 111.
5 Ibid., p. 90.
6 Derek Wood and Derek Dempster, *The Narrow Margin*, p. 470.

CHAPTER 8

1 Webster and Frankland, op. cit., I, p. 152.
2 Ibid., p. 154.
3 Ibid., p. 129.
4 Ibid., pp. 161, 162.
5 Ibid., p. 159.
6 Ibid., p. 226.
7 Ibid., pp. 182–5.
8 Ibid., pp. 239–45
9 Ibid., p. 257.

CHAPTER 9

1 Major-General I. S. O. Playfair, *History of the Second World War: The Mediterranean and Middle East*, II, p. 124.
2 Ibid., III, p. 52.
3 Ibid., pp. 220–1.
4 Winston S. Churchill, *The Second World War*, IV, p. 390.

CHAPTER 10

1 John Gwyer, *History of the Second World War: Grand Strategy*, III, i, p. 90.

CHAPTER 11

1 Samuel Eliot Morison, *The History of United States Naval Operations in World War II: The Rising Sun in the Pacific*, p. 128.

CHAPTER 12

1 Webster and Frankland, op. cit., I, p. 369.
2 Ibid., II, p. 12.
3 Ibid., p. 20.
4 Ibid., p. 145.
5 Ibid., p. 70.
6 Ibid., III, p. 103.

BIBLIOGRAPHY

The following lists include books which have proved useful as sources and a selection only of books for further reading. Dates are not necessarily the dates of first editions.

I THE DEVELOPMENT OF AERONAUTICS AND AVIATION FROM THE EARLIEST UNTIL RECENT TIMES

BABINGTON-SMITH, Constance, *Testing Time: a Study of Man and Machine in the Test-Flying Era* (London 1961)

BACON, Gertrude, *Balloons, Airships and Flying Machines* (London 1905)

BOUCHÉ, A., See Dollfus, C.

BOWERS, P.M., See Swanborough, Gordon

BRETT, R.D., *The History of British Aviation, 1908-14* (London 1934)

BROOKS, P.W., *The Modern Airliner: Its Origin and Development* (London 1961)

CHAMBE, R., *Histoire de l'Aviation* (Paris 1948)

CHANUTE, O., *Progress in Flying Machines* (New York 1894)

DOLLFUS, C. and BOUCHÉ, A., *Histoire de l'Aéronautique* (Paris 1942)

DORMAN, G., *Fifty Years Fly-Past: From Wright Brothers to Comet* (London 1951)

DUHEM, J., *Histoire des Idées aéronautiques avant Montgolfier* (Paris 1943)

Histoire des Origines du Vol á Réaction (Paris 1959)

FRANCILLON, R. J., *Japanese Aircraft of the Pacific War* (London 1970)

GATLAND, Kenneth W. and KUNESCH, Anthony M., *Space Travel* (London 1953)

GIACOMELLI, R., *Gli Scritti di Leonardo da Vinci sul Volo* (Rome 1936)

GIBBS-SMITH, C.H., *A History of Flying* (London 1953)

The Wright Brothers (London 1963)

The Invention of the Aeroplane, 1809-1909 (London 1966)
Leonardo da Vinci's Aeronautics (London 1968)
Clément Ader: His Flight-Claims and his Place in History (London 1968)
Aviation: An Historical Survey from its Origins to the End of World War II (London 1970)

GOLDSTROM, J., *A Narrative History of Aviation* (New York 1930)

GRAHAME-WHITE, C. and HARPER, H., *The Aeroplane, Past, Present and Future* (London 1911)

GRAY, Peter and THETFORD, Owen, *German Aircraft of the First World War* (London 1962)

GREGORY, H.F., *The Helicopter* (London 1948)

HARPER, H., See Grahame-White, C.

HART, C., *Kites: An Historical Survey* (London 1967)

HART, I.B., *The World of Leonardo da Vinci* (London 1961)

DE HAVILLAND, Sir Geoffrey, *Sky Fever* (London 1961)

HAYDON, F. Stansbury, *Aeronautics in the Union and Confederate Armies* (Baltimore 1941)

HODGKINS, E., See Magoun, F. A.

HODGSON, J.E., *The History of Aeronautics in Great Britain* (London 1924)

INSTONE, Alfred, *Early Birds* (London 1938)

KUNESCH, Anthony M., See Gatland, Kenneth W.

LAMBERMONT, Paul with PIRIE, Anthony, *Helicopters and Autogyros of the World* (London 1970)

LANCHESTER, F.W., *Aerodynamics* (London 1907)
Aerodynetics (London 1908)

LANGLEY, S.P., *Experiments in Aerodynamics* (Washington 1891)

LEASOR, James, *The Millionth Chance* (London 1957)

LEWIS, Peter, *British Aircraft, 1809-1914* (London 1962)
The British Bomber since 1914 (London 1967)

LEY, W., *Rockets, Missiles and Space Travel* (London 1951)

LINDBERGH, C.A., *The Spirit of St Louis* (London 1953)

LORIN, René, *L'Air et la Vitesse* (Paris 1919)

LUSAR, Rudolf, *German Secret Weapons of the Second World War* (London 1959)

MCFARLAND, Marvin W. (Editor), *The Papers of Wilbur and Orville Wright*, 2 vols (New York 1953)

MAGOUN, F.A. and HODGKINS, E., *A History of Aircraft* (New York 1931)

MILBANK, Jeremiah, Jnr, *The First Century of Flight in America* (Princeton 1943)

MORRIS, L. and SMITH, K., *Ceiling Unlimited: The Story of American Aviation from Kitty Hawk to Supersonics* (New York 1953)

MOUILLARD, L.-P., *L'Empire de l'Air: Essai d'Orthinologie Appliquée à l'Aviation* (Paris 1881)
NEON (pseudonym), *The Great Delusion* (London 1927)
OBERTH, Herman, *Wege Zur Raumschiffahrt* (Munich 1929)
PENROSE, Harald J., *British Aviation: The Pioneer Years* (London 1967)
PIRIE, Anthony, See Lambermont, Paul
PRITCHARD, J.L., *Sir George Cayley: The Inventor of the Aeroplane* (London 1960)
PUDNEY, John, *Laboratory of the Air* (London 1948)
ROLT, L.T.C., *The Aeronauts* (London 1966)
SANTOS-DUMONT, Alberto, *My Airships* (London 1904)
SAUNDERS, H.ST.G., *Per Ardua: The Rise of British Air Power, 1911-1939* (London 1944)
SEIFERT, K.D., *Otto Lilienthal: Mensch und Werk* (Neuenhagen 1961)
SHUTE, Nevil, *Slide Rule* (London 1954)
SMITH, K., See Morris, L.
SPANNER, E.F., *The Tragedy of 'R.101'* (London 1931)
SWANBOROUGH, Gordon and BOWERS, P.M., *United States Navy Aircraft since 1911* (London 1968)
THETFORD, Owen G., *Aircraft of the Royal Air Force, 1918-1957* (London 1957)
British Naval Aircraft since 1912 (London 1971)
See also Gray, Peter
TISSANDIER, G., *Histoire des Ballons et des Aéronautes Célèbres*, 2 vols (Paris 1877-90)
UCCELLI, A., *I Libri del Volo di Leonardo da Vinci* (Milan 1952)
VAETH, J. Gordon, *Graf Zeppelin* (London 1959)
VOISIN, Gabriel, *Mes Dix Mille Cerfs Volants* (Paris 1961)
WALLACE, Graham, *Flying Witness: Harry Harper and the Golden Age of Aviation* (London 1958)
WEISS, J.B., *Gliding and Soaring Flight* (London 1922)
WHITEHOUSE, A., *The Early Birds* (London 1967)
WHITTLE, Sir Frank, *Jet* (London 1953)
WYKEHAM, Peter, *Santos-Dumont, A Study in Obsession* (London 1962)

2 THE APPLICATION OF AIR POWER FROM THE FRENCH REVOLUTION TO THE END OF THE FIRST WORLD WAR

a AIR HISTORIES, NARRATIVES, EYE-WITNESS ACCOUNTS, MEMOIRS AND REMINISCENCES

ASHMORE, Major-General E. B., *Air Defence* (London 1929)
BARING, Maurice, *Flying Corps Headquarters, 1914-1918* (London 1968)

BISHOP, Major W. A., *Winged Warfare* (London 1968)

BISHOP, W. Arthur, (Son of the foregoing), *The Courage of the Early Morning* (London 1966)

BOYLE, Andrew, *Trenchard: Man of Vision* (London 1962)

COLE, Christopher, *McCudden, V.C.* (London 1967)
(ed.), *Royal Air Force, 1918* (London 1968)
(ed.), *Royal Flying Corps, 1915-1916* (London 1969)

FREDETTE, Major Raymond H., U.S.A.F., *The First Battle of Britain, 1917-1918* (London 1966)

GAMBLE, C.F. Snowden, *The Story of a North Sea Air Station* (London 1967)

GIBBONS, Floyd, *The Red Knight of Germany* (London 1927)

GRAY, Peter and THETFORD, Owen, *German Aircraft of the First World War* (London 1962)

GRINNELL-MILNE, Duncan, *Wind in the Wires* (London 1926)

HAYDON, F. Stansbury, *Aeronautics in the Union and Confederate Armies* (Baltimore 1941)

JONES, H.A. and RALEIGH, Sir Walter, *History of the Great War: The War in the Air*, 6 vols (London 1922-37) (vol. I by Sir Walter Raleigh)

LEE, A.G., *Open Cockpit* (London 1969)

LEWIS, Peter, *The British Bomber since 1914* (London 1967)
Squadron Histories: R.F.C., R.N.A.S. and R.A.F., 1912-59 (London 1959)

LORIN, René, *L'Air et la Vitesse* (Paris 1919)

MACMILLAN, Norman, *Sir Sefton Brancker* (London 1935)

MORRIS, Alan, *Bloody April* (London 1967)
First of the Many (London 1968)
The Balloonatics (London 1970)

MORRIS, Captain Joseph, *The German Air Raids on Great Britain, 1914-1918* (London 1969)

NORMAN, Aaron, *The Great Air War* (New York 1968)

POOLMAN, Kenneth, *Zeppelins over England* (London 1960)

RALEIGH, Sir Walter, See Jones, H. A.

ROLT, L.T.C., *The Aeronauts* (London 1966)

SAUNDERS, H.StG., *Per Ardua: The Rise of British Air Power, 1911-1939* (London 1944)

TAYLOR, John W. R., *C.F.S.: Birthplace of Air Power* (London 1958)

THOMPSON, Sir Robert, *The Royal Flying Corps* (London 1968)

VIGILANT (pseudonym), *German War Birds* (London 1933)

b NAVAL AND MILITARY HISTORIES, NARRATIVES, EYE-WITNESS ACCOUNTS, MEMOIRS AND REMINISCENCES; POLITICAL AND GENERAL BACKGROUND STUDIES

AMERY, L.S. (Editor), *'The Times' History of the War in South Africa, 1899-1900*, 7 vols (London 1900-9)

ASPINALL-OGLANDER, C.F., *History of the Great War: Gallipoli*, 2 vols (1929-32)

BACON, Admiral Sir Reginald, *The Dover Patrol, 1915-1917* (London n. d.)

BARKER, A.J., *The Neglected War: Mesopotamia, 1914-1918* (London 1967)

BEAVERBROOK, Lord, *Men and Power, 1917-1918* (London 1956)

BLAKE, Robert, *The Unknown Prime Minister: The Life and Times of Bonar Law, 1858-1923* (London 1955)

(ed.), *The Private Papers of Douglas Haig, 1914-1919* (London 1952)

BLUNDEN, Edmund, *Undertones of War* (London 1928)

CALLWELL, Major-General Sir Charles E., *Field-Marshal Sir Henry Wilson: His Life and Diaries*, 2 vols (London 1927)

CHURCHILL, Winston S., *The World Crisis*, 4 vols (London 1928-9)

CORBETT, Sir Julian and NEWBOLT, Sir Henry, *History of the Great War: Naval Operations*, 5 vols (London 1920-31) (vols IV and V by Sir Henry Newbolt)

EDMONDS, Sir J. E., *History of the Great War: Military Operations, France and Belgium*, 9 vols (London 1922-48)

FISCHER, Fritz, *Germany's Aims in the First World War* (London 1967)

GARNETT, David (Editor), *The Letters of T. E. Lawrence* (London 1938)

GEORGE, David Lloyd, *War Memoirs*, 2 vols (London n.d.)

GOUGH, Hubert, *The Fifth Army* (London 1931)

GREY OF FALLODON, The Viscount, *Twenty-Five Years*, 2 vols (London 1925)

GUINN, Paul, *British Strategy and Politics, 1914-1918* (Oxford 1965)

HANKEY, Lord, *The Supreme Command, 1914-1918*, 2 vols (London 1961)

JELLICOE, Admiral of the Fleet the Earl, *The Grand Fleet, 1914-16* (London 1919)

JOFFRE, J.-J.-C., *Mémoires, 1910-1917* (Paris 1932)

LUDENDORFF, General Erich, *My War Mémoirs, 1914-1918* (London 1918)

MAGNUS, Philip, *Kitchener: Portrait of an Imperialist* (London 1958)

NEWBOLT, Sir Henry, See Corbett, Sir Julian

NORTH, John, *Gallipoli: The Fading Vision* (London 1936)

OGLANDER, C.F. Aspinall-, See Aspinall-Oglander, C. F.

RITTER, Gerhard, *The Schlieffen Plan* (London 1958)

ROBERTSON, Field-Marshal Sir William, *Soldiers and Statesmen*, 2 vols (London 1926)

SEYMOUR, Charles (Editor), *The Intimate Papers of Colonel House*, 4 vols (London 1926-8)

SPEARS, Major-General Sir Edward, *Liaison 1914* (London 1931)

TEMPERLEY, H.W.V., *A History of the Peace Conference of Paris*, 6 vols (London 1920-4)

TERRAINE, John, *Douglas Haig: The Educated Soldier* (London 1963)
The Western Front, 1914-1918 (London 1964)

TUCHMAN, Barbara, *The Guns of August* (New York 1962)

WOLFF, Leon, *In Flanders Fields* (London 1959)

3 THE APPLICATION OF AIR POWER FROM THE END OF THE FIRST WORLD WAR TO THE THRESHOLD OF THE NUCLEAR ERA

a NAVAL, MILITARY AND AIR HISTORIES, NARRATIVES, EYE-WITNESS ACCOUNTS, MEMOIRS AND REMINISCENCES

ARNOLD, General H. H., *Global Mission* (New York 1949)

BAILEY, Jim, *The Sky Suspended* (London, n.d.)

BEHRENS, C.B.A., *History of the Second World War: Merchant Shipping and the Demands of War* (London 1955)

BRAGADIN, A.M., *Che ha fatto la Marina? 1940-1945* (Milan 1950)

BRICKHILL, Paul, *The Dam Busters* (London 1951)

O'BRIEN, Terence H., *History of the Second World War: Civil Defence* (London 1955)

BUTLER, J.R.M., *History of the Second World War: Grand Strategy, II* (London 1957)
History of the Second World War: Grand Strategy, III, ii (London 1964)

CALDER, Angus, *The People's War: Britain, 1939-1945*(London 1969)

CATE, J.L., See Craven, W. F.

CHENNAULT, C.L., *The Way of a Fighter* (New York 1949)

CHURCHILL, Winston S., *The Second World War*, 6 vols (London 1948-54)

COAKLEY, R.W., See Leighton, R. M.

COLLIER, Basil, *History of the Second World War: The Defence of the United Kingdom* (London 1957)
The Battle of Britain (London 1962)
The Battle of the V-Weapons, 1944-1945 (London 1964)

CONNELL, John, *Auchinleck* (London 1959)

CRAVEN, W.F. and CATE, J.L., *The Army Air Forces in World War II*, 5 vols (Chicago 1948-51)

DAVIN, D.M., *Official History of New Zealand in the Second World War: Crete* (Wellington 1953)
DAVIS, Kenneth S., *The American Experience of War, 1939-1945* (London 1967)
DEMPSTER, Derek, See Wood, Derek
DERRY, T.K., *History of the Second World War: The Campaign in Norway* (London 1952)
DEXTER, David, *Australia in the War of 1939-1945: The New Guinea Offensives* (Canberra 1961)
DIBOLD, Hans, *Doctor at Stalingrad* (London 1958)
DORNBERGER, Lieutenant-General Walter, *V-2* (London 1954)
EHRMAN, John, *History of the Second World War: Grand Strategy, V* (London 1956)
History of the Second World War: Grand Strategy, VI (London 1956)
EISENHOWER, General of the Army Dwight D., *Crusade in Europe* (London 1958)
ELLIS, Major L. F., *History of the Second World War: The War in France and Flanders, 1939-1940* (London 1954)
History of the Second World War: Victory in the West, 2 vols (London 1962 and 1968)
FITZGIBBON, Constantine, *The Blitz* (London 1970)
FRANKLAND, Noble, *The Bombing Offensive against Germany: Outlines and Perspectives* (London 1965)
See also Webster, Sir Charles
GALLAND, Adolf, *The First and the Last* (London 1955)
GIBSON, Wing Commander Guy, *Enemy Coast Ahead* (London 1946)
GLEASON, S.E., See Langer, W. L.
GOUTARD, Colonel A., *The Battle of France, 1940* (London 1958)
GREENFIELD, Kent R., *American Strategy in World War II: A Reconsideration* (Baltimore 1963)
(ed.), *The United States Army in World War II*, volumes listed under names of authors.
(ed.), *Command Decisions* (New York 1959)
GRINNELL-MILNE, Duncan, *The Silent Victory* (London 1958)
GUDERIAN, H., *Panzer Leader* (London 1952)
GWYER, J.M.A., *History of the Second World War: Grand Strategy, III, i* (London 1964)
HARRIS, Marshal of the Royal Air Force Sir Arthur, *Bomber Offensive* (London 1947)
HEYDTE, Baron von, *Daedalus Returned: Crete, 1941* (London 1958)
JACOBSEN, H.-A. and ROHWER, J., (Editors), *Decisive Battles of World War II: The German View* (London 1965)
JOUBERT DE LA FERTÉ, Air Chief Marshal Sir Philip, *The Third*

Service (London 1955)
Rocket (London 1957)
Birds and Fishes: The Story of Coastal Command (London 1960)
KELLY, Denis, See MacLeod, Roderick
KEMP, P.K., *Fleet Air Arm* (London 1954)
KIRBY, Major-General S. Woodburn, *History of the Second World War: The War against Japan*, 5 vols (vols I to IV, London 1957-65)
LAWRENCE, W.J., *No. 5 Group R.A.F.* (London 1951)
LEE, ASHER, *The German Air Force* (London 1946)
The Soviet Air Force (London 1952)
(ed.), *The Soviet Air and Rocket Forces* (London 1959)
LEIGHTON, R.M. and COAKLEY, R.W., *Global Logistics and Strategy, 1940-1943* (Washington 1955)
LONG, Gavin, *Australia in the War of 1939-1945: To Benghazi* (Canberra 1952)
Australia in the War of 1939-1945: Greece, Crete and Syria (Canberra 1953)
MCCARTHY, D., *Australia in the War of 1939-1945: South-West Pacific Area, First Year* (Canberra 1959)
MCKEE, Alexander, *Strike from the Sky* (London 1960)
MACLEOD, Roderick and KELLY, Denis (Editors), *The Ironside Diaries* (London 1962)
MANSTEIN, Field-Marshal Erich von, *Lost Victories* (London 1958)
MATLOFF, Maurice and SNELL, E. M., *Strategic Planning for Coalition Warfare* (Washington 1953)
MEDLICOTT, W.W., *History of the Second World War: The Economic Blockade*, 2 vols (London 1952 and 1959)
MERRIAM, Robert E., *The Battle of the Ardennes* (London 1958)
MIDDLETON, Drew, *The Sky Suspended* (London 1960)
MILNER, S., *Victory in Papua* (Washington 1947)
MITCHELL, Brigadier-General William, *Our Air Force: The Keystone of National Defense* (New York 1921)
Winged Victory (New York 1925)
Skyways (New York 1930)
MOOREHEAD, Alan, *African Trilogy* (London 1944)
MORISON, Samuel Eliot, *The History of United States Naval Operations in World War II*, 15 vols (Boston 1947-62)
American Contributions to the Strategy of World War II (Oxford 1958)
The Two-Ocean War (Boston 1963)
MORTON, Louis, *The Fall of the Philippines* (Washington 1953)
OWEN, R., *Tedder* (London 1952)
PERCIVAL, Lieutenant-General A. E., *The War in Malaya* (London 1949)

PHILIPPI, A. and HEIM, F., *Der Feldzug gegen Sowjetrussland* (Stuttgart 1962)

PLAYFAIR, Major-General I. S. O., *History of the Second World War: The Mediterranean and Middle East*, 6 vols (vols I to IV, London 1956-62)

RENTZ, John N., *Bougainville and the Northern Solomons* (Washington 1948)

Marines in the Central Solomons (Washington 1952)

RICHARDS, Denis and SAUNDERS, H. StG., *The Royal Air Force, 1939-1945*, 3 vols (London 1953-4)

ROHWER, J., See Jacobsen, H.-A.

ROSKILL, Captain S. W., *History of the Second World War: The War at Sea*, 3 vols in 4 parts (London 1956-61)

The Navy at War, 1939-1945 (London 1960)

Naval Policy between the Wars, 2 vols, I (London 1968)

SAUNDBY, Air Marshal Sir Robert, *Air Bombardment* (London 1961)

SAUNDERS, H.StG., *Per Ardua: The Rise of British Air Power, 1911-1939* (London 1944)

See also Richards, Denis

SCHRÖTER, Heinz, *Stalingrad* (London 1958)

SCHULMAN, Milton, *Defeat in the West* (London 1947)

SLESSOR, Marshal of the Royal Air Force Sir John, *The Central Blue* (London 1956)

SLIM, Field-Marshal the Viscount, *Defeat into Victory* (London 1956)

STACEY, Colonel C. P., *Six Years of War: The [Canadian] Army in Canada, Britain and the Pacific*, 3 vols (Ottawa 1955-60)

SUNDERMAN, Major James F., U.S.A.F. (ed.), *World War II in the Air: The Pacific* (New York 1962)

World War II in the Air: Europe (New York 1963)

TAYLOR, Telford, *The Breaking Wave* (London 1967)

TEDDER, Marshal of the Royal Air Force the Lord, *With Prejudice* (London 1966)

THOMAS, Hugh, *The Spanish Civil War* (London 1961)

VERRIER, Anthony, *The Bomber Offensive* (London 1968)

WALLACE, Graham, *The Flight of Alcock and Brown* (London 1955)

R.A.F. Biggin Hill (London 1957)

WARLIMONT, Walter, *Inside Hitler's Headquarters, 1939-1945* (London 1964)

WATSON, Mark S., *The War Department: Chief of Staff: Prewar Plans and Preparations* (Washington 1950)

WEBSTER, Sir Charles and FRANKLAND, Noble. *History of the Second World War: The Strategic Air Offensive against Germany*, 4 vols (London 1961)

WERTH, Alexander, *Russia at War, 1941-1945* (London 1964)

WESTPHAL, Siegfried, *The German Army in the West* (London 1950)

WHEATLEY, Ronald, *Operation Sea Lion* (Oxford 1958)

WIGMORE, L., *Australia in the War of 1939-1945: The Japanese Thrust* (Canberra 1957)

WILMOT, Chester, *The Struggle for Europe* (London 1952)

WOOD, Derek and DEMPSTER, Derek, *The Narrow Margin* (London 1961)

WYKEHAM, Peter, *Fighter Command* (London 1960)

b BACKGROUND STUDIES

ACHESON, Dean, *Present at the Creation* (London 1970)

AVON, The Earl of, *Full Circle* (London 1960)
Facing the Dictators (London 1962)

BULLOCK, Alan, *Hitler, A Study in Tyranny* (London 1952)

BUNDY, McGeorge, See Stimson, H. L.

CHANDOS, The Viscount, See Lyttelton, Oliver

CLARK, Ronald W., *Tizard* (London 1965)

COBHAM, Alan, *Skyways* (London 1925)

DOUHET, Giulio, *The Command of the Air* (London 1943)

EDEN, Anthony, See Avon, The Earl of

FEIS, H., *The Road to Pearl Harbor* (Princeton 1950)
The China Tangle (Princeton 1953)
Churchill, Roosevelt, Stalin (Princeton 1957)

GOWING, M.M., See Hancock, W. K.

HALL, H. Duncan, *History of the Second World War: North American Supply* (London 1955)

HANCOCK, W.K. and GOWING, M.M., *History of the Second World War: British War Economy* (London 1949)

HIGHAM, R., *Armed Forces in Peacetime: Britain 1918-1940, A Case Study* (London 1963)

HOAG, C.L., *Preface to Preparedness: The Washington Conference and Public Opinion* (Washington 1941)

HULL, Cordell, *The Memoirs of Cordell Hull*, 2 vols (London 1948)

ICHIHASHI, Y., *The Washington Conference and After* (Stanford 1928)

JONES, F.C., *Japan's New Order in East Asia* (London 1954)

KENNAN, George F., *American Diplomacy, 1900-1950* (London 1959)

LANGER, W.L. and GLEASON, S.E., *The Challenge to Isolation* (New York 1952)
The Undeclared War, 1940-1941 (London 1953)

LEAHY, Fleet Admiral W. D., *I Was There* (New York 1950)

LONDONDERRY, The Marquess of, *Wings of Destiny* (London 1943)

LYTTELTON, Oliver (Viscount Chandos), *The Memoirs of Lord Chandos* (London 1962)

MUGGERIDGE, Malcolm (ed.), *Ciano's Diary* (London 1947)
(ed.), *Ciano's Diplomatic Papers* (London 1948)
MURPHY, Robert, *Diplomat Among Warriors* (London 1964)
NAMIER, L.B., *Diplomatic Prelude, 1938-1939* (London 1948)
Europe in Decay (London 1950)
In the Nazi Era (London 1952)
POSTAN, M.M., *History of the Second World War: British War Production* (London 1952)
ROOSEVELT, Elliott, *As He Saw It* (New York 1946)
SCHWARZ, Urs, *American Strategy: A New Perspective* (London 1967)
SHERWOOD, Robert E., *The White House Papers of Harry L. Hopkins* 2 vols (London 1948)
SHIRER, W., *The Rise and Fall of the Third Reich* (London 1960)
SIMON, The Viscount, *Retrospect* (London 1952)
STIMSON, H.L. and BUNDY, McGeorge, *On Active Service in Peace and War* (London 1948)
TEMPLEWOOD, The Viscount, *Ambassador on Special Mission* (London 1946)
Nine Troubled Years (London 1954)
Empire of the Air (London 1957)
TREVOR-ROPER, H.R., *The Last Days of Hitler* (London 1947)
(ed.), *The Bormann Letters* (London 1954)
WATKINS, K.W., *Britain Divided: The Effect of the Spanish Civil War on British Political Opinion* (London 1963)
WELLES, Sumner, *The Time for Decision* (London 1944)
WHEELER-BENNETT, J.W., *The Nemesis of Power: The German Army in Politics, 1918-1945* (London 1953)

4 AIR POWER AND THE NUCLEAR AGE

ADAMS, Michael, *Suez and After* (Boston 1958)
AMRINE, Michael, *The Great Decision* (London 1960)
ANDERSON, Oscar E., Jnr, See Hewlett, Richard G.
ARON, Raymond, *Paix et Guerre Entre les Nations* (Paris 1962)
BALDWIN, Hanson W., *The Great Arms Race* (New York 1958)
BATCHELDER, Robert C., *The Irreversible Decision* (Boston 1962)
BAWLY, Dan, See Kimche, David
BEAUFRÉ, André, *The Suez Expedition, 1956* (London 1969)
BLACKETT, P.M.S., *The Military and Political Consequences of Atomic Energy* (London 1952)
BRODIE, Bernard, *Strategy in the Missile Age* (Princeton 1959)
BUTOW, Robert J. C., *Japan's Decision to Surrender* (Stanford 1954)
BYFORD-JONES, W., *The Lightning War: The Israeli-Arab Conflict, 1967* (London 1967)

BYRNES, James F., *Speaking Frankly* (London 1947)

CLARK, Ronald W., *The Birth of the Bomb* (London 1961)

COMPTON, A., *Atomic Quest* (New York 1956)

ETZIONI, Amitai, *The Hard Way to Peace: A New Strategy* (New York 1962)

Winning Without War (New York 1964)

FINER, Herman, *Dulles over Suez* (London 1964)

GARTHOFF, Raymond L., *Soviet Strategy in the Nuclear Age* (New York 1958)

GAVIN, Lieutenant-General James M., *War and Peace in the Space Age* (London 1959)

GOWING, Margaret, *Britian and Atomic Energy 1939–1945* (London 1964)

GROUEFF, Stephane, *Manhattan Project* (London 1967)

GROVES, Lieutenant-General Leslie R., *Now It Can Be Told* (New York 1962)

HALPERIN, Morton H., *Limited War: An Essay on the Development of the Theory and an Annotated Bibliography* (Cambridge, Mass. 1962)

HEWLETT, Richard G. and ANDERSON, Oscar E., Jnr, *A History of the United States Atomic Energy Commission* (University Park, Pa. 1962)

JONES, F.C., *Japan's New Order in East Asia* (London 1954)

JUNGK, Robert, *Brighter than a Thousand Suns* (London 1958)

KAHN, Herman, *On Thermonuclear War* (Princeton 1960)

Thinking about the Unthinkable (New York 1962)

KASE, Toshikazu, *Eclipse of the Rising Sun* (London 1951)

KAUFFMANN, William W. (ed.), *Military Policy and National Security* (Princeton 1956)

KIMCHE, David, *The Sandstorm: The Arab-Israeli War of 1967* (London 1968)

KING-HALL, Commander Sir Stephen, *Defence in the Nuclear Age* (London 1958)

KISSINGER, Henry A., *Nuclear Weapons and Foreign Policy* (New York 1957)

The Necessity for Choice (New York 1961)

LECKIE, Robert, *The Korean War* (New York 1962)

MIKSCHE, F.O., *The Failure of Atomic Strategy* (London 1959)

MORGENSTERN, Oskar, *The Question of National Defense* (New York 1959)

NUTTING, Anthony, *No End of a Lesson* (London 1967)

OSGOOD, Robert E., *Limited War* (Chicago 1957)

An Alternative to War or Surrender (Urbana, Ill. 1962)

POKROVSKY, Major-General G. I., *Science and Technology in Contemporary War* (New York 1959)

REES, David, *Korea: the Limited War* (London 1964)

SCHELLING, Thomas C., *The Strategy of Conflict* (Cambridge, Mass. 1960)

SCHWARZ, Urs, *American Strategy: A New Perspective* (London 1967)

SOKOLOVSKII, Marshal V. D. (Editor), *Soviet Military Strategy*, (Englewood, N.J. 1963); another translation published as *Military Strategy: Soviet Doctrine and Concepts* (New York 1963)

TAYLOR, General Maxwell D., *The Uncertain Trumpet* (New York 1959)

TRUMAN, Harry S., *Year of Decisions, 1945* (New York 1955)

INDEX

DATE